PELICAN BOOKS

THE ISRAELIS

Amos Elon is considered among Israel's most prominent journalists by both readers and colleagues. He has gained himself this unique reputation by, among other things, his distinctive polemical style. It would not be an exaggeration to say that in the Western world Mr. Elon, more than others, is identified as the spokesman for the liberal Israeli intelligentsia. He is also the author of *Journey Through a Haunted Land: The New Germany*; *Between Enemies* (with Sana Hassan); *Herzl: A Biography*; *Herzl: A Play* (with Dore Schary); *Timetable: A Novel*; and *Flight into Egypt*.

AMOS ELON

THE ISRAELIS

FOUNDERS AND SONS

PENGUIN BOOKS

PENGUIN BOOKS
Published by the Penguin Group
Penguin Books USA Inc.,
375 Hudson Street, New York, New York 10014, U.S.A.
Penguin Books Ltd, 27 Wrights Lane, London W8 5TZ, England
Penguin Books Australia Ltd, Ringwood, Victoria, Australia
Penguin Books Canada Ltd, 10 Alcorn Avenue,
Toronto, Ontario, Canada M4V 3B2
Penguin Books (N.Z.) Ltd, 182–190 Wairau Road, Auckland 10, New Zealand

Penguin Books Ltd, Registered Offices:
Harmondsworth, Middlesex, England

First published in the United States of America by
Holt, Rinehart and Winston 1971
First published in Canada by
Holt, Rinehart and Winston of Canada Limited 1971
This edition first published in Israel by Adam Publishers 1981
Published in Pelican Books 1983

10 9 8 7 6 5 4 3 2

LIBRARY OF CONGRESS CATALOGING IN PUBLICATION DATA
Elon, Amos.
    The Israelis.
    Previously published: New York: Holt, Rinehart, and
Winston, 1971.
    Bibliography: p.
    Includes index.
    1. National characteristics, Israeli. 2. Jewish-
Arab relations. 3. Israel—Politics and government.
I. Title.
DS126.5.E4195 1983   956.94   82-22366

ISBN 0 14 01.6969 5

Printed in the United States of America
Set in Electra

FOR BETH

Contents

FOREWORD TO THE NEW EDITION

Books that last are very likely those that explode with a delayed impact, Cyril Connolly suggested in *Enemies of Promise*, "an inquiry into what makes a book last ten years." When *Enemies of Promise* was reissued after eleven years, Connolly was understandably quite pleased. It is with a similar pleasure that I welcome the new edition of *The Israelis*, ten years almost to the day after its first publication in 1971. Its reissue is not necessarily proof of the rightness or wrongness of its main arguments, the point is rather that above all, there is a continuing need to argue about them.

The debate itself is a vital stage in the progress of Israel toward maturity and to a sense of identity commensurate with the times. It is a process more difficult here than in most places, and probably more painful. When *The Israelis* was first published, some of the more strident voices in the controversy surrounding some of its arguments illustrated the great difficulty we experience as individuals and as a collective, to arrive at self-identity. In the intervening ten years, not a few illusions have been shattered here and suggestions that were seen by some as outrageous at the time will more likely be met today with equilibrium. And yet the difficulty of which I speak, to arrive at some consensus regarding our self-identity as a people (and through such consensus to a little peace and quiet in the realm of ideology), continues today.

On the surface, this is not surprising. We share this difficulty with other new nations. It is true, we are an ancient people. But at the same time, we are a new nation. As a new nation, Israel was born under tragic circumstances, which none of her founding fathers could have foreseen, a catastrophe unique in history. The intellectual roots of Zionism are to be found in the French revolution, and in the romantic waves of social messianism that swept Europe in the wake of that revolution. For a people as self-assured as the Jews, and as proud of their uniqueness as a civilization, such ideological dependency upon other movements is not an easy thought. Nor is the debate made any easier by the realization, even today only half admitted by most, that without a Hitler, there might never have been a modern state of Israel.

The national ethos of Zionism was, of course, influenced also by Jewish religious traditions that had been secularized in the nineteenth century. But its main strength was derived from European sources. Before Theodore Herzl's *Judenstaat* ("An attempt at a modern solution of the Jewish problem," Vienna 1896), the four major tracts of Zionist thought were imitative reactions by Jews to the national resurgence of other peoples. Yehuda Alkalai *(The Third Redemption)* wrote under the influence of the Greek War of Independence. Leo Pinsker's *Autoemancipation* was written under the impact of Bulgarian independence. Moses Hess, in *Rome & Jerusalem*, responded, as is suggested by the title, to the first triumphs of the Italian *risorgimento*; his heroes were Garibaldi and Mazzini. Z. H. Kalisher's *Seeking Zion* drew its inspiration from the Polish nationalists among whom he lived in his home town of Poznan. Herzl himself went to school with the German nationalists of the Wilhelm era, and adopted their values after the Dreyfus Trial. His great model was Bismarck.

The social vision of Zionism was not inspired by the prophets, as is often erroneously thought, but by the humanist principles of western European liberalism and by the dreams and strivings of Russian radicals and revolutionaries, Tolstoyans, socialists and others aspiring to a society, not merely just, but supremely just.

As time passed Zionism too became another example of the proof that contrary to the naive assumption of many nineteenth-century radicals, revolutions cannot be programmed. What was planned by Herzl as an orderly exodus came as a desperate escape. What was intended by the early pioneers as a kingdom of the just, has emerged as a society marked by contradictions, ethnic tension, clashes between the religious and the secular, a mixture – perhaps all too human – of true believers and cynics, the naive and the corrupt. And what is probably the most problematic feature of today's Israel, given the hopes and expectations of its founders, the continued occupation of the West Bank of the Jordan and the Gaza Strip affords liberty to one people and oppression to another. Even had there been no wars, the inevitable contradictions between dream and reality would have been painful; as it happened the wars have made it even more so.

Like other new creatures, we are a very self-conscious, perhaps even excessively self-conscious, people. The self-consciousness probably explains the sharp division of opinion among us, a division more acrimonious, I think, than in many other democracies. We are unable to decide, not only "Who is a Jew?" but "Who or what is an Israeli?" The problem of identity is not merely a kind of childhood disease, as is sometimes thought, but rather an important step in the growth of nations. It is a less bothersome problem to old, established nations, such as the French, the Swedes or the English, whose sense of self has grown almost unconsciously over the centuries from more precise (or at least less controversial) ethnic, cultural, territorial and religious entities. Yet even older nations have experienced deep and powerful crises of identity. In the case of Israel, the crisis is compounded by the fact that in the eyes of the generation of founders the state was never an end in itself but a means to realize social and cultural ideals infinitely more noble than that infamous ideology of sacred egotism which, in our lifetime, has been the gravedigger of Europe, and, indirectly, of its Jews. The enlightened nationalism of the founding fathers has been shunted aside in recent years to make way for an explosive mixture of pseudo-patriotic chauvinism and medieval pseudo-religious orthodoxy. This has been one reason, among others, that Israel has taken on the cast of pariah state in recent years. I am convinced that this was not inevitable, and hope that in this book I have shown why.

Israel, in her short life, has been continually disturbed – or, as some might say, made more interesting – by nervewracking events and violent changes of mood. The dramatic upheavals and storms so characteristic of public life have become even more numerous and more dramatic in the ten years since the first publication of this book. At home, the upheaval of 1977, when for the first time since the early 1930s, the political parties left-of-center were defeated by the parties right-of-center, led by Menachem Begin, a former terrorist who had been regarded as a "fascist" rabblerouser by David Ben Gurion and his fellow founding fathers. The extent and possible meaning of this upheaval become apparent in those chapters of the book that describe the political and moral makeup of the founders. The historical perspective might help to explain the surprise of the victors as well as the bitterness of the vanquished, and perhaps also, the fact that in the elections of 1981, the labor party began to recover.

Externally, events have been not less tumultuous in the ten years that have passed since *The Israelis* was first published: The Yom Kippur War, the rise of Palestinian nationalism, the peace treaty with Egypt. These events have not made this book and the issues it discusses any less topical. The contrary is true.

The Yom Kippur War ended that curious vacation from reality, a euphoria into which many of us had floated in the aftermath of the 1967 war, and against which this book, I think, warned. Few events can be as debilitating as a great victory.

One of the more controversial arguments put forward in *The Israelis* was my contention that two "just causes" have clashed over a single piece of real estate, and that the only solution is to divide that real estate between them. Peace is possible only as the result of mutual recognition and compromise between the Israeli and Palestinian national movements. This remains a minority view. But the self-image of Israel so prevalent in the early seventies, as a mini-power in absolute control to pursue its interests and goals regardless of the sensitivities of others – that dangerous view seems to have largely disappeared in the wake of the 1973 war. It does not mean that the way we see ourselves since then – at times rather paranoically – is less dangerous or more realistic than that which preceded it.

The peace treaty with Egypt has drastically changed the basic conditions of Jewish life here since the beginning of the Return in the latter part of the nineteenth century. Notwithstanding a few exceptions, whose importance the Zionist settlers tended to overestimate, the Arabs and their leaders consistently and often violently opposed the Return, almost from its first day. They were not against Jews settling here and there as individuals. But as a political movement, the Zionists were always regarded as an enemy to be destroyed as quickly and as thoroughly as possible. Most Zionists at most times preferred to overlook the importance of this enmity. At least until 1947, or 1948, there was an element of comfort and convenience in this oversight, which pushed aside doubts and fears as well as considerations that might have braked and partially paralyzed the movement at its onset. Eliezer Ben Yehuda, the father of modern Hebrew, was not the only one to feel a crisis of conscience upon disembarking for the first time in Jaffa, in 1882, and noted in his diary: "Dread! Dread! I suddenly broke... I come to this country as a proselyte, a stranger... remorse rose in the depths of my soul."

Nearly one hundred years would pass before President Sadat's pilgrimage to Jerusalem and the subsequent signing of a peace treaty between Egypt and Israel. With this treaty not only 100 years of rejection and 31 years of war would end, but the largest and most powerful and developed Arab state recognized that Israel and the Israelis belong to this area, not only as individuals but as a political entity. In President Sadat's words to the Israeli Knesset: "In all sincerity I tell you we welcome you among us with full security and safety... We used to reject you... Yet today I tell you and I declare it to the whole world that we accept to live with you in permanent peace..."

It is still difficult to fathom the full importance of this change which comes after a century of hostility, total rejection and intermittent bloodshed. Yet here it is and with it comes the almost universally held view that the separate peace with Egypt will not last unless it becomes part of a process leading to peace with other Arab states, and above all between Israel and the Palestinian people.

The rise of Palestinian nationalism, the third event of great importance since this book was first published, confronts Israel with challenges both political and moral. The political dilemma is influenced by regional and global factors. It reflects the world's growing subservience to the oil producing countries and the conflict between the two superpowers. These are relatively new factors in the history of Israel and of Zionism.

The moral dilemma, by contrast, has been a familiar one since the early 1920's, when in the aftermath of the Balfour Declaration, the first attacks were launched against Jewish settlers by Palestinians, then called, variously, bandits, marauders, or rebels. Today they are called terrorists and "so-called guerillas of the PLO." It is a problem which has been with us, in one form or another, since the beginning of the century. It will not simply disappear by force alone, nor by linguistic tricks. It does not condone murder and terror to say that the Palestinians have a case. Two national movements have clashed in this country over possession of the same land, two rights, two kinds of justice; the only way to resolve the conflict, the only just and practical solution, would be to partition the country between them. I have attempted to show in this book how difficult it is for one people to understand the nationalism of another. But at the same time I would reason that if such peoples wish to survive they must make the serious effort to understand. Every reconciliation begins with empathy. I believe that this remains our great duty.

Some readers will wonder and protest at the absence, or deletion, of this or that item or event in the historical narrative. They will undoubtedly be right. My excuse is a simple one. The material has been selected to illustrate, not to exhaust, problems. This is a test-drill, not an excavation in order to expose all. This is not a history of Zionism, nor a biography of some of its main figures. It is a polemic. The selection is deliberate and perhaps arbitrary. It is, in the first instance, an exercise in self-awareness. It reflects one Israeli's view of himself, his people, their past and present, and suggests his hopes for the future.

Jerusalem, September 1981   A.E.

PART ONE

Founders

1

A PARADE

> I set out to be a farmer—and I think I made
> quite a good farmer. Yet I have spent most
> of my adult life as a soldier, under arms.
>
> MOSHE DAYAN, 1968

So moving was the scene in Jerusalem on May 2, 1968, that some people in the vast crowd wept. Many more felt their blood quicken in a mood of rare exultation. Israelis were commemorating the twentieth anniversary of their independent state; they were also celebrating their year-old victory in the Six Day War of 1967. There was dancing in the streets and old-timers wandered starry-eyed through the teeming squares. According to newspaper reports the next morning, the remarks most often heard were: "It's wonderful! It's almost unbelievable!" Other people were more circumspect and said: "Let us hope it lasts."

It had already lasted twenty years since Independence; fifty, since Britain had recognized Palestine rather vaguely in the Balfour Declaration as a "national home" for the Jews; almost a century since the beginnings of modern Jewish colonization on desolate and malaria-ridden swamplands some ten miles from the Mediterranean Sea, in the Turkish *sanjak* (sub-district) of Jerusalem. Twenty, fifty, or even a hundred years may seem a fleeting moment in the course of human history. In the lives of people it is a very long time. Few Israelis could remember a more massive celebration, nor one as touching and spontaneous as this; yet it was overcast by a strange melancholy.

Israelis are not normally a reticent lot. On the contrary, their exuberance is proverbial. Sons of immigrants, or immigrants themselves, predominantly of Eastern European or "Oriental" origins, they combine the heartiness of Slavs with the emotionalism and lively bearing usually associated with people of the Mediterranean, and make Israel one of the noisiest countries on earth. But scenes such as those that occurred on that particular Independence Day had rarely been seen before. Strangers kissed on the street, homes were thrown open to out-of-towners, middle-aged matrons joined with giddy teen-agers who danced and sang to the accompaniment of homemade drums.

Only eleven months before, four Arab states—Egypt, Syria, Jordan, and Iraq—had concentrated enormous, threatening forces opposite Israel's long, exposed borders. Total Arab strength, at least on paper, had vastly outnumbered that of Israel. The Arabs had twice as many troops, over three times as many tanks, and more than three times as many combat aircraft.* At the same time Arab leaders had threatened genocide and destruction. One much-quoted Arab rabble-rouser, Akhmed Shukeiry, head of the Palestine Liberation Organization, had announced: "Those native-born Israelis who will survive the war will be permitted to remain in the country. But I don't think many will survive."

More careful with his words but hardly less ominous in his threats, President Nasser of Egypt had proclaimed that the very existence of Israel was "in itself an act of aggression." The Syrian Defense Minister, General Hafiz al-Assad, had declared: "The army, which has long been preparing itself for the battle and has a finger on the trigger, demands in a single voice that the battle be expedited . . . . The time has come to wage the liberation battle . . . ." Iraqi troops, already stationed on Jordanian soil, had been told by their deputy Chief of Staff: "Au revoir in Tel Aviv and Haifa!" In the streets of Cairo the mobs had run amok for days, crying for blood into the microphones and cameras of international television reporters. Egyptian television broadcasts, easily received in most parts of Israel, had driven this message home to tens of thousands of Israeli viewers. They heard the wild chants, and saw the war flags inscribed with black death skulls, and the faces of the mob as it screamed for war.

For two or three weeks prior to the Six Day War, Israelis had shared a sense of anguish and dread as deep as only a nation of

---

* Reliable estimates in May 1967 put the combined strength of Egypt, Syria, Jordan, Iraq, Lebanon, and Saudi Arabia at 482,000 troops (mostly regulars), 2,180 tanks, 848 combat aircraft. Israel's strength was estimated at 264,000 troops (mostly reservist), 800 tanks, 300 combat aircraft.

refugees can feel, down to the marrow of their bones. The incredible victory in the field alleviated the anguish but at the moment of victory there was a marked absence of gaiety. The routing of three Arab armies—more numerous and better equipped—by a force of hastily mobilized reservists had elicited little pride of triumph. The army of reservists, mobilized overnight, had quietly returned home, tired rather than festive, disgusted with war rather than elated by its outcome. Few Israelis had indulged themselves in the luxury of self-congratulation; most people had simply been relieved to have survived.

The reticence of eleven months before now gave way to a celebration more massive than anything seen in the twenty-year history of the state. All the emotions that had been subdued under a veil of shock and surprise, now, almost a year later, suddenly surged forward. For one or two days, in May 1968, they swept the masses like spring fever.

Jerusalem sits atop the central mountain-massif of Palestine; on a good day it is possible to see mountaintops fifty miles away, swimming in the distant heat on pillows of pellucid air. This was such a day. The weather was mild. For Jerusalem it was the best time of the year. The hilltops and valleys in and around this mountain city were not yet parched by the summer sun, but freshened by the green of a brief spring. Under a brilliantly translucent sky that hung over the city like a tent of spun silk, the ancient ramparts gleamed in a steady, blazing light of crystalline clarity. Rooftops, ruins, towers, terraces, and street poles were covered with flags.

One could see beyond the fluttering flags, down to the Wilderness of Judea, across the Jordan Valley to the mountains of Moab, luminous and bare. The Wilderness of Judea had been the home of the prophets in biblical times and from Moab Moses had been shown the Promised Land. The Wilderness was now occupied by Israeli armed forces; Moab was part of the Kingdom of Jordan.

Loudspeakers were turning the crowded, gaily decorated streets and squares into giant music halls. Everywhere there was singing and dancing. Yet, with all the merriment and pride of triumph or possession, for many of those present the paean of victory held ironic overtones. The war had borne many fruits, sweet and sour. The sweet ones were obvious, for the third Arab-Israeli War, lasting just six days, had ended in a crushing Arab defeat. The Arabs had lost a vast arsenal which was not yet replenished by their Soviet friends. Israel had new borders, strategically safer than before. Before the war, the border had been less than twenty miles away, and Tel Aviv had been within firing range of Jordanian artillery. The city and its suburbs, with almost half of Israel's population, could count on less than five minutes' warning before the start of air raids launched from Egyptian air fields in Sinai.

The roles were now largely reversed. Israeli forces stood less than thirty miles from Amman, thirty-five miles from Damascus, and seventy miles from Cairo. The war which the Arabs had hoped easily to pursue into Tel Aviv and Haifa had spun around and reached into their own suburbs and backyards. The great Egyptian cities and ports of Suez—Ismailiya, Port Fuad, and Port Said—were within firing range of Israeli artillery along the East Bank of the Suez Canal.

These were the sweet fruits of victory. The sour ones were not less obvious, and in the mouths of many Israelis the delicious flavor of success was tempered by the accompanying bitterness of futility and frustration. Triumph was mixed with terror; war had resolved some of Israel's immediate concerns, but military success had scarcely affected the need for peace and reconciliation with her Arab neighbors. In the immediate aftermath of victory, most Israelis had expected a final peace settlement with the Arabs within days, or weeks. Now, nearly a year later, they realized the vanity, or the naiveté of such hopes. It has been said that wars never "solve" problems. Wars have "settled" and still "settle" human affairs. But in settling one problem they invariably create new ones as grave or even graver than before. Few wars in recent history illustrated this truth as pointedly as the Arab-Israeli example of 1967. It deepened rather than allayed the Arab sense of outrage at the establishment and success of a state which, in their eyes, seemed a foreign intrusion. The war saved Israel from extinction, but it remained a beleaguered fortress state. Israel had more than quadrupled the territory under its control, but it had conquered more land and people than it knew what to do with.

In the territory now under its control, the population differed drastically from that of the pre-war period. The aim of Zionism had always been to establish a *Jewish* state in Palestine. This is what Israel was, for all practical purposes, up until the war of 1967. Now, by a brutal twist of fate, things were suddenly different. At war's end, more than a

million hostile, or at best deeply resentful and suspicious Arabs, former Jordanians or residents of the Gaza Strip, had come under Israeli
rule. Even as the crowds danced in the streets of Jerusalem, sappers
were moving about empty lots with electronic devices, looking for
time bombs and button mines. Cars were stopped, passers-by questioned, ladies' handbags checked. Arab nationalists, members of the
terrorist El Fatah group, had vowed to disrupt the Independence Day
celebrations. The irony of the situation was inescapable. Israelis, who
had themselves been terrorists only a quarter of a century before in
their struggle against the British, were now dismissing the Arab guerrillas as "thugs" and "corrupt racketeers."

The outskirts of Jerusalem were cordoned off by a vast force of
army and police searching for hidden weapons. In the Arab sector of
Jerusalem, incorporated into Israel as a spoils of the war, armed
guards sat on rooftops; soldiers, submachine guns slung over
their shoulders, patrolled the narrow lanes and covered bazaars of
the Old City. The shops were closed.

The night before there had been fireworks and more dancing in the
streets in the Jewish sector. Pop bands had played at street corners
and thousands had whirled in the hora. It had been a perfect night for
sleeping out, and many people simply lay down on sidewalks, exhausted after the dancing. Others had spent the night in parks and
empty lots, sitting around huge bonfires, singing folk songs with their
slow, melancholy tunes. Few drunks were seen; alcohol is not a popular vice among Israelis. But with that peculiarly Israeli exuberance that
feeds mainly on resources of mood and on nerves rather than liquor,
the celebrating masses were turning the entire city into one vast fair
ground.

In the morning the streets were still so filled with people that traffic
was at a standstill in the downtown area and in much of the residential district as well. The crowd was estimated at 600,000; one of every
four Israelis was there. Throughout the day people continued to
stream in from all parts of the country. Old-timers and newcomers;
dark-skinned immigrants from Arab countries, lighter-skinned immigrants from Central Europe; men with high-set Slavic cheeks and
short, curly raven-black hair; tall, pink-faced immigrants from the
Anglo-Saxon countries; *kibbutzniks* and bankers; day laborers who
earned £1450 per month and lived in public housing apartments, and

members of the new, wealthy bourgeoisie who came in their sleek Mustangs and Buicks from the richer residential areas of Jerusalem and Tel Aviv, from their houses along the Mediterranean coast and on the upper ridge of Haifa's Mount Carmel.

The city's 60,000 Arab residents shuttered their windows and stayed home. In Jerusalem on May 2, 1968, one man's triumph was another's tragedy. Leaders make mistakes but the price is most often paid by the people. If, in the fateful morning hours of June 5, 1967, the King of Jordan had not blundered into the war on Nasser's side and had instead heeded Israel's urgent appeal (through the United Nations and the American ambassador) to stay out of the fight, there would not have been Israeli forces now in the Arab sector of Jerusalem, nor elsewhere on the occupied West Bank of the River Jordan. There would have been no annexation by Israel of the Arab sector of Jerusalem. The Arabs of Jerusalem would not, in effect, have been second-class citizens of a Jewish town that was reunited by force of arms.

During the actual days of fighting, eleven months earlier, the Arab population of the Jordanian-held sector of the city had remained singularly passive. Although Arab Jerusalem had been a hotbed of nationalism for over half a century, during the war itself only Jordanian troops had done any fighting. Most of these troops had been Bedouin from the East Bank. Impassively, the civilian population had watched the conquest of their city. Only a few months before the conquest, pro-Nasserite demonstrators in Jerusalem had screamed for war with Israel; but when a blood bank was set up on the eve of hostilities, not a single donor had come forth. When the occupiers entered the Arab sector in their tanks and half-tracks, thousands of Arabs, young and old, had greeted them with traditional Arab hospitality ("Welcome, welcome!") and with calls of *Shalom! Shalom!*

There were no calls of *shalom* now. A few weeks earlier, twelve members of an underground terrorist cell that had planted a bomb in a Jerusalem movie house were arrested by the police. A number of prominent Arab civic leaders, including the former mayor, had been expelled to Jordan by the Israeli authorities. As Jewish Jerusalem celebrated a few hundred yards away, Israeli troops patrolled the deserted lanes of the Old City. From time to time an anguished pair of eyes would peer through windows or shuttered doors. From the city's mosques, the tape-recorded voices of muezzins echoed as usual over the stone roofs, through a forest of television antennas. But on May 2, 1968, few Moslems showed up for prayer. Over Amman radio came an announcement that this was a day of mourning, and of contemplation for revenge.

In the morning the Israeli air force staged a fly-past. It was followed by a grand military parade. In the preceding weeks the parade had been the subject of a heated public controversy. A considerable number of Israelis felt sure that this was not the best way to celebrate the event. Three wars in a lifetime of conflict had turned Israelis into a nation of amateur soldiers, disciplined to the rigors of frequent and long years of service in the army reserve, reconciled to living in a fortress state. But military paraphernalia still regularly evoked massive uneasiness. There had been considerable public soul searching as to the wisdom of staging a show of military force. Supporters of the parade said that it enabled the nation to express its gratitude to the soldiers. The protesters answered that only totalitarian countries indulged in such displays; military parades belonged to Moscow, Madrid, and Cairo.

In the middle of the public controversy, the opponents of the military parade received some support from an unexpected source. While watching the finals of a colorful cross-country walk called the *Tzaada*—a popular sport imported from Holland which annually brings out thousands of participants of all ages—General Chaim Barlev, Chief of Staff, commented that such a fete would probably be a much more fitting way to celebrate future Independence days than the traditional display of guns, tanks, and political brass. The country had outgrown the stage, General Barlev thought, where it needed public shows of military might to reassure itself.

The controversial parade of 1968 did indeed become the last display of its kind in Israel. The critics had not been totally unsuccessful and subsequent Independence days were staged as civilian events. But on that occasion, eleven months after the war, Israelis thoroughly enjoyed themselves. Settled on plastic cushions in the wooden grandstands, and in ever larger numbers along the parade route across the city, the crowds greeted the armed forces with tremendous roars of applause. Leading the fly-past were a few dozen Israeli-produced Fouga Mystère jet trainers. During the war they had substituted for missing light, ground-support bombers. As such, they had contributed heavily to the routing of Egypt's technically superior armored corps. Flying low over the rooftops of the city, tailing smoke clouds in the national colors of blue and white, they formed a huge Star of David in the sky.

Next came, in quick succession, formations of French-built Mirage Three fighter-interceptors, Votour bombers, and American-built Sky-hawks, the planes which, in the early hours of the war, had knocked out the larger, but unalert, air forces of Egypt, Syria, and Jordan and thus had determined the war's outcome. There were transport planes and helicopters, and a lone Russian MIG 21 which had been flown to Israel two years earlier by a defecting Iraqi pilot.

Then the ground forces moved up, headed by armored units, troop carriers, half-tracks. Clumsy steel monsters, heavy Patton and Centurion tanks plowed up the asphalt; their crews in battle fatigues stood in open turrets, smartly saluting. Next came a column of war booty; Russian-made tanks and cannons passed the grandstands, their gun barrels drooping in an expression of defeat. The tanks were followed by captured Russian rockets, troop carriers, and trucks.

So heavy was the roar of the equipment that the audience sat in silence. Less dramatic, but infinitely more colorful, were the marching columns which followed the booty. There were paratroopers in green camouflage uniforms and red berets, flying cadets and sailors, pretty girl soldiers in near-miniskirts, infantry units, signalmen, and engineers. Each unit was preceded by a massive formation of flag carriers stepping in smart unison. Now the crowd really stirred; silence gave way to outbursts of cheers. Neatly turned out in their tight-fitting sand and grass-colored uniforms, their pants tucked neatly in their boots and their sleeves rolled up, the marchers passed, looking incredibly young. Their average age was nineteen. Israel is such a small country that in the vast crowd there were few who did not have a son or daughter, brother, cousin, friend, or neighbor marching past the grandstands.

Slowly the parade moved down the slopes of Mount Scopus to the walls of the Old City. It continued along a winding route across the New City to where its suburbs merge with the outskirts of Bethlehem. The route had been selected for reasons of traffic regulation, and to give the largest number of people a chance to watch it in relative comfort. Yet like almost everything else here in the ancient city of Jerusalem, the route also evoked rich historical associations. The Romans had taken this route in A.D. 70, when they sacked Jerusalem, burned it down, and began the dispersion of the Jews that is not yet over. Before the Romans, the armies of Nebuchadnezzar had come the same way, down the slopes of Mount Scopus toward Mount Moriah, where Solomon's Temple had stood. Later came the Byzantines, the Arabs, the Crusaders, the Mamelukes, the Turks, and the English. All had followed the same track, from Scopus to Moriah, with a regularity that seemed dictated by topography, and which the Israeli victory parade was now taking almost inadvertently.

At certain historic sites, though they are only dust and stone, the most self-righteous conqueror can be haunted by spirits which constantly hover in men's imagination. Nearly a thousand years earlier, another conquest of Jerusalem—by the Knights of the First Crusade—had resulted in the ruthless slaughter of its Moslem (and Jewish) inhabitants. It was this bloodthirsty Christian fanaticism that in the 11th century had re-created the fanaticism of Islam. The Jewish conquerors of modern Jerusalem were not Crusaders, but bewildered men and women fighting for their survival as individuals and as a nation. They had felt threatened; hitting back, they succeeded beyond their wildest expectations. The Jewish conquest of Jerusalem precipitated no outrage, no massacre, yet none was needed to kindle the ever-growing fires of Arab hatred. National passions were strong enough.

In the main grandstands, against a dramatic background of waving flags, blazing emblems, and distant mountains, Israel's aging power elite watched the parade go by. The entire government was there, headed by the President and flanked by scores of septuagenarian and octogenarian settlers, the last of the first, remnants of Jewish immigration to Palestine in the early part of the century.

For the old leaders, this was an hour of achievement such as is given to few men in public life. Their record was probably unparalleled in modern history, for these old veterans in the grandstand had not only revolutionized their society but also to a large extent created it. Israel had come into being contrary to all prevailing reason, in the course of their own lifetimes, on new territory, through a modern

Völkerwanderung of outcasts and idealists. Such things had happened before, of course, but never so quickly, within the life span of a generation of founding fathers. Other immigrant communities that were established overseas, on new territories, had enjoyed the powerful military and political support of a mother country. The Zionist settlers had accomplished their task alone, with only financial aid from their co-religionists abroad.

An observer of the scene must pause here. Let him rest his spotlight on these old men and women, as they sit perched upon wooden planks, perspiring uneasily in the sun. For their stormy lives reflect much of the drama and grandeur as well as the irony and tragedy of the moment. From the circumstances of their lives, their achievements, their pious dreams and illusions, there emerges a saga not merely political, but human and dramatic. With few exceptions the veterans are now in their seventies and eighties. Their skins are parched, their taut faces lined by deep furrows, their heads snow white or bald. Remnants of a small group of Eastern European romantics, they are now stooped, burned out by the fires of their youth, and yet surrounded by the sovereign power of a nation which half a century before had been but a figment of their wild imagination. Their lives exude a curiously mixed air of matter-of-factness and romance, of eccentricity and conventionality. Earlier in this century— as obscure figures in now forgotten Zionist discussion groups in Poland, White Russia, and the Ukraine—they had helped to begin the sequence of events that was culminating that day. They were now seeing the efforts of their long lives come to fruition, but in a way and form which few had ever expected. Nearly all had come to the country before 1914, or immediately after World War I, as young men and women. Most had left behind relatively well-to-do middle-class homes. Their hard-working but generous fathers and doting Jewish mothers hoped that their sons would become academicians or go into business. Instead, the sons settled on the land as farm laborers. Dressed in rags, they frequently went hungry, were regularly stricken down by attacks of typhoid and malaria, and were often forced to defend their farms against armed Arab neighbors.

In the late 1920s the future leaders gradually passed on to trade union work, journalism, and politics. Their lives were totally dedicated to a cause. Some directed the fiscal affairs of their settlements, managed workers' sick funds, or purchased land for resettlement. They colonized hard, arid, seemingly impossible desert and mountain regions. Some worked as organizers of a clandestine defense force; some ran an underground route for illegal immigrants in defiance of British immigration regulations. Others tirelessly toured Jewish communities abroad to collect the huge funds necessary to finance it all. They had little time for their families; their wives were often engaged in similar work. Few had hobbies; hardly anyone pursued a sport. With the tenacity which Latins devote to love and Frenchmen to food, they pursued and served the idea of Zion Revived. Socialists and Zionists, they were secular rabbis of a new faith of redemption. Their main relaxation consisted of composing argumentative, quarrelsome, ideological diatribes against one another upholding the superiority of one notion of socialism, or Zionism, or an amalgam of both, over all others. Even when in office they lived frugally on ridiculously low incomes. Their salaries were tied to the wage scale of farm or industrial workers and graded not according to rank, but according to the number of dependents. Only occasionally were salaries augmented by expense accounts, and even then tastes remained modest. A ready-made suit in New York, purchased at a discount from a sympathetic Jewish tailor, a few nylon shirts, a transistor radio or electric hand mixer—at a time when such luxuries were unavailable in Israel—were their most cherished personal possessions. But when it came to The Cause—a *kibbutz*, a school, a party, a land reclamation agency, a community center—their capacity to raise, and occasionally squander, enormous sums of money, was boundless. They developed fund raising to an art both rare and fine. Jews have always answered generously to appeals for help. But the skill of these men in putting that tradition to work has probably never been equaled.

Resolute and resourceful abroad, at home they often fought one another with a ferocity that seems to characterize the in-fighting of most revolutions. In their lifetime, historical processes normally much longer had shortened sensationally. They had lived their Utopias in their own lives. There were moments when it was difficult for them to believe what they had done. In one short lifetime, a modern welfare state had grown up in what had been a backward, partly barren, thinly populated Ottoman province. In one short lifetime, a nation, spirited and cohesive, had developed out of a horde of frightened refugees, the outcasts of Europe, survivors of concentration camps and primitive, half-literate masses from the shoddy souks of the Near East and North Africa. A common language, painfully resurrected from the dead, had emerged from a babel of tongues. In one short lifetime, big cities, theaters, orchestras, ballet troupes, had sprouted in a profusion rarely found in much larger nations. Zoos, ports, and airfields, industries, superhighways, traffic jams, great universities; all were the realization of their dreams.

Those still alive and present at the twentieth-anniversary celebration were old, tired, and not a little confused. Some sat on the grandstands with their middle-aged sons and grandsons. Others saw their heirs marching by below on the hot asphalt. The President reviewed the troops from a small wooden stage, upon which a few armchairs had been placed. At seventy-nine, President Zalman Shazar was a small, portly, white-haired, kindly old gentleman of great personal charm. He was now hardly more than a political figurehead; in past decades he had played a considerable role, first as a Zionist agitator, later as Israel's first Minister of Education. He was a prolific writer and poet in Hebrew, Russian, and Yiddish. A public speaker of great fervor and effectiveness, his speeches sometimes lasted up to ten hours. Once, in the 1930s, in Tel Aviv, he was so carried away by an argument in favor of social democracy that he stepped over the edge of the stage and fell three feet into the orchestra pit.

Shazar was a nationalist of the old, liberal style, reminiscent of a Mazzini or a Masaryk. He was a socialist of the democratic pre-revolutionary Russian school. By temperament and intellectual background Shazar was almost interchangeable with the liberal socialists, mensheviks, or social-revolutionaries who in the fateful spring of 1917 had tried to make both socialism *and* democracy work in Russia, until such radiant designs were shattered in the agonies of civil war and bolshevik repression. With all his commitment to modern socialism, he was steeped in the traditions of the former Jewish Pale of Eastern Europe. Few Israeli politicians combined so well the idealistic fervor of social democracy and religion, Hassidism and poetry, Zionism and Sabbatean Messianism.

Shazar was born in 1889 in the little Russian hamlet of Mir, near Minsk. Mir burned down a few years after his birth. His family then moved to the nearby town of Stoibitz. There the small Jewish community was coming into ever-increasing contact with its Russian neighbors; its simple life was overshadowed by the revolutionary strivings that seized the country at that time. Shazar later wrote in a moving memoir: "What one's soul absorbed at that period of one's fresh youth is sealed forever with love's fire . . . its effects never cease."

The distinguished Hassidic family from which he came was just beginning the transition from orthodox Judaism to European culture. Families like this were producing in almost equal numbers leading Zionist pioneers and socialist revolutionaries. Not infrequently, as with Shazar, the two movements overlapped. His underground work in Russia ended in a Czarist jail. Discharged, he went to Palestine in 1911, to work briefly as a farm laborer in Galilee. He returned to Russia to do his military service, but was soon discharged on medical grounds. Russian universities at that time were closed to most Jewish young men, so Shazar went to Germany to study. He returned to Palestine and settled there permanently in 1924.

Flanking President Shazar on the main grandstand were Premier Levi Eshkol and his Minister of Defense Moshe Dayan. Eshkol, already a sick man (he was to die within a year), was a man of great moderation and considerable political skill. He had succeeded the fiery Ben Gurion as Premier in 1963. Dayan, a former general, was the architect of Israel's victories in her last two wars, 1956 and 1967. It was hard to imagine two more different men.

Eshkol, at seventy-two, was a man of the old, passing order of wider Jewish loyalties. Dayan, though he often claimed, "I am first a Jew, and an Israeli only second," represented a new locally bred, locally oriented generation of hardened, morally disillusioned younger men, self-reliant, asking no man for sympathy and with little of their own to give. At fifty-three, tough and competent, Dayan conformed to a somber ideal of perfection not untypical of the modern world. He had been in four wars, and in frequent border skirmishes between. He often said he feared he might have to go to war again. His oval head was balding. His face was smooth and sun-burned; his cheekbones high; his thin, sensuous lips sarcastically dropped to one side, cutting a diagonal frown across his boyish face. Even when he smiled, the drooping left corner of his mouth lent his expression an unexpected air of enigmatic bitterness, irony, and a little disdain. The foreboding black patch over his left eye seemed part of the mute, melancholy landscape, an incarnation of its rocky, arid surface.

Eshkol was a sociable, rather garrulous, and marvelously witty, experienced party functionary, widely liked, but not much respected. His heavy figure, his broad, relaxed, fleshy face, with something like a reflection of well-earned contentment, suggested patience, humor, an easy-going temper, and the benevolence that comes of a lifetime of reconciling antagonistic views. Dayan, a lone wolf in politics, was much admired for his war record but feared for alleged dictatorial tendencies. Eshkol, a typical committee man, aimed at consensus; he was given much to compromise, for which he had earned a not undeserved reputation of flabbiness in action and indecision at time of crisis. He was the butt of innumerable political jokes. According to one of the better-known anecdotes, when asked by a waiter in a café whether he would like coffee or tea, he stammered a while, and finally blurted: "You know what, make it *chetzi-chetzi* (half and half)."

Dayan, openly contemptuous of committee work and "unnecessary blabber," was a believer in lone decisions, for which he was prepared to shoulder all responsibility. Eshkol was a political tactician; he owed his position at the helm of the current national coalition to his colleagues' fear of stronger men and to his own talent for reconciling opposites within a cabinet comprised of right and left, religious and secularists, hawks and doves. Dayan, impatient of normal party procedure, was in the cabinet despite Eshkol's opposition. He had come to his present post a few days prior to the 1967 war. He owed his position to the exigencies of war and the fears generated by crisis. Shortly after his appointment on the eve of the war, he said: "One hundred thousand Egyptian soldiers were necessary to put me into the cabinet."

Eshkol spent most of his public life as a trade union man; as head of the Department of Colonization, he initiated and directed vast irrigation schemes. He was Ben Gurion's Minister of Finance. His life was forged by the ever-growing effort in construction during the past fifty years. Dayan had been a military man from his earliest manhood; his life was forged by war. Eshkol was an early immigrant while Dayan was a first-generation *sabra*, the second child born in the country's first *kibbutz*, Degania, on the shore of the Lake of Galilee. Eshkol had lost his father in a Russian pogrom; he remembered huddling in a tightly shuttered home as a child, hiding from ransacking, raping Cossacks.

He carried in his heart the gloom and sardonic humor, the lack of certainty of the Diaspora. Dayan had lost his left eye in one war and his only brother in another. He grew up in a hard frontier atmosphere, where men did not hide behind shutters but often kept their lives because they fought for them. An Australian officer who was present when Dayan lost his eye in battle during the British advance to Vichy Syria, in 1941, later wrote: "What a pity that this courageous lad— who used to cast one eye down to the plow while the other was on guard—will now possess only one eye. Will that eye be turned to Mars?"

Although Eshkol and Dayan were scarcely on speaking terms, there was little animosity to be seen as they sat, flanking the kindly old head of state, exchanging pleasantries with him and gracefully acknowledging the salutes of the passing troops. Eshkol, slightly bent as he slouched in his seat, wore a gray business suit and dark tie. Dayan, in his general's uniform, sat stiff as a stick, not out of miltary decorum, but because of the plaster corset he wore as the result of a back injury he had recently suffered while engaged in his favorite hobby of archeology. A hole he had been digging in search of antiquities had suddenly caved in and buried him in the debris. He was unconscious and near suffocation when uncovered; he was rushed just in time to a nearby hospital. His ribs were broken and his spine injured.

Other survivors of the fast-shrinking group of founding fathers were sitting close by on another stand reserved for VIPs. There was Golda Meir, at seventy, the Grand Old Lady of the ruling labor party, Israel's first ambassador to Moscow, and a former foreign minister. She had arrived in the country in 1921 from the United States, where she had been a schoolteacher in Milwaukee. But as a native of Czarist Russia, she too had childhood memories of the sound of hammers boarding up doors and windows against marauding Ukrainian peasants and the clatter of the rearing horses that the Cossacks rode through Jewish streets in Kiev as they put houses to the torch. "If there is any logical explanation necessary to the direction which my life has taken," she once said, "maybe this is the explanation: the desire and determination to save Jewish children, four or five years old, from a similar scene, from a similar experience."

Her arrival in Moscow in 1949 precipitated a massive street demonstration by tens of thousands of wildly cheering Jews, a spontaneous outburst unprecedented in the history of the Soviet Union. As Minister of Foreign Affairs (1955–1965) she had been second only to the Premier in her influence. She was now temporarily out of office, having resigned her last executive post because of age, health, and general fatigue. Yet within a year—in what would be an extraordinary display of energy and recovered health—she would be succeeding Eshkol in the premiership. The slightly square, somewhat masculine, heavy-set body, the nicotine-stained fingers of an inveterate chain smoker, the powerful nose and impatient manner contrasted oddly but not unpleasantly with a homely face of extraordinary softness, a warm and pleasant voice, and the simple gray bun of a grandmother. Her deep soft eyes with their look of almost childish sincerity concealed an iron will matched by few of the men in whose midst she sat.

A little farther down the grandstand there were additional survivors of the generation of founders. The "quiet little great," they had stayed out of public life, to remain on the land where they watched their children and grandchildren till the fields they themselves had cleared of boulders and drained of swamps in the first decades of the century. Most of the marching soldiers were hardly aware of the roles the old men had played in an earlier, less publicity-conscious age. They probably did not even know their names; had they been told, they probably would have vaguely smiled.

Many of the marching soldiers were sons of Oriental immigrants, dark-skinned young men of Moroccan or Iraqi origin, and as uncomprehending of the East European Zionist mystique of the founding fathers as Sicilian or Polish immigrants must have been of the ideology of the New England puritans in America. The young marchers of European origin were also, in a way, a new breed. The old group was already losing active communication with them. The veterans spoke a language, both in form and essence, that sounded strange to these young men. To those who had grown up to take Israel for granted, the frequent talk of "Zionist ideals" or "national renaissance" had begun to sound like so much abstract nonsense. In their parlance *Tzionut* (Zionism) had become synonymous with blather.

Sitting on the VIP grandstand, but unknown to most onlookers, was Dayan's father, Shmuel, who had arrived in 1908 from the Ukraine as a teen-ager with the second wave of immigrants. Shmuel

Dayan had rebelled early against the extreme collectivism of the first *kibbutzim*. In the early 1920s he had co-founded the rival, but less collective, cooperative settlers union—the *moshav*—which in later years went on to vastly outnumber the more doctrinaire *kibbutz*. He had retired from parliament in 1959, when his son, Moshe, entered. The old Dayan, in his plain khaki trousers and yellow, open-necked shirt, was in town from his farm in Moshav Nahalal to watch the troops salute his triumphant son. He too would die within the year.

Nearby sat Yitzchak Tabenkin, who had left his native Russia in 1905 to become a co-founder of the powerful *Kibbutz Meuchad* movement. His small, roundish face was covered by a beautiful white beard; he had turned to mysticism in his old days. Next to Tabenkin was the Speaker of the parliament, Kadish Luz. Luz was a native of Bobruisk, a Jewish town in Byelo-Russia famous for its rabbis and institutions of learning. While still in Bobruisk, Luz founded a training farm for prospective Zionist pioneers. He served with the Czarist army in World War I and later became an officer in the Red Army. Luz left the Soviet Union in 1920 and settled in Palestine as a road worker. He co-founded a *kibbutz* and stayed in charge of its cowshed until 1948.

In the front row, on a padded chair placed especially for her comfort, Rachel Yanait Ben Zvi watched the parade go by. A frail, thin old lady of eighty-one, she was the widow of Israel's second President, Yitzchak Ben Zvi. Rachel Ben Zvi was a pioneer and a political figure in her own right. She played a prominent role in Zionist affairs from the time she first arrived in the country in 1908. Even before that, despite her relative youth, she had been a veteran of underground socialist and Zionist work in Czarist Russia. At the age of seventeen she had been arrested by the Russian police for participating in a clandestine socialist meeting. At her release from prison more than a year later, her apprehensive father had assured the director of the prison: "I promise you, sir, that she will stay out of trouble from now on. We will keep her home." But the young girl had broken in: "No, I will not!" She had then gone on to tell the warden, "But have no worry; I have no use for this Russia of yours. I don't need it. We have our own country—the Land of Israel."

Her parents, hoping to divert their young firebrand to more sober pursuits, sent her to St. Petersburg to study. There, in 1908, she later recalled, she was sitting with her books at the Hermitage Library, when she was suddenly seized by so strong a desire to become a pioneer girl in Palestine that she left her books on the table, ran home, packed her things, and took the first train south. At the Black Sea port of Odessa, while waiting for a boat, she encountered Chaim Nachman Bialik, the leading Hebrew poet of the time and a resident of Odessa. Bialik asked her, "But what will you *do* in Palestine?" She answered him: "I will live."

On a stand far away from the other celebrities, sharing the benches reserved for paying foreign tourists, but known nevertheless by all around him, sat one of the main heroes of the drama, the old man of Israeli politics, David Ben Gurion. He had spent the last five years in semi-retirement at his desert retreat, a little wooden hut on the edge of Kibbutz Sde Boker. He was still pursuing an angry, acrimonious feud with his successor, Levi Eshkol. He himself had picked Eshkol as his heir as premier and warmly recommended him to his party; yet he now considered him "perfidious," even dangerous to the well-being of the state, "immoral," and a "shocking liar." As a result of this running feud, he refused to take his seat on the main grandstand, and sat with his old friend, Teddy Kollek, the Mayor of Jerusalem.

David Ben Gurion had run the affairs of the new state from its inception in 1948. Before 1948, with a terrible simplicity of vision and single-mindedness of purpose, he had led the community of Jewish colonists and urban settlers on the road to self-determination and independence. He was now eighty-two years old. Aging, but singularly alert, Ben Gurion was still taking his daily five-mile constitutional. He was an old man of small height, but his unassuming figure, short and stocky, came with a pair of direct, incredibly bright, steel-blue-gray eyes that were the true index of his fiery temperament. Even at this advanced age they exuded an air of frightening determination. His legs were shorter than they perhaps should have been; they enhanced the imposing vigor of his sturdy frame. His high forehead was covered by an almost feminine mane of flowing white hair. His strong chin, which he normally thrust forward in an expression both puzzled and defiant, was set on a thick, short neck. His pink, smooth leatherlike skin made him look more and more like an American Indian as the years passed.

David Ben Gurion, born David Grien in 1886, was a native of

Plonsk, a small town some forty miles northwest of Warsaw in Czar-
ist-ruled Poland. He was the sixth child of Sheindle and Avigdor
Grien. The mother died while the future premier was still an infant.
The father was a provincial lay lawyer and notary public. His main
task was to write petitions for illiterate peasants and to act as go-
between on affairs with the authorities.

In 1906, seized by an irresistible urge, the young David Grien left
his father's house. He was twenty at the time, and already transfixed
by a dream that would not leave him his entire life. With only a small
knapsack on his back, he traveled by fourth-class train to Odessa,
continued in steerage across the Black Sea and down the eastern shore
of the Mediterranean. Three weeks after his departure from Plonsk,
travel-stained and weary, he was finally rowed ashore onto the rocky
port of Jaffa. The promised land, as it appeared to him that day, was a
small dusty town of some 15,000 Arabs and 3,000 Jews engaged in
petty business. Ben Gurion did not like Jaffa; he found it filthy and
depressing. He did not even stop overnight when he came off the ship
after his long journey. He continued on foot across barren and
swampy sand dunes which would subsequently become the traffic-
choked metropolitan area of greater Tel Aviv with a population of
more than one million, to the nearby colony of Petach Tikva.

Petach Tikva, today a city of 100,000 and an important industrial center, at that time was a small village of a few hundred
souls. A muddy path led through its single street. Ben Gurion spent
his first night in a workers' hostel, a wooden shack with straw mats.
He did not sleep. In a lyric mood that would be seen less and less in
later years, he wrote:

> I did not sleep. I was among the rich smell of corn. I heard the
> braying of donkeys and the rustling of leaves in the orchards. Above
> were the massed clusters of stars clear against the deep blue firma-
> ment. My heart overflowed with happiness as if I had entered the
> realm of joy. . . . A dream was celebrating its victory. I am in Eretz
> Israel, in a Hebrew village in Eretz Israel, in a Hebrew village called
> *Petach Tikva* ("Gate of Hope").

He hired himself out as a field worker to farmers who had settled in
Petach Tikva some twenty or twenty-five years earlier. Economically,
Petach Tikva was still a shaky enterprise. The farmers' deficits were

covered by generous donations from Baron Edmond de Rothschild of Paris. There were no subsidies for the hired laborers and their lives were especially harsh. Malaria was a frequent visitor, as was hunger. In a letter to his father a short time after his arrival, Ben Gurion wrote: "But who is to complain, to sigh, to despair? In twenty-five years our country will be one of the most blooming, most beautiful and happiest; an old-new nation will flourish in an ancient-new land. Then we shall relate how we fevered and worked, hungered and dreamed." The revolution he was contemplating was to take much longer to achieve.

It is not customary to speak of Zionism as a revolution. But, if revolution connotes a sudden, far-reaching change, a major break in the continuity of development, the word is certainly applicable to modern Zionism.

As a revolution, Zionism profoundly affected the lives of men. It gave people, thus far powerless and disenfranchised, a measure of power to decide their own fate. In an hour of extreme need, when others were reluctant to seriously help them in their agony, the Zionist revolutionaries taught Jews to help themselves. The Zionist revolution took a great many people out of near medieval serfdom and within less than half a century it afforded them the dignity of free life in a rebuilt country and the opportunities inherent in a modern, egalitarian welfare state. In the *kibbutzim* it realized (with greater success than had been possible elsewhere) a utopian society, which, on a limited scale, still expresses some of the noblest aspirations of mankind. It also gave people a new language; and in many ways, an entirely new culture. It changed not only their socio-economic structure, but their climate, cuisine, and geography as well.

The Zionist revolution failed in one of its major aims. It did not automatically secure Jews from assault. But a people, who for centuries had been the helpless prey of innumerable massacres by religious and political bigots, were at least now in a position to undertake their own defense.

Every revolution has its price, of course, and the Zionist revolution was no exception. By a brutal twist of fate, unexpected, undesired, unconsidered by the early pioneers, this price was partly paid by the Arab inhabitants of Palestine. The Arabs bore no responsibility for the centuries-long suffering of Jews in Europe; yet, in the end, the Arabs were punished because of it. The price extracted was heavy; it is impossible to measure it in terms of human bitterness and suffering. Whatever their subsequent follies and outrages might be, the punishment of the Arabs for the sins of Europe must burden the conscience of Israelis for a long time to come.

The exact number of casualties inflicted on both sides has never been ascertained. It is estimated that about 80,000 (four-fifths of them Arabs) have died in the minor skirmishes and major Arab-Jewish wars over Palestine in the last fifty years.

Approximately 1,300,000 Jewish immigrants entered the country in the years between Independence and 1967; of them, some 1,150,000 remained. At the same time roughly 600,000 Palestinian Arabs lost their homes and became refugees. Jews and Arabs have since accused one another of having caused this tragic exodus by calculated measures. There is an element of truth in both charges, and yet the basic cause lies in neither argument. Many left their homes, as is common with peasants everywhere, to evade what they hoped would be temporary hostilities. Often they moved just a few miles, to the next village, only to flee again as the fast-moving forces caught up with them. Some were ordered to leave, either by their short-sighted leaders, or, less frequently, by the advancing Jews.

They and their children have since multiplied to more than 1,300,000. In 1970, over 500,000 of the 1948 refugees still led wretchedly poor lives in miserable United Nations refugee camps. In the years between 1949 and 1967 the Arab states had used the refugees as political pawns and refused to do anything serious about their resettlement. The roles were reversed after 1967, when many of the refugee camps came under Israeli rule. Now Israel used them as political pawns and did little or nothing toward their permanent resettlement.

An additional 200,000 Arabs fled from their homes on the West Bank of the Jordan as a result of the Six Day War of 1967. Some left in the face of advancing Israeli troops, who urged them to remain, others left for Transjordan after the cease-fire on June 10. The tragedy of the Arab refugees is one of the most excruciatingly bitter prices exacted by Zionism.

This is not how the Zionist pioneers had intended it. Quite the contrary, they had hoped that two nations, Jews and Arabs, could live together peacefully and amicably for the benefit of both. To the centuries-old Jewish conflict with Christianity, a new, unprecedented collision—between Judaism and Islam—was added. This is the second great price of Zionism. It is a conflict likely to continue and deepen for a considerable time and may last generations.

Moslem-Jewish relations, of course, were not exactly rosy even before Zionism. The so-called Golden Age of Jewish-Moslem cooperation in the Middle Ages is at least partly a myth. It was propagated for pious reasons during the past fifty years by those who hoped to soften the severity of the Arab-Jewish conflict by holding up an image of past brotherhood. Islamic societies were never as tolerant of Jewish minorities as is often claimed. Jews, like Christians in the Moslem world, were always second-class citizens. In countries such as Yemen, Iraq, and Morocco, they were subjected to severe repressive measures.

But in the East there had never, or almost never, been a pogrom of Jews. There had not been hatred of Jews based on purely racial grounds, as in Europe. In this sense, the Arabs had never been "anti-Semitic." They were now beginning to be. The Arab-Israeli conflict was producing a species of Arab anti-Semitism never before seen. This newly generated anti-Semitism was making it almost impossible for Jews to continue to live in Arab countries. Even Moslem countries which were not Arab, or geographically so remote that they had never been involved in the Palestine conflict, were affected. In countries as different and distant from one another as Iraq and Morocco, Tunis and Yemen, Jews had been settled for centuries, even before the arrival of Islam. The Arab-Israeli conflict forced almost a million Jews to leave the Islamic countries. Of them, about two-thirds, mainly the poor, have found their way to Israel.

The early Zionists proclaimed their hope to "normalize" Jewish life. They wanted to take a holiday from Judaism as it had existed throughout two millennia. But as the Arab-Israeli conflict intensified, with little if any hope of reconciliation, it became evident that even in Israel there was to be no holiday.

In the hour of triumph, on Israel's twentieth anniversary (a century since the beginning of modern Zionism), there was a growing awareness among Israelis of their dismal predicament. The speeches delivered on that day were full of somber warnings of hard times still to come. Another war was generally, even placidly, considered "inevitable," perhaps within two or three years, and Israelis awaited it like the visit of a tedious and meddling mother-in-law. Some said that a war every five or ten years was the price they must pay if they wished to survive.

In previous years there had always been a widespread assumption among Israelis that peace with the Arabs was possible. In the immediate aftermath of the 1967 war, the belief in imminent peace reached a euphoric peak. It lasted only a few months. Contrary to most people's expectations, the Arabs refused to make peace. Now the bitter conflict dividing Arabs and Israelis was not expected to end in a single lifetime, nor even perhaps in the lifetime of the next generation. Some Israelis were saying that "nothing we could safely offer in concession is likely to satisfy the hurt pride of the Arabs." A few were claiming that they understood the Arabs. "After all, we took a country they considered their own. If I were an Arab I would probably be as adamant as they." Ben Gurion, who, in the 1920s had often stressed the need for Arab-Jewish accommodation—for which he had been criticized by Zionist right-wingers as a deracinated cosmopolitan and doctrinaire socialist—now empathized with the Arab *fedayeen*. Privately, the old statesman who had spent his entire life in the accomplishment of Zion was saying that if he were a young Arab, he might also be one of the *fedayeen*.

The new fatalism was well echoed by Moshe Dayan. In a short autobiographical piece written for the American magazine, *Esquire*, he reflected with some bitterness on that part of his life which seemed to him "misspent." With characteristic candor, Dayan wrote:

> In one important way my life has been a failure. . . . I set out to be a farmer—and I think I made quite a good farmer. Yet I have spent most of my adult life as a soldier, under arms. I . . . was born in 1915, in a *kibbutz* near the Sea of Galilee. It had been a malarial swamp. My father and his fellow pioneers had cleared several acres, and now, after centuries of neglect they had been made fruitful again. Farming, for me, is not only a means for living but also a [moral] concept.

Dayan wrote that in his heart he still abided by this concept of the early pioneers to cultivate "another acre of swamp and desert, and yet another acre. Thus by constructive efforts would we renew the contact between our nation and our ancient homeland." Yet although he wanted to be a farmer, he had been a soldier since the age of sixteen.

"Although we [now] are on the Suez and on the Jordan," Dayan wrote elsewhere, "and despite our readiness for far-reaching concessions it still holds true that if we wish to continue our work against their will there is no escape from bloody sacrifice. We are doomed to live with [the Arabs] in a state of permanent belligerency. Perhaps this is undesirable; but such is reality."

This was a new, harder language, rarely heard in the early, more optimistic pioneering days. Only a handful of hard-boiled realists of power—decried by most settlers as dangerous and "un-Jewish" immoralists—had used such language. The early settlers fatally misjudged the situation. They came to a country which, in their eyes, was empty, or almost empty—a common optical illusion among Europeans in the late nineteenth century. They saw themselves as a progressive, socialist force. If they anticipated difficulties, they expected them to be with "international capitalism," with the colonial powers, the Ottoman Empire and its British successor. Yet, Turkey's opposition ended with her defeat in World War I, British opposition at the conclusion of World War II. The early settlers misunderstood the Arabs of Palestine and the neighboring countries.

Of course, they also had the misfortune to arrive too late on the scene. What might have been considered natural and right in 1830, or 1850, was beginning to be questionable by the time the first Zionist colonists set foot in Palestine. Fifty, or eighty, years before, it might have still been possible to settle Palestine without too much ado. But the Zionist pioneers started out in 1881. Their claims were recognized internationally in 1917 and 1920, not in 1800 or 1830.

Nor could they have begun earlier, for Zionism was as much a product of the new age of nationalism as was its Arab protagonist. The clash in Palestine was not between natives and colonialists in the ordinary sense, but between two nationalist movements. Both were, in their own way, "right" and "natural." The fault, if there was one, lay less with the men directly involved on both sides than with the new world of ferociously hostile nation-states in which they lived. If men had higher aims there would have been no Palestine conflict, nor, probably, "Jews" and "Arabs."

If, in this conflict between two nationalisms, Israel seemed to persevere, it was not solely through the exertions of her people, or because of international support and sympathy. In a curious way, the Arabs had been among her best allies. Had they agreed, in 1919, to accept *a* Jewish homeland in their midst, as stipulated in the Balfour Declaration, a Jewish minority, moderate in size, would in time have been absorbed into an Arab Palestinian state. A few years later the British proposed a mixed Palestine legislative council that would have paved the way to a predominantly Arab, independent Palestinian state. The proposal was accepted by Chaim Weizmann, who later became first President of Israel. Weizmann's opponents on the militant, right wing of Zionism attacked his acceptance as a betrayal of the Zionist dream. In accepting the proposal, Weizmann felt he was remaining loyal to the liberal traditions of world Jewry. Yet even this much the Arabs refused. Had they agreed, the Jews would probably have remained a minority forever; at best, they would have enjoyed a parity status within a mixed Palestinian state, perhaps like the Maronites in Lebanon. By shutting their eyes completely to the motives of the Zionists and by refusing all compromise with them—the Arabs were courting their future disasters.

If, in 1937, the Arabs had agreed to the Peel Commission report which proposed a lopsided partition of the country into a tiny free-city-of-Danzig-type Jewish state, and a large Arab one, they would probably have swallowed the autonomous Jewish area within a generation. The Woodhead Commission report of 1938 proposed an even smaller Jewish autonomy; both reports were rejected by the Arabs. The White Paper of 1939, issued mainly to win Arab sympathies away from Nazi Germany, seriously curtailed Jewish settlement and immigration; but the Arabs did not accept it. The plan of 1946 to admit no more than a final 100,000 Jewish immigrants from Displaced Persons camps in liberated Europe was again rejected by the Arabs. Only in 1968, after three lost wars, did the United Nations Partition Plan of 1947 begin to look reasonable to the Arabs. Yet in 1947 the Arab states had flatly turned it down and had dispatched their armies into Palestine in an abortive attempt to prevent its implementation. After the first war, they might have accepted the armistice lines of 1949. After the second war, they still could have accepted the status quo of 1957, which implied the borders of 1949 plus freedom for Israeli shipping in the Gulf of Aqaba. If they had accepted the status quo of 1957, there would have been no war in 1967, and no Arab defeat.

These are speculative observations but not entirely senseless when weighed against the alternatives. Following the war of 1967, Israel was in control of 88,000 square kilometers, as against 20,250 square kilometers before the war, or eighteen times as much as the area allocated to the Jews by Lord Peel's first partition proposal of 1937.

The late King Abdullah of Jordan was one of the few Arab leaders acutely aware of this strange alliance of cause and effect between Arab intransigence and Israeli territorial expansion. He wrote in his memoirs that Zionism not only relied upon the European countries who wanted to get rid of their Jews, but upon Arab extremists who refused any settlement as well.

After the complete rout of the Egyptian army in 1967, it was thought—to paraphrase Lenin's remark—that the tens of thousands of fleeing Egyptian soldiers had voted for peace with their feet. But Arab leaders soon announced that another war was "inevitable"; in the long run they expected to arrive at victory by patience and perseverance and by the sheer weight of numbers. Was this a realistic estimate or one more pipe dream? If the 1967 war had been decided by Israel's technological superiority, the results of the next war—even without the use of nuclear weapons—depended even more heavily upon technological factors. Given the prevailing national growth rates, the technological gap between Israel and her adversaries was likely to grow even wider than it had been in 1967.

Herman Kahn and Anthony J. Weiner in their study, *The Year 2000*, speculated on the extent of this growing gap. They may have oversimplified; they probably underestimated the effect of the unpredictable human equation. Nevertheless their figures indicate a trend which appears to be plausible. By the year 2000, Israel, with a gross national product of $5,839 per capita, is expected to be within the "post-industrial stage," a cybernetics-controlled "learning society." At the same time, Egypt, with an expected GNP of only $480 per capita, is expected to remain, at the bottom of the ladder, a "partially industrialized" society.

In the Six Day War of 1967, the Israeli people came of age. It was their third war. The 1948 war of independence had been harder to win; but it had taken place before the arrival of mass immigration.

The 1948 war had been a unique moment of grace; during their first war with the Arabs the Israelis had been able to rely upon the support of both the United States and the Soviet Union. In the 1956 Suez war they had fought in collusion with England and France. This time they stood alone. When most was at stake, they could stand up and shape their own future. They proved it to others, but above all to themselves. The 1967 war was a military victory; the psychological effect was even greater. For Israelis it marked the transition from adolescence to maturity.

The war changed not only Israel's position in the Near East, but even more so the Israelis' self-image. As the army of hastily drafted civilians rolled up to the Suez Canal, the men in the tanks and armored trucks knew it was the end of an era.

For most Israelis, the almost century-old debate over the rightness or wrongness of Zionism reduced itself to a purely academic matter. Must there be a Jewish state? If so, where? Or should the Jews remain dispersed among the nations? For all practical purposes, such questions became irrelevant and obsolete. There was now a state. Israel was a nation, resourceful and cohesive, whatever the argument over Zionism. For Israelis it was no longer a discussion of theory but an issue of survival. No longer a matter of doctrine, but one of personal security. Opponents of Israel claimed that this was a political, not a moral argument. But then it could be argued that preservation of life is the highest morality. For Israelis there was no other place to go.

They had won a great victory, at no small cost to themselves in human life, and in what is often dearer than property—nerves. The war had come after a long period of excruciating anxiety. The tension burst like a long-infected abscess. Yet, as a people, they did not lose an inner sense of balance. They had overrun a hostile population of more than one million Arabs, who came under Israeli rule and added to the 290,000 Arabs already living in their midst. But as conquerors they remained civilized. There were few outrages, only a few cases of pillaging and wanton destruction. Few had expected such enormous territorial gains; most were conquerers against their will. The military interfered as little as possible in the internal affairs of the occupied territories. Administration by the army was a curious mixture of non-chalance and bad conscience. To most Israelis the occupied areas quickly became an almost inexhaustible tourist attraction. There were some who almost seemed to say, "Forgive us for winning," as they frantically overpaid shopkeepers, waiters, and taxi drivers in an apparent attempt to appease.

The war added self-assurance. At the same time it created concerns of a new order and shattered myths of moral self-righteousness. There was little bragging and much compassion for the loser. In his victory address, given when he received an honorary degree from the University of Jerusalem, General Yitzchak Rabin, chief of the armed forces during the war, spoke of the fighting soldiers' "incomplete joy." They had seen with their eyes not only the glories of victory but also its price. "Their comrades beside them bleeding ... and I know that even the terrible price our enemies paid touched the hearts of many of our men." After the war there were soldiers who told press interviewers that when they saw the frightened Arab refugees escaping their homes, trekking on hot roads off to a neighboring country, women, children, and old men, thirsty and hungry, dragging only a bundle of clothes behind them, they felt sick: "I could not help thinking of the Jew in the Diaspora."

Even as they were gloriously victorious, into the hearts of many Israelis were born new doubts. These doubts and hesitations were a reflection of the human condition in an extreme form. They bore witness to men bound by moral principle but because of their limitations unable to put them into practice. There was a grand debate about the future of occupied Arab territories. Should they be annexed? Is it fitting for Israelis to sit as masters? Or should these territories simply be held in collateral against eventual peace talks with the Arabs?

The tragedy was that there were no real peace talks. There was no settlement, not even the beginning of one. A limited settlement was blocked by the Israelis themselves; they insisted upon direct negotiations which would lead up to a fully fledged peace pact. They could not bring themselves to agree to some interim, indirect understanding on co-existence. Future historians may blame them for having blocked what might have been the beginning of a process. For the Israelis this was not enough, not a sufficiently safe arrangement to evacuate their newly won strategic strongholds in the occupied areas. But if the Israelis remained where they were, it was naive to believe that a colonial rule, however enlightened, could give the Arab masses confid-

ence in Israel or make them forget that Palestine was "stolen" from
them by the Zionists. With an Arab population of more than 1.3
million against their own 2.5 million, the Israelis were faced by almost
equally unpleasant alternatives. At worst, the complete domination of
Arabs by Jews. At best, an uneasy federation of hostile communities,
pulling the country apart at the seams. Given either alternative, there
would be recurrent terrorism.

Some Israelis in years past had dreamed of a bi-national state. This
was still a possibility, but only a theoretic one. Jewish supporters of
bi-nationalism had never met any reciprocal action from any Arab
party. This lack of Arab reciprocity finally totally discredited their
position within Israel as well. Moreover, a bi-national state had recently been shattered on nearby Cyprus, the only place where it had
been tried in modern times, under more auspicious circumstances
than in Palestine. Hardened by strife, embittered by a thousand disil-
lusions heightened by their adversaries, few Israelis were now prepared
to take that risk. The Israeli-Arab writer, Attalah Mansour, borrowing
an Oriental image, described the plight of the Israelis thus: "Instead
of stepping on the snake that threatened them, they swallowed it.
Now they have to live with it, or die from it."

After every revolution in human affairs the question is asked: Was
it worth it? Could not its advantages have been purchased at a lower
price? The early Zionists were of that pure species of revolutionaries
who live in their own world of radiant obsessions and abysmal fears.
They initiated events of great consequence; at the same time they
responded to the pressures of Jewish misery abroad, pressures which
assumed an irresistible force with the breakdown of European civilization under Hitler. It is true that revolutionaries are often less concerned with man than with what disturbs him. Some revolutionaries
entertain an image of reality that is partly artificial; they believe it
implicitly and often make the scenery real to others as well. The early
Zionists certainly had their share of unreal images, but less so, it
would seem, than other revolutionaries of our brutal time. No revolution is ever an unmixed good or an unmitigated evil. The Zionist
revolution was no exception, whatever may have been the pious hopes
of its originators. It affords yet another illustration to the claim that
revolutions, like the human will itself, cannot be programmed.

As it removed some dangers, it created new ones. As it saved some from misery, it heaped sorrow upon others. It caused the physical reconstruction of a land long barren through neglect, ignorance, and decay. But countries, in flower or in waste, are no end in themselves; what counts is the people who inhabit them. In this respect the Zionist revolution was a mixed blessing. It must be measured by the kind of society it implanted or by the better opportunities it created for the persecuted of Poland and Russia, the survivors of Nazi Germany, and the downtrodden ghetto dwellers of the Orient, to live "not safely but active and free" as Goethe made his protagonist say toward the end of *Faust*. It must also be measured by the misery it has brought upon the original inhabitants of Palestine. Compared to other wars of national liberation the amount of suffering generated by Zionism may have been smaller, quantitatively speaking. But this is a political argument, not a moral one.

Nobody has been, as they claimed, absolutely right. Neither the Jews who were driven by necessity, nor the Arabs who were hopelessly caught up with them. Neither the Zionists who at first ignored the Arabs and later talked themselves into believing that it was in their power to make the Arabs happy, nor the Arabs who never for a moment stopped to consider seriously whether some kind of modus vivendi with the Jews was not possible after all. Wrong were those Zionists who thought there was no future and no safety anywhere for Jews as Jews except in their own state; and wrong were the anti-Zionists who extolled the supra-national mission of the Jews and relegated them to skeptics-on-duty in a world of atavistic tribal attachments. Wrong were the anti-Semites who taunted the Jews and thought they were cowards unfit for war or plow. Mistaken were the assimilationists who considered Jewry an anomaly which must disappear except as a religious sect. Unrealistic also were those who held both sides of the stick and called upon Jews to either remain Jews and emigrate to Israel or assimilate promptly and disappear without an ethnic or religious trace. Life was stronger than the simplicities that were generated by the disasters and complexities of the times, and made a mockery of them all.

2

A CHEKHOV PLAY
BY DUERRENMATT

Almost everyone comes from Kikel.

—MEYER WEISGAL, 1944

PRESIDENT, WEIZMANN INSTITUTE

Israelis are a hybrid people. The modern colonization of Palestine began almost a century ago with the arrival of the first Russian and Rumanian settlers. Jews have since flocked here from all corners of the earth and have brought with them their distinctive habits, cultures, and traditions. Statisticians list one hundred and two countries of origin.

This extreme diversity has left its deep marks everywhere. It has affected people and politics as well as the physical environment. Parts of Israel today resemble outposts—or caricatures—of Iraq, Galicia, or Baden-Wurtemberg. One plunges everywhere into a maelstrom of people of sharply different backgrounds and cultures. Affected as they are by a shared social experience, climate, and nutrition, the prevailing disparities are still widespread and profound. In 1965 more than half the adult population still used one of a dozen different languages as the main instrument of communication.

And yet, overriding the dissimilarity are a number of unifying forces of great strength and perseverance. They are an important element in this story; by examining their roots, much as a botanist dissects a plant, a light is shed on some of the crucial factors of Israeli life. Religion is one of them. As a church, Judaism is notoriously disorganized and decentralized into a profusion of independent, equal rabbinical authorities; yet it is still more uniform in doctrine and observance than the various sects of Christianity and Islam. Moreover

33

Judaism has always meant much more to Jews than faith and strict observance of The Law. Secular Jews have often tended to view Judaism as less concerned with the world as it is than with what it should be. This tendency to moralize in politics easily ties in with the more utopian streaks of modern Zionism; together they form a main component of the Israeli temper.

Nationalism is another unifying force. It is an important article, even though a prototype was patented in the Jewish name a very long time ago. The atavistic tribalism of the ancient Hebrews and its "sacred" connection with a promised territory, their ethnic arrogance and God-ordained exclusivity, certainly played a role, at least indirectly, in the development of modern nationalism. But the present form of Israeli nationalism was adopted by the Jews of Europe from the peoples among whom they lived.

Modern Jewish nationalism started in Eastern Europe during the second half of the nineteenth century. In the previous chapter we have seen that as colonists the Jews were latecomers. As nationalists they were latecomers as well. Of all the national minorities that populated Eastern and Central Europe in the nineteenth century, the Jews were the last to succumb to the lure of their own piece of cloth nailed to a wooden stick. If nationalism was a deplorable aberration of the mind, a recrudescence of tribalism which the enlightenment had hoped to overcome, the Jews were among the last who held out to give emancipation a working chance. When that chance failed, or was too slow to succeed, they adopted local colors. If the spirit of the humanist enlightenment had won, there would have been no Zionism.

Zionism has been called a form of "collective assimilation." As a people, the Jews wanted to be like all the "other peoples." Assimilation and conformism certainly played a role; but so did convictions born of bitter experience. Zionist nationalism was a form of Jewish self-defense and a plan for a better future. It derived from French positivism, German idealism, and Russian populism. It was imported into Israel from Europe by the early pioneers along with modern agricultural implements and industrial technology. It is presently reinforced by the prevailing external threat. The Arabs by their continuing enmity have reduced it to that most basic of human instincts, the will for self-preservation.

Equally important as a unifying force is the dominant political culture. For a people as diverse as this, the moral postulates of society display a series of surprisingly uniform patterns. They are expressed above all in political life and in education. The patterns were set at the beginning of this century by the first waves of Eastern European immigrants. This was Israel's formative period. Its influence has • proven decisive; it has left a mark as indelible as that imprinted by the Pilgrim Fathers in the early stages of the American republic. Ethnically Israelis may be a hybrid; as political creatures they are children of the special world of nineteenth-century Eastern Europe. Many branches have been grafted onto the original trunk, but the trunk is rooted in Czarist Russia, Poland, and the Austro-Hungarian empire.

To say that as political creatures Israelis are children of nineteenth-century Eastern Europe is of course an oversimplification. If taken too narrowly, the argument becomes contrived and ultimately absurd. And yet it is not altogether frivolous. It is not the only key; but as the most important single aid to the understanding of a complex background, it must not be dismissed as altogether superficial. A noteworthy parallel, by way of illustration, can be found in the early history of the American colonies. Of all the forces responsible for the founding of Massachusetts, the most important were obviously those generated by the crisis faced by the English puritans during the reign of Charles I. The crisis which confronted Eastern European Jewry during the reign of the last three Czars played a similar role in the beginnings of Zionism; it exerts a powerful and continuing influence on modern Israeli culture.

The Viennese journalist and playwright Theodor Herzl played a key role as founder of the World Zionist movement; important as his role was, popular histories of Israel usually overestimate his ultimate impact on events. The roots of modern Israel are not in the cosmopolitan *fin de siècle* Vienna of Herzl and Freud, Berta von Suttner or Arthur Schnitzler, Otto Weininger, Robert Musil, or Karl Kraus. Herzl, somewhat naively, hoped to transplant into the proposed Jewish homeland his own sophisticated milieu of witty intellectuals, *bohémiens*, and philosopher-businessmen; he did not envisage the structural changes, the social and cultural revolution, postulated by the leftist Zionists of Russia. Many of the latter were socialists; Herzl was a conservative believer in aristocratic government. The Eastern European Zionists wanted Palestine, but Palestine was not Herzl's first choice. He recognized its force as a "powerful legend"; but initially he considered Palestine unsuitable for his scheme because of its climate, its lack of opportunity for expansion, and its dangerous proximity to Europe. He was not interested in creating another self-centered nation-state. He rather hoped for a community of multi-national loyalties. He was largely ignorant of Jewish traditions. "What is Jewish culture?" he once asked impatiently. He wanted many official languages, especially English and German. He was not interested in the romantic revival of Hebrew nor in the re-creation of the "historical Hebrew peasant" as were the Zionists of Eastern Europe. This would have been to him like arming a modern army with "crossbow and arrow."

"Do you really suppose that we shall get Palestine?" he once asked the fiercely passionate Russian Zionist Ussishkin, for he was too civilized, too sensitive, not to entertain at least some doubts.

"Yes," answered Ussishkin, "and if you don't believe it there is no place for you at the head of this movement." Toward the end of his days his own movement rebelled against him. Herzl's influence on the makeup and climate of the future state was marginal compared to the lasting impact of his Eastern European followers.

— The peculiar institutions of Israeli society, its intellectual climate, are inexplicable without considering the stirrings of nationalism and populism in nineteenth-century Eastern Europe. The idea of modern Israel was conceived in the light of the national awakening of Poland, Lithuania, and the Ukraine, of the Serbs, the Czechs, the Finns, and the Slovaks, but above all in the revolutionary climate prevalent in Russia between 1880 and 1920. From Russia came Israel's founding fathers; the Zionist Labor movement was born in Minsk in 1902 and has controlled Israeli politics without intermission from the early 1930s until today. We shall see that it was a product as native of Russia as Populism (Narodnism), Menshevism, and Bolshevism.

This is the source of much that is admirable today in Israeli life, as well as problematical. Much of what Israelis and outsiders admire or admonish, extol as a unique achievement of the human spirit, or dismiss and deplore as anachronistic and ultimately harmful grew out of and is still profoundly affected by the political and moral climate of Eastern Europe prior to World War I. Traces of that time are evident everywhere. We find them in politics, social ideology, cuisine, religious behavior, and the key concepts of national identity.* In the day-to-day life of Israel, in the flavor of its politics, its traditions of social radicalism, the manners of its people, their passionate argumentativeness, their belief in ideology, their incorrigible addiction to theoretical formulation, their worship of labor and soil and the virtues of simple peasant life, even in their attitude to the industrial West—a mixture of envy and disgust, provincial admiration and self-righteous superiority—in all these, echoes of Eastern Europe reverberate like an old tune through a cacophony of ultra-modern electronic music.

This is one reason Israel seems at times to the outsider, or to the more impatient native, so old-fashioned a young country; with all its novelty and frantic activity—a paradox of dynamic immobilism. It is a museum of nineteenth-century ideas in a twentieth-century setting; a Chekhov play by Duerrenmatt.

In the peculiar social and ideological world of nineteenth-century Eastern Europe, the more dynamic members of the Jewish minority responded to their oppression in one of several ways: some emigrated to the United States; some entered revolutionary movements; a third and smallest group joined clandestine, usually socialistically oriented Zionist organizations, and hoped eventually to emigrate to Palestine. A few thousand actually did emigrate; many more just talked. Those who did go staged a "utopian withdrawal to their own past" through an act of sheer will power. In a marvelous leap against time they became the founders and future rulers of Israel. Chaim Weizmann, the first President of Israel, was once asked by a British commission by what right the Jews claimed possession of Palestine. He is said to have answered: "Memory is right." Other nations too have occupied lands and then abandoned them. The point is that they did not remember, but the Jews never forgot Palestine.

Did it all start, then, in the first century with the beginning of the

---

* When Meyer Weisgal, the future president of the Weizmann Institute of Science, was asked in 1944 how he liked the country, he replied: "Of course I like it, almost everyone comes from Kikel" (a small Jewish townlet, *shtetl*, population 1,500—in Poland, where Weisgal was born).

Yitzchak Gruenbaum, a future Minister of Interior, reported angrily: "What do you mean by everybody?"

"Where do you come from?" asked Weisgal.

"Well, I grew up in Plonsk" (another *shtetl*, population, 2,800), answered Gruenbaum.

first great dispersion of the Palestinian Jews throughout the Roman Empire? Or in the second century when the last Jewish uprising was put down by the Romans? History is a seamless web; the choice of starting points is always arbitrary. Jews have always remembered and longed for their ancestral homeland. Palestine was almost never without Jewish inhabitants, even under the Crusaders who began their rule by slaughtering them. In this sense Zionism is as old as the Diaspora.

There always existed among Jews a kind of *ur*-Zionism. In the course of the Diaspora it assumed a purely religious character, metaphysically connected with the End of Days and the Coming of the Messiah. Mystical Zionism always prompted Jews to go as settlers and as pilgrims to the Holy Land. But this was no more a national movement than were the pilgrimages of Christians.

As a political force, rather than an eschatological mood, Zionism dates back only to the last century. It was a *risorgimento* for Jews: it fed upon the general ideological milieu even more than on ancient religious heritage. Half a century earlier the poet Heinrich Heine had written: "*Wie es sich's christelt so jüdelt es sich*" ("as it christens so it jews"). Heine meant manners in general; Jewish nationalism illustrated that truth in the political field as well. Jewish nationalism had its unique features, of course, as was natural with people of so ancient a history and a "national" religion of its own. An acute nostalgia for the past was inherent in all romantic thought. But in its essence Zionism was a new beginning rather than the sudden politicalization of an ancient religious idea. The Jewish religious establishment was bitterly opposed to Zionism. From a religious point of view political Zionism was the great Jewish heresy of the nineteenth century. It was a populist uprising against the Jewish "establishment" as well as against the conditions imposed upon Jews of all ranks by their host nations.

Israel is the result. Robert Michels wrote that every nation has two dominant myths, the myth of origin and the myth of mission. The crucial experience which lies at the origin of Israel as a modern state was the persecution generated by the failure of emancipation and democracy in Europe. Its myth of mission was the creation of a new and just society. This new society, as envisaged by the early pioneers, was to be another Eden, a Utopia never before seen on sea or land. The pioneers looked forward to the creation of a "new man." A

3

EASTERN ORIGINS

> Through a historical catastrophe—the de-
> struction of Jerusalem by the Emperor of
> Rome . . .—I was born in one of the cities
> of the Diaspora. But I always deemed my-
> self as one who was really born in Jerusalem.
> —S. Y. AGNON
>   Nobel Prize acceptance speech, 1966

A traveler making his way through European Russia during the last half of the nineteenth century viewed a strangely gray, desperately backward, sorely depressing, monotonous land. Human habitations were pitifully squalid. The traveler might also have noticed the fabulous homes and careless abandon of the ruling feudal aristocracy, or the intense intellectuality, rarer in the West, of a few well-to-do. But these lucky few lived their lives apart, on a different star. The fundamental and most enduring feature was, as Leon Trotsky has written, the slow tempo of development; it led to economic backwardness, primitive social forms, and a low level of welfare.

Nor was nature more inviting. The northwestern belt between Warsaw, Minsk, and Vitebsk, which at that time was one of the main population centers of world Jewry, was an immense lowland of forest and marsh with patches of primitive cultivation in between. As it rose almost imperceptibly toward the Urals in the east, it was all flatness and seemingly unlimited space, dull and inert; only where the sullen monotony was broken by a sudden profusion of lakes, rivers, and thick forests of spruce and Scotch pines was there a certain somber beauty.

There were relatively few cities. The countryside was teeming with wretchedly poor, illiterate peasants; they lived under the crushing double yoke of superstition and autocratic government. It was a classic nineteenth-century example of an overpopulated countryside. Overpopulation halted economic development, reduced savings, and kept living standards low. The barbaric brutality of the Czarist regime was tempered, or sometimes worsened by the most corrupt civil administration in Europe. Natural reserves had not yet been properly exploited. Russian backwardness at that time could be measured by the fact that the entire foreign trade of such a vast and potentially rich country amounted to less than a third of that of tiny Belgium. The peasants had been emancipated by the "liberal" Czar Alexander II in 1855 but in many cases freedom remained on paper. It was the middle ages surviving into the nineteenth century; rampant everywhere were the twin conditions of poverty and hopelessness.

The climate made it even worse. "It isn't exactly cooperative," Yephkhodor in Chekhov's *Cherry Orchard* drily commented. For most of the year it meant either ice, snow, slush, mud, or dust. Winter lasted up to six months, with snow covering the land and severely limiting human activity. Spring set free the frozen rivers, swamps, and lakes and simultaneously spread seas of deep heavy mud and slush which added further hardship to outside movement. The briefest of summers could bring days as stiflingly hot as in southern deserts; dust storms and huge dust clouds hovered low in the air, covering the meager crops and often ruining them. Autumn meant violent winds; it saw the reappearance of the mud. Nature itself joined forces with the sterile apparatus of Czarist oppression to inflict a terrible punishment on people and country alike as though for some primeval sin. Survival was an achievement.

It was here, against this dreary bleak background, that in the nineteenth century millions of Jews eked out a meager, miserable existence. They were wedged in as aliens between Poles and Lithuanians, White Russians and Little Russians (as the Ukrainians were called), Letts, Rumanians, Magyars, Germans, Slovaks, and Carpathians, a multitude of diverse people whose separate and often contradictory aspirations were beginning to rock the foundations of great multi-national empires. All were, as a rule, savagely hostile to one another. But above all they hated and suspected the Jews and subjected them to severe oppressive measures.

Most Jews were dispersed over an area roughly corresponding to the present Soviet Republics of Byelo-Russia, Ukraine, and Lithuania and the eastern districts of present-day Poland. Here was the great Jewish captivity of Eastern Europe which has since disappeared through emigration, assimilation, or in the gray, sick-sweet-smelling smoke of Treblinka, Auschwitz, and Sobibor. In 1897 it still numbered more than seven million people. About five million of the most miserable lived under Czarist rule; the rest inhabited adjacent areas of Austro-Hungarian Galicia, Hungary, and Rumania. They were not, in any reasonable sense, newcomers to the region. Some of their ancestors had lived in these parts from Roman times, others since the seventh century. Jews had been living in Hungary even before their present host nation arrived on the scene. In the eighth century the Kingdom of the Khasars, professing Judaism, had flourished in southern Russia. But the majority were descendants of Jews who had wandered east from the twelfth century on in order to escape the slaughter, pillage, and blood-accusations rampant in the Rhine and Danube valleys during the Crusades.

They were an extremely proud and stubborn people. With only a gesture—conversion—they might have saved themselves from banishment and death. Some doubtlessly converted; many more did not. In the thirteenth century Boleslav V the Chaste, King of Poland, invited them to settle in his territories. Boleslav wanted to encourage trade and economic growth. He granted the Jews a liberal charter of self-government. The Jews considered the King's invitation a great act of charity. They brought with them their own language and folkways, a "tradition on wheels" (Isaiah Berlin) which they had preserved almost intact and would continue to preserve for the next six centuries. During this period they became a middle class of tradesmen, artisans, and stewards; despite their wretched poverty they constituted a major civilizing force in an area still largely on the fringes of European culture.

By 1887 the Jews amounted to about 4 or 5 percent of the general population of Czarist Russia and slightly more than 10 percent in Galicia itself. As they constituted a cohesive ethnic group, separate and distinct in almost every way, inhabiting limited areas where they were often the majority or near majority, there was fertile ground for Jewish nationalism. Jews lived by themselves and mostly for themselves in concentrated clusters. They were officially classed as "aliens" (*inordsy*—those of another race), together with certain primitive Asian tribes. Jews were required by law to limit themselves to the so-called Pale of Settlement, the *Tcherta ossjedlosti*; here, according to the technical definition, Jews were "permitted to reside permanently." In other regions only special categories of Jews, academics, or rich merchants could live temporarily.

Inside this Pale of Settlement the Jews lived in tight clusters containing anywhere from a few hundred to a few thousand souls, a people within peoples, clinging tenaciously to their own traditions, liturgy, diet, and even dress. They had a religion of their own. In contrast to the other ethnic groups around them, they shared this religion with no other people. Their religion was an "exclusive," or national, one. They spoke their own language, Yiddish, a Middle High German vernacular imported by their forefathers from the Rhineland in the thirteenth century, interspersed with Hebrew, Polish, and Russian. Its preservation over the centuries turned out to be of crucial importance.

Nineteenth-century nationalism was nearly always tied to language, which was held to embody a people's innermost soul. Early in the nineteenth century Yiddish suddenly developed from an unwritten tribal vernacular to a forceful and vastly popular vehicle of literary expression. Mendele Mocher Sefarim and Sholom Aleichem ("the Jewish Mark Twain") were its recognized masters at the time. Few Jews were as yet fluent in the language of their Russian, Polish, or Lithuanian neighbors. The little they knew was restricted to a few handy words and phrases for use in business or rare dealings with the state bureaucracy. But in sharp contrast to the host of surrounding peoples, Jewish men were often literate in Yiddish and had at least a reading facility of Hebrew. The revival of Hebrew ran parallel to the development of Yiddish as a language of literature. Under the influence of romanticism, Hebrew, like other ancient languages such as Greek and Gaelic, was rediscovered for secular purposes. Yiddish was still a richer and more expressive idiom. But Hebrew breathed the magic of past glory, ancient wisdom, and sunny days in the East. As a language it was still not "fully alive," even though for centuries it had served as a *lingua franca* for Jewish scholars and businessmen. Only much later, in Israel, was Hebrew transformed from the frozen language of prayer and sacred study to the

modern instrument of communication it is now. But there were beginnings; for the first time in centuries Jews were putting Hebrew to
secular uses.

Though touched by the winds of change as were all who lived in
Eastern Europe at that time, the Jews of the Russian Pale lived the
highly traditional, rigidly orthodox, closely knit life of their forebears.
Life revolved around the family, the synagogue courtyard, house of
study, small workshop, weekly market day, poor house, ritual bath,
old-age home, and communal burial society. It was an "island culture." Its stronghold was the *shtetl*, or small townlet. The *shtetl* was
neither town nor village but a thing in between, a kind of regional
market center. There were thousands of such *shtetl* all over White
Russia, the Ukraine, southern Lithuania, Galicia, and Poland; small,
isolated, semi-rural, semi-urban communities of little shopkeepers,
wholesalers, peddlers, artisans, innkeepers, and distillers, along with
the so-called *Luftmenschen*, those "living on air," beggars, idlers, wait-
ers-on-Providence, and dreamers.

Many *shtetl* were wholly or predominantly Jewish. Napoleon, as he
entered the predominantly Jewish city of Vilna, is said to have called
it the "Jerusalem of Lithuania." Some were "university *shtetl*," such
as Volozhin, a seat of great rabbinical learning which attracted masses
of students. Others rarely had contact with the outside world except
economically. Their inhabitants dwelt not in Russia but in their
dreams; or as Maurice Samuel, the historian of the *shtetl* has written,
they lived "in the holy land," either in the distant past or in the
Messianic future. Their festivals were tied to the Palestinian climate
and ancient Hebrew calender. Though in the middle of Russia or
Poland, in their hearts they were residents of an imaginary Jerusalem.
Daily they repeated the ancient prayer: "I believe with all my heart in
the coming of the Messiah; and even as he delays nevertheless I
expect him every day." S. Y. Agnon, the writer, whose work reflects
and echoes the life and death of his native *shtetl*, Buczaz, expressed a
kind of transcendental truth when he announced, many years later, in
his Nobel Prize acceptance speech: "Through a historical catastrophe
—the destruction of Jerusalem by the Emperor of Rome, and the exile
of Israel from our country—I was born in one of the cities of the
Diaspora. But I always deemed myself as one who was really born in
Jerusalem."

Other *shtetl* were mixed settlements with strong Jewish minorities. Whether as majority or minority, Jewish communities retained a large measure of local autonomy. Real power and authority lay with the national non-Jewish majority. Even in predominantly Jewish towns and hamlets there were always representatives of the national government—policemen, tax collectors, judges, drafters for the military. But in day-to-day affairs, even the smaller Jewish communities maintained a kind of self-government. It was based largely on the principle of voluntary consent, which later on was to exert a powerful influence upon the political culture of modern Israel. Jewish self-government in the *shtetl* was exercised through the assembly in the synagogue, which was a kind of Town Meeting. Its instruments of power were the *kahal*s (community boards) and *chevra*s (societies). As early as the seventeenth century these self-governing bodies succeeded in making elementary education—centered on the Bible and Talmud—practically universal for *shtetl* Jews. Between the ages of five and thirteen every boy attended school, regardless of his social standing or economic position.

Every *shtetl*, down to the smallest hamlet, had its voluntary societies. Their main tasks were to aid the sick and to provide education to poor boys and dowries to orphaned girls. Some *chevra*s issued interest-free loans to the needy; others provided free shelter for the transient visitor. There were, of course, considerable differences between rich and poor, even more between learned and unlearned; but neither wealth nor erudition conferred any caste privileges. Wealth, though scarce, was held duty-bound to social purpose; its supreme expression was charity acquitted with tact. If practice deviated at times from principle, as happened more and more frequently with the sharpening of social differences in the nineteenth century, the moral tone continued to be set by the ethical precepts of religion. Later on these precepts were to play a role in the development of the social ethos of Zionism.

The tone of *shtetl* life lies at the root of the extraordinary charitable traditions of the wealthy Jewish community of America; the support of this community proved crucial to the establishment and survival of Israel. In one form or another the heritage of *shtetl* life still affects the tenor of public debate in Israel, the revulsion against caste privileges, the commitment to social welfare and to an extreme form of egalitarianism. In the *shtetl*, "life was with people." Simple human solidarity was the *shtetl*'s source of strength to survive as an island culture surrounded by hostility. A ghost of the *shtetl* lingers on in the modern living institutions of Israel.

To describe so briefly the Eastern European Jewish world of a century ago, solely as a backdrop for events to come, is a risky undertaking. Now that the *shtetl* has disappeared there is an inclination to view it through tinted spectacles of sentimentality, blissfully floating on roseate Chagallesque clouds. This is not how people saw it at the time. Even before the great wave of pogroms began in the 1870s, life in the *shtetl*, as indeed in all Russia, was hard and grudging.

As the nineteenth century progressed, the position of Eastern European Jews as middlemen for a backward feudal economy was gradually undermined by new marketing techniques, the emancipation of serfs, and the growth of banking and credit. Jews were not permitted to play a useful role in the new mercantilistic age. The Czarist authorities subjected them instead to ever-increasing restrictions and civil disabilities. Their occupational structure became increasingly lopsided, an "inverted pyramid," top-heavy with so-called "non-productive" middlemen of all sorts. Jewish intellectuals and reformers became obsessed with the idea that their co-religionists were dangerously and immorally "unproductive." Their obsession was destined to exercise a profound influence on the social ethos of Zionism.

The occupational pyramid of Eastern European Jews as a whole was never actually as lopsided as was claimed. For example, of those engaged in industry and crafts in Galicia, 25 percent were Jews, two and one-half times their share in the general population. In the Russian Pale of Settlement, where Jews represented 4 to 6 percent of the population, 21 percent of all factory workers were Jews. Proportionately, the number of Jews engaged in commerce in Russia was smaller than in Western European countries.

But what mattered most psychologically was that within the Russian Pale and Galicia almost all middlemen were Jews. Later economic theorists would take a different view and see the Jewish peddlers as proto-bourgeois pioneers of trade, men of no little courage, who penetrated a closed, superstitious feudal world, often with new goods and new ideas. At the time, however, cruder concepts of productivity prevailed in economic thought. Anti-Semites joined Karl

Marx in calling Jewish middle-men "parasitic peddlers" and "unproductive hucksters." At a time of economic change and growing social, racial, and nationalist antagonism, the position of the entire Jewish community was becoming less and less viable. To some extent the Jews of Eastern Europe were identical to and identified with the people among whom they lived; to a larger extent they were different. Chaim Weizmann said that they were becoming "a disembodied ghost of a race without a body," inspiring suspicion, which in its turn bred hatred.

Weizmann's hometown was Motol, located on the marshy plains surrounding Minsk. Motol was a mixed community, comprising some 500 Russian and 200 Jewish families. The Jews lived in a separate section of town, "for the sake of comfort, security and company," as Weizmann later wrote. In Weizmann's eyes it was one of the "darkest and most remote corners of the Pale of Settlement." A master of vivid description and quick wit, Weizmann grappled for words in his memoirs and wrote that he found it "hard" to convey to a modern Westerner "even a vague notion" of the dismal way of life of the people of Motol, their special trades, their shocking poverty, their strivings, and their terrible loneliness.

Maurice Samuel, a native of Eastern Europe, gave this description of the hamlet *shtetl* of Kasrielevky in the district of Poltava, from whence come also the homely inhabitants of the tales of Sholom Aleichem:

> Kasrielevky is also Kozodoievka and Bohopolie and Bohslav and any one of a hundred Jewish or half-Jewish centres in old White Russia. The town itself is a jumble of wooden houses clustering higgledy-piggledy about a market place . . . . All around is the spaciousness of mighty Russia, but Kasrielevky is as crowded as a slum. . . . The congestion is not produced by external pressures alone. There is internal shrinkage too. What are they shrinking from? Perhaps the . . . formlessness of space, perhaps the world of the uncircumcized, perhaps the brutalizing influence of untamed nature. They fear the bucolic. . . .
> They are the greatest talkers in the world; and for a neat epigram, an apt Biblical quotation, an ingenious piece of commentary, a caustic phrase, or a good story, they are ready to pawn their ragged capotes.

The streets of Kasrielevky were labyrinthine, narrow, bent, and folded "as thesis dribbling into an anti-climax." Here stood the synagogue, the several prayerhouses, the ritual bath. Here the peddlers and merchants made a meager living buying livestock and vegetables from the peasants selling them in exchange for the produce of the cities. Was it a living? It depended naturally (says Maurice Samuel) on what you call a living. "A genuine Kasriel was content to say: 'Well, it's better than nothing ...' Yerechmiel Moses, the Hebrew teacher, blind in one eye and shortsighted in the other used to wear spectacles without lenses. Asked why, he would answer triumphantly, 'Well, it's better than nothing isn't it?' "

Those who were not shortsighted, nor blind in one eye, could not sustain such philosophic equanimity, but instead prepared for rebellion.

In the last half of the nineteenth century, the *shtetl* was rapidly decaying. Shalom Jacob Abramovitz (1836?–1917), who wrote under the pen name of Mendele Mocher Sefarim ("Mendele the Book Peddler"), and was the great epic poet of Eastern European Jewry, summed up the situation: "It is an ugly life, without pleasure or satisfaction, without splendor, without light, a life that tastes like lukewarm soup, without salt or spice." His bitter novels, based on life in Eastern Europe, are crowded with the pitiful, calamitous products of social decay: *luftmenschen*, flea-covered beggars and vagrants, fools, idlers, quacks and hypocritical rabbis, feeble old folk, forsaken wives, heartless rich and corruptible poor, bankrupts, peddlers in despair, losers, ne'er-do-wells, and ridiculous dreamers. Some critics have seen in Mendele's work a case of Jewish self-hatred bordering on anti-Semitism. None have denied his basic and redeeming quality of love and deeply felt identification with his tragi-comic heroes, or the sharpness of his eye. True to the epic tradition, Mendele reveled in the astonishing and curious. Mendele was a didactic novelist, given to exaggerated generalizations; he wanted to improve the dismal condition of Jewish life at a time of growing disintegration. He assumed that life's ills were a measurable deviation from a sane standard and thought it possible to overcome this gap through a rational program of Jewish education and social reform. He was a precursor of both Jewish nationalism and Jewish socialism in Eastern Europe. Toward the end of his life, while on a visit to Vilna, in Lithuania, an admiring audience presented him with two gifts: a red flag and a prayer shawl with phylacteries. The presentation was a dramatic premonition of things to come.

For Jews and Gentiles the medieval world was coming to an end. Both Gentile and Jewish writers intimated the end might be violent. "Man must live for something better," cried a drunken gambler in a famous passage of Gorky's *Lower Depths*; in his incoherent stammering he echoed the agony and helpless frustration of Czarist Russia. In Feierberg's *Le'an* (*Whither?*), perhaps the widest read Hebrew novel of the time, the case for a Zionist exodus to Palestine was presented by—of all people—a lunatic. In a wild synagogue scene in *Le'an*, "Crazy Nachman" pronounced all Europe "sick." He reminded the flabbergasted Jews, who had gathered in the synagogue for prayer, that they were not Europeans, but Levantines. They must quit Europe and found a "new society" in Palestine.

It was the end of the Romanov regime; the Jews were hopelessly caught up in its labyrinthine contradictions and Kafkaesque absurdities. The Pale of Settlement had been formally instituted by Catherine II following the first and second partition of Poland when three million Jews came under her direct rule. The five Czars who followed her on the throne of Russia governed by whim and a blend of brutality, weakness, paternalism, and political blindness. Their single consistent aim was to preserve the autocracy.

As in most other fields they had no consistent policy in regard to the Jews. Jews could never be sure where it was safe to live; the Pale was widened and narrowed at whim. Nor could they easily decide what professions to follow; they were alternately excluded and reincluded in them. One Czar tended to encourage the Russification of Jews, another was absolutely against it. One Czar encouraged Jews to become farmers but refused to allow them to own land, in the same way that he liberated the serfs but would not permit them to be free peasants. In the eighteenth century a federation of semi-autonomous Jewish *kahals* extended over a wide territory of Poland, Lithuania, and the Ukraine. The Czars broke this up but did not grant to Jews the civil rights of other Russian subjects. Alexander I relaxed some of Catherine's restrictions. He permitted Jews to pursue any occupation and to attend Russian schools. But after the Congress of Vienna he reversed himself and ordered the Jews out of the professions and back into the Pale. He died before he could carry this out but his successor, Nicholas I, put his plan into practice with deliberate speed. Within a few years thousands of Jews were made homeless and penniless, banned from professions and banished from the cities to the Pale. Nicholas I introduced special military conscription for Jews, to last twenty-five years. Before he died in 1855 the Pale of Settlement had shrunk to half its original size; its Jewish population had meanwhile grown by almost 50 percent.

The ascent to the throne of Alexander II, the "liberal Czar," brought a false dawn of hope. Alexander baldly reversed his predecessor's measures; he freed forty million serfs, ended the twenty-five-year military conscription for Jews and opened schools and universities to them. In the Pale of Settlement Alexander II was hailed as the "Czar liberator." Some of the wealthier Jews benefited from the new measures; some lived in the cities as opulent merchant princes; a few acquired baronial titles from impecunious German principalities. But their improved status was as far removed from that of their fellow Jews as was the glittering Czarist court from the life of the average Russian.

Alexander's liberalism came to an end with the Polish revolt of 1863. Alexander was blown up in 1881 by a group of desperate young anarchists. Three of those involved in the conspiracy bore Jewish names. The next Czar, Alexander III, was completely in the hands of ultra-reactionary churchmen and nobles. His chief adviser was the fanatical anti-Semitic Slavophile, Pobedonostsev. Pobedonostsev, a former professor of constitutional law and from 1880 Procurator of the Holy Synod, was the official state philosopher of the theocracy. He considered democracy a leprous disease and parliamentarianism the "great lie of our time." Pobedonostsev sponsored anti-Jewish riots as a popular diversion from the miseries of daily life. Tolstoy petitioned him in the name of Christ to pardon the assassins of Alexander II. Pobedonostsev answered: "Our Christ is not your Christ. To me Christ is the man of energy and truth who heals the weak; your Christ shows lineaments of weakness, is himself in need of healing."

Pobedonostsev also had his formula for solving the Jewish problem. It was simple and in its time quite famous: "One-third emigration, one-third conversion, and for one-third, death." Thousands of Jews who had lived twenty or thirty years in Moscow were suddenly expelled. They were forced to sell their property almost overnight. Those who delayed were shipped back to the Pale in prison trains. From now on, even within the Pale, Jews were restricted to towns: "It was as if all the Jews of Russia were to be violently crowded in and piled on top of one another like grasshoppers in a ditch," wrote an observer. "There they were to be miserably crushed together until the fruitless struggle for life should have done its work."

Inside the Pale of Settlement there were now about 4.8 million out of a total of 5.2 million Russian Jews. Even in the towns within the Pale where they were still permitted to live, and where they constituted vast majorities, Jews were now made ineligible to serve on city councils. In towns where Jews constituted 80 percent of the population, the percentage allowed to attend high school could not exceed 10 percent. The combined effect of poverty and overcrowding created a crisis of such magnitude that hundreds of thousands would have died of hunger had not the mass emigration to America begun at the same time.

In the decade between 1884 and 1894, the number of Jews lacking minimum means of livelihood arose to 27 percent of the Jewish population. Almost 40 percent were living on dole. Two or three decades earlier the average Jew had still been somewhat better off economically than the average Russian peasant; by 1887 a government inquiry commission stated that "90 percent of the Jews are a proletariat of such poverty and destitution as is otherwise impossible to see in Russia." There were two or three similar reports, circulated by one branch of the Czarist bureaucracy, while other branches were at the same time designing measures to compound the evil. On the margin of one such report, the Czar scribbled the comment: "But we must never forget that the Jews crucified our saviour and shed his precious blood."

Following a particularly savage outburst of persecution, tolerated by the government, a deputation of privileged Jews visited the Czar. They hoped to extricate an imperial statement deploring the riots. The Czar replied that the riots were the fault of the Jews themselves, as they insisted on continuing to "exploit the Russians." At about this time a Russian word entered the international lexicon: *pogrom* (devastation), or a violent outrage against a particular ethnic group.

The wave of pogroms which swept Russia between 1881 and 1903 were partly government-inspired and partly government-ignored. Havoc spread because army and police either stood idly by or showed up at the scene too late; the pogroms happened either through design or through inefficiency. For those who were killed, maimed, raped, robbed, or made homeless, such fine distinctions made little difference. The wave of horror swept from Warsaw to Odessa, through hundreds of villages and small towns, with a violence not seen since the Crusaders had littered their route to the Holy Land with corpses of Jews.

"From their hiding places in cellars and garrets the Jews were dragged forth and tortured to death," wrote Michael Davitt, the Irish nationalist leader who had gone to Russia to investigate.

> Many mortally wounded were denied the final stroke . . . in not a few cases nails were driven into the skull and eyes gouged out. Babies were thrown from the higher stories to the street pavement . . . Jews who attempted to beat off the attackers with clubs were quickly disarmed by the police. . . . The local bishop drove in a carriage and passed through the crowd, giving them his blessing as he passed.

Modern readers, versed in the details of concentration camps, death factories, and nuclear weapons, are frequently left unmoved by contemporary accounts of pogroms in Kishinev or Homel, Zhitomir, Odessa, and Kiev, or tales of smaller outbursts of violence and arson at the turn of the century in hundreds of towns and hamlets throughout White Russia and the Ukraine. In the quieter days of 1890 or 1900 the sudden slaughter of forty or fifty innocent men, women, and children, innocent except for their being Jewish, was so traumatic a shock that everywhere in Eastern Europe Jews began to change their entire outlook on life. More and more Jews searched for radical solutions. After the Kishinev pogroms of 1903, Chaim Nachman Bialik, the greatest Hebrew poet of the time, wrote in a fit of poetic rage that the devil himself had not yet invented a fitting revenge for the blood of a small child.

Elsewhere in Eastern Europe, in Galicia and Rumania, the pressures of internal decay and external menace were different only in degree; the crisis was equally serious, if less dramatic. Galicia, with some 811,000 Jews in 1910, about 10 percent of the population, was a province of the semi-liberal multi-national Austro-Hungarian empire. Austria-Hungary at the end of the century was an anachronism in a world of new, fiercer loyalties.

Nowhere in Europe did nationalities, languages, and cultures present as complicated a pattern as here; nowhere was the link between nationalism and religion so pronounced. Jewish nationalism sometimes fed upon Polish nationalism and vice versa. Poles and Jews shared a common mystique of stateless, ex-territorial nationhood, of chosenness, sin, atonement, and redemption. Israel Belkind, one of the earliest Zionists (he migrated to Palestine in 1882), remembered that his best friend in school had been a Polish boy. "We would share all our secrets. Together we would discuss our futures. We resolved then and there that when we grew up, each would serve his respective nation and country. I would go to Palestine to work for its redemption; he would work for the redemption of Poland."

It was natural for Jewish nationalism to be as tied to religious allegiance as was that of the Poles or Ruthenians. For Jews, as for others, there had been historical precedents. Forms of Jewish self-government, with quasi-popular elections, had existed in Galicia in the middle ages. The Council of Four Lands (Posnan, Krakau, Lublin, Vohlin) had been a kind of Jewish *seym* (parliament) within the Polish crown lands. Until 1776 a semi-autonomous "Jewish directorate," headed by the Chief Rabbi, with its own system of taxation, had been in existence.

Here too, as in nearby Czarist Russia, a sense of Jewish separateness was fed by strong bonds of common heritage, language, diet, costume, and liturgy. An added impetus in Austria-Hungary was the greater exposure to the free flow of ideas from the West. A young Jew growing up there at the end of the nineteenth century, absorbed, along with the Torah, a sense of heroic nationalism from the Polish works of Mizkevitch and a knowledge of German poetry and German philosophy. He also acquired a memory of past horrors and pogroms that haunted the Jews of an area historically ravaged by Eastern invaders. In the 1880s, the twentieth of Sivan on the Jewish calendar was still observed as a fast day by the Jews of Eastern Galicia to commemorate pogroms perpetuated between 1648 and 1650 by the Cossacks under Bogdan Chmielnitzki. The sense of national identity was further intensified by the close proximity of Russia. Everywhere in the little towns of Galicia, Jewish refugees from the East were spreading horrendous reports.

As elsewhere in Eastern Europe, the Jews of Galicia lived in separate communities. These would often be as "Jewish" as any small town in Israel today. Within these small, closely knit communities— slightly "Westernized" *shtetl*—Jews frequently formed a majority. Under the more liberal Austrian regime they exercised their rights by appointing their own mayors and city counselors. In 1876, forty-five Galician cities had absolute Jewish majorities; ten were governed by Jewish mayors. At the turn of the century Jewish Galicia was becoming a unique storehouse of creative energies, which overflowed to the capitals and universities of the West. The Jews of Galicia produced an unusually high number of great scientists and painters and writers of note—Freud, Soutine, Buber, Agnon, Joseph Roth, to name only a few.

Yet with all their civil and cultural advantages, the material plight of Galician Jews was equal to, if not worse than, that of the Jews of Russia. They too saw their traditional positions eroded by a changing economy which presented them with fewer and fewer opportunities as a middle class of petty tradesmen, stewards, and artisans. (Only a few were farmers.) The percentage of Jews engaged in commerce, though considerably lower than in Russia, was high enough to create unbearable frictions. Population growth combined with economic crisis to produce famine. Five to six thousand Galician Jews starved to death annually.

In Russia, meanwhile, the predominant reaction of Jews to their predicament was one of growing gloom. The first Russian pogroms prompted such men in the West as Ernest Renan and Victor Hugo to raise a voice in protest, but the greatest Russian writers, Turgenev and Leo Tolstoy, remained silent. Turgenev, like Dostoyevsky, was openly anti-Semitic. Tolstoy's resources of compassion were apparently exhausted by the suffering of the Russian muzhik. Yet if the educated and enlightened did not protest against the pogroms, who would? The silence of men like Tolstoy added to the anguish of the Jews. An eyewitness described a prayer service in a St. Petersburg synagogue following the riots of 1882.

The preacher was drawing a sombre picture of the life of Israel today when suddenly burst forth a long sigh, as if from one heart, spreading in the synagogue. Everyone wept. Old and young, poor and rich, clerks, doctors, students, and, needless to say, women, cried. The sigh lasted two to three minutes, a general cry of agony bursting forth. The rabbi could not finish his sermon. He stood on the rostrum, and covering his face with his hands, wept like a child.

Hebrew and Yiddish letters soon reached a nadir of bleak depression rare even in modern literature. Only twenty years earlier, in the 1860s, upon the liberation of the serfs by the "liberal Czar," Alexander II, the Hebrew poet J. L. Gordon could still write ecstatically:

> Now hath the dawn come forth
> The sun has risen, darkness has fled.
> Bright light shineth all over men,
> It has touched *us* also.

Whatever was left of such optimism faded quickly after 1881. J. C. Brenner, a remarkable essayist and novelist who was later killed by Arab rioters in Palestine, wrote that Jews were reduced to leading a sheer biological existence, like ants. "Why should we fear death," cried Bialik, "when his angel rides our shoulders, his bit between our teeth?" The poet Tschernichovsky saw his fellow Jews as "walking corpses, the rot of the human seed."

The prevailing despondency was not improved by gratuitous advice from outside. After the next great wave of pogroms in 1903, Tolstoy finally denounced the outrages as a "direct result of the propaganda of falsehood and violence which our government conducts with such energy." Tolstoy's only advice to the Jews was that they must ensure their salvation by closely following the rule: "Do unto others as you would that others should do unto you." He counseled them to "fight the government . . . by virtuous living."

4

THE POWER OF IDEAS

> Dream and deed are not as different as many
> think. All the deeds of men are dreams at
> first, and become dreams in the end.
>
> —THEODOR HERZL
>
> POSTSCRIPTS, *Altneuland*

This then was Eastern Europe at the turn of the century, Lenin's great "prison of nations." The Jews, like others, were trying to break out. "What is this freedom, by which so many minds are agitated," asked Pobedonostsev, the apostle of Czarist authoritarianism, ". . . which leads the people so often to misfortune?"

For Pobedonostsev, freedom was a leprous disease; for the revolutionaries it meant social justice; for the liberals, civil rights. It would bring self-determination for the suppressed Letts, Finns, Poles, and Ukrainians. For the Jews it was first and foremost a chance to escape discrimination, looting, murder, rape, and arson.

Jews began to break out of the Pale under Alexander II; they would not be forced back into it under his successors. Barred from the universities and high schools after 1887, most young Russian Jews were forced to study at home. A reader of Israeli biographical dictionaries is immediately struck by the unusually high number of Russian-born members of the generation of founding fathers whose secular education is listed simply as "private tuition." The few young Jews whose parents were more well-to-do went abroad to study. There were Russian-Jewish students at all of the main universities of Germany and Switzerland; they mingled with the Russian students, sharing their revolutionary atmosphere. The Czarist regime, by shutting them out of Russian universities and forcing them to study abroad, exposed Jewish students to a liberal atmosphere likely to increase even further their resentment of Russian conditions. Geneva, Bern, and Heidelberg were breeding grounds for political alignments destined to play a role in Israeli politics thirty and fifty years later.

At home, oppression achieved results that were not intended. The more the Jews of Russia were oppressed, the more they clung to their distinct ways; the more they were thrown together into areas of forced residence of ever-diminishing size, the more they sought refuge in the narrow confines of orthodox religion, or in Messianic dreams or in radical avenues of escape.

There were mainly three such avenues. By far the most popular one was emigration to the West. America was an obvious choice. New York was the "promised city," a new Jerusalem beyond the seas. There are few reliable statistics from the first half of the nineteenth century, but immigration was restricted because of transportation difficulties and the as yet unshattered hope for internal reform. However, Hebrew and Yiddish tracts extolling the glories of freedom and economic opportunity in America circulated in the Pale as early as 1825. In the years between 1800 and 1870 only some 7,500 Jews are thought to have risked the hazards of a journey thousands of miles across continental Europe and the sea.

The Odessa pogrom of 1871 was a turning point. During the 1870s more than 60,000 East European Jews escaped to the West, 40,000 of them to America. In the 1880s, 200,000 went to America; in the 1890s the figure rose to 300,000. Between 1900 and 1914, some 1,500,000 Jews left Russia for America, and Russia was not the only place in Eastern Europe which Jews and others were leaving. In 1880, some 686,000 Jews lived in Galicia under the quasi-liberal Austro-Hungarian regime; during the next thirty years, 236,000 left. It was a mass movement of unheard-of proportions, comparable only to the Irish exodus after the great famine. Within less than forty years, almost one-third of all Eastern European Jews went forth in search of a new lease on life in the western countries and America.

Their departure did not necessarily improve the lot of those who remained behind. To a large extent the Pale was an economy within an economy. In the *shtetl*, Jews lived off one another. The energetic, more dynamic element left, and even remittances from abroad could not alleviate the dire consequences of a shrinking market.

Politics was a second avenue of escape. Its ultimate end was revolution. Radical politics would have come naturally to many Eastern European Jews, even if, as Jews, they had not been singled out for persecution. Historically, Jews were the most urban of all the ethnic groups of Russia and Poland; as a result, they engaged in that most urban of all human activities—politics. As outsiders they had fewer prejudices and emotional restraints, more enthusiasm for daring concepts of change and renewal. The Messianic dream of justice on earth was an integral part of their religious heritage, and in the case of many young people led to political radicalism. Rebel and rabbi were more closely related to one another than they seemed at the time. The police records of one department for the years 1873–1877 list radicals arrested, tried, and sentenced: 279 nobles, 197 sons of priests, 117 sons of high officers, and 68 Jews. "From the pusillanimous people that the Jews were some thirty years ago," wrote a contemporary observer, "there sprung men and women who threw bombs, committed political murders and sacrificed their lives for the revolution." Minority groups—Letts, Finns, Poles, Georgians, Armenians, and Jews —contributed far beyond their proportionate share of recruits for the revolution; the Jews surpassed all other minorities. Between March 1903 and November 1904, 54 percent of those sentenced for political offenses were Jews. Lenin confided to his sister Anna a high appreciation of Jews as revolutionaries. "Russians," he said, "were too easy going, too readily tired of the revolutionary struggle. Jews, on the other hand, with their stubbornness and fanaticism, made excellent revolutionaries."

Almost half of the delegates to the second Russian Social Democratic party congress of 1903 were Jewish. In addition there were at the congress the delegates of the *Bund*, a Jewish workers' party affiliated with the Social Democrats. Together they must have constituted far more than an absolute majority. (The *Bund* nevertheless walked out because the other Jews, including Trotsky, were not "Jewish" enough for them and refused to recognize their ethnic interests.) Thomas G. Masaryk, in his book *Spirit of Russia*, gave the following figures of dues-paying members of the Social Democratic party in 1906: Russians, 31,000; Poles, 26,000; Letts, 11,000; Jewish *Bund*, 30,000.

Most contemporaries were struck by the predominance of Jews

among the leaders of the main revolutionary parties. Such was their preponderance—Trotsky, Zinoviev, Kamenev, Sverdlov, Sokolnikov—that both before 1917 and after, the revolution was widely considered part of a world-wide Jewish conspiracy. It was not, of course; and yet one is almost tempted to say that, to a very considerable degree, it was the Russian Jews fighting back. Leon Trotsky (né Bronstein), standing trial after the abortive revolution of 1905, stated as much in his defense speech. His attitude to Zionism was negative; he said: "I am a revolutionary, not a Jew"; and yet his famous speech at the trial stands as a moving battle cry by one member of a persecuted Jewish minority who grew up in the pogrom-ridden regions of southern Russia.

> What we have is not a national government but an automaton for mass murder . . . if you are telling me that the pogroms, acts of incendiary and violence . . . that everything that happened in Twer, Rostov, Kersk, Sjedletz, Kishinev, Odessa, Bialstock, was part of the governmental system of the Russian empire—well, yes, then I share the opinion of the prosecution that in October and November we armed ourselves against the governmental system of the Russian empire.

The third avenue of escape was Jewish nationalism. It was a reaction not only to Jewish suffering but also to the emergence of other national movements. Herzl's *Jewish State*, published in 1896, was his response to the anti-Semitism generated by the Dreyfus trial. The four main tracts of the Jewish national revival prior to Herzl were clearly reactions to the successes of other nationalities. Yehuda Alkalai's *The Third Redemption* (1843) reflected its author's response to the Greek war of independence. Moses Hess's Zionist tract *Rome and Jerusalem* (1862) responded, as is suggested by the title, to the first success of modern Italian nationalism. In *Seeking Zion* (1862), Zvi Hirsch Kalischer, a rabbi in Posen, familiar with Polish national strivings, extolled his people to "take to heart the examples of the Italians, Poles, and Hungarians." Leo Pinsker published his *Auto-Emancipation* (1882) under the impact of the Russian pogroms and also of Bulgarian independence. An early Zionist leaflet circulating in Rumania in 1883 stated: "The slaves of America have been liberated. The Russian serfs have been emancipated. Bulgaria is freed. The time has come to work for the liberation of Israel as well."

Like other intellectual and political movements in Russia and Poland at that time, Jewish nationalism was strongly influenced by Western ideas, and in particular, of German romanticism. It was in part a defensive reaction against them. Under the spell of romanticism, Russian nationalists insisted upon the "uniqueness" of the mystic essence of their folk, what the Germans were calling *Eigenart*. Within this exclusive realm, populated by foggy, prehistoric, and often pagan and barbaric archetypes, the Jews had no place—not in Germany and not in Russia. The romantics held that nations were possessed by immutable "eternal spirits." States were seen not as free political organizations set up for rational purposes of security and economic well-being, but as biological, superhuman personalities. Within that state philosophy, even assimilated Jews found themselves left out. The new mystique of race was often a "democratic" substitute for the old mystiques of class.

Soon, partly in self-defense, partly because they could not remain immune to current fashions of thought (Russia at that time was considered an intellectual province of Germany), Jews adopted similar romantic conceptions. Stripped of the right to share in the mystic essence of the "national soul" of Russia or Poland, of Rumania or the Ukraine, Jews preserved their dignity by insisting upon the singularity of their own national archetype. "Myth" was the fashionable word of the time; volumes were written on the "soul" of Spain, of Russia, or of the German folk. A parallel development among Jews was the rediscovery of Hassidism, an unofficial "earthy" trend in Judaism, free of the "anemic" intellectualism of the rabbis.

Fichte's *Reden an die Deutsche Nation*, having been ignored for a few decades, was becoming fashionable again among German intellectuals, and thus found its way to Eastern Europe too. Fichte proclaimed the German mission to realize an ideal community on earth; he claimed it was a task for which Germans were particularly suited, for, in spite of subjugation under Napoleon and assimilation of alien ways, they had preserved their integrity as a people. Hans Kohn, the historian and one-time member of an influential Zionist club at the University of Prague, says in his memoirs that young Jews "transferred Fichte's teaching" into the "context of our own situation ... we accepted his appeal to bring forth the ideal community by placing all the power of the rationally and ethically mature individual at the service of his own nation."

On a more extreme level, the Hebrew essayist Micha Joseph Berdi-
chevsky (1865–1921) pronounced the prophets and sages as gravedig-
gers of "true" Judaism. True Judaism, he felt, was better represented
by the barbaric strength and colorful myths of the sinful kings of
Jerusalem and Samaria, those who "wrought evil in the eyes of the
Lord" and roused the ire of Isaiah. This was Nietzsche, partly even
Wagner, translated into Hebrew. Saul Tschernichovsky, second only
to Bialik in modern Hebrew poetry, stood "before the Statue of
Apollo" and, bowing to it, turned away from the God of Israel to
worship a tribal idol of soil and blood: "El Shaddai, the Lord of the
desert, who led Canaan's daring conquerers" and whom "dried up"
rabbinical Jewry had strangled in the "fetters of prayer strap."

Jewish nationalism, the third avenue of escape, was closely related
to the second, social revolution. Zionism and revolution grew intertwined in Laocoön complexity, within the history of Russian radicalism. A large part of the Jewish national revival actually occurred
within the inner circle of the Russian revolutionary parties, particularly within the *Bund* of Jewish Workers. *Bund* was a Yiddish-speak-
ing labor movement affiliated with Lenin's Revolutionary Social
Democratic party. Lenin bitterly criticized the ethnocentrism of the
Bundists. Plekhanov called them "Zionists afraid of a sea voyage." Un-
daunted, the men and women of the *Bund* strongly affirmed Jewish
nationhood; they favored a form of cultural and quasi-political autonomy for Jews within a pluralist, socialist federation. This was the
point of division between the Bundists and the Zionists; the latter
demanded their own country. The *Bund* wanted "national" control of
schools, press, and the arts.

As a clandestine trade union, with a non-Zionist but clearly nation-
alist orientation, the *Bund* had strong popular support within the
Pale.* The *Bund* soon became a source of growing concern for the
Czarist authorities.

The Zionists—committed as they were to a solution beyond the

---

* The *Bund* caused more social unrest than non-Jewish trade unions. Jewish workers
in the Pale struck twice as often as workers in Russia generally. They had one of the
highest strike records in Europe. Between 1900 and 1904, of every thousand Jewish
workers, 58 struck; of every thousand Russian workers, 26. Parallel figures for other
European countries were: Germany, 11; Belgium, 14; England, 15; Austria, 21; France,
30.

borders of Russia—were formally outside the more narrow confines of the Russian revolutionary movements. Unlike the *Bund* they went their own separatist way. Yet they, too, fell into a wide spectrum of parties, of which the most "right wing" was still somewhat left of the Russian bourgeois liberals. Toward the end of the century, the radically socialist "left wing" of Zionism became dominant; it soon began to play a leading role in the colonization of Palestine. The socialist Zionists, as they were being called, were not affiliated with any one of the revolutionary parties, as were the Bundists. Yet they, too, were within the wider circle of insurgents. They shared with both socialists and anarchists a deep faith in social revolution; in the Zionist version, revolutionary salvation was possible only in Palestine. In Palestine, under socialism, the future would take care of itself and resolve all of Jewry's social and national problems.

By temperament, inner motivation, or upbringing, the young socialist Zionists in their clandestine clubs throughout Russia were hardly distinguishable from other radicals. Isaiah Berlin equated them with the "revolutionaries, populists, Honest Men, students, New People, terrorists, seminarists, cadets, reds," or whatever else they were called in Czarist Russia before 1917. They shared prison cells and hopes for the moral rejuvenation of man with other Russian revolutionaries. For instance, Gregory Gershuni, a leader of the Social-Revolutionary party (S.R.) in Kiev preached individual terror, yet participated in strictly non-violent fund-raising efforts for Zionist colonies in Palestine.

Jewish families were often split by socialists of the "pure" and the "Zionist" variety. The same people often moved back and forth from one group to another, with an apparent ease that sometimes belied the bitter antagonism between them. "Zionist" and "international" socialists nevertheless debated each other ferociously, especially at foreign universities. At one such meeting, the speaker for the "internationalists" was Parvus-Helphand, a Russian Jew who, to emphasize how international the world had become, pointed to his jacket and exclaimed: "The wool in this jacket comes from Angoran sheep; it was spun in England and woven in Lodz. The buttons come from Germany, the thread from Austria!" The speaker was heavily gesticulating at this point and the seam of his sleeve suddenly burst. One student immediately jumped up: "And the tear on your sleeve comes from the pogrom of Kishinev!"

Bundists and Zionists were even more bitterly opposed to each other, because they had so much in common. Zionism and Bundism were both products of the national awakening within the Pale, an awakening at the same time cultural, political, and social. Both movements were wed to Utopia; in each, discussions were marked by a peculiarly venomous and violent verbal imagery that combined Russian earthiness with talmudic hair-splitting. To some extent this is characteristic even today in Israeli political discussions. Students of turn-of-the-century Russian politics will recognize a familiar tone in the raised voices and bitter acrimony which echo through the Israeli Parliament.

Bundists considered Zionism a "dangerous illusion," the "socialism of idiots." Zionists accused Bundists of living in a fools' paradise. They would never be granted the autonomy they strove for; they were slaves of the Gentile world, its intellectual bootlickers. Both Bundists and Zionists had strong popular support. As they competed for public favor, Bundists grew gradually more "national" and Zionists more "socialist" until, years later, the iron fist of Stalinism crushed them both.

Trotsky opposed both Zionism and Bundism. He lashed out against the "hysterical sobbings of the sentimentalists" and proclaimed as early as 1904 the "bankruptcy of Zionism." Later he shifted ground somewhat. He told an interviewer in 1937 that after Nazism (and Stalinist anti-Semitism) it was difficult to believe any longer in assimilation. He still maintained that Zionism "by itself" was no solution. But even under socialism, he thought, it might still be necessary for the Jews to live in a territory of their own.

Jewish nationalists, both socialist and liberal, reached this conclusion more than half a century earlier. There were differences of opinion among them. Some viewed the future paradise of liberty and justice on the banks of the Mississippi River; others could see it only on the Jordan. All agreed with Mazzini that without a country of your own, "you have neither name, voice, nor rights nor admission as brothers into the fellowship of peoples. You are the bastards of humanity."

During the Odessa pogrom of 1881, Moses Leib Lilienblum, a former teacher at an orthodox religious seminary, was hiding from the rioters in the cellar of his barred-up house. A few years earlier he had turned his back on orthodox religion and had become a devotee of Russian positivism, with its disdain of metaphysics—a good carpenter, who can produce a solid chair, is better than a thousand philosophers. Now, at the age of thirty-seven, he was attending a Russian gymnasium in order to acquire a general, secular education.

"I am glad I have suffered," he wrote in his diary on the seventh of May, one day after the riots. He described the scene, when the rioters approached his house:

> The women shrieked and wailed, hugging their children to their breasts, and did not know where to turn. The men stood by dumbfounded. . . . At least once in my life I have had the opportunity to feel what my ancestors felt every day of their lives. Their lives were one long terror, why should I experience nothing of that fright? . . . I am their son, their suffering is dear to me and I am exalted by their glory.

It was not the first pogrom he had heard of but the first he had personally witnessed. What shocked him even more was the fact that "cultured" Russians, university students, and high school boys participated in the bloody riots. The experience changed his entire outlook and set him firmly on the course of Jewish nationalism. He quit his studies at the Russian gymnasium. "It was not a lack of high culture that was the cause of our tragedy," he wrote, "for aliens we are and aliens we shall remain, even if we become full to the brim with [Russian and secular] culture." Lilienblum became the first prominent ideologist of Jewish nationalism in Russia. He inspired the first pioneers who left Russia in 1882 to settle in Palestine. "Why should we be aliens in foreign lands," he wrote, "when the land of our forefathers is not yet forgotten on the face of the earth, is still desolate and capable . . . of receiving our people. We must purchase much land and innumerable estates and slowly settle them."

Jews in the Diaspora had always dropped pennies into little collection boxes for the support of rabbinical scholars who studied the Torah in the Holy Land. Lilienblum was probably the first who thought of using the same technique to raise funds for the purchase of land in Palestine. "Whoever wants to support the national idea," he wrote in 1883, "will contribute one kopek a week, to be saved for a given period in special boxes in every home, for the settlement of

Eretz Israel. In a year this will add up to thousands of rubles. It is also possible to earmark given percentages of the sums donated in the synagogue, at weddings, at funerals of the rich, and so forth. Perhaps a Jewish lottery can be set up. . . . In a word, it is possible in some way or other to collect . . . huge sums to buy many large holdings in *Eretz Israel* from the Turkish government." As a start Lilienblum hoped to collect ten million rubles; he planned the establishment of "three hundred colonies," irrigation works and roads. Such an enterprise, he felt sure, would inevitably lead to a kind of political autonomy.

Israel celebrates the memory of its spiritual fathers by calling street names after them. There are Lilienblum streets today in all the larger cities. In Tel Aviv, Lilienblum Street is, appropriately enough, the heart of the banking district, for the embittered scholar from Odessa was probably the inventor of the modern Jewish fund drives for Israel.

Lilienblum was not the first prophet of Jewish nationalism. Throughout the nineteenth century the idea was reoccurring to non-Jews and Jews, to poets and businessmen, Protestant clergymen, visionary idealists, promoters. Even some politicians thought of Palestine as a solution to the "Jewish problem." Napoleon, according to the *Moniteur,* published a proclamation in 1799 in which he invited the Jews of Asia and Africa to assemble under his flag and "reestablish ancient Jerusalem." It was for this reason, he announced, that he was marching into Syria. As far as is known, no Jews heeded his call.

The leader of the Decembrist uprising of December 1825 in Russia, Pavel Pestel (hanged soon after), proposed the resettlement of Jews in Palestine, not out of love but to get rid of them. In Prussia similar thoughts crossed the mind of the German nationalist Heinrich von Stein. In France the socialist Fourier proposed to test his idea of cooperative settlements (*phalansteries*) in a kingdom of "Judea" or "Lebanon" which would be set up with funds supplied by generous Jewish millionaires. We encounter in Fourier not only a first premonition of the future link between Zionism and utopian socialism (some of his ideas were later realized in the *kibbutz*), but also of the unholy alliance between anti-Semitism and Zionism. Like Pestel, Fourier was a vehement anti-Semite.

Above all, poets were fired by the idea of Zion revived. In England Byron wept for those ". . . by Babel's stream, whose shrines are desolate, whose land a dream." As his heart went out to the subjugated

Greeks, so it did to the homeless Jews: "The wild dove hath her nest, the fox his cave, mankind their country, Israel but the grave."

Spiegelberg, in Friedrich Schiller's *The Robbers*, poring over Josephus Flavius' ancient history of the Jews, called out to Karl von Moor: "Drink, fellow, drink ... how would it be if we were Jews and restored the kingdom ... isn't that a shrewd, courageous plan? We issue a manifesto in the four corners of the earth, and take to Palestine all who do not eat pork."

On a different level there was Lord Shaftesbury in England who believed himself to be acting under divine inspiration. He proposed to Palmerston a restoration of the Jews in Palestine. With supreme Victorian self-confidence he envisaged an Anglican Palestine, populated by Jews converted to the Church of England out of sheer gratitude. In America, a businessman named Mordecai Emanuel Noah laid the foundation stone for the Jewish Commonwealth of Ararat on Lake Michigan, but nothing came of it. There is a temptation to dismiss such moves as irrelevant curiosities. But the nineteenth century, more than any before it, was under the powerful influence of small sects and lonely eccentrics publishing tracts after a lifetime spent in public libraries. Moses Hess was one of them.

Moses Hess was Lilienblum's main precursor in the nationalist camp, although at the time unknown to him. Hess was an assimilated German Jewish socialist. Like his contemporary Heinrich Heine, he spent much of his life in exile in Paris. He was the first Zionist Communist and for some time he was a close collaborator of Marx and Engels. Hess was no isolated little autodidact cowering in a distant corner of the Russian empire, he was in the very mainstream of current Western European progressive thought.

Hess did not believe in violent revolution but in peaceful evolution, not in eternal economic laws but in individual decision. Marx savagely mocked Hess for his "utopian sentimentalism." Hess, in *Rome and Jerusalem* (1862) strongly pressed for a socialist Jewish commonwealth in Palestine. He espoused a "practical ethic" of love, voluntarism, and harmonious cooperation between free men.

Repelled by the materialism and middle-class egotism of his family, he refused to join his father's business. He married a Cologne prostitute, less out of love than as an act of restitution to a victim of the crimes of bourgeois society. He saw in history a struggle between the forces of altruism, love, and justice and those of egotism and oppression. In *Rome and Jerusalem* he called upon Jews to reaffirm their nationality. In their own country they must prepare for the socialist "Sabbath of History," which would liberate them and all mankind.

Another German Jewish socialist, Ferdinand Lassalle, also came close to affirming Jewish nationalism but not as avowedly as Hess. Lassalle, at the age of sixteen, upon hearing of a ritual murder charge hurled at the Jews of Damascus, wrote in his diary:

> The oppressions which caused the Swiss to rebel, were they greater? Was there a revolution more just than that of the Jews of that city, if they would rise up, burn Damascus, blow up the towers and *kill themselves* together with their torturers? Cowardly people, you do not deserve a better lot! The crushed worm twists and bends, but you bow deeper. You don't know how to die, to destroy; you do not know what is just vengeance; you don't know how to be buried together with your enemies and tear them apart even in a fit of agony.

Hess's way to Zionism was different from that of Lassalle or Lilienblum. No pogrom or similar harrowing personal experience led this cosmopolitan intellectual to publish *Rome and Jerusalem. Rome and Jerusalem* was as forceful a statement in favor of Jewish nationalism as was ever written. It prompted Herzl to write in 1901: "Everything we have tried already is written there."

Earlier in his life Hess had believed that Jews should assimilate, even convert. He now came to the conclusion that this was impossible, even dangerous. His basic idea was that just as Italians were reuniting so Jews must find one another and reunite in their own land. He was convinced that "every Jew, whether he wants or not, is solidly tied in with his own nation." There was no other possibility for Jews to be truly free except in their own state. Only there would Jews "again exercise an influence upon the whole of mankind .... It is only with a national rebirth that the religious genius of the Jews, like the giant of the legend touching Mother Earth, will be endowed with new strength and again be inspired with the productive spirit." According to Hess a national renaissance was only possible through a return to "productive" work on the soil within the framework of a just order, without social hierarchies, in cooperative units.

In Hess we meet for the first time that fusion between ethical socialism and enlightened nationalism, which was to play a role in the future development of socialist Zionism. At Hess's funeral in 1875, French, German, and Polish socialists followed the coffin. One mourner, speaking at the open grave, said: "Rest in peace, my friend. What you desired, we shall fulfill. . . . In thousands of hearts you have become immortal, your memory shall revive each time a wretched proletarian will seek help in your ideas."

In 1962 Hess's remains were transferred to Israel and in a state ceremony Hess was reinterred on the shore of Lake Galilee, alongside the first pioneers who in 1908 had established the first *kibbutz* nearby. His gravestone in the cemetery of Cologne had borne the inscription: "Hess, father of German Social Democracy." Speaking at his new graveside, in 1967, Israel's President Zalman Shazar eulogized him as "one of Israel's founding fathers."

During the 1880s few people in Russia read Moses Hess's Zionist writings. Nor in all likelihood were his readers more numerous elsewhere. *Rome and Jerusalem* was largely ignored when it came out. In Russia it was not books but the prime forces of life—fear of hunger and fear of death—that drove young Jews to radicalism. Nor were radical solutions haunting only the minds of young hotheads.

Leo Pinsker was a distinguished physician in Odessa. In 1881 he was already sixty years of age. His youth had coincided with the years of repression under Nicholas I (1825-1855). But Pinsker's father had somehow managed to evade the restrictions of ghetto life. Pinsker was one of the lucky few who attended a Russian high school and then received a medical degree from the University of Moscow. Moreover, he had been decorated by the Czar for services rendered in the Crimean War. Most of his adult life he had believed that Russia would gradually become a constitutional monarchy with social progress and equality for all.

For him, as for Lilienblum, the pogroms of 1881 were a turning point. He too was shocked above all by the participation in the riots of "cultured" elements, seminarists, students, even left-wing intellectuals of the *Narodni* movement, and by the role played by leading newspapers in whipping up the mob.

If Pobedonostsev hoped to drown the revolution in Jewish blood, some of the Populists (*Narodniki*) echoed his views, at least as far as the Jews were concerned. A number of Populists were openly anti-Semitic. Others were not discouraged by the pogroms, because the pogroms seemed to prove that the phlegmatic peasants could be turned against the existing order. In a public statement of August 30, 1881, the executive committee of the "Narodniya Volya" called upon the Russian masses to rise up against the "corrupt Yids." The Jews were described as the greatest cause of the suffering of the people, the poor muzhik's disaster, the townman's scourge. Deeply shocked, Pinsker decided that Jews, even if they wanted to assimilate, would never be allowed to. Anti-Semitism, he concluded, was an incurable disease, its main cause the homelessness of the modern Jew.

"To the living," he wrote, "the modern Jew is dead, to the native-born he is a stranger, to the long-settled a vagabond, to the wealthy a beggar, to the poor a millionaire and exploiter, to the citizen a man without a country, to all classes a hated competitor." Jews must therefore once more become a nation, and possess their own territory. He did not much care where that territory was. Palestine was one possibility but not the only one. Like Herzl fifteen years later, Pinsker was not driven by a secularized version of the ancient religious yearning for the land of Zion. His was a rescue operation, not a movement for national revival on historic soil.

Pinsker went to Western Europe in search of supporters. He found none. A year later, he published his program anonymously in a pamphlet entitled *Auto-Emancipation—an appeal to his people by a Russian Jew*. It was written not in Russian but in German and appeared in Berlin. Perhaps Pinsker thought that despite their sufferings the Jews of Russia were not yet ready for his views. He was soon proven wrong.

Pinsker's pamphlet appeared in 1882. In the same year a group of young men, mostly students, gathered in Kharkov and formed the "Lovers of Zion," or BYLU, an acronym for *Bet Yaacov Lechu V'nelcha* ("Oh House of Jacob, come ye, let us walk," Isaiah, 2:5). It was the first cell of an organization that was to be instrumental in launching a first wave of emigrants to Palestine. Historians like precise dates for great and imprecise events; 1882—the year Pinsker's pamphlet was published and the Lovers of Zion was formed in Kharkov—will do better than any other as the opening year of the Zionist colonization of Palestine. In the following decades thirty-nine colonies were founded in Palestine, heavily subsidized by Baron Edmond de Rothschild of Paris.

"Everywhere we are rejected, we are pushed out from everywhere. We are considered aliens," said an early public announcement by BYLU. "Is all hope really lost? Oh no! Judea shall rise again. Let our own lives be an example to our people. Let us forsake our lives in foreign lands and stand on firm ground in the land of the forefathers. Let us reach for shovels and plows," the statement continued, echoing a Jewish version of narodnism, "*We educated must be the heroes who go into battle at the head of the people*."

The Lovers of Zion held their first national convention in 1884, in the small town of Katowitz across the German border, out of the reach of the Russian secret police. The Lovers of Zion were enthusiastic Pinskerites. And Pinsker, who attended, was slowly converted by them to the idea that the separate territory for Jews could not be just anywhere but must be in Palestine, since this was the "instinctive" wish of the people.

In distant America the poetess Emma Lazarus welcomed Pinsker's pamphlet. But the German-speaking Jews of Western Europe, for whom he had written it in the first place, largely ignored it. Among those in the West who did become acquainted with Pinsker's ideas, the reaction of Adolf Jellinek, the Chief Rabbi of Vienna, was typical. He advised Pinsker that he was in shock and should urgently see a doctor. Pinsker's plan could not be carried out; it was "a joke," Jellinek said. More realistic ways must be found to alleviate Jewish suffering.

"I don't see any other solution," Pinsker said.

"But progress, civilization!" exclaimed Jellinek. "Russia cannot forever remain as reactionary as it is."

The conversation between the two men took place in Vienna in the spring of 1882. At that time a young Jewish law student by the name of Theodor Herzl was attending the University of Vienna. He was a good-looking, dandyish young man, son of a wealthy Budapest family, making the rounds of literary salons. In his spare time he wrote plays and feuilletons (sketches in a light and whimiscal vein), only to have them rejected time after time. A thoroughly assimilated Jew, he belonged to the German nationalist student union Albia. He dreamed of making a future for himself in German letters, his law studies merely the concession of a dutiful son of good bourgeois upbringing to his wealthy father.

Thirteen years later, in 1895, Herzl was already a well-recognized playwright and foreign correspondent for Vienna's leading liberal paper, when under the shocking impact of the Dreyfus trial he suddenly arrived at the same conclusion that Pinsker had reached in 1881. When Herzl first expounded his idea to a close Viennese friend, the friend's reaction was strikingly similar to that of Rabbi Jellinek. He told Herzl that he was under shock. He should urgently see a doctor.

Herzl, like Pinsker, was a disappointed liberal. He came to consider anti-Semitism an incurable social disease. Racial fanaticism and national self-righteousness were indelible traits of European society. In *The Jewish State*—the first Zionist pamphlet ever to attract widespread attention—he proposed an orderly exodus of Jews to an as yet unidentified territory.

Although the Zionist movement existed before Herzl, he gave the fledgling movement charismatic leadership, a working organizational machine, and a recognized place on the map of international politics. The rich Jews of the West by and large dismissed his message, as they had ignored Pinsker's. Baron Edmond de Rothschild of Paris, though actively supporting Jewish settlement in Palestine for the past thirteen years, at first refused to see him. But for the poor Jews of the East he became a new Moses.

Herzl overestimated the power of personal diplomacy. His elaborate negotiations with European kings and statesmen and with the Ottoman Sultan came to naught. The British Colonial Office offered him Uganda for Jewish settlement. Herzl accepted but the scheme was vetoed by the Zionist organization he himself had created. He underestimated the primeval force which drew the Zionists to Palestine and only Palestine. He died of a heart disease in 1904. The next powerful impetus to Zionism would come from the region where it mattered most, Eastern Europe.

Imagine, then, these small groups of passionate young men, living restively under an alien regime which not only did little to prevent riots but on occasion actively encouraged them; young men and women in their late teens and early twenties, embittered by their exclusion from the universities and high schools, strongly influenced by the radical fervor of their immediate intellectual environment. Children of their time and place, there were seized like their Gentile contemporaries by a passion for ideas so powerful that in the words of one, it "filled all my waking hours and made everything else appear almost obscenely irrelevant . . . the only thing which really counted was the need to put our ideas into practice."

The Russian Populist Stepniak, whose pen name was Sergei Krav-chinsky, described in his novel *The Career of a Nihilist* the mood of one young Jew after the 1881 pogrom:

> We Jews, we love our race, which is all we have on earth. . . . Why should I love your peasants who hate and ill-treat my people with blind barbarity? Who tomorrow will perhaps loot the house of my father . . . and brutally assault him as they have done to thousands of other poor hard-working Jews? As to the upper classes, why! what but contempt can one feel for such wholesale cowards. No, there is nothing in your Russia worth caring for. . . .

Zionist study circles and clandestine clubs soon sprouted in hundreds of cities all over Russia. They were a form of Jewish popu-lism, a "back to the people" movement nearly as mystical as its Russian counterpart. The simultaneous growth of the various clubs was largely spontaneous. Some were soon calling themselves "parties" or "movements"; they constituted a disconnected network with little if any coordination. Members were often surprised to learn that else-where others were active along similar lines. The Zionist World Con-gress, which began to convene regularly after 1897, afforded a first opportunity for members of these groups and splinter groups to know one another. The Congress, however, did little to increase any unity among them. By the turn of the century the clubs had become so numerous and so hopelessly splintered in ideological and personal argument that it became increasingly difficult to properly sort them out; today it is almost impossible.

There were "reds," eager to participate in the clandestine work of the socialist revolutionary parties; and "blues," anxious to stay out but nevertheless committed to an even more radical socialist policy. There was a bewildering medley of in-between groups committed to various hair-splitting compromises; Marxist and non-Marxist socialists; anarch-ists and syndicalists; Yiddishists and Hebraists; unconditional supporters of Palestine as the future homeland and territorialists who would accept Uganda or territory in Australia or America. There were religious reformers and traditionalists. Some wished to combine the national renaissance with a complete change of existing social forms, beginning with the family and ending with economic institutions; others were ready to stop at agrarian reform. There were liberal groups waiting for a victory of the Russian constitutionalists and hoping that under them it would be possible to arrange an orderly exodus of poorer Jews to their Palestinian homeland. In 1906, in Pinsk, under the influence of Polish nationalists and the terrorist Armenian Socialist party, a secret caucus of Zionist socialists decided to speed things up and finance the redemption with the booty of armed robberies. It was called the *Yiddisher Nationaler Terror* (Jewish National Terror). As far as we know, nothing came of it.

Whatever their other differences, one notion was shared by all Zionist socialists. They saw the Jewish worker crushed by the twin pressures of "exploiting capital" and the exclusive nationalism of the majority. The "Jewish worker" was therefore seen as the natural "pioneer" or "vanguard of Zionism."

There was probably no current thought, from Nietzsche to Kropotkin, from Marx to Adler and Tolstoy, which did not find its echo in one of the Zionist parties or clubs. But it is probably fair to say that by the first decade of the twentieth century a majority of these clubs had moved left of center, and were committed to a more or less radical program of socialist reform.

Many cabinet ministers in the first several Israeli governments, as well as the country's first three presidents—Chaim Weizmann, Yitzchak Ben Zvi, and Zalman Shazar—began their political careers in a Zionist club in Russia or Galicia at the turn of the century. This was the political school to which they had gone; its blind spots and ideals, its hopes and dreams, passions and prejudices, were to pursue them throughout their lives. Some of its qualities they were to bequeath to their future native-born heirs.

The impact of these clubs and youth groups on young Zionists in the little towns of Galicia or Czarist Russia was well described by David Horowitz, a future president of the Bank of Israel:

> We were getting more and more divorced from the existing environment. We expressed our utter lack of faith in it by citing Dante's

introduction to the *Inferno*: "Lose all hope, ye who enter here." But in the Labor Zionist youth movement we created for ourselves an ideal world, new free and noble. We dreamed of Utopia—the Labor Zionist movement was the gate that led to it.

A characteristic leaflet, issued in Lvov about 1904, reads:

Jewish workers of all countries unite behind the banner of Poalei Zion! Brothers and sisters of the workers' class! We see before us two great and powerful movements: on the one hand socialism which seeks to liberate us from economic and political slavery; and on the other hand Zionism which seeks to liberate us from the yoke of the Diaspora. Both affect us greatly. Both promise us a glorious future. Both are vital for us as life itself. . . .

The leaflet went on to say that while in the past it may have been necessary to choose one of the two, in recent years Zionism had turned socialist while socialism recognized national rights. Therefore socialism and Zionism now complemented one another . . . .

Jewish workingman and working woman, all the exploited, oppressed and those who live by the sweat of their brow . . . let us unite and declare:
Down with assimilation!
Down with capitalism!
Down with anti-Semitism!
Long live the international proletariat!
Long live Jewish freedom!
Long live socialism!
Long live Zionism!

Pinsk, Minsk, Homel, Yekatrinoslav, Odessa, or Kishinev, the scenes not only of pogroms but also of Russian revolutionary ferment, were centers of activity for the nascent Zionist left, the ephemeral groups from which later grew the various Israeli labor parties. Another such center was Poltava, in the southwest. Yitzchak Ben Zvi, second Israeli President and a native of Poltava, described it as a quiet market town, full of gardens and orchards, "no industry and no proletariat," with little social or political unrest. The Czarist government by chance had picked Poltava as a place of exile for revolutionary agitators. Among them Ben Zvi remembered the famous writer Korolenko and especially Martov, the one-time collaborator of Lenin, editor of the influential *Iskra* and later leader of the Mensheviks. Young Poltavans easily came under their influence. The concentration of brilliant revolutionists, moving freely about town with little else to do but write and engage in argument, created some "ferment among the learning youth, Russian-Ukrainian as well as Jews," wrote Ben Zvi. "Illegal circles were set up, a social-democratic and a social-revolutionary circle, a Ukrainian-revolutionary circle, an anarchist circle, and others. The learning youth ... sons of the Jewish middle class, followed the new ideas and joined the bandwagon of the Russian revolution."

It was in Poltava that Ber Borochov, a young twenty-five-year-old Jewish intellectual, already expelled from the Social-Democratic party for Zionist deviationism, developed a theory fusing orthodox Marxism and Zionism, socialist revolution and nationalism; it appealed to many young Jews who were equally committed to both doctrines but found it difficult to reconcile the two.

To a modern reader, Borochov's writings seem tedious; his reasoning artificial and contrived. Borochov's ideas must have seemed infinitely more meaningful at a time when the Communist faith was as yet untarnished by later practice. To appreciate his impact we must remember that he wrote during a period of rising Messianic fever. Marxists regarded their movement as part of the final struggle over a world tyranny when all peoples would be renewed and history brought to its consummation.

Borochov's Marxist vision of Zionism seemed to evolve logically from a proper reading of *Das Kapital*, a conclusion which Marx would have doubtless himself reached had he only put his mind to it. In this "Marxist" view of the Diaspora, Borochov saw Jewish misery mainly as the result of adverse "process of production," what Marx had called "*Produktionsverhältnisse*." By this he meant that being "ex-territorials" without a country of their own, Jews were being inevitably pushed out of "primary" economic fields (agriculture, mining) to "secondary" fields (commerce or light industry). Not being "productive," the Jewish proletariat was incapable of rallying together as a social force; without territory, it lacked the strategic base for a normal class struggle. For Pinsker and Herzl, improving the lot of the Jews was fraught with psychological and political difficulties. Borochov saw only economic ones. Pogroms were "explainable" in terms of historical materialism in the same way Marx and Engels had explained wars. Borochov saw the Jewish proletariat of Eastern Europe as a

Promethean figure, chained to a social and national misery by his "unproductivity"; socialism meant improved *Produktionsverhältnisse*, but for Jews, he thought, this was possible only on autonomous territory. Emigration was thus *"stychic"* (independent of human desire, a blind force of nature); to forgo the likelihood that emigration would simply reproduce elsewhere the same conditions of misery, the Jews must in the end move to an underdeveloped country. Palestine was such a country, and because it was also underpopulated, in Palestine the problem was likely to be finally solved.

Zionism (i.e., emigration to Palestine) hence became as "inevitable" for the Jews as was the coming of socialism for mankind in general. Left-wing Zionists eagerly clung to "Borochovism." Half a century later, the Israeli government went to some lengths to induce the Soviet government to permit the transfer of Borochov's remains from Kiev (where he had died, at the age of thirty-six, in 1917) to Kinneret, on the Lake of Galilee, where they were reinterred in a national shrine alongside those of Moses Hess.

Ben Zvi, who grew up with Borochov in Poltava and shared his early political career, later wrote in glowing terms of him as "the teacher" of a whole generation of Zionists. For Ben Zvi himself the moment of truth came during the abortive revolution of 1905, shortly after the publication of Borochov's tract, "The National Question and the Class Struggle."

When the revolution broke out in October 1905, even sleepy Poltava began to stir. A mass meeting was held on the main square to celebrate the event. Leaders of the local Social Democrats, the Social-Revolutionaries and the Ukrainian Socialist party appeared on the terrace of the new municipal theater. Among the speakers was the twenty-year-old Ben Zvi, who addressed the meeting on behalf of the Zionist socialists. In his memoirs he described the moment as one of the most dramatic of his life. He was standing on the terrace and praising the revolution; some ten thousand people were listening below. But "as I spoke . . . there appeared in my mind's eye the living image of Jerusalem, the holy city, with its ruins, desolate of its sons" (he had seen it on a short trip during the 1904 school vacations).

At that moment I asked myself: *Whom am I addressing?* Will my listeners here in Poltava understand me, will they believe? Are we, the Jews, *real partners* in this revolution and in this victory? Will this revolution, which promises salvation to the Russians, bring salvation for us Jews too? Why am I here and not there? Why are we all here and not there? As these questions arose in my mind I could no longer free myself from them; and as I finished my speech I no longer thought of this demonstration and of the victory of the Russian Revolution but of *our Jerusalem*. That very hour I reached the absolute decision that my place is in the land of Israel, and that I must go there, dedicate my life to its upbuilding, and as soon as possible.

Such were the notions born in the minds of a few energetic young men, full of a missionary zeal, in the very midst of revolutionary euphoria. Even stronger was the mood of disappointment which followed the failure of the 1905 revolution and the subsequent wave of persecutions. Both helped to launch a second wave of emigration to Palestine. It proved much more decisive than the first wave and changed the whole nature of the Palestinian enterprise.

Shortly after Ben Zvi's public appearance the Czarist police searched his home. They found a case of dynamite belonging to a secret Jewish defense organization. Ben Zvi escaped in time; his family was arrested and exiled to Siberia. Ben Zvi went to Palestine; an avowed socialist, he dismissed as cowardice the possibility of joining one of the local revolutionary parties. It was "escape to the strong camp," undignified for proud Jews.

The new literature reflected the new nationalism. In this sense, too, Zionism paralleled the development of nationalism in Europe. In Ireland, in Italy, in Germany, in Poland, and in Greece national liberators always stood, as it were, on the shoulders of poets—Shelley's unknown "legislators" of the age. Hebrew poets served a similar role. Like the Irish literary revival, the revived Hebrew literature not only summarized people's feelings but was itself an active agent of change. Chaim Nachman Bialik was the greatest among the new Hebrew writers.

None before Bialik nor after has expressed the Jewish will to live in words and rhymes of such beauty and poetic force; he is rightly known today as *the* national poet of Israel. Within the Pale of Settlement Bialik's poems went from hand to hand, as printed copies were rare. Some poems circulated by hectograph, a system still used in Russia sixty years later for the distribution of underground poems. Ben Zvi in his memoirs described the "tremendous impression" made upon young Jews by Bialik's *Poems of Wrath*, written immediately after the Kishinev riot:

"If there be any justice, let it shine now!" Bialik in one of his most celebrated poems, "City of Slaughter," exhorted the young. He and his fellow poets of the Hebrew literary revival wrote passionate poems extolling Palestine. The poems were filled with yearning for the ancient homeland; their imagery was marked more by a wistful hope to regain something lost than by the desire to discover anything new. The poets had never seen Palestine, nor in all probability any reliable prints or water-color reproductions. And yet in their mind's eye they clearly saw a land, its rivers and its mountains, its flowers and birds, and they poured this image into hot poetry. Under the iron sky of the north they sang of sunny Galilee; in the vast flatlands of the Ukraine they dreamed of the craggy mountains of Judea. They "were seeking with their souls" the Land of the Jews, as Goethe's Iphigenia, on the island of Tauris, was seeking the Land of the Greeks.*

It has been said that young Russians of that time, more so than other people in Europe, were extremely sensitive to literary influences; young people would suddenly change their entire way of life after reading a single poem or pamphlet. "Two books set me on my present course," a pioneer in Palestine wrote in his diary in 1907, "the Communist Manifesto and a slim volume of poems by Chaim Nachman Bialik. I shall never forget the first day I read Bialik's

> Rise, wanderer in the desert, get out of the wilderness.
> The road is still long, the battle's still great!

I knew then and there what I had to do."

In 1902 Bialik wrote that this was "the last generation of slavery

---

* A forgotten poem in Russian by Ilya Ehrenburg, recently rediscovered, suggests that not only Zionist or ethnic writers were touched by the idea of return, but also one as distant from Zionist or Jewish affairs as Ilya Ehrenburg. The poem "To the Jewish People" appears in a volume entitled *I Live* (published 1911, St. Petersburg). Ehrenburg does not mention it in his memoirs nor is it listed in official Soviet bibliographies.
> . . . Gather your offsprings, the weak and feeble,
> And go thee to the fields of Jerusalem the lofty,
> Where happiness was yours in the years of thy youth.
> There cast thy eye o'er your desolate fields,
> And move thy rusty plow.
> And there, under the olive trees, there
> Perhaps you'll find your peace after the years of pain.
> But if to die the fates have doomed you,
> Do not in foreign lands give up your soul.
> But only there, there where you've seen youth's beautiful morning,
> Just there, just there where happiness once was yours.

and the first of salvation." Throughout Eastern Europe young Jews
were responding to this call.

The second wave of pioneers to Palestine started in 1905 and lasted
until 1914. Compared to the massive exodus to America, the pioneers
to Palestine represented a mere trickle; a few thousands only as against
one and one-half million. A personal and active commitment to Zionism was clearly a minority solution, as an involvement in underground
Communist activity must have been.

After the pogroms, appeals from Palestine by some of the earlier
pioneers circulated in the Pale of Settlement. "From Palestine we call
upon you: Come!" The sixteen-year-old Shmuel Dayan, father of the
future general, read one of these appeals and declared it was "a consolation to an aching soul." Soon afterward he left. Berl Katzenelson,
another young man who would emerge as a leading ideologist of the
Zionist labor movement in Palestine, explained his decision to go to
Palestine: "Not out of Zionist faith but out of humiliation, stubbornness, unwillingness to be part of that generation (of Jews) who did
not even have the strength to die an honorable death."

In Plonsk, a small *shtetl* southwest of Warsaw in Czarist Poland,
the eighteen-year-old Shlomo Zemach* went off to his Talmud School
in the morning and did not return home. He ran away to Palestine
with three hundred rubles, stolen from his father, carefully sewn into
the lining of his coat. With no papers he crossed the Austrian border
illegally, with a group of immigrants bound for America. Someone
named Samuel Hirstein lent him his Austrian passport. This was
common procedure at the time; after use, the passport would be sent
back to its owner by mail from Palestine. But when Zemach presented
his new passport to J. D. Berkovitz, head of the Zionist liaison office
in Vienna, whose endorsement was necessary to obtain a Turkish visa,
Berkovitz's first reaction was to telephone the police. "Swindler!" he
screamed, for the real Samuel Hirstein happened to be his nephew.
Zemach, quick-witted, interjected: "Isn't your honor the renowned
author, translator of Herzl's *Jewish State* into Hebrew?" Berkovitz
somewhat calmed down. "Something human began to light up in the
little elephant's eyes." Seeing his advantage Zemach quickly drove his

* Later a well-known Israeli writer and literary critic.

point further home: "Mr. Berkovitz, it is you who caused all this, you who are responsible for this forgery. If it were not for your translation of Herzl's *Jewish State*, I would not have gotten here."

Another young man in Plonsk, David Grien (who soon afterward changed his name to Ben Gurion), defied his father and announced his imminent departure for Palestine. A short time before he had written: "We take with us (to Palestine) young and healthy arms, the love of work, an eagerness for free and natural lives in the land of our forefathers, and a willingness toward frugality." He wanted to "redeem" and build Palestine with his own hands, there to create "a model society based on social, economic and political equality."

It was not an isolated mood. In the small towns of White Russia, the Ukraine, and Russian-controlled parts of Poland, hundreds of young men and women were packing their little bags. They bid their parents farewell, or simply ran away from home. Their departure was sporadic and disorganized. No man, no ministry, planned it. Individuals and small groups of friends just started moving. They embarked at Odessa or Trieste and in Constantinople or Port Said they changed for slow cargo vessels, or occasional passenger boats bound for Jaffa in Ottoman-controlled Palestine.

5

FOUNDING FATHERS

> Every country is endowed with a character-
> istic feature . . . Russia and its steppes, Italy
> and its Gondolas. What is the distinctive
> feature of this country? Perhaps it is you,
> or the life you lead, which is unreal and
> based upon an arbitrary rule. . . .
>
> —YITZCHAK SHENHAR
> *Perason (An Unwalled City)*

Jaffa, as the first Jewish colonists saw it in the 1880s, was a small
cluster of houses, built of mud and porous sandstone, perched un-
evenly on low mounds of ruins, the accumulated debris of innumerable previous civilizations. The site is one of the oldest continuously
inhabited places in the world. It is mentioned in the list of port cities
conquered by Thutmosis III around 1600 B.C. To the "haven of
Joppa" cedars of Lebanon were sent in floats for the building of
successive temples in Jerusalem; the Jewish king Jonathan Maccabeus
besieged Jaffa in the second century B.C. and "won it." It fell successively under Greek, Roman, Crusader, Saracen, and Turkish rule.

Today Jaffa is a rundown section of Tel Aviv, which began as its
suburb in 1908. Abandoned by most of its Arab population during the
bitter house-to-house fighting of 1948, it is now inhabited mostly by
lower-middle-class immigrants from Bulgaria, Rumania, and the
North African countries. A small picturesque medieval section, overlooking the harbor no longer used, has recently been restored as a
quaint tourist attraction with the usual art galleries, souvenir shops,
and cafes.

In the 1880s Jaffa was a much more important place than it is today. It was the main seaport and trade center of Palestine, the pilgrim's gate to Jerusalem. Steamers moored at some distance from the shore; passengers and cargoes were ferried by rowboat through a succession of dark protruding rocks (believed to be those to which Andromeda was chained by the dragon) to land at an open roadstead with wooden storehouses and a customs shed manned by Turkish officials. With a population of about 8,000 Arabs and 2,000 Jews, Jaffa was the largest city along the entire Mediterranean coastline between Beirut in Lebanon and Port Said in Egypt.

As they disembarked at Jaffa, many early pioneers were of a fault-finding and complaining disposition. Many arrivals recorded their shock at the Oriental confusion, the noise and the squalor of Jaffa, its filthy bazaars, its thoroughly corrupt Turkish administration, its swarms of sore-eyed children, moneychangers, peddlers, beggars, flies, and lepers, its wild-looking porters and dragomans who haggled with pilgrims and tourists over the price of a mule ride up the hills to Jerusalem. "The stench drove me sick," a colonist arriving in 1882 remarked. When Ben Gurion landed at Jaffa, twenty-four years later, his reaction was similar. "I left Jaffa as soon as I could, a few hours after I arrived. This was not my idea of the new life. It was worse than the Plonsk I had come from."

East and northeast of Jaffa, for about a mile or two, were orchards and orange groves; their produce was already being exported to the European market. A small German farming settlement, established in 1867 by Protestant pilgrims from Würtemberg over the ruins of an older, abandoned colony of American pietists, thrived nearby. Its quaint, German-style peasant houses were surrounded by flower beds and shaded by green trees—a rarity in those days. Its imported cows produced small quantities of fresh milk and butter, which were even rarer and fetched good prices from the small community of European vice consuls and men of affairs at Jaffa.

Beyond this German settlement, "civilization," as the early colonists understood the word, was largely nonexistent. Here was the swampy coastal plain, a silent, mournful expanse, ravaged by centuries of warfare, fever, piracy, and neglect, and bearing the pockmarks of a tragic history like few other landscapes on earth. This was the ancient land of the Philistines. Its rivers and ancient waterways were clogged up, producing large swamps infested by malaria flies; the soil was rich enough but frequently given over to weeds; its ancient towns, which in antiquity had held over a million inhabitants, lay in ruins, buried under wandering sand dunes. In the seventeenth century an ancient forest of oak trees had still covered parts of this coastal plain, but most trees were by now chopped down. Fever and sea pirates had long since driven a large part of the population to take refuge in the eastern hills; for some centuries now, the coastal plain, except for a few villages, was sparsely populated. In the coastal plain there was much *aradi muat* (Turkish for "dead land"), so called in Ottoman law because it was untilled and belonged to nobody. The title to such land was acquired by tilling it "with government permission," which was at times available through bribery. The existence of so much uninhabited and relatively cheap land on the swampy coastal plain made settlement easier for the early colonists.

In the hills further east the scene was much more inviting. There were almond and olive trees, shepherds with flocks of sheep, and small villages with famous biblical names—but Moslem populations—perched on stony hilltops. Their way of life, food, dress, their daily implements—from sickle to wooden plow and threshing sledge—hardly seemed to have changed from the days of the Bible. Here was the heart of the Holy Land, but as an eighteenth-century English pilgrim wrote in his diary, "terra sancta being the name only, for all holiness is banished therefrom." Here the Canaanites offered human sacrifice to Moloch; here Joshua called upon the sun to lengthen the day of battle; Deborah sang her savage song of victory; and the prophet, "who was among the herdsmen of Tekoa," proclaimed his message of universal peace and justice; here Jesus was crucified; here the Romans massacred the Jews; the Persians massacred the Byzantines; the Crusaders massacred the Saracens; the Turks the Arabs; and Napoleon, in 1799, only eighty years before, brutally massacred the Turks, who now in the late 1800s were maintaining a loose control over the country.

In the nineteenth century, travel to Palestine was becoming easier and relatively safer than at any time since the days of the Roman Empire. In the second third of the century the country gradually opened up to European tourism. Soon an enormous travel literature sprang up. Hundreds of volumes were written, frequently in a tone of breathless excitement and adorned with beautiful woodcuts and etchings, lovingly bound in leather and goldleaf. In England alone, the number of pious Holy Land travel books published between 1840 and 1880 is estimated at more than 1,600. Some are still highly readable today; they are an indispensable source of information on life and scenery in Palestine before and during the arrival of the first Jewish settlers.

Most of these travel books were, of course, of a very special kind. In England they were part of the Evangelical revival, when eighteenth-century rationalism was giving way to revelation and Hellenism to Hebraism. Travelers, whether Catholics, Presbyterians, Methodists, or orthodox Jews, in most cases were seeking evidence to prove a special creed, and frequently little else besides. Mark Twain, who came storming and muckraking through Palestine in 1867, noted that the pilgrims "could no more write dispassionately and impartially about it than they could about their own wives and children."

There was a curious difference between Jewish travelogues of nineteenth-century Palestine and parallel accounts by Christian Protestants, especially English and American. The latter frequently stressed the fabulous beauty of the land of milk and honey. Jews as a rule fixed a sad eye upon its ruin and destruction, "a habitation of dragons and a court for owls." For Jews the country sat in sackcloth and ashes. For them it was part of God's punishment to his people for their sins; and like the destruction of the Temple in Jerusalem, a reason to atone and humbly pray for the coming of the Messiah. Most Jewish travelogues stressed the bleakness of the landscape; their authors lamented with Isaiah and cried for the return of "the teats, the pleasant fields, the fruitful vine" of days gone by.

Wherever they looked they saw but thorn and thistle, ruined cities, dens of wild animals, and death's shadow upon forsaken palaces. Jewish travelogues of the time are pervaded by grim images. "Ah, the roads of Zion are desolate," Dr. Louis Loewe, a Jewish traveler noted in 1838. From a distance the city of Jerusalem looked "great . . . Moslem houses of prayer give it much beauty," but as one approached the city its "desolation increased and wherever I looked I saw only caves and ruined stone, where in antiquity, perhaps, glorious palaces had stood—the markets I passed on my way to the Street of the Jews were narrow and horrible as in the cities of Egypt."

The Viennese physician and radical liberal writer Ludwig August

Frankl, a participant in the revolution of 1848, visited Jerusalem in 1856. The city looked to him like "a pilgrim, grey with age who has come here and sunk down to die; his pain has turned into stone like that of the mother whose children had been throttled by the wrath of God."

Many Jewish travelers were given to similar reflections and much of what they wrote was patently absurd. Jerusalem in 1855 had a population of 15,000 people, of whom some 6,000 were Jews. Though primitive by European standards it was certainly not "forsaken." Despite the preponderance of archeological remains, it was a living city; it is highly questionable whether it really "lay in ruins." Whatever may have been its faults, and however different the contemporary taste, the situation of Jerusalem must certainly have been as majestically beautiful as it is today. Yet few of the Jewish travelers were sensitive to that.

Christian travelogues often set a strikingly different tone. To English and American travelers, Palestine was the charmed land of David's lyre, Isaiah's strain and Jacob's might, of Abraham's faith and Jesus' love. Like the Jews, Christians permitted an image of the past to transfigure present reality; they were as deeply romantic but saw diametrically opposite landscapes. Their vision was equally clouded by wishful thinking. William Blake in 1804 dreamed of building Jerusalem on England's green and pleasant land; some of his countrymen traveling through Palestine a few decades later actually saw the green and pleasant fields of England in the most unlikely corners of Jerusalem. As astute an observer as George Adam Smith, whose *Historical Geography of the Holy Land* (1894) is still one of the most useful and delightfully written books on the subject, was reminded of Scotland in the stony and mostly dry, uncultivated hills of Samaria—a rare lapse in an otherwise meticulously accurate account.

Edward Lear, the Victorian landscape painter, visited Palestine in 1857, and was commissioned by the Prince of Wales to make a painting of Jerusalem. His painting, executed in mute and delicate colors, pictured a city of exquisite beauty. Yet, privately, in a letter to Lady Waldegrave, he called Jerusalem "that vile place! For let me tell you, physically Jerusalem is the foulest and odiousest place on earth."

The vast collection of nineteenth-century travelogues, especially those written by pious Englishmen and Americans, is filled with dreamed-up scenes. Modest hills lift their crowns to heaven; the Jor-

dan River, rarely wider than thirty feet, is seen as a great and mighty
stream. Local *felahin* are compared to the ancient patriarchs. The
country abounds with handsome young Davids tending sheep as they
amiably converse with their Jonathans. *Felahin* women are tall, grace-
ful, and queenly, like Madonnas in Renaissance paintings. ("She is
not tall, but short, not beautiful, but homely," Mark Twain mock-
ingly interspersed, and one is strongly tempted to agree with him.)
Travelers further embellished the landscape by superimposing—as on a
doubly exposed film—fantastic scenes resurrected from history and
literature. In their mind's eye some travelers staged wonderful phan-
tom pageants. As they stood on the bare hills of Galilee or Judea, they
summoned kings and prophets from their graves, flowers and trees
from the dry rocks, and glorious palaces from their ruins, mixing
dream and reality to a point where the two became indistinguishable.
In the nineteenth century Palestine exercised a fatal spell upon its
beholders; Jews or Gentiles, it clouded their vision to fit an inner
image.

All this is, of course, very old; as old as most literature written
about this land. The only safe conclusion to be drawn from the
conflicting evidence of nineteenth-century descriptions must be a trite
one, that there was a little truth in both cases. Christian travelers
rarely stayed for any length of time; even when they did they rarely
exposed themselves to all the rigors of the place as deliberately as did
the Jews. Inevitably, their impressions were rosier. The Jewish settlers
of the early period have left extensive accounts of the depressing
environment they had come to live in. We must judge them in their
context.

The Jewish settlers exchanged relatively sheltered lives in urban
surroundings for work in agricultural settlements. There is a strong
temptation to assume that as they were ignorant of country life elsewhere, they exaggerated its rigors in the new land. Their imagination
was fired by the brilliant image of Zion rebuilt in glory. Everyman
shall peacefully and comfortably "sit under his vine and under his fig
tree" (Micah 4:4); it was an image imported from the Diaspora and
enhanced by a populist idealization of country life, by the reformer's
impatience and the progressive's social program. It clashed with existing reality and invariably made it appear much worse.

Palestine had none of the external glamour and amenities of nearby Egypt, where the first seeds of European progress had been sown by Napoleon's expeditionary force in 1799. In Egypt, following the opening of the Suez Canal in 1869 and the takeover of the country by the British in 1882, a thin veneer of Westernism was forming in the larger towns. There were beginnings of an upper-middle class, the first trains, hotels, imported goods, a few local factories, and other modern services. These were superficialities, but even of such there was scarce little, or nothing at all, in Palestine of the 1880s or 1890s. Travelers hardened by the rigorous exertions of a grand tour through the Orient would return from Palestine to Egypt relieved, happy at last to reach a comfortable bed with no bugs, clean hot water with which to wash, and competent doctors to tend the various diseases they had contracted on the way.

Economically Palestine was lagging behind its northern and eastern neighbors, Lebanon and Syria. In Lebanon, the autonomy enforced by the Western powers in 1864 had stimulated cultural and economic development, particularly in and around the port of Beirut, while Palestine still remained a relatively backward, neglected, and certainly more remote province of the Ottoman Emprie. The gradual penetration of Palestine by Jewish colonists was undoubtedly facilitated by this backwardness; elsewhere it would perhaps have met sooner with greater local opposition. This was a stroke of luck for the early colonists as was the abundance of so much unpopulated swampland along the coastal plain. At the same time it did not make their lives easier.

And yet in Palestine things were also slowly changing. Following two centuries of local strife, invasions, and general disorder, there were signs, at mid-century, of growing political stability. Public safety had increased considerably; for the first time in many centuries it was possible to travel in the countryside unarmed. The economy was expanding; it was boosted by lavish expenditures by Jewish philanthropists and Christian religious orders and foundations; some of the latter served as agents for the European powers, Prussia, England, France, and Russia, who competed for political advantage and pounds of flesh from the rapidly disintegrating cadaver of the Ottoman Empire. For the country as a whole, but more so for a small part of its urban population, the advantages of this competition began to show. In the 1860s and 1870s modest beginnings of a relative prosperity began to appear in the cities. The economy was still largely based on maize, wheat, sesame, and olives; the increasing population was supported by a parallel increase in the area under cultivation. Agricultural exports of fruit were beginning, and briefly, as a result of disruptions caused by the American Civil War, of cotton as well. The population of Palestine probably more than tripled in the nineteenth century, mostly as a result of Arab immigration from neighboring countries. In 1900 it reached 600,000.

As recently as 1845, one grumbling tourist had complained that in the whole of Palestine there was no wheeled transport. In 1869 the first rough road was cut in the mountains between Jaffa and Jerusalem. In 1893 a single-track narrow-gauge railway began plying the same route. Such amenities of course mostly benefited the foreigners and a small number of townsmen. The majority of Palestinians still traveled on foot or on the back of a donkey. People walked from Jerusalem to Jaffa, from Jaffa to Galilee. Many of the Jewish settlers, partly on principle, mostly because of lack of funds, were still doing so as late as 1920. Native peasants by and large remained miserably poor. Their deep suspicion of all governmental authority was the result of bitter past experience; this inbred suspicion exposed them to brutal extortions by kinsmen and feudal robber-barons in the towns who "volunteered" to represent their interest with the hated authorities. When the Turkish government made it compulsory to register land property, suspicious peasants permitted local sheiks and notables to register in their stead. Vast stretches of land—mainly in the plains— "legally" became the property of a few feudal overlords. Some exercised their "legal right" and sold the land. At the same time, they acted as creditors and tax collectors. The peasants of Palestine, exploited and frequently squeezed dry by such a combination of formidable forces, were slowly becoming one huge class of serfs. It was estimated in 1910 that 80 percent of all land in Galilee, and 50 percent in Judea, was owned by a small, diminishing number of large landowners.

Early Jewish settlers, newly arrived from the centers of radical unrest in Eastern Europe, and full of ideas of justice and reform, were undoubtedly shocked by this state of affairs: nevertheless they greatly benefited from it. Here was another basic fact, which, like the general retardedness of the country, helped them in their fortunes. Much of the land bought up for Jewish settlement by individual settlers, by philanthropist promoters like Baron de Rothschild of Paris or by public funds collected by the Zionists abroad, was acquired from absentee Arab landlords. By 1900 Jews had purchased 218,000 dunams of land; by 1914 the total area owned by Jews had grown to 419,000 dunams; 220,000 dunams were under cultivation (4½ dunams equal one acre).

When, in 1881, the first new settlers from Russia and Rumania, the Lovers of Zion, began to arrive in the country, a small Jewish community was already there. The Jewish community of Palestine—even after the Roman purge—had never ceased to exist. Jews had always lived in Palestine. In recent years it has been claimed that some of these Jews were direct descendants of the ancient Hebrews; most of those who were there in 1881 were of more recent origin. From barely 10,000 in 1800, the number had grown to 12,000 in 1850 and to 25,000 in 1881. A few were native-born descendants of Spanish refugees who had been admitted in the sixteenth century by Suleiman the Great at the time of the Inquisition. The majority were pious scholars who had come to the Holy Land to pray and die. Jews had always considered that to live and pray in the Holy Land was a *mitzva* (sacred duty) that was bound to speed the coming of the Messiah. Moreover, from the sixteenth and seventeenth centuries, nearly every reform or revivalist movement in Judaism had been accompanied by a small stream of immigrants to Palestine. Somehow reformers looked to gain strength in their rebellion against the prevailing orthodoxy by direct personal contact with the sacred soil.

Most Jews lived in the "four holy cities," Hebron, Safed, Tiberias, and Jerusalem. They were partly supported by charities, partly engaged in small business and in a few crafts, such as stone masonry which seems to have been almost a Jewish monopoly. In the middle of the nineteenth century they became the target of frantic but fruitless efforts by missionaries to convert them to Christianity.

Living in small, closed communities, fanatically orthodox, they were suspicious of all change, and above all of political Zionism, which they regarded as a sinful attempt to force the hand of God. A remnant of this ancient community survives to this day in the Mea Shearim quarter of Jerusalem and is called *Neturei Karta*—"Guardians of the City."

In 1881 the Jews of Palestine numbered approximately 6 percent of the total population, but in Jerusalem they constituted almost a majority (they achieved this status in 1914). It is difficult to arrive at a balanced judgment of this pre-Zionist Jewish community. Outside of its own narrow circle of orthodox supporters, few people at the time had anything good to say about it. The Zionists' judgment was especially severe; their opinion was colored by the fact that the old Jewish community of Palestine reminded them of the ghettoes of Eastern Europe from which they had escaped. They felt that here again was that "unproductive" life, divorced from the "soil," responsible for Jewish misery abroad. The old community was hopelessly split into *Sephardim* and *Ashkenazim*; the latter were further split into hostile sects which fought one another on matters of doctrine as much as over shares of charity funds.

Herman Melville visited Jerusalem in 1857. The Jews of Jerusalem, he wrote were "like flies who have taken up their abode in a skull." Ludwig August Frankl, who toured Palestine in 1856, found the *Sephardim* of Jerusalem colorful and quite attractive, but because they could not even maintain a religious school (*Talmud Torah*) of their own, he judged them more miserable than the poorest and smallest Jewish community of Europe, which "would be ashamed not to have one." The situation of *Ashkenazi* Jews, of Russian and Polish origin, was even more pitiable to Frankl. He called them "unpleasant" and ascribed that quality to their "well-known ugly Polish costume and the dirt clinging to it"; he disliked their excruciating ungraceful manner, their "grimacing" and "superciliousness in conversation." Frankl deplored their poverty and superstition, their reliance on charity, their fatalist refusal to improve their situation by learning useful crafts. He himself helped to create a trade school with funds supplied by a Viennese philanthropist, but his hopes were not high.

Fifteen years later his pessimism was echoed by a well-known English explorer, Colonel T. S. Conder of the Palestine Exploration Fund, who favored a Jewish restoration in Palestine. He dismissed the Jews of the pre-Zionist community as incapable of realizing such a feat. They were, he wrote, "too bound by the iron chains of Talmudic law." Their veneration of "the past seems to preclude the possibility of progress or improvement in the present."

Yet, only nine years later, in 1879, a group of orthodox Jews broke out of their narrow confines, purchased a stretch of swampy land in the coastal plain, and became farmers. Their settlement was close to the malaria-infested River Yarkon, eight miles from the Mediterranean coast. The settlers were warned by a Greek doctor in Jaffa against settling in the swamp. "Over this entire blue and silent expanse of land I did not see a single flying bird," wrote the doctor. ". . . the place must be so bad and rotten that even birds of prey, always obeying an inner instinct, take care not to approach the spot." The settlers ignored this warning. They named their settlement Petach Tikva (literally, "the valley of gloom for a *Gate of Hope*," Hosea 2:15). It was the first modern Jewish settlement. Today it is a city of more than 100,000 inhabitants and a part of the greater metropolitan Tel Aviv.

But when Salman David Levontin, the first of the new Lovers of Zion from Russia, landed at Jaffa only three years later in March 1882, Petach Tikva lay abandoned; malaria and Turkish officialdom, which had been deeply suspicious of this enterprise, combined to make life so miserable that the settlers, who were not used to farming anyway, quickly gave up.

Levontin, twenty-five years old, a former bookkeeper and bank clerk in Kremenchug in the district of Poltava, southern Russia, was a young enthusiast who turned to Palestine under the traumatic shock of the pogroms of 1881. There are always complex motives that lie behind the seemingly grandiose simplicity of great beginnings. Levontin was a dedicated Zionist, an inspired dreamer who had married a rich girl. His marriage, as was customary in those days, was an arranged affair; he had met his bride for the first time under the marriage canopy. Within the next five or six years, in the course of a few unhappy transactions, he had lost most of his wife's ample dowry. When the pogroms broke out, he was ready for a new start. But he was sensationally different from the vast majority of other young men in similar circumstances. What set him apart was the fact that he did not go off to seek his fortune in America, as was customary, but to Palestine, where only a madman would have gone in search of riches. Palestine in 1881 was infinitely more hopeless a proposition and desolate a place than Tierra del Fuego would seem in our own jet age.

Levontin was a sturdily built, good-looking young man, with

dreamy large eyes, sensual lips, a trimmed mustache and bushy, round beard. He has left a moving memoir of his first year in Palestine (*To the Land of our Forefathers*, written only two years later, in 1884). Its opening line—" *'Sorry, sir,' said the hotel attendant in Kharkov. 'I cannot permit you to stay here, the orders of the Chief of Police as regards Jews are very firm . . .'* "—relates a humiliating incident a few months before his departure. Levontin, on a trip to Kharkov, had been thrown out of his hotel room. A Jew of the Pale of Settlement, with marked papers, could not remain in Kharkov even on a temporary visit.

Those interested in origins will find in Levontin's story a fascinating mixture of accident and deliberate intent that is the hallmark of true drama. His first embassy to Palestine was exploratory. He carried letters of intent from two groups of prospective settlers back in Kremenchug and Kharkov. Elaborately scripted on parchment in Hebrew, the letters echoed the two main motives of awakening a Jewish nationalism at the time—a yearning to revive past glories and an urge to escape present horrors. The men of Kremenchug wrote:

> We the undersigned who wish to go out to the Land of Israel (may it soon be built and restored) in order to establish a colony of farmers with our own financial means, are dispatching this learned envoy, elected by common consent, the honest and true lover of his people Salman David, the son of Yehuda Levontin, to explore the land and observe its essentials and gain a clear knowledge of climate and soil conditions . . . government and population and all details essential for every man among us to the purpose of transferring our residence from hither thither. . . . We ask all concerned. . . .

The men of Kharkov, reflecting the second motive, wrote:

> The condition of our brethren here and compelling reasons aroused our hearts to send the present envoy, the lover of his people, the generous man, Mr. Salman David Levontin, to explore the Holy Land and ascertain, is there a stretch of land to buy, to establish with government permission, colonies for our persecuted brethren. . . .

Eleven men signed the first, and twenty-six the second, letter. But the signatories apparently soon became discouraged or lost interest; for when Levontin found a stretch of 3,340 dunams of sandy virgin land some twelve miles southeast of Jaffa, only two of his Kremenchug backers and none of those at Kharkov actually signed up for shares. The land was bought at 13.37 francs the dunam, a total of 45,925 francs or 1,837 pounds sterling. Following Petach Tikva, this was the second great land purchase by Jewish settlers. It set a pattern for future acquisition: the land was unoccupied; it was owned by absentee landlords, the two brothers Mustapha and Mussa el Dejani, scions of a wealthy Arab family of Jaffa which had acquired it only a decade earlier for only 10 percent of the sale price; and it was bought through a ruse. As would frequently happen in the future, the transaction could not be openly carried through in an ordinary way. Four years before, following the Balkan War, the Congress of Berlin had formally instituted the dismemberment of the Ottoman Empire; the Turkish government in Palestine, wary of all foreigners, had warned against such sales by its representatives in Czarist Russia. Strange as it may sound, the Turks probably suspected a secret Czarist design behind the Lovers of Zion to seize control over the Holy Land.

A few days after Levontin's arrival at Jaffa, an order was issued prohibiting the sale of Palestinian land to Russian and Rumanian Jews. The land was therefore registered under the name of a British subject, Chaim Amsalag, a Jewish native of Gibraltar, who at that time acted as British vice consul at Jaffa. Half of the price for the land was paid by an elderly, rich relative of Levontin, who had just arrived in Palestine from Nikolayev. Childless, Zvi Levontin responded to his young nephew's appeal to "establish a name and memorial for yourself in the holy land of the forefathers." Too old to farm, he earmarked 360 dunams of his land for poor settlers; they would repay him in five annual installments and the proceeds would finance construction of a synagogue in the new colony.

The other half was paid for and taken by young Levontin with eight other young Lovers of Zion from Russia who had come to Jaffa independently of one another and then assembled to settle on the land. One was Joseph Feinberg, a native of Sevastapol; he was twenty-six years old and a graduate of the universities of Heidelberg and Munich. Comfortably employed as a chemical engineer at a sugar refinery in southern Russia, he too was goaded into action by the pogroms of 1881. In Kiev he saw the Czarist governor ride into town on his horse, greeting the rioters and being hailed in return. Like Lilienblum he was less shocked by the riots than by the support they

enjoyed among "cultured" Russians; he concluded that the enlightenment was an illusion, that assimilation was impossible and anti-Semitism a law of nature.

Lilienblum gave Feinberg a letter of introduction to Levontin; he
caught up with him in Jaffa. This sophisticated scion of a wealthy
family and graduate of a good German university, who spoke four
languages fluently, was a professional to whom the entire world stood
open. He might have gone, and probably would have succeeded, anywhere. In background and motivation he was not untypical of his
fellow settlers. All had already broken out of the narrower confines of
ghetto life; all were on the verge of assimilation; all were relatively
well off. They paid for their shares of the new land in ready cash.
Their assets were between 400 and 600 pounds sterling. (Although at
the time this seemed a lot of money, it barely paid for both the land
and the first inevitable mistakes in tilling it, as well as for the digging
of wells.)

The new colony was called Rishon le-Zion (*The First to Zion* . . .
that bringeth good tidings to Jerusalem," Isaiah 41:27). The settlers
loaded their packhorses with tents, tools, and supplies of food and
drinking water and moved out from Jaffa early in August 1882, singing
hymns and offering prayers of thanksgiving. Levontin, lying on his
overcoat the first night and looking at the bright stars above, was
seized with melancholy doubts. Already he "felt passionately in love"
with the new place. It was, he wrote,

> the love of a prodigal son who returns to his home but finds that his
> father is gone . . . tears poured out of my eyes; my heart and soul
> trembled. My home and rest are in this place; here is the cradle of
> my youth . . . but my brothers, where are they? Will they really gather
> from the far places of the earth? I remembered the Lovers of Zion
> meetings at Kremenchug and Kharkov, the fiery speeches, the prom-
> ises. . . . *But where are they?* These hands of mine, used only to
> holding a pen and calculating profits and losses, will they be capable
> of handling a plow to produce bread for me, my wife and my children?
> Do I sacrifice my dear ones on this altar? Have I the right? Will I
> be at all useful . . .

As he thus pondered, his servant and interpreter, a Jew from Jerusalem, interrupted his thoughts. He pointed to the tents which some

Arab bedouin had pitched on a distant sand dune, and said: "When you build your houses and settle here . . . they will come, in the dark of night . . . to plunder and murder."

Although it hardly seemed so at the time, 1882 was an eventful year in the history of the Zionist settlement of Palestine. Levontin and his group were only the first. Throughout the summer and fall, prospective settlers continued to arrive. Petach Tikva, abandoned three years earlier, was resettled by newcomers before the year was out. On the southern ridge of Mount Carmel a group of Rumanian Lovers of Zion purchased and settled Samarin, the future Zichron Yaakov. Another group went further north to Upper Galilee, attractive to them because of its more European climate; after jogging through barren mountains on the backs of donkeys for almost a week, during which time one woman gave birth to a child, and much energy was wasted in quarrels with their Arab guides, the settlers reached a spot east of Safed and founded Rosh Pinna (literally, "Head Stone," the stone which "the builders refused is become the headstone of the corner," Psalms 118:22). Other colonies, in the north, south, and west on the coastal plain, soon followed.

Equally important, perhaps, was the fact that, in 1882, the British seized control over adjacent Egypt. This was a first step toward the extension of their rule to Palestine, which in turn led to the Balfour Declaration of 1917 and its recognition of a Jewish national home in Palestine.

Third, in that same year of 1882 there arrived in Palestine an obscure scholar from Lithuania named Eliezer Perlmann. Perlmann settled quietly in Jerusalem. He adopted a new name, Ben Yehuda; returned his passport to the local Russian Consul; and, unperturbed by the Consul's retort that it was obviously not so, announced that Perlmann was dead.

This slightly-built, twenty-four-year-old philologist, whose constitution had been sapped by an early attack of tuberculosis, but whose nature was as hard as steel, lived under the ruthless tyranny of an idea —the revival of Hebrew as a spoken language. In his youth Ben Yehuda had been an orthodox rabbinical scholar. As a teen-ager he had renounced his studies to become a self-confessed "Russian nihilist." The Russian populist's classic tract, *What Is to Be Done*, became his Bible; Chernishevsky and Lavrov, his "rabbis." After his arrival in Jerusalem he did for Hebrew what Korais, the brilliant Corfu school-teacher, did for modern Greek. Korais invented an intermediary language between that of ancient Greece and the current argot of his day. Ben Yehuda searched classic Hebrew literature for words to be used in a modern context. The very first word he created was *millon* (dictionary), a derivative of *milla* (word). Another early coinage was *leumiut* (nationalism). In his memoirs he noted that there was one thing that he regretted all his life: "I was not born in Jerusalem, nor even in the land of Israel."

Looking back, Ben Yehuda dramatically staged the decisive moment of his life at "midnight," shortly after the Russian-Turkish War of 1878. He had been at home, reading a Pan-Slavic tract by candlelight. Suddenly he realized the lesson implied for a small people like his own, and the imperative need to immediately "re-create Israel and its language upon the home soil. . . . " When he first broached this idea to an acquaintance, Ben Yehuda (like Pinsker and Herzl after him) was warned that he was sick and must consult a doctor.

Ben Yehuda's wife knew no Hebrew; while still on shipboard he told her that in Palestine they would speak nothing but Hebrew. He ruthlessly kept his vow. When his first son, Itamar, was born (by a curious coincidence on the same day the colony of Rishon le-Zion was founded) he became the first child in centuries to hear only Hebrew from both his parents and almost nothing from anyone else, for he was kept isolated from all human contact lest the purity of his Hebrew be spoiled by alien sounds. His mother, though weak and ailing, agreed to her husband's demand not to hire a servant in order that the child might hear nothing but the holy tongue. "We feared the walls of our home, the spaces of our room, lest they echo the sounds of a foreign language . . . and reach the child's ear . . . we wished to keep all foreign sounds distant. . . ."

It was a risky undertaking. The language was still archaic. Many words indispensable in modern intercourse were missing. The child had no playmates; until his third year he remained almost mute and often refused to utter a word.

Ben Yehuda's wife died in 1891 of tuberculosis that she had contracted from her husband. Ben Yehuda, undeterred by the tremendous opposition from almost everyone he knew, remained firm, and by his fanaticism proved that Hebrew could become a language fit for ordinary daily usage. Sympathetic teachers in Jerusalem, Jaffa, and the new colonies joined his cause. Soon the children in all the new colonies spoke Hebrew fluently; while it was frequently a second language for them, after Yiddish, Russian, or French, it was "alive."

Many new settlers who followed in the steps of Levontin and Feinberg had been university students caught up by the double influence of Zionism and Russian populism; they interrupted their studies to go off to settle in Palestine as farmers. One pioneer, discussing works by two high priests of Russian populism, Alexander Herzen's *Who Is Guilty*? and Chernishevsky's *What Is to Be Done*, noted in his diary: "So agitated were young Russian revolutionaries by these books, that they decided to 'go to the people' and cause a revolution in their lives. The Russian people exist and live on native soil; (Jews) must re-create everything from scratch: the work, the land, the people and the society."

The ideas of Russian radicalism affected the new colonies from the beginning with varying results. An early manifesto by the Kiev Lovers of Zion denounced private ownership of land as the greatest evil of civilization; its authors warned the settlers against building Palestine on the "rotten basis" of the old world order. One charter forecast the extreme collectivism of the future *kibbutz*: ". . . one fortune for the entire society. No man has private property. Also his things, his clothes and whatever he may bring with him or receive from his home belong to the entire society."

Actually, none of these socialist and cooperativist ideas were put to practice at this early stage. With all their imported theories, the earliest settlers found Palestine a sobering experience. In reality most colonies quickly gravitated to private ownership of land, capitalist profit, and the exploitation of cheap (native Arab) labor. It was explained as the only realistic policy and was at least partly imposed from without. For within less than two years after settlement, in 1883, most of the newcomers were close to bankruptcy and some even to starvation. Baron Edmond de Rothschild of Paris came to their rescue.

Edmond de Rothschild (1849–1934) was one of the least known scions of a famous family of financiers, a dandy who through his

Palestine venture inadvertently played a greater role in history than any of his more famous namesakes. He was inclined to leave the making of money to his brothers and cousins, and preferred rather to spend it as he saw fit. What seemed at the time an eccentric charity proved in the end a decisive political act. But for his lavish support of the early settlers, the Jewish colonization of Palestine would have started much later, perhaps even too late to succeed.

In October 1882 he willingly responded to the plea by Joseph Feinberg of Rishon le-Zion for a modest loan of 25,000 francs toward the digging of wells in the colony. He did so, as he later put it, as an "experiment" to see if it was possible to settle Jewish farmers in Palestine. The colonies soon became his main charity, surpassing even his generous support of French arts in general and the Louvre in particular. Between 1884 and 1900 he spent an estimated £1.6 million on purchase of land and the construction of houses for the colonists; he invested also in training and machinery, livestock, waterworks, and the like. His total expenditure has been estimated at £10 million. His entire property in Palestine was later turned over to the colonists or earmarked for a foundation which today supports various educational enterprises, including instructional television. Rothschild became a kind of benevolent feudal lord who owned villages and peasants in the Holy Land (the colonists were guaranteed a certain minimum income); he insisted upon tight controls through an extensive network of baronial overseers and administrators.

Rothschild's paternalism was of a type prevalent among many nineteenth-century philanthropists. In his vineyard he grew a Bordeaux-type wine. He resented his colonists' European clothes and wanted them to wear the local Arab dress; he insisted they observe meticulously the Jewish Sabbath, dietary and other laws of orthodox Jewish religion, which he himself—though not his pious wife—ignored. It is doubtful whether he ever hoped for a "Jewish state"; he was interested in "creating centers where Jewish intellectual and moral culture could develop." He met Herzl only once, for one brief and disastrous conversation. He considered Zionism dangerous both for the Jews of Europe and for those in his colonies, as it exposed them to accusation of not being "patriotic" Frenchmen, Russians, or Turks. His overseers were imported from France. They were professionals, thoroughly business-minded, deeply suspicious of the settlers whom they frequently accused of laziness and of harboring dangerous "Russian anarchist ideas." Bitter quarrels were common between the settlers and the Baron or his overseers.

In later years Rothschild's opposition to political Zionism mellowed. Weizmann quoted him as saying: "Without me Zionism would not have succeeded. But without Zionism my work would have been struck to death."

Rothschild's administration kept a tight reign in the colonies, and, at least for a while, set the pattern of things. It was not socialist or cooperative, as some of the early Zionist Populists had hoped, but "colonial" in the accepted contemporary sense of that word. By 1902 there were already twenty-one colonies (eighteen others lay temporarily abandoned), with a total population of almost 5,000. All but a few were still subsidized by Rothschild. Some were beginning to show signs of prosperity, with fine, tree-shaded houses, schools and kindergartens, synagogues and parks, local periodicals, public libraries, amateur theatricals, etc.

A traveler in these colonies would probably not have found them much different from the English, French, or Dutch settlements in Kenya, Algeria, and the East Indies. Their economy was based largely on the supply of cheap native labor. It came from neighboring Arab villages as well as from farther-away places in Syria, Egypt, or the Horan in Transjordan. By 1889, barely seven years after its founding, the colony of Zichron Yaakov on Mount Carmel had 1,200 Arab workers serving a population of 200 Jewish settlers. In Rishon le-Zion —formerly an almost barren, waterless spot—an eyewitness reported that the first group of forty Jewish settler families attracted close to 300 Arab families of migrant laborers who squatted in courtyards or built shacks in the immediate neighborhood.

This imbalance precipitated an enormous *crise de conscience* abroad. Visiting Zionists noted with chagrin that some of the settlers were adopting the uglier aspects of colonialists elsewhere. They seemed no longer to conform to the original ideal of farmers who themselves tilled the soil, a work which, to the Zionists, was healthy and rejuvenating, both for the individual and the community; more and more were beginning to "resemble business entrepreneurs." According to one critic, some even "played cards at home while their Arab laborers did the work." Much of the criticism of the purists was doctrinaire or naive, full of the easy cleverness of those who observe a torturous experiment from a safe and comfortable distance. "How far they are from the life of the simple farmer," complained one visiting literateur from a Polish Hebrew periodical, who promptly returned to Warsaw. "How far they are from the life of the simple farmer who tills his land with his own hands without buying food (sic) and without worry that he may not find a buyer for his crop. When will this dire sight disappear? When shall the seed be sown from which will grow Israel's salvation?"

By 1902 the colonists, being human, were thinking above all of their own needs and not exclusively of a Jewish national revival in Palestine. They had become experienced in the hardships of life in Palestine; they had little patience for advice rendered gratuitously, they felt, from abroad by those who themselves were not willing to come.

In 1883, Zeev Vladimir Dubnov, a settler in Rishon le-Zion, described the early ardor of the settlers in a letter to his brother Simon, the well-known Jewish historian. He wrote that his aim was perhaps "magnificent and sublime" but "not unattainable. It is to inherit the land of Israel in time and to restore to the Jews the national independence they were robbed of two thousand years ago." Such passions did not last long. That two or three hundred settlers could imagine in 1883, as Vladimir Dubnov did, that they were about to "inherit" the land was a madly fantastic dream in the first place. Cortez took Mexico with a few hundred men only, but behind him lay the resources of an empire.

The Jewish settlers had little behind them beyond a loose network of peripatetic discussion groups. Moreover, Palestine and Syria by 1883 had already become a focus of imperialist Russian, French, German, and British designs, and a breeding ground for native nationalism as well. The first settlers were alone in a strange environment; if it was not yet as hostile as it would be a few decades later, it was nevertheless extremely difficult. They had no farm training. Rejecting Europe and settling in the ancient land of Canaan, tilling the barren fields, and singing hymns—all this had been a euphoric experience. Like most romance, it was of brief duration. Within a few years, even months, disenchantment set in. Even Levontin, the first of the new settlers and leader of Rishon le-Zion, returned to Russia after only eighteen months. A year later he sold his share of the land to Rothschild. His wife and mother had opposed his Palestine schemes from the beginning; the two women insisted upon accompanying him to Paris to complete the deed of sale, fearful that fantasy might again overtake him and he would change his mind in the last moment. Twenty years passed before Levontin returned once again to Palestine, as a functionary of the fledgling Zionist bank.

According to contemporary reports, a great number of settlers—or their sons—left the country. Some returned to Russia and Rumania. Others wandered off as far as Kenya, America, South Africa, and Australia. Re-emigration was hotly debated in the colonies. In the cemetery of Hadera, an early colony founded in the swampland of Sharon, where many first settlers died of malaria, the tombstone of a Peretz Herzenstein bears the inscription:

> He was his country's loyal son
> Until his final breath.
> His dying words to his children were
> Your country do not leave.

Those remaining relied more and more on cheap Arab labor and frequently turned away Jewish newcomers eager and willing to work. Some of the uglier aspects of colonialism everywhere became more and more common. "What the hell are *you* doing here!" a farmer in Rishon le-Zion hissed at a newly arrived young Zionist from Poland who was waiting with a group of Arab laborers in the main square of a colony for employment as a field hand. "Can't you find yourself a better place than among those blacks?" Moreover, by 1904, the majority of settlers had begun to doubt the Zionist dream could be fulfilled in Palestine. Newcomers would often be met in Jaffa by grumbling old settlers: "Madman! Irresponsible dreamer! Why have you come here? Go back to Russia, or move to America!"

Herzl died in 1904; in Europe his World Zionist movement was on the verge of disintegration. Even Eliezer Ben Yehuda, the great fanatic of the Hebrew revival, became a so-called territorialist, a supporter of those seeking a territory in Uganda or Brazil as the site of the future Jewish national home. Ben Gurion recalls that his greatest shock upon arriving in Palestine in 1906 was to hear of Ben Yehuda's defection.

It was precisely at this low point in Zionist morale that the second wave of emigration from Russia was instigated by the pogroms of 1903 and the abortive revolution of 1905. This new influx was the "Second *Aliya*"; its men and ideas decisively changed the course of events.

The first wave of settlers, or those who remained of it, were slowly integrating into the economy of the country. Tiring of nationalist aspirations, they "lived with the Arabs" as colonial employers. The newcomers, for reasons of socialist doctrine, vehemently protested this "exploitation of Arab labor." They said that Jews must build their homeland with their own hands and not draw capitalistic profits from the employment of aliens. Their theorizing was a mixture of doctrine and self-interest, for they also desperately needed those jobs for themselves and were prepared to work for native wages.

In retrospect it seems that had the earlier settlers persevered in their course the Jewish population of Palestine, though growing, would have eventually become a wealthy colonial minority to be expropriated and expelled by the resurgent Arabs. The separate society and independent institutions created by the newcomers after 1905 in the end proved strong enough to avert such a possibility.

These newcomers were young and mostly unattached. Few married or bore children during their first fifteen years of settlement. Rabbis of a new secular faith, they were full of the fervor of Russian revolutionism which they transposed to Zionism with a tenacity and zeal such as had never fired the settlers of the first wave. Their missionary faith was stronger; above all they had been educated in a different political school. They produced leaders; they had "ideologists," whose dominant role was reminiscent of that of the clergy in puritan New England. They were burning to work on the land, but an overriding preoccupation, at least among the leaders, was with abstract ideas and with the organization of political power to put their ideas into practice. Almost the moment they set foot on land they began to form overseas branches of their Eastern European-based political parties. Two main groups emerged, the Marxist *Poale Zion* and the non-Marxist labor party, *Ha'poel Ha'tzair*.

The two parties opposed one another with a religious ferocity. The total membership of both did not exceed a few hundred until after 1914 and their frequent "national conferences" were attended by almost the entire membership.

The Hebrew Social Democratic party, *Poale Zion*, the party of Ben Gurion and Ben Zvi, considered itself as part and parcel of the international, revolutionary proletariat. "We are the party of the Palestinian working-class in creation, the only revolutionary party of the Jewish worker in Turkey," ran a party announcement published in Jaffa a short time after the first two dozen members disembarked at Jaffa. The men and women of *Poale Zion* considered themselves engaged in a "class struggle" in Palestine, although the country had no industry, hardly any workers, and no capitalists to speak of. Ben Zvi later rather pompously wrote: "Prognosis preceeded reality and therein lay its glory." He took for granted the support of the "international proletariat"; in his eyes it followed logically from the precepts of Marxism. If it was not immediately forthcoming, that was certainly only a temporary aberration, a misunderstanding which would soon be cleared up in an atmosphere of international solidarity. One *Poale Zion* leader delivered a series of lectures in Jaffa called "The Prophet Elijah and the Class Struggle in Ancient Israel."

Poale Zion defined its Marxist doctrine in a curious document entitled "Platform of Ramle, 1906"—so called after the little town on the Jaffa-Jerusalem highway where it was formulated, in the upstairs room of an Arab camel-driver's *khan*, or caravansery. A more improbable setting can hardly be imagined as the background for such a discussion. It was a clandestine meeting. In Ramle, and under Turkish rule, there was no real need for such secrecy, but the participants—a dozen or so recent arrivals, including Ben Gurion—kept up the Russian tradition of revolutionary conspiracy. They argued three days and two nights. The wording of the end product was in part a Zionist paraphrase of the *Communist Manifesto*:

> The history of mankind is the history of national (*sic!*) and class struggle . . . the natural and historical conditions of the process of production divide humanity into societies and classes . . . in the revolutionary process (in Palestine) an important role is played by the productive forces among the Jewish immigrants. . . .

Early in 1907 this "platform" was expanded to include (1) a demand for "public ownership of the means of production" (through the waging of a class struggle) and (2) ". . . with regard to the national problem, the party seeks political autonomy for the Jewish people in this country." This was later watered down to "create in Palestine a Jewish settlement, concentrated in its land and independent in the *economic* sense." For many newcomers the trappings of national sovereignty were less important than their ideal of a new, economically and socially just society.

Of all the amorphic groups who competed for membership among the newcomers, *Poale Zion* was probably the furthest left. But it was only a matter of degree. The majority, whether they adhered to this group or to another, whether formally "Marxist" or not, were importers of social revolution. Revolution was a hope, a mood, a dream, a program; as the new settlers traveled steerage from Russia to Palestine, they carried it with them in their knapsacks, like Napoleonic soldiers their marshal's batons. Many were driven to these shores by the shattered hopes of 1905. What had so dismally failed in Russia, some now hoped would succeed in one of the more destitute corners of the Ottoman Empire—a safe haven for Jews, and a new paradise to boot. A kingdom of saints, a new world purged of suffering and sin. In this they would fail; but in the course of trying out their fantasy they forged reality as few men have in modern history. When, almost half a century later, the state of Israel was declared, at its helm stood the gray-haired survivors of that early group; a puritan oligarchy whose members had persevered, who had neither run away nor dropped from sight nor died. And because they had forced their will upon history they succeeded in making it.

6

BEGGARS WITH DREAMS

> This is the secret which I hide from every-
> one. I am at the head of only boys and
> beggars . . . with dreams.
>
> —THEODOR HERZL

> To be a Zionist it is not necessary to be mad,
> but it helps.
>
> —CHAIM WEIZMANN

Even a brief glance at their lives reveals an essential difference which separates many contemporary Israelis from the men and women of the Second *Aliya*. They were true believers. Contemporary Israelis lack the simplicity of their faith. They were moved by ideological convictions, by elaborate abstractions which were frequently divorced from any perceivable reality: modern Israelis are motivated by self-interest and the brutal realities of power. The early pioneers were dreamers; their innocence gave them great strength; courage came from inexperience. Modern Israelis are likely to be weakened by hindsight.

The early pioneers went to school with the idealists of the nineteenth century, for whom things were simpler than they are to us. Never were people more sure that they were on the right track. Some inevitably rationalized their action by reference to religious ties; but most were decidedly irreligious. One avowed atheist wrote shortly after his arrival in 1907: "What I do is not God's will—for I do not believe in God—but what simply is right morally and in practice absolutely necessary." The basic assumptions of their youth, derived almost exclusively from an Eastern European setting, remained with them throughout their lives.

When the first wave of settlers arrived in 1882 from Russia and Rumania, the greatest difficulties were still relatively far off; even in 1906, few of the young enthusiasts of the second wave had an inkling of the bitter struggles and hopeless complications still before them. Unburdened by such knowledge, they proceeded upon their tasks with an energy that was made possible only by a sense of total self-righteousness and awareness of a higher purpose.

They were children of their time, as we are of ours. It has been said of the Russians of that period that they were the only people of Europe who lacked the "cement of hypocrisy." In this sense, too, the pioneers of the first and second waves were genuinely typical of their age, though it would be a mistake to think of them as a crowd of faceless conformists. Each had his own reasons, both personal and ideological, for coming, staying, or leaving. As a whole, those who arrived with the Second *Aliya* were not "tougher" than the earlier settlers. A very considerable number very soon left the country as had many pioneers of the first wave—tired, sick, unable to adapt in what often seemed a community of deranged fanatics; unable to stand the climate, the hard work, or the food; disappointed, or simply because of a change of mind.

Arrival in the country was often a depressing anticlimax. Herzl had envisaged the disembarkation as a dramatic event. His blueprint had sounded almost like a tourist brochure: "When the land comes into sight the flag is raised. . . . All must bare their heads (!) . . ." At disembarkation all must "wear the yellow tag." Elsewhere he wrote that the settlers' arrival would compare to the Exodus of Moses as a "Wagnerian opera compares to a *Singspiel* by Hans Sachs for Shrove Tuesday." The reality was neither Wagnerian nor a *Singspiel*, but rather often just a letdown. Embarrassing scenes frequently occurred at the open roadstead in Jaffa. Groups of arriving pioneers, enthusiastically coming ashore, at times even kissing the dusty ground as they fell upon it, would mistake those assembled on the quay for members of a welcoming party. In fact, the latter were simply preparing to embark on the same ship to go back to Europe. It was not the most encouraging first encounter.

Some contemporaries have put the number of those who left at 60 to 70 percent. David Ben Gurion, who arrived in 1906, has even spoken of 90 percent. We are concerned with those who remained, and who eventually came into power; the hardened residue, the toughest, who held out, surviving, one is tempted to say, in a Darwinian process of natural selection.

They were marked by a terrible sincerity and by an almost inhuman sense of rectitude. Inveterate diarists and eager composers of polemic articles, they have left a vast body of written material. S. N. Eisenstadt has noted that "never have so many volumes of polemics been written about so many subjects by so few men in such a short time." They were extremely self-conscious in their roles. Some, like Ben Gurion, recounted their own feats in the third person, à la de Gaulle. With few exceptions not a glimmer of doubt flashes through this voluminous output. On a summer night in 1910, J. C. Brenner, the writer, who arrived with the pioneers of the second wave, was walking with some friends at the farm at Ben Shemen where they worked. Suddenly Brenner dropped to the ground. He clutched in his fists a few clods of earth, kissed them, and with tears in his eyes exclaimed: "Land of Israel, will you be ours? Will you really be ours?" The cause was never questioned; only the power of mean and petty humans to sustain it.

Brenner himself felt such inadequacy most acutely. His letters reflect his own tortured hesitations before he finally went to Palestine. It took him nearly three years to decide. The irony in his letters strikes a refreshingly candid tone among the letters—otherwise so emphatic—of the time:

September 1, 1906: ". . . I am a typesetter . . . ready to go [to Palestine] at anytime. But who knows what will happen there? . . . What do I care for London, what do I care for Jerusalem?"

September 4, 1906: ". . . As for Eretz Israel, it seems that my position is clear. I would go if I knew that I would be able to do something decent there. . . ."

October 10, 1906: "As for my journey to Eretz Israel, I have decided to come in any case. . . . But please explain: (1) Is there a decent Hebrew printing press in Jaffa? (2) Is the censorship difficult? (3) Does one suffer a lot from the Turkish officials and the Arab neighbors? (As for suffering at the hands of our Hebrew brethren—I know.)"

November 6, 1906: "When I consider the matter, [my] possibilities in Eretz Israel are terribly doubtful: censorship, and no money,

and a new place and the present atmosphere of Eretz Israel, and
its Jews, etc. etc."

November 15, 1906: "I have decided to postpone my decision to go to
Eretz Israel for a full year at least."

March 25, 1907: "[I am a man] who sees no glimmer of hope . . .
I'll go to Palestine, but not as a believing and hopeful Zionist,
but as a man who misses the sun. I want to work as a field laborer."

July 20, 1907: ". . . To Palestine I will not go. I hate the Chosen
People, I hate the dead Country, the so-called Land of Israel,
Fie! . . ."

December 26, 1907: "I want to move. In the past I thought about
Palestine. Now I have decided to go to Galicia [Poland]."

March 16, 1908: ". . . I'll go to Palestine. . . . But I won't stay long."

September 18, 1908: "You are going to Palestine . . . But what will
you do there? I would go to New York. . . ."

January 27, 1909: "Today I leave Galicia [for Palestine]."

Some pioneers of the second wave have described their decision to
emigrate to Palestine in almost mystic terms. "Everything was suddenly crystal clear; the fog parted, my entire body shook with excitement. . . . It was as if I had suddenly awakened from a bad dream. I
knew what I had to do. Nothing else mattered."

Others claimed that at the very moment they set foot in Palestine
they had been "reborn." Ben Gurion started to count his years afresh
from that date on, considering everything that preceded it a waste of
time. "I wish that the remaining years shall not go up in smoke," Berl
Katzenelson, the labor leader, wrote shortly after his arrival, "and that
the *real* life will soon begin."

The poet Bialik wrote to the pioneers: "The very dust will come
alive under your bare and sacred feet." This indeed was how they felt
in the ecstasy of the first months or years, even before the barren fields
they had sown turned green, or the virgin hills they had cleared of
boulders were covered by forests. There is an ecstatic quality in the
letters and notes written at the time by pioneers. There are the usual
terms such as "homecoming" and "rebuilding," but other, stranger,
descriptions occur: notions of return to the "womb" of history, and

even to Zion the "betrothed." One spoke solemnly of his desire to achieve a "libidinous link with the soil." In Jewish liturgy there were always frequent references to a mystical "betrothal" between Israel and its promised land; this was now given a modern, personal, and political meaning.

Although most had hardly more than a rudimentary command of the language, the pioneers were fanatical Hebraists. Disembarking at Jaffa, Ben Gurion and many others—like Ben Yehuda in 1882—vowed never again to use a foreign language, but to speak only Hebrew. While such solemn vows were frequently impractical and often broken, they were sometimes kept with a stubborn will and an inhumanity that shocked only the non-initiated. When Ben Yehuda's aged mother, who spoke no Hebrew, arrived in Palestine shortly before her death, Ben Yehuda, who had not seen her in years, refused to talk with her in a language she could understand. (Nevertheless, he is said to have broken his vow—in speaking French with Baron Edmond de Rothschild on one of the latter's visits to the country.) In a makeshift clinic for malaria-struck pioneers, a girl patient who spoke Russian in a delirium was rudely chastised by the nurse for not using Hebrew.

Hebrew was more than a language. The insistence on its usage reflected a program, an attitude to life, to history, and to society. Johsua Altermann, a pioneer of the Second *Aliya*, was working in the Rothschild vineyards at Rishon le-Zion. The Baron's overseers ran the farm rather high-handedly and shared their employer's disdain of Hebrew and political Zionism. A few persisted in speaking Yiddish only. Altermann played deaf.

> Until his orders are translated to Hebrew I just would not do what he wanted.
> One day he again told me in his Rumanian-accented Yiddish to close a wine tap. I decided to keep it open even if he exploded with anger. He repeated his order. I went on asking him in Hebrew: "What are you saying?" By this time he was furiously screaming in Yiddish: "Vermach den Kran!" Again I asked calmly "What is it that you want me to do?" And all this time the wine was pouring out before our eyes.

After much screaming back and forth between the two, the overseer finally shouted in Hebrew:

"Shut that tap you idiot! And get out of here immediately!" I closed
the tap and said: "Now I know what you *are*." Nevertheless he fired
me. That day I knew that I had not been defeated but, to the contrary, had been gloriously victorious.

Technically speaking, they were colonists. Yet by temperament,
motivation, circumstance, and choice they differed sharply from other
emigrants of that period who colonized Australia, Africa, Canada, or
the United States. They were not in search of fertile land, gold,
unlimited opportunity, or steady employment in a fast-expanding
economy. Nor were they sent by chartered companies or governments
anxious to rid themselves of surplus populations, expand the territories under their control, or make the flag follow the trade.

This was colonizing without a motherland, an attempt to establish
a state without the backing of state power; it was also a dramatic
reversal of the then current village-to-city trend. Some of the early
pioneers of 1882 had dreamed of industry and commerical enterprise;
the newcomers after 1905 turned to agriculture. They became farmers
less for practical than for ideological reasons. They thought little of
profits, at least in the first period; they were trying to live a theory. It
might have been easier and quicker to develop trade and industry; but
for ideological reasons they did not. The pioneers believed that nations, like trees, must be "organically" rooted in the soil and that
anti-Semitism was a result of the "unnatural" occupational structure
of Jews in Eastern Europe.

Properly speaking, they were immigrants. But the Messianic temper
frequently breeds its own special language and the new arrivals rarely
used that word. Instead, echoing the American "pilgrim," they referred to themselves as *olim*, a near-mystic term supercharged with
emotion, primeval faith, and historic associations. It means, "those
who ascend" who go on pilgrimage, rise above earthly desires. Immigration into Palestine was called *Aliya* (literally "ascension"), hence
"First *Aliya*," "Second *Aliya*," etc.

Those *olim* who went into agricultural work were called "*chalutzim*," literally, "vanguard," but in the current Hebrew usage
charged with ecstasy such as was never associated with the closest
English or American equivalent "pioneer." In America, the "pioneer"
ethos stressed individuality, daring, go-gettism. In modern Hebrew,
"*chalutz*" connotes above all *service* to an abstract idea, to a political

movement, and to the community. A biblical term, it meant not only "to pass over armed before the Lord into the land of Canaan" (Numbers 32:32) but also liberation, exaltation, expedition, rescue. The ecstatic quality of being a *chalutz* was well reflected in a popular Yiddish song:

> We are, we are, we are
> Pioneers, Pioneers! (*Chalutzim! Chalutzim!*)
> On burning fields
> On barren fields of waste.
> The first to arrive
> Like swallows in spring
> We believe . . .
> We'll cover the stony fields
> With golden bloom.

The term *chalutz* soon served as basis for derivatives such as do not exist in other languages: chalutzism, chalutzistic approach, chalutzistic culture, education, values, and even *chalutzistic* morality. Cumbersome portmanteau words of considerable imprecision but of such tremendous emotional force that they are still widely used in Israel today. The pioneers of the second wave saw themselves less as nation builders than as *chalutzim* of a new social order.

Their orthodoxy was of that peculiar, innocent optimistic kind which was a common trait of nineteenth-century reformers. The idea of progress which had remained for such a long time a mere speculative toy became in the nineteenth century an operative principle. The pioneers of the second wave deeply believed in the possibility of human progress, a faith which may seem naive today only because we are governed by a different set of immediate historical memories. It was before the Russian Revolution and before Marxist Leninism degenerated into the Stalinist and post-Stalinist police state, a process which, borrowing the words of Shigalev in Dostoyevsky's *The Possessed*, started from "unlimited liberty" and ended in "unlimited despotism." It was before two world wars were waged "to end all wars"; before nationalism emerged not as Mazzini had hoped, as a vehicle of liberal humanism, but as a recrudescence of tribal savageries unprecedented in their ferocity; before the ennui engendered by the modern welfare state. It was the simpler, more hopeful world of yesterday. No problem seemed insoluble, if only properly analyzed and approached through the tenets of this or that philosophy.

Life for them was a perpetually striving, an incessant training course. Like so many Russian Populists they lived under an obsessive urge to conquer *themselves*, to fashion and forge their personalities after some great ideal, an ideal that was often taken from literature. Their letters and notes frequently express a powerful desire to discover the meaning of existence. This pursuit at times overshadowed their commitment to Zionism; but frequently the two achieved a near-mystic union. They were convinced that every man had a unique mission to fulfill in life and the first step was to define it. Zvi Schatz was a twenty-three-year-old worker at Migdal, on the Lake of Galilee, who, in his spare time wrote deeply melancholy Russian poetry. In 1913 he noted in his diary that "never in my whole life have I felt as far from human perfection as now, and never has there been in me as strong and deep a desire to begin deliberate work to perfect myself towards the great ideal of moral improvement."

For many young men and women who arrived with the second *Aliya*, the magic key to a true perception of the self was physical labor. It was the beginning and end of morality. Like Levin in *Anna Karenina* they worked in the fields with scythe or shovel and decided they were finally beginning to understand life itself, communing with its deepest mysteries. In conquering work they were conquering themselves. There is a characteristic story of the young, frail, and pale girl who insists upon doing a man's heavy field work on a hot *Chamsin* day, digging trenches in difficult soil. She is taken on by a reluctant farmer on a trial basis; upon being told that she has passed the test and is accepted for work, she collapses, exhausted, in near-hysterical laughter of joy. This story later served as the backdrop for a successful Israeli play (*Kinneret, Kinneret* by Nathan Altermann) much as the fall of the Bastille served as the backdrop for many a nineteenth-century play on the French Revolution. Today the scene may seem unduly melodramatic, its heroes "too positive" for the modern taste; yet it clearly echoes the mood of the years 1905–1914.

The poetess Rachel Bluwstein (1890–1931)—a former art student who worked as a farmhand in Palestine in the years between 1908 and 1913—could easily have been the girl in Altermann's story. She wrote of "making music with the shovel and painting on the soil." Others wanted "to be slaves to the soil . . . kneel and bow down to it daily. Nurse its furrows until even the stony clods will yield a blessing."

"What is the point of your working as a laborer in Palestine?" the parents of Noah Naftulski complained in a letter written in 1907. "After all you are only twenty-two years old . . . you still have many possibilities to succeed in life; it is not yet too late. . . ." Naftulski was a gifted young man; barred as a Jew from the Russian gymnasium, he had taught himself mathematics, botany, and biology. He left for Palestine in 1906. His parents pleaded with him to try now to enter a Western European university. Young Naftulski wrote back: "There is a hidden delight in God's treasury . . . its name is labor; blessed is the man who has found it."

He adorned his letter with dried red poppies, from the fields of Petach Tikva where he worked. "These days of April," he wrote, "when everything around you is covered by ice and the bitter cold is raging, here the soil of our land is covered with flowers, and by the curing, soothing sun of spring. . . ." Naftulski and his fellow pioneers sang together what was probably the leitmotiv of their generation,

> Work is our life's elation
> From all troubles the salvation,
> Yah-hah-li-li labor mine!

and would immediately pass on to melancholy Russian songs. But if they sang of the Volga, their thoughts were on the Jordan. Many shared a feeling of holy orders. Levi Ben Amitai, after slaving all day in the heat of the Jordan Valley, visualized himself dressed in

> a shirt of clean white cloth
> and in the company of priests I take my place
> and on the table find my bread and broth.

In some of the pioneers of the second wave, physical labor assumed an almost transcendental meaning; it afforded most of the psychological satisfactions commonly supplied by religion. The word *avoda* in Hebrew means both labor and worship. Labor was worshiped. The harder it was, in terms of pure exertion—and at times it led to total exhaustion—the more it was held up as a means to realize one's true self. Not all, of course, worked with the same amount of sincerity. Every religion has its hangers-on, its phonies and hypocrites. S. Y.

Agnon, the novelist who later became the first Israeli to win a Nobel Prize, lived in Palestine at that time, and cast a skeptical eye upon the scene. In his novel *Tmol Shilshom* set in Jaffa and Jerusalem of the time, he ironically distinguished between those who came to work and those "who came to write a great book on labor."

The great prophet of the religion of labor was Aaron David Gordon. His influence was considerable and lasted for decades, long after his death in 1922. Like Tolstoy in later life, Gordon abandoned his family in order to commune with nature and soul. At the age of forty-seven, a weak and ailing man with a flowing white beard, he became a manual laborer in the fields of Palestine. He quickly attracted a large following among the young pioneers, who called him *Hazaken*, the old man. His teaching was a curious amalgam of cabalistic mysticism, populist agrarianism, Zionism, and socialism, in that order of importance. He preached that only through hard physical labor could a man be redeemed. He called upon his fellow pioneers to become "zealots of labor." This was their only cure as men; as Jews they must not live by their wits but by their sweat. Gordon slaved by day in the fields. At night he would join the young workers in dancing the *hora*, and while intoning a monotonous Yiddish refrain, *"frailich! . . . frailich! . . . frailich! . . ."* (Joy! . . . Joy! . . . Joy! . . .), would whip himself and his fellow dancers into a state of near ecstasy. He wrote:

> In my dream I come to the land. And it is barren and desolate and given over to aliens; destruction darkens its face and foreign rule corrupts it. And the land of my forefathers is distant and foreign to me, and I too am distant and foreign to it. And the only link that ties my soul to her, the only reminder that I am her son and she my mother, is that my soul is as desolate as hers. So I shake myself and with all my strength I throw . . . the [old] life off. And I start everything from the beginning. And the first thing that opens up my heart to a life I have not known before is labor. Not labor to make a living, not work as a deed of charity, but work for life itself . . . it is one of the limbs of life, one of its deepest roots. And I work. . . .

Gordon worshiped labor, the soil, and the nation as cosmic forces; he viewed "society" as a sheer mechanical, unstable entity. Man, instead of theorizing, must "enter the great university of labor, where heaven and earth and all of nature are creating a new human species."

A modern reader is inevitably disconcerted by all this worship of irrational cosmic forces, of nature and sweat with undertones of "blood and soil" theories consciously or unconsciously derived from the romantic precepts of German nationalism. A parallel exists but it must not be carried too far. Gordon was a pacifist. He had a profound horror of all bloodshed, of force, and of all government. There were no racial or militaristic features whatsoever in his teachings. In the tradition of Tolstoy and of the Hebrew prophets he did not believe in state power or politics, but in ethical action by the individual. The Jews had been the first to say that the individual was created in God's image. "We must amplify this," Gordon wrote hopefully, "by saying that the nation must likewise be formed in God's image."

Many pioneers of the second wave were puritanical, or, to use an overworked word, idealistic. They adhered to the ascetic tradition of the Russian Populists. Poverty was cultivated with an elaboration and a ritual that almost seemed to defeat the original purpose. Food was deliberately plain, consisting mainly of bread, olives, vegetables, and soup, prepared in communal workers' kitchens. Clothes were unadorned, demonstratively proletarian in a Russian style. Settlers wore Russian *rubashka* shirts and heavy boots, adding an occasional *keffiya*, the Arab headdress, as a concession to the Oriental environment. One well-known figure of the period, Israel Giladi, refused to wear shoes and walked barefoot as a matter of principle. His feet were covered with scratches and nasty wounds but he insisted stubbornly and said: "Our feet must get used to the soil of the Land."

Some donned Russian student caps or went out to work in their dark blue, former Russian school uniforms, the sleeves worn to mere threads and metal buttons replaced by short bits of string. Luxury, even the little there was of it in a largely primitive land, was despised. Simplicity of style and manner was extolled. Weak tea served in tin cups was the main form of indulgence.

They were deeply resentful of the "luxuriousness" of life among the already established farmers of the first immigration wave. Shlomo Zemach, a close friend and native of the same Polish town as Ben Gurion, resented the "two-story" houses of the early settlers of Rishon le-Zion (they were certainly nothing but modest) and complained: "Why must they raise their seats so high? These are not the modest abodes of farmers that I had hoped for." The letters and memoirs of the newcomers are full of shocked references to the "materialism" and alleged "decadence" of the earlier settlers. The young Zemach was attracted by the wives and daughters of the farmers with their "heaving bosoms," shapely arms, legs, and hips; but he comments disparagingly in his memoirs upon their silk and cotton fineries. He resented the men's white cork hats, their formal ties and shorts of woven wool, and their women perfumed and made up. "It broke my heart," he wrote. "This was not how I had imagined the settlers in the colonies."

In the wine-growing areas where many of the new pioneers worked, wine and other alcoholic beverages were cheap, frequently free. Nevertheless there was apparently very little drinking; there is so little reference to it in the vast body of memoirs and letters, that one suspects either deliberate abstinence or else a puritanical reluctance to admit what was probably a breach of good form. Most of the pioneers were young men and women in their late teens or early twenties. They led ostensibly free lives, vehemently contemptuous of bourgeois prejudice, and men and women frequently shared quarters. Yet, with few exceptions, their memoirs are marked by a curiously sexless quality. Contemporary descriptions read like annals of monastic orders. Occasionally a reader comes across confessions such as, "I blushed deeply," "I was tense," or a casual reference to voluptuous women and girls with long, attractive hair. But despite the near-absolute freedom under which they lived, promiscuity was apparently rare; long and rather melancholy platonic relationships, accompanied by the exchange of keyed-up poems and emotional letters, were common. Few formal marriages were contracted by young pioneers before 1922. This was later rationalized by economic reasons—poverty, unemployment, etc. But at the time, a purely ideological resentment of the bourgeois institution of marriage prevailed.

Few of the pioneers stayed in one place longer than a few weeks or months; most wandered from one colony to another. They worked during the daytime and argued at night with their fellows, and thus gained among the already established First *Aliya* farmers a not undeserved reputation as vagabonds with dangerous socialist and anarchist ideas. Some refused to specialize, even in agriculture. All work except the most difficult, the most menial and closest to the soil, was treated with disdain. Legend has it that the men of the Second *Aliya* were highly educated intellectuals who took to the plow. It is not borne out by the facts. A few were; most were not. Whatever they may have done later, there were no academics among the pioneers who settled on the land as laborers between 1906 and 1914. Their formal level of education was surprisingly low. According to a poll among those still living in the late 1930s, few had had more than a primary education; none were university graduates.

This was only partly a result of restrictive measures against Jews at Russian high schools and universities; in part it was by deliberate intent. The Russian revolutionary milieu, in which they had grown up, had implanted in their hearts a deep contempt for "careerism." By this was meant everything mean and egotistical; the pioneers expanded the term to embrace individual improvement as well, through formal education and vocational training. There was some resentment in the ranks when, in 1912, Ben Gurion and Ben Zvi went off to study law at the University of Istanbul, albeit with party headquarters approval. It was hard to think of a more "bourgeois" calling than the study and practice of law. But the two future leaders had a better-developed sense of politics than many of their contemporaries. Ben Gurion hoped to be able to run later for the Ottoman parliament as representative of the Jewish settlers in Palestine.

There were other differences between the more unworldly Second *Aliya* colonists and those who were emerging as their leaders. An important contrast was the growing sense of pragmatism on the part of Ben Zvi and Ben Gurion. As early as 1909, while others were practicing the "religion of labor," Ben Zvi and Ben Gurion helped to organize a secret defense organization. Ben Zvi's description of the organization's first meeting is full of forebodings of things to come. The meeting took place in Ben Zvi's room. "Mats, spread out on the floor and a few wooden crates served as armchairs and desks . . . one feeling seized all those present . . . they gathered up courage (and they knew) that not by word of mouth shall the nation be saved, nor shall a country be rebuilt by speeches. 'In blood and fire Judea fell, in blood and fire it shall rise again!' "

Ben Gurion (later a moderate, non-Marxist Social-Democrat) in those days led the extreme left-wing Marxist *Poale Zion* party. But apparently sooner than many others, Ben Gurion freed himself from the shackles of abstract Marxist ideology. Looking back in later years he claimed that within a few hours of his first arrival in the country he had already lost his patience with "meaningless abstract talk." He recollected that a short time after his disembarkation he had stopped for a drink in a workers' hostel in Jaffa. A fellow pioneer engaged him in debate on "Marxist historical determinism." "I thought he had gone out of his mind," Ben Gurion remembered. "Here I am, finally in the Land of Israel and he is trying to turn my head with historical determinism. He was a *Poale Zion* man, you know. I got up and left."

Ben Gurion related this story more than sixty years after the event and there may be a grain of wishful reminiscence in it. And yet his recollection reflects the mood, the implicit approach which pervades much of his writing after he settled in the country even before World War I. He remained committed to one basic precept of Marxist Zionism: the working class, because of its "progressive" nature, is and will be the vanguard of the Jewish renaissance.

But as time passed, Ben Gurion's concerns revolved more and more around national, and less and less around social, issues. He was one of the few hard-headed realists among the dreamers of his group. With the advent of Nazism in Europe, the more utopian features of the Zionist enterprise were overshadowed by the bitter necessity of rescuing the Jews of Europe. Hitler seized power in Germany in January 1933; although it was not immediately realized, the Jews of Europe were doomed. A year later Ben Gurion was elected chairman of the Jewish Agency for Palestine.

In the beginning the pioneers of the second wave hardly differed from other eccentric Europeans who made the Holy Land into a testing ground for their various ideological obsessions. Throughout the second half of the nineteenth century groups of pious American, Swedish, and German Protestants had tried to settle in the Holy Land in mystic communities similar to those of the early Christians.

By 1900 close to 20,000 pilgrims were arriving in the country annually. The majority were poor Russian peasants seeking to compensate for a lifetime of wretchedness at home as serfs or semi-serfs with a few days or weeks of ecstatic bliss in God's own country. They crawled on their knees through the mud along the Via Dolorosa in Jerusalem. Barefoot and in rags they walked across the country in great hordes, waving banners and crosses and singing hymns as they immersed their tired, dusty bodies in the waters of the Jordan or in the lake of Galilee, where the ruins of their huge shedlike dormitories can be seen to this day.

The Jewish pioneers often merged with the pious pilgrims, fundamentalists, hermits, and would-be prophets from abroad, one more group of foreign eccentrics among many. Their activities, along with those of others, were followed by the natives with a mixture of greed and incredulous wonder. All foreigners were protected by their consuls. Under the Ottoman system of capitulation, foreigners were beyond the reach of local courts of law. They were tried by the consuls even in cases where one of the litigants was a native. Most Jewish immigrants were Russian subjects. The Russian Consul, for reasons of Czarist imperialist policy, jealously guarded their rights and even their interests with an impartiality that, had it been more common in Russia, might have prevented their coming to Palestine in the first place.

Such Turkish bad will or suspicion as there was was often circumvented through bribery and inefficiency. Most Jewish settlers of the second wave received Turkish landing permits for short visits only. They were legally bound to leave after three months. This restriction —opposed by the consuls—was ignored; at any rate, it was rarely enforced. Nor was a more stringent policy called for. Few outsiders, at that early time, paid much attention to the Zionist settlers' politics and programs; there were even settlers who refused to treat such programs seriously.

The Turks, if indeed they were aware of the fantastic schemes and deliberations among members of the two labor parties, chose to ignore them or else did not take them very seriously. From time to time measures were taken to cut off the immigration of Russian Jews but the measures were usually ineffective. During a debate on Zionism, instigated in 1911 by Arab representatives to the Ottoman parliament, the Grand Vizier Ibrahim Pasha contemptuously dismissed the Arabs' complaints. He called the Zionists "ridiculous dreamers," "a handful of charlatans," incapable of achieving a Jewish government in a socialist Palestine. The very idea that a few dozen farm laborers might succeed in such a venture was too ridiculous for words.

For the Turks, as for most realistic outsiders, it was, of course, extremely difficult to treat with any gravity the handful of Jewish teen-agers from Russia, who milked cows and drained swamps during the day and at night sat under portraits of Herzl and Karl Marx, heatedly debating the constitution of the future socialist republic of Jewish Palestine. Most rational observers would have been strongly tempted to treat the handful of Zionist workers with the same bewildered benevolence they would give to a group of Russian Orthodox pilgrims ecstatically claiming to see a vision of Christ upon the slow moving waters of the Jordan.

It was natural that the early Jewish colonies should attract a considerable number of colorful personalities with pet solutions for the ills of mankind. All or almost all came from that vast reservoir of desperate hopes created by the ideological and political turbulance of Eastern Europe. Roving anarchists joined Russian Social Democrats on-the-run; itinerant revolutionaries came with no precise program but a strong temperamental commitment to change. There were nationalists and internationalists, Marxist socialists and non-Marxist socialists, disciples of every leading trend in Russia at that time. Only Czarists were not represented. Everywhere among the newly arrived workers in the colonies one found copies of underground Russian magazines; at night the dim, kerosene-lit tent encampments would resound with deep male voices singing melancholy Russian songs of insurgence. Their involvement with Zionism was at times quite incidental. Shlomo Lavie has reported a conversation he held with a group of fellow workers in Petach Tikva in 1907. They had asked him to a party in their wooden shed where they maintained a kind of commune.

"No, no, we haven't come back to history [like the Zionist romantics]," said one. "We have come to the people who live here. Jews and Arabs alike. Our job is to forge them all into one revolutionary, proletarian mass. But let us talk about this later," he added amiably. "Now let's drink 'tchai' and taste these biscuits."

Another conversation is reported by Zemach. In 1905 he shared a shed with a fellow worker at Rishon le-Zion who was a dedicated Tolstoyan.

"I am not a Zionist," he told Zemach. "No, certainly not. I am above such things."

"Well, why have you come here?" Zemach wondered.

"I . . . this is a land without order and without authority . . . here a man can live as he pleases . . . here is true *svoboda*" (freedom, in Russian).

There were globe trotters and avowed pacifists, draft dodgers of the Japanese-Russian War of 1905 and Jewish disciples of Tolstoy; fanatic vegetarians repelled by all violence, exalting celibacy, detesting all formal organization, and repudiating the idea of the state, established religion, and most modern comforts as well. They cultivated long-flowing beards and let their hair grow over their naked shoulders. Some wore only clothes of self-spun, rough gray flax, and when they were not barefoot, shoes made of cloth.

Such people rarely stayed long; some found their way eventually to America. Others perished later in Soviet prisons. A considerable back-and-forth movement continued until the late 1920s among those unable to decide where true salvation lay, in Palestine or in Russia. But even as eccentric transients, they left an indelible mark upon the society of pioneers in its early stages.

It was an enterprise which itself defied all norms. Of the many eccentrics some became legends even in their own lifetimes. It is significant for the development of the Zionist mystique that such popular heroes at times owed their fame less to their commitment to abstract salvationist ideas than to a strong appeal to the romanticism of toughness. Sooner than others they conformed to the new ideal of the "un-Jewish" Jew, as strong and hardy and courageous as the Gentiles were held to be and, according to the Zionist myth, as the "diasporic" Jew was not. One such popular hero was Ezechiel Chankin, a former housepainter in the Ukraine. He had been persecuted by the Czarist police for organizing armed resistance during the pogroms of Homol. Evading his pursuers, he escaped in 1904 to Palestine. Here he became a lone hunter in the desert, a kind of Jewish T. E. Lawrence, who lived with the Bedouins and adopted their ways. Chankin personified the Zionist rejection of city life. He was the embodiment of the "return to healthy nature," albeit in a rather extreme form. His contemporaries considered him a new, pagan-type Jew, a welcome reincarnation of the historic Hebrew savage. "In him there breathed the spirit of ancient Nimrod," President Ben Zvi wrote admiringly, "of David and Jonathan, the brave hurlers of arrows." Chankin died of yellow fever.

Michael Halperin was another *chalutz* who, for similar reasons, caught the fancy of the early society of settlers. He came from a very wealthy family in Vilna; his father owned citrus plantations in Palestine. The son, mounted upon a magnificent white horse, a sword in one hand and a red flag in the other, led the plantation's Arab and Jewish workers in strike against his father. He reveled in show of physical prowess. In 1911 a traveling Italian circus performed in Jaffa; among its exhibits was the usual caged lion. During a performance Halperin entered the beast's cage. As the lion calmly sat by, he sang the Zionist hymn "Hadtikva" to prove to the assembled Arab crowd that Jews are a valorous and absolutely fearless lot. He was a big, burly man with an unusually strong physique, high cheekbones, blue eyes, a thick blond beard, and long yellow hair falling over his shoulders, half Samson, half Russian muzhik, and a good prototype of the future *sabra* syndrome. He, too, traveled a great deal among the Bedouins; he urged his fellow *chalutzim* to marry Bedouin women and convert their kin to Judaism. In such fashion he proposed setting up a powerful tribe of Jewish Bedouins to "conquer Palestine with the sword."

In the 1910s, thirty years after the beginning of Jewish colonization, Zionist pioneers were still commonly referred to by the Arab natives as "Moscobites." The settlers, weary of lengthy and certainly complicated explanations, rarely objected to this appellation, and frequently used it themselves. Some Arabs, upon learning who they really were, contemptuously called them by the name traditionally reserved for Jews in the Orient, *"Wallad al Mitha"* (Children of Death, i.e., not really alive, not manly, not courageous). This misconception was to prevail among the Arabs for over half a century; and some are not yet freed of it today.

There are few instances in modern history when the image of things overshadowed reality as thoroughly as it did in Palestine during the first half of the twentieth century. One can think of no other country where a utopian state of mind persevered for so long a time. If the Arabs shut their eyes to reality, many pioneers of the second wave shut their eyes to the Arabs. They lived among themselves in workers' camps—closed communities that often resembled isolated religious orders. Contacts with the Arab natives were few. It was as if the *chalutzim* deliberately banished the Arabs from their minds.

As their legend grew—success is always a great mythmaker—the men and women of the Second *Aliya* assumed an almost superhuman aura. Modern observers weary of the terms *heroism*, *dedication*, *selfless idealism*, which were and frequently still are used to describe them. One suspects that the truth was much more complex.

It has been asserted that political men displace their private motives onto public objects. The unusual men and women who came to Palestine as pioneers in the first two or three decades of this century were not beyond such human frailty. Pure, innocent, naive idealism played a part, but also in all probability so did a tremendous parent-child conflict. Hebrew letters of the time abound with overt and covert references to the generation gap.

> Do not listen, son, to a father's preaching,
> And shut your eyes to mother's pleas. . . .

the poet Shimonovitz wrote in a well-known poem. Fathers' precepts were too "moderate," he wrote, not dynamic or revolutionary enough; mothers were excessively cautious.

In later years, after the destruction of Eastern European Jewry in the Nazi extermination camps, after the disappearance of that unique world of culture, language, habit, and faith, former pioneers tended to sentimentalize their early years at home, their antecedents and families—many of whom had fallen victim to the Nazi rage. But it is a fact that not a few of the early pioneers ran away from home. Those who later wrote memoirs invariably related their escape to an "ideological" disagreement with their fathers over Zionism. One wonders if such "disagreement" did not reach deeper.

Ben Gurion left his father's home in Plonsk at the age of twenty. His mother, of whom he later spoke adoringly, died in his infancy. In the many volumes of historical essays and personal recollections that he produced over the years, Ben Gurion is curiously reticent about his father, with whom he seemed to have had little if any personal rapport. On one occasion he confessed to a "problematic" situation, but would not go into details. It would be haphazard to read too much into this fact but still it is worthwhile to note that the young man, whose attitude to his father seems to have been a problem, who in effect left home to pursue a grand political and social idea, soon afterward decided to adopt a Hebrew surname, and of all possible alternatives, picked the name Ben Gurion, literally, "Son of a Lion."

Ben Gurion's change of name was not an isolated case. On the contrary, he followed a Zionist tradition, already well established in

1906, and one which continues to this day. The Zionist mania for renaming was too widespread to be dismissed as a mere bagatelle. The new names they chose were too suggestive to be ignored as elements in the complicated jigsaw that represents the transient sensibility of an epoch. Names are elementary symbols of identity. They are seldom the heart of the matter, but they often shed a sharp light on where that heart can be found.

Names are rooted in the deepest layers of mythical thought and feeling. The sphinx compelled Oedipus to name himself. At the end of their struggle, the angel renamed Jacob, Israel. A Zionist settler, in changing his name from Grien to *Ben Gurion*, or from Rachmilewitz to *Onn* ("Vigor"), was not only Hebraicizing a foreign sound. He was in fact re-enacting a piece of primitive magic, reminiscent of the initiation rites of certain Australian tribes, in which boys receive new names at puberty and are then considered reborn as men and the reincarnations of ancestors.

Eliezer Yitzhak Perlmann (Ben Yehuda), the father of modern Hebrew, was the first Zionist settler who formally changed his name. Ben Yehuda adopted his new Hebrew name a few days after his arrival in Jerusalem in 1882; the former Russian nihilist not only Hebraicized his name but was such a stickler for form that he made the Turkish authorities issue him (at the age of twenty-four) a brand new birth certificate. Ben Yehuda returned to the subject in his memoirs. He summed up his change of name in a few ecstatic lines: "I felt I had been reborn. My link with the diaspora had been severed." Ben Yehuda had reincarnated in himself a mythic ancestor. "Resurrection for the people of Israel and the Hebrew tongue in the land of the forefathers!"

In later years the Zionist passion for renaming amused or annoyed outsiders, and often confused insiders. It has been suggested that Israel needs an encyclopedic *Who Was Who*? The zeal for renaming —themselves, places, even the calendar—has of course been shared by many revolutionaries in history, from the English puritans to the Russian Bolsheviks and the national leaders of the new Afro-Asian states.

A great many Zionist name changers were affected by their frustration and fears, or hopes and innermost wishes. Many new names, of course, were simply translations from the German or Russian into Hebrew. Thus Silber or Silbermann renamed himself *Caspi*; Stein became *Avni*. Other names were selected for their pleasant sound, and meant nothing in particular. Sometimes the new names were chosen for their biblical associations—geographical locations and proper names (not infrequently heroic, such as *Avner* or *Yehoshua*). In other cases the new name was inspired by the cult of agriculture, by national or personal notions of strength and rebirth. The new names, inspired by ideology or not, reflected the emotional climate of the time. The same fervor to live the revolution body and soul which, during the French Revolution, gave birth to *Libre-Constitution* as a proper name, apparently prompted a considerable number of Zionists to adopt such "programmatic" names as *Amichai* ("my people lives"); *Amiad* ("my people forever"); *Ben Ami* ("son of my people"); *Ben Artzi* ("son of my country"); and the like.

There is an old Jewish custom of changing the name of a very sick man in the hope of cheating the angel of death. Thus it may be more than accident that so many Jewish refugees from lands of persecution —even more often their sons—have shown a proclivity to redefine themselves with names that denote firmness, toughness, strength, courage, and vigor: *Yariv* ("antagonist"); *Oz* ("strength"); *Eytan* ("firm," "solid"); *Tamir* ("towering"); *Lahat* ("blaze"); *Kabiri* ("tremendous"); *Hod* ("splendor," "majesty"); *Barak* ("lightning"); *Tsur* ("rock"); *Nechushtan* ("brazen"); *Bar Adon* ("son of the master," or "masterful"); or even *Bar Shilton* ("fit to govern"). There were also a few who cast off ancient Jewish names like Levy, Mizrachi, and Cohen, to adopt new ones less reminiscent of the Diaspora and more reminiscent of a prehistoric dawn; former Levys or Cohens are now known as *Keynan* (a derivation of Cain); *Marom* ("sky"); or *Kidan* ("javelin thrower").

Equally common are the so-called "agricultural" names. They enjoyed a special popularity in the earlier stages of settlement when transforming Jewish townspeople into farmers was still the essential element of Zionism. Even those who remained lawyers and clerks "transformed," their names: *Karmi* ("of the vineyard"); *Kimchi* ("flour"); *Dagan* ("corn"); *Regev* ("clod of earth"); *Sadeh* ("field"); *Yogev* ("husbandman").

Local place names constitute a distinct category of popular names— *Carmel*; *Galili*; *Sharon*; *Yerushalmi*; *Elat*; *Yavnieli*; *Elon*; and the like.

Not a few name changers were attracted by high mountains, peaks, and ranges: *Sinai; Hermon; Atzmon; Gilboa; Tavor*. In other countries, mountains are sometimes called after great men; in Israel, men more often call themselves after great mountains.

For many settlers, the new surnames were mythic symbols of a personal and collective rebirth; for a few, they served compensatory needs. The widespread adoption of local flora and place names reflected the frantic desire of the settlers to become one, in body and name, with the landscape of their regained patrimony, its rivers and mountains, its trees and its thorns.

The parents of some of the early pioneers were, in broad context, Zionists. To be a Zionist meant, and still means, different things to different people. It was, and still is, one thing to call oneself a Zionist, and another to pack up and move to Palestine. One suspects that in most cases, even "Zionist" parents were reluctant to approve of their children's decision, if not strongly opposed to it. Many pioneers later remembered violent scenes at home. Some reported that as the estrangement from the parental home grew, "the movement" (i.e., the local Zionist youth club) gradually became a second home for them, a "substitute family." Parental tactics naturally varied from case to case.

In his period piece, *Tmol Shilshom* (*Only Yesterday*), set in Palestine before World War I, Shmuel Yoseph Agnon, an eyewitness, wryly noted that "some [of the newcomers] ran away from home, others were sent by their parents in the hope that they will ascertain with their own eyes that there is no substance in this land of Israel." The mood was well caught in a song by Avigdor Haimeiri, very popular in the 1920s, which combined sentimental melodrama of the classical "Jewish mother" theme with the stark realities of life:

> A tearful mother writes a letter
> To my good son in Jerusalem!
> Your father's died
> Your mother's sick, ah!
> Come home to the Diaspora.
> Come home dear son
> Come home, come home, come home beloved son
> Come home, come home to where there's spring.
> Oh come!

and the tearful son's response:

> Dateline Jerusalem, nineteen twenty-four
> Forgive me mother
> Though you are sick
> To the Diaspora I will not return
> If you love me
> Join me.
> I will not be a wanderer once more.
> I will not ever budge from here
> I will not budge, I will not budge.
> No!

The ambivalence of relations with their parents must have weighed heavily on the early pioneers. It pursued them for a long time. It may very well be at the root of the future attitude toward their own children. The former rebels against their parents were notoriously lenient toward their own offspring. For at least three or four decades the newly established educational system was marked by an almost obsessive desire to avoid parent-child conflicts at great cost. Children of the first generation born in the country frequently could do no wrong; their permissive parents often bent over backward to satisfy every whim. Such leniency was explained at first as a response to the findings of the best, most progressive theories in child-rearing. Psychologists of a later, more detached period have tended to think of these explanations as a rationalization. Second- and third-generation Israelis with less harrowing memories and/or feelings of guilt display a markedly tougher attitude toward their children.

A pure, and thoroughly wholesome thirst for adventure must also lie somewhere behind the officially recognized motives of idealism and selflessness. Although it was rarely admitted—the very idea of adventure clashed with the professed puritanism of the settlers—it is immediately apparent as we pursue the immigrants' trek from the relatively comfortable and stodgy surroundings which they left voluntarily, crossing illegal borders to their new, constantly changing abodes in the still undeveloped land of their dreams.

A decade or two later there would be a greater readiness to admit to a variety of motives. "We left home in the happy feelings of floating on the waves of real life," David Horowitz, the future president of the

Bank of Israel, wrote in a letter to his parents soon after his departure from Lvov, Poland, to Palestine. "Of wanting to give a lot to life and take a lot; to scrape as much of it as possible, to worship the God of youth and its ecstasy, to approach life with the eternal demand—all or nothing. We thirst for strength, tension, overflowing life, liberty and intoxicating beauty."

Many pioneers were teen-agers, barely nineteen years old. They sought a kind of freedom which was probably much more intensely personal than they cared to admit "ideologically." In Palestine, beyond rendering service to an idea to which many felt passionately committed, there was also a chance to get out from under the pressure of parental authority, to live wildly independent lives, or so it seemed. Many were northerners from dismal slummy little towns in the Pale of Settlement who loved to sleep outdoors, to revel in the brilliant stars spread out across the dark blue sky and the soft breeze that came in from the sea. Most memoirs are full of moving passages praising the glories of the eastern nights. Natives of grim Polish provinces and the cold, landlocked Russian steppes, they luxuriated in the fine, white, sandy beaches that were as yet unspoiled by tar and urban sewage. They made extensive use of them in their spare time. Inveterate hoboes, they were constantly on the move during their first years in the country. Few stayed in one place longer than a few weeks or months.

As he walked one day with a friend, Berl Katzenelson, the future labor leader and ideologue, remarked: "In the final analysis we are all. *adventurers*. . . ." His use of that word is noteworthy. In its contemporary Russian usage it was far from conveying anything complimentary or romantic. Though doubtlessly uttered in half-jest, it nevertheless stands as a rare instance of cool, detached lucidity in that ideologically overburdened period.

In their dress, as in their way of life and manner of work, they displayed a strong bohemian quality. Ben Zvi, the future President, and his girl friend Rachel (he formally married her more than a decade later) lived in an abandoned ruin on the outskirts of Jerusalem. In this ruin the Central Committee of *Poale Zion* held its meetings; Ben Gurion, a frequent visitor, would engage Ben Zvi in heated discussion.

The household consisted of a straw mat and a few wooden crates.

"What does a man need more?" Rachel Ben Zvi writes in her memoirs, describing life in Jerusalem prior to World War I: "Why should we tie ourselves to a routine way of life? Why bother to cook and amass furniture? This our household does not require too much bother. In a minute the straw mat is aired, the tin cups are rinsed, everything needed is done and we are at full liberty. . . ."

Although hard work was taken up as an almost religious rite, performance was at times lacking. The pioneers seemed to have more enthusiasm than patience. Arthur Ruppin, who directed the Zionist settlement office in Jaffa, complained of their "lack of constancy at work." He found the youngsters lacking in "precision"; they were never on time. Ruppin, the former Prussian *Assessor* (assistant judge), resented their "emotionalism" and "tendency for prolonged debate." They were, he admitted in his diary, "strangers" to him, and in more than one way, for "they did not understand my German and I understood none or little of their Hebrew and Yiddish." Yet publicly he defended the newcomers who were widely accused—and not without reason—of being "Russian anarchists" with "dangerous revolutionary" tendencies. For, as he put it, "I finally came to the conclusion that their sincere enthusiasm for agriculture as the basis for the Jewish national home was an asset of great value which must be carefully guarded."

As early as 1907 the Dutch Zionist and banker Jacobus Kann, after a tour through the colonies, worriedly noted the influx of "restless elements, their heads filled with social democratic anarchist theories." Kann conceded that they too had a right to settle in the colonies. They must even be aided, "for they come from the countries of persecution." But he felt it important to reserve all positions of influence and leadership for those of "proper upbringing" and a "solid education." The new "restless elements" did not qualify.

Ruppin, with all his criticism of the newcomers, obviously did not share this view. Earlier than other non-socialist Zionists from the west, he sensed instinctively how deeply social passions were intertwined with the awakening of nationalism among these young Jews from Eastern European lands of persecution and poverty. It was possible to secure their collaboration, he felt sure, "only if we do not degrade them to the level of mere foot soldiers, but instead elevate them to the rank of partners in the colonizing enterprise." When a group of "restless elements," employed on a farm administered by Ruppin's office, clashed with his overseer and declared a strike, Ruppin sided with the strikers and fired the overseer, in whose eyes, Ruppin complained, the workers "were nothing but hired employees." Ruppin readily agreed to let the workers run the farm themselves on a communal basis. This was the beginning of the *kibbutz*, which soon became the single most powerful cultural force of the entire Zionist enterprise. Ruppin continued to support it. He was called upon repeatedly to defend the *kibbutz* against conservative Zionist dignitaries and donors abroad, who suspected that behind it there was a heinous conspiracy controlled by the Bolsheviks preparing for world revolution.

Apart from wanting to secure the good will of the restless newcomers, Ruppin, the non-socialist, had good practical reasons to support and finance this foray into Utopia. There was little available land for settlement and even fewer public funds. Individual farming required a measure of prior training. Subsidized individual farmers, even if they turned out failures, were difficult to get rid of. Groups were cheaper to train, and, as they were composed mostly of enthusiastic teen-agers with no dependents, cheaper also to house and feed.

The appearance of the *kibbutz* at this particular time is noteworthy. Morally "perfect" communal communities dedicated to this or that utopian ideal—from the Essenes of antiquity to the Doukhobors of Russia, the Harmonists or Mormons of America, and the Flower Children of today—have appeared regularly in history at times of crisis and during marked transitory periods. In the case of the *kibbutz*, practical and ideological factors of varying force combined to give it a longevity and a place in the general community seldom achieved by similar utopian experiments elsewhere.

Henceforth the men and women of the *kibbutzim*, and later their children, more than any other group would symbolize the "new Jew." They have never averaged more than 8 percent of the population in Israel, and for most of the time never exceeded 4 percent. But more than any others they have personified the ideals of labor Zionism which at least up until 1945 were the dominant themes of Israeli nation building. With all their hairsplitting the socialist Zionists shared the aim of not only reconstructing a land and creating a haven for the persecuted, but of establishing a "good," "just," even "morally perfect" society as well. In retrospect, such a combination of aims may seem unduly presumptuous. In view of later events, it may appear to have been tragically short-sighted and naive. And yet there is no other single key that explains subsequent events, so large a part of Israeli behavior in the following years, or for that matter, the moral crisis that marks Israeli society today and which in all likelihood will plague it for a long time to come.

Consider, then, the early Zionist pioneers, the *chalutzim* of the second and third wave of immigration (1905–1924), hardworking and argumentative, obstinate, exuberant young men and women in their teens or early twenties, isolated within their communities, slowly making headway but still more like a secular priesthood spreading a gospel that few could accept. In retrospect one notices a number of curious parallels between the *chalutzim* and the hippies, yippies, or *enragés* who made their appearance more than half a century later in the industrial societies of the West. On the surface, the *chalutzim* were the hippies of the beginning of this century.

Of course, like all oversimplifications of this type, the comparison cannot be driven too far; however striking some likenesses may appear, the differences are immediately obvious. But taken merely as an indication of similarities in mood, psychology, and moral motivation, it should not be dismissed as altogether frivolous. The *chalutzim* were neither the first nor the last youngsters in history to search for the millennium and work for it through individual, voluntary action.

The experience of the early *chalutzim* is lent an added interest if we remember their role later on. The hippy rebels of an earlier age became the *establishment* of a later one, and a rather rigid and conservative *establishment* at that. At least half the members of the first Israeli constituent assembly in 1948 were veteran *chalutzim*; a third were members of *kibbutzim*, although the *kibbutz* population at the time hardly exceeded 5 percent. The uniqueness of this situation becomes apparent if we imagine a similar overrepresentation of Doukhobors, Tolstoyan mystics, Harmonists, Shakers, and members of like utopian communities in the parliaments and cabinets of the United States and Russia, where such communities also flourished in the nineteenth century.

Most *chalutzim* came from predominantly middle-class backgrounds. They deliberately opted out of established society in pursuit of a new life predicated upon a seemingly impossible dream. In their private papers and memoirs there is ample proof that they sought far more than the immediate, rather humdrum, down-to-earth aims of their particular Zionist faction, e.g., "another acre under irrigation," "another cowshed," "another settlement." Important as these aims were, they were not infrequently of lesser concern to them. Many *chalutzim* sought a "psychic community" in which their own identity could be redefined, and social and personal relations would be based on love. Theory was not always put into actual practice, but there is no reason to doubt the genuineness of the sentiment.

Opting out of established society, they fanatically rejected even external facets of the old life. Such facets included alcohol, and frequently tobacco, the cinema, dancing, and even decent table manners. As they rejected some external manners, they ritualized others. This was especially true in their dress. The role of dress in the history of revolt goes back to Adam and Eve, and is well known in modern times, from Gandhi's *dhoti* to the Mao jacket. The *chalutzim* despised jackets and dresses. Jackets and suits were the abominable symbols of the decayed and hypocritical world they had escaped. The men wore rough cotton shirts, sometimes embroidered at the neck in the Russian peasant style, which fell loosely over bulky shorts and widened like skirts at the knees. Many women wore trousers. Men's neckties were banned, as they would be years later in Barcelona during the brief rule of the Anarchists in 1936. In some *kibbutzim* common shower rooms for men and women were maintained on into the 1940s.

Like many people overly committed to politics, the leaders, in their lives and manners, often combined such obsessions with an amazing lack of personal sentimentality. Ben Zvi married his wife in between two sessions of the party's Central Committee. Ben Gurion, using the time during his expulsion from Palestine by the Turks at the outbreak of war to make speeches in America for *Poale Zion*, met and married a young nurse in New York in 1918. Soon afterward Ben Gurion abandoned her almost penniless and in the sixth month of her pregnancy in order to volunteer for the Jewish Legion, which was being organized by the British to assist in the occupation of Palestine. Paula Ben Gurion, a warm-hearted Jewish girl of unusual vivaciousness, was as far from Zionism as most of her fellow members in a lower East Side "study group on anarchism" which she attended faithfully twice a week before being swept off her feet by the visiting Palestinian exile.

A number of extraordinary letters written by Ben Gurion to Paula at that time reflect in Ben Gurion the curious mixture of moving tenderness and cruel will power. The letters throw a fascinating light on the motivations of the small group of leading *chalutzim*, who at that time were exiled or preparing for new action in British-occupied Palestine. They also supply an unusual insight into the character of a man so totally committed to his politics, so absolutely obsessed by his dream, that anything merely human becomes sheer trivia outside of its assimilation to The Idea.

In one letter written shortly after leaving his pregnant wife to her own devices, Ben Gurion commiserates a bit sheepishly with her over the "immense difficulties" and the "great suffering" he has caused her. He assures Paula (and one can only guess the tenor of her complaints, for her own letters to him are unavailable) that he left her not because he did not love her enough. "I loved you even *before* I married you, and you know it, *even though I never told you.** My love has since grown ... you are my saint, the suffering angel hovering over me unseen." Next he compliments her on her courage.

> What you did is infinitely greater than anything which I and others are doing and your sacrifice is so great that *sometimes* I want to take off my hat to you and bow down deep. . . . I did what I had to do, for your sake too, and I assure you, my dear Paula, that a time will come—and it is not far away—when you will share this feeling and you will understand.
>
> I did not want to give you a *small, cheap, secular* kind of happiness. I prepared for you the great sacred human joy achieved through *suffering and pain*. To the greatest joy of my life, I have become convinced *that you were born* for such happiness ... to suffer together with me for a great cause and you deserve that I bow my head before you. *Therefore* I love you so dearly ... I know you were not ready for the suffering and hard test ... but I know you well enough to be certain that you will carry this heavy burden. Dolorous and in tears you will arise to the high mountain from which one sees vistas of a New World, a world of gladness and light, shining in the glow of an eternally young ideal of supreme happiness and glorious existence,

* Author's italics.

a world only few will be *privileged* to enter, for only rich souls and deep hearts are *permitted* entry there. I know that your soul is rich and your heart great enough for the superb world and the superb life that I want to prepare for you.

In one letter, stressing the "heavy burden I have placed on you," he requests rather blatantly: "Inform me how much I owe you." In another he asks her to write freely and not be concerned that she may worry or frighten him unduly. "I am perhaps not too strong physically but I am able to bear everything and nothing can break me spiritually." Three months later, when Paula in his absence gave birth to a daughter, he named her *Geula*, meaning, literally, "Salvation."

Such sentiments—although perhaps less elitarian in spirit—were shared, as we have seen, by many pioneers of the second wave: disdain for "small, cheap, secular" kinds of happiness; a desire to mount high peaks of chiliastic faith, to open glorious vistas of a "new superb life" in a new, vaguely autonomous Jewish community in Palestine, based on a Messianic blend of Zionism and socialism. The Messianic sentiments became even more pronounced with the arrival of the next, third wave of immigrants, between 1919 and 1924.

As a mass movement the Third *Aliya* was mainly a result of the Balfour Declaration of 1917. The British declaration, and its subsequent endorsement by the League of Nations, legitimized by international law what had been since 1881 the haphazard experiment of a few enthusiastic amateurs. However, it was not the only reason for the coming of the third wave.

If the second wave of immigration had, at least partly, been a result of the abortive Russian revolution of 1905 and of its bloody concomitant of pogroms, the dislocations caused by World War I were a crucial reason for the third. Another important reason was the growing disappointment with the results of the successful Russian revolution of 1917. In the beginning, as William Henry Chamberlin has pointed out, there was a grim although most probably quite accidental retribution in the fact that "the last Czar died very much as many Jewish families had perished during the pogroms of 1905 . . . [and] that the Czar's chief executioner was a Jew and . . . most of his assistants . . . Letts." But people do not live by symbolic accidents. The revolution and its immediate aftermath inflicted terrible suffering on the Jewish population of the former Pale of Settlement. Most historians agree that the Jews suffered more than the population in general. In the Ukraine alone the number of Jewish casualties has been variously estimated between 60,000 and 130,000. There, and elsewhere, the violent upsurge of peasant anarchism caused a series of pogroms far more devastating in ferocity, number of victims, and destruction than anything that preceded them under the Czar.

The immigrants of the third wave came mostly from Eastern Europe. They are the first about whom more or less reliable details are known. The third wave totaled some 35,000; it included an unusually high number of unattached men and women in their early twenties. Of them, 14,685 were young bachelors; 2,826 young marrieds. Approximately one-third of those who arrived soon left. Again, a process of selection occurred. Left behind was a hard core of those either committed beyond recall or else too tied by circumstance. Ideology played the greatest role in the development of the modern Israeli psyche; the feeling of having no alternative was the second largest factor.

The spirit of the third wave was passionately anti-authoritarian. Formal government by professionals was an anathema. The new *chalutzim* wanted to be free men, operating in federated, voluntarily established communes of like-minded enthusiasts, subject to the most direct, grass-root democracy imaginable. No man should be master; all men must have an equal share in government. Their idea of participatory democracy was derived from the best part of the European revolutionary tradition—the council system, which Hannah Arendt has called "the always defeated but only authentic outgrowth of all revolutions since the eighteenth century." Their faith seems less naive if we remember how isolated their company still was in those early days and how small the society was in which it functioned.

And yet it will not come as a surprise to students of utopian ventures that such libertarian ideas frequently clashed with rigid principles of service and modes of personal behavior. These were imposed by majority decisions, at times so excessively intolerant of minority views that people holding slightly divergent opinions often found it impossible to live under the same roof or even in the same settlement. Splits, splinters, and desertions were common. There is little that can be as demanding and restricting to an individual's liberty as service to an extreme form of libertarianism. The demands of chalutzism must have come as a terrible burden to all but the strongest spirits. Its requirements were defined in a characteristic 1923 statement:

> *Chalutzism* is not sacrifice but Fulfillment. It is the marriage of inner-most, subjective strivings and objective values.
>
> The *chalutz* is an "Individualist." His act satisfies his very own, basic drives for a new life.
>
> The *chalutz* is the socialist (commune-man) *par excellence*. He wants the commune, because, without it he could not be an individual; for only within the commune can the "new life" flower, *among* humans, not merely *within* them.
>
> In the *chalutz* individualism and collectivism unite in a natural-or-ganic manner, not in an ideological one. And so is proven, that the "contradiction" between individual and commune is a Eu-ropean lie . . . as he fulfills himself, the *chalutz* fulfills the Idea. Within him is abolished the polarity of individual and commune, as well as the polarity of Body and Spirit, Being and Value.

Joseph Trumpeldor*, a veteran of the Russo-Japanese War who settled in Palestine in 1912, a prominent pioneer, vegetarian, and former adherent of Tolstoy's ideas on pacifism, is said to have given this rather chilling definition of the ideal *chalutz*:

> We need men prepared to do everything . . . we must raise a genera-tion of men who have no interests and no habits. . . . Bars of iron, elastic but of iron. Metal that can be forged to whatever is needed

---

* Trumpeldor (1880–1920) is said to have been the only Jewish officer in the Czarist army. He was elevated to this rank after the Battle of Port Arthur for acts of unusual bravery, during the course of which he lost a hand. In World War I he served in a Jewish unit fighting with the British in Galipoli. A well-known figure in his lifetime, he became a national hero after his death in battle aganst Arab insurgents in Galilee. His death in action afforded the fledgling Jewish community of Palestine—and Zionists everywhere—their first heroic legend. Other pioneers before Trumpeldor had died in defensive action. Trumpeldor's story was charged with all the powerful symbols of courage, dedication, unflinching valor and famous last words that often go into the makings of national myths. His dying words were: "It is good to die for our country." Some say these words were uttered in jest, his last utterance being a hefty Russian curse. Throughout his life he remained closely attached to all things Russian, and in 1914 left Palestine because, as a Czarist officer, he could not bear to remain in a country formally at war with Russia. A few months before his death he noted in his diary: "If only the Gogols, the Dostoevskies, and other Russian writers could have seen these brave, determined lads, their Jewish types would certainly have been portrayed differently . . . forty brave lads standing fearlessly at their post, facing an angry sea of [Arab] rebels" (Joseph Trumpeldor, Diary, January 10, 1920).

for the national machine. A wheel? I am the wheel. If a nail, a screw or a flying wheel are needed—take me! Is there a need to dig the earth? I dig. Is there need to shoot, to be a soldier? I am a soldier. . . . I am the pure idea of service, prepared for everything. I am not tied to anything. I know only one rule—to build.

In the early twenties a group of *chalutzim* established a Labor Brigade and named it in honor of Joseph Trumpeldor. Its discipline, fortunately, was considerably less rigid than that envisaged in the Trumpeldor program cited above. Nor, considering the nature of recruits, could it be otherwise. In the eyes of a majority of the *chalutzim* such ideals were as much out of pace with the spirit of the times as was Trumpeldor's carefully preserved officer's uniform. The Trumpeldor Labor Brigade was a kind of youth movement dedicated to anarcho-syndicalistic principles. The lack of human beings "hard and flexible as iron" and as easily forged to "whatever is needed for the national machine" was made up in many instances by an unfailing ecstatic enthusiasm.

The Joseph Trumpeldor Labor Brigade aimed at the conversion of the entire country to one great *kibbutz*, owned and self-governed by members engaged in agriculture and industry. It was felt that with the realization of this plan there would be little need for government or coercion, as people would realize an unheard-of freedom through independent, loosely federated collective and cooperative bodies owned and directly controlled by their members. The men and women of the Labor Brigade frequently shared their income and all their personal possessions on a collectivist basis; they lived in tent encampments and hired themselves out as construction workers, road gangs, and swamp-drainage teams. In 1921 they formulated as their goal the "Reconstruction of the country through the creation of a general commune of Jewish workers"; in 1925 they went further and envisaged "the establishment of a national center of labor for the Jewish people and a communistic society in the country." Vague feelers were put out to establish "political" and even "military" cooperation with the new Union of Soviet Socialist Republics, but they met with no response.

Many Brigade members later found their way to the *kibbutzim*. At least one of the present three great *kibbutz* movements— Ha'kibbutz Had'meuchad, with a membership in 1970 of close to 26,000, is directly traceable to the Brigade. Membership in the Brigade never exceeded 665 at one time, but the total number of *chal-*

utzim who passed through has been estimated at 2,000. Many later achieved considerable prominence in Israeli politics.

Some Brigade members gave up on the possibility of creating a voluntary communistic society within what was by 1926 obviously a capitalistic British colony. A few dozen returned to the Soviet Union, where they were permitted briefly to set up similar brigades in the Crimea and the Ukraine.* Later, under Stalin, many were imprisoned in slave labor camps and killed.

In Palestine the romance of the Labor Brigade and its road gangs lingered on for years. Already in the twenties it counted as a status symbol to have one's address at a certain kilometer on this or that road under construction, where one of the labor communes of the Brigade had pitched its tents.

An aristocracy in rags: "Now, more than forty years later, it seems to me that of all winters I passed in Palestine, the one of 1920–21 was the coldest and rainiest," Hillel Dan** a laborer on one of the road gangs, wrote. Newcomers frequently arrived at camp straight from the boat. The first job was to find a tent.

> We found one with torn flaps. Beds in those days were two iron bars tied to a wooden board. Even those were luxuries to us, for we had none. So we gathered a few pieces of broken plywood and put them on the ground. I remember how jubilant we were when one day we found a whole piece of plywood which could serve us as a real bed. . . . After a few days our [European city] shoes were disintegrating in the mud. They were not made to protect the feet of road workers. It was impossible to get other shoes . . . soon most of us moved about with feet bound in rags of cloth. . . .

In later years, even brief membership in the select fraternity of men who had paved, say, the Haifa-Jedda or the Afula-Nazareth roads, became a note of aristocratic distinction and frequently a key to political advancement. In 1954, thirty years after the event and six after the attainment of independence, almost half the leading politicians in the ruling labor party and a third of all senior officials in government, in the trade unions, in the nationalized or union-owned industries, had been, in the twenties, construction workers, laborers in

---

* Even though they were native Russians, their language continued to be Hebrew. Their settlement in the Crimea was called *Via Nova*, Esperanto for "New Life."

** Later chairman of Israel's largest industrial holding company, the trade-union-owned Solel Boneh.

road gangs, or members of bizarre communes, near-mystic brother-hoods of men in rags deliriously serving an idea. Few would have suspected in them the budding cells of a future power elite.

One of the most fascinating of these brotherhoods which sprung up in the early twenties was that of Bittania. The commune of Bittania was located in the Jordan valley, romantically perched on a dry, stony hilltop overlooking the opaque surface of the Sea of Galilee. It is hard to imagine a softer, more dreamy landscape or one as mystically trans-figured on a hazy day. Here, in the tranquil, soft atmosphere of the Lake of Galilee, Jesus had preached a religion of love and had prom-ised the heavenly kingdom to all who are wretched and poor; in the first century, according to Josephus, the area surrounding the lake had been a virtual Eden of fragrant flowers, fruit trees, and fountains; however, when the first Jewish colonists arrived it was largely barren and dangerously infested by malaria. Here, within a short distance from Bittania, the dreamers of Kinneret had established the first *kib-butz* in 1909.

In Bittania proper there was nothing picturesque whatsoever. It was a dismal, slumlike conglomeration of dirty tents and shabby, wooden huts surrounded by a few dreary vegetable beds. The men and women of Bittania—the commune numbered some forty or fifty members—came mostly from Galicia. There they had belonged to the Zionist youth movement *Ha'shomer Ha'tzair*, which in later years would be-come strictly Marxist, even pro-Stalinist in orientation,* but in those early days members still upheld a curious hodgepodge of ideas derived in varying proportions from Karl Marx, Sigmund Freud, Martin Buber, Hans Blueher, and Gustav Wyneken, the German apostles of the then fashionable *Jugendkultur*. *Ha'shomer Ha'tzair* was strongly influenced by the *Wandervogel* movement, with its romantic worship of nature, its cult of eroticism and disdain for bourgeois values.

The men and women of Bittania called themselves an *edda*

---

* Up until Khrushchev's speech at the Twentieth Party Congress of the Soviet Com-munists, most members of *Ha'shomer Ha'tzair* ignored Stalin's terror. Although they remained passionate Zionists throughout this time, even Stalin's persecution of Jews and Zionists was dismissed as a temporary aberration in an essentially just and peace-loving system.

(congregation). "To remain pure we must extricate ourselves from
the abyss of conformity," began a *Ha'shomer Ha'tzair* statement, cited
by David Horowitz.

> Perhaps we shall be the first torrent of youth to remain young forever;
> humanity's first chance to escape failure. Let us go far between moun-
> tains and deserts to live in simplicity, beauty and truth. Perhaps our
> new *edda* will be the nucleus of a new culture of new relationships
> between humans leading communal lives. We shall be the pioneers
> who shall carry the revolution through to the masses of miserable Jews,
> who will stream to the country to live by our principles. Let us create
> a new land of Israel free from the shackles of European capitalism
> and of the diaspora. . . .

The members of Bittania were of predominantly solid middle-
class origins. Some had been to college; nearly all had completed good
Polish or Austrian *gymnasiums*, and most spoke two or three languages fluently. Their leader was a slim young man by the name of
Meir Wald who soon Hebraicized his surname to Yaari. He was
simply called Meir by his disciples. He was a man of extraordinary
intellect, personal magnetism, and suggestive power; his lean ascetic
face was pierced by a pair of fiery eyes; a shock of black hair fell over a
high forehead. He was the unchallenged guru of his group. His disciples sat at his feet in concentrated admiration, a charmed circle of
initiates.*

David Horowitz, one of the few who broke away, later recorded his
reminiscences with a dispassionate detachedness rare among former
pioneers of that early period. He compared Bittania to a "monastic
order without God." It was no simple matter to be accepted as a
member; candidates passed a trial period, a kind of novitiate. Horowitz likened Bittania to a "religious sect . . . with its own charismatic
leader and set of symbols, and a ritual of confessions in public reminiscent of efforts by religious mystics to exorcise God and Satan at one
and the same time."

* In later years Yaari became the chief ideologue of Mapam, one of the three leading
Israeli labor parties. He never accepted executive office. Yaari preferred to continue
the role of guru, and his pronouncements were still made in a spirit of near-religious
ritual. In 1965, in response to a newspaperman's question, he said that as long as he,
Ben Gurion, and another aged *kibbutz* leader and former member of the Labor Brigade—Yitzchak Tubenkin—were alive, no internal Israeli political development could
seriously harm the country.

For although the men and women of Bittania spent from ten to fourteen hours a day working hard in the fields, such exertions of the body were considered as trite side phenomena of the "real life." Everyone knew, says Horowitz, that the real life at Bittania "began in the evening." After a frugal meal in the communal dining shed, members engaged in the *sicha* (literally, *sicha* means "conversation"). In reality, it was a prolonged session of monologues and near-hysteric public confessions where members bared their innermost secrets, sexual anxieties and dreams, doubts, yearnings, and perplexities. At some sessions written records were kept; some were later incorporated into a private limited edition which is still not available to the general public. It is one of the most fascinating authentic documents of the period, and is here used as a source for the direct quotations which follow.

Daily sessions usually began with a half-hour period of silent contemplation at which Meir Yaari presided. "Who art thou, man?" a participant once called out to Yaari, according to the published record, "you who have such power and daring to force me this very minute to step out of my soul—one step above it and myself!"

Another exclaimed: "I beseech you, I beseech you, brethren, teach me true love! True love! I want to be sacrificed on its altar." The communal idea went so far that sexual intercourse between two individuals was considered a despicable act of selfishness unless the two lovers later verbally shared their feelings at *sicha* with the entire commune. A man's private sexual life was considered "the spiritual property of the entire commune." Even though there could not have been much time for love-making after ten to fourteen hours of work and three to six hours of *sicha*, and although mutual attraction was undoubtedly dulled by close and constant proximity between the sexes in circumstances not overly aesthetic, a kind of catharsis was achieved by this obsessive sharing. Members "sat up til dawn . . . we confessed to each other. It was like pure prayer bursting forth from heart to heart. . . ." On one occasion they called it their "night of atonement." On another a member exclaimed that "in Bittania a book was opened to us which was different from the usual; it was the soul of man."

The land they tilled they called their bride; they were its "bridegroom who abandons himself in his bride's bosom . . . yes, thus we abandon ourselves to the motherly womb of sanctifying earth." And

Yaari summed up: "In this last hour of usage, before our wedding night, we bring as holy sacrifice to you, earth of our fulfillment, these our very lives, our daily lives in the Land of Israel; our parents, children, brothers, our poverty and wealth. ..." Speakers sometimes fainted from excitement at the rostrum; girls seized by sudden fits of hysteria jumped to their feet and ran from the room crying. "There were times when I feared that collective madness would seize this lonely congregation," Horowitz writes. The published annals record such outcries as: "Oh save me for the distant image of the congregation of blood! Save me from the stifling burden of morality! Tamar ... daughters of Lot ... where are you!" "I do not want to be an artist! Matter I want to be!" "Table, oh mine table! Never have I seen you so square! I love you, and in the hour of fulfillment how could I forget you!"

In retrospect the commune of Bittania certainly seems more bizarre than the others. But was it? The men and women of Bittania were on the whole more articulate than the rest of the pioneers. They made a fetish of their "openness" and left a revealing written document testifying to their inner struggles and debates; members of other communes, less articulate or more discreet, have not.

Men commonly considered to be "in their right senses" would scarcely have settled as communards either in Bittania or in one of the other early communes. Weizmann, although he was a non-socialist, perhaps even anti-socialist liberal, was fascinated by the communards. ("To be a Zionist it is not necessary to be mad, but it helps.") He often said that he felt better among the communards than among the Jewish settlers in the towns. To Weizmann, as to a number of other leading liberal-bourgeois Zionists, the communards' incessant search for a "new, just society" seemed one guarantee that the Zionist enterprise would not end as "just another nation-state" or, as Ruppin said, "another Albania."

The physical and psychological strains of ushering in a new culture based on "beauty, justice, and love" must have been considerable. The communards were mostly young men and women in their twenties. In contemporary photographs we invariably see them as looking much older: weary, lined, exhausted, slumped over tin plates in shabby communal dining rooms, or bravely smiling into cameras out on the dusty fields. It does not come as a surprise to learn that next to disease, which was rife, suicide was also rampant in the early communes. Contemporary publications obliquely refer to this or that deceased as "the victim of bitter circumstance." In *Kehilatenu*, the published annals of the Bittania group, an anonymous member is quoted as telling the commune: "I would like to tell you about myself . . . about my 'today.' My tomorrow is shred in bleakness; for me the sun has set . . . darkness is approaching . . . I do not fear it . . . I reach for it with my hand, imploring, 'take me please . . . your cold breath on my burning chest . . . rest.'" One member of Bittania shot himself; he was found dead with a volume of Dostoyevsky's *The Brothers Karamazov* by his side.

In Bittania, as in most other communes, life for most settlers continued to be hard and frequently quite primitive. In 1926 Arthur Koestler abruptly abandoned his studies at the University of Vienna and joined the communal settlement of Hepbzibah. He has recorded his initial shock at the commune's "ramshackle dwellings in which only the poorest in Europe would live as an alternative to the discarded railway carriage."

It is hard to visualize today the contours and features of an environment that has since been so radically reshaped. Large stretches of country were still barren, traversed only by dirt track. Traffic moved slowly, much of it on camelback or by "diligence," a horse-drawn wagon similar to those used in the American West a few decades earlier. Medical services were improving, but disease was still rampant. There was hardly a *chalutz* who escaped malaria. It was before the advent of DDT or cheap and simple preventative drugs. Struck by the gnawing fever, the only thing to do was to wait and suffer. It was easier to bear the malaria during the day than at night. Levi Eshkol remembered attacks of fever at night which gave him terrible nightmares. With recurrent attacks the whole system of the body weakened and became less resistant to other diseases. Dysentery, rheumatism, typhoid, skin and eye diseases were all common.

Among those who remained in the communes, the single most important compensation for enduring such hardship was the deep sense of satisfaction that comes from a knowledge of personal achievement and participation in an extraordinary drama. Nor was the sense of great drama confined to those who participated, or only to Zionists. Ernst Toller, the poet and leader of the abortive Communist uprising of 1918 in Bavaria, visited the communes in the mid-twenties. He summed up his feelings in a dedication he inscribed for one of the pioneers in a volume of his poems:

> "Wer keine Kraft zum Träumen hat
> Hat keine Kraft zum leben."
> (He who has no strength to dream,
> has no strength to live.)

The third wave of immigration came to an end in 1924. It is customary to count only two more *Aliyas*. The fourth wave (1924–1929) brought in some 68,000 immigrants, mostly small businessmen escaping anti-Semitic measures in Poland. Again, more than one-third of them re-emigrated. In 1927 the number of those leaving (5,071) exceeded the number of those who arrived (3,034). Everything from 1930 to 1939 is today called the fifth wave. It mounted in the thirties with the rise of Nazism in Germany and culminated in the great masses arriving after Independence in 1948.

There is something arbitrary in all such distinctions between different waves of immigration. History is a continuous thread, although in its retelling it becomes convenient to cut it here or there. For our purposes the important thing to note is that the first waves of immigrants—until about 1930—with all their bizarre quaintness, were crucial in the development that came later. Because there was nothing or little before them, no subsequent wave of immigration had as deep an influence on future social structures as the Second and Third *Aliyahs*. They set a pattern of politics and society, of habits, passions, and prejudices, that add up to what one loosely calls national character. Henceforth, at least in the eyes of the founding fathers, all latecomers had to fit themselves to it.

As in America, the first waves of immigrants developed a set of attitudes and values so powerful that even today, when the passage from pioneer society to modern industrial state is nearly complete, one still associates them with Israeli politics and manners. It will suffice to mention a few outstanding examples: (1) the party system —its unique centrality in political life; (2) the strong belief in equality; (3) the continuing informality and simplicity in manners, dress, and language; (4) the agrarian ritual; (5) the belief in voluntary action; and (6) the notion of an official (Zionist) "state ideology."

In the investigation of new societies it is, of course, often impossible to follow with any conviction the old logic of cause and effect. In Israel, too, events crowded upon events; accidents overshadowed solemn intention. It was often only long after the original event that the pieces seemed to fall into place. The twenties were a heyday of social experimentation, not since surpassed. Ironically, such experiments were largely financed by generous contributions from conservative philanthropists abroad, who normally would have been among the staunchest opponents of the socialist kind of society that was being tried out here. Yet most of the social and political institutions which give present-day Israel a measure of singularity in the world stem from this early period.

First and foremost, is the continuing predominance in Israeli politics of the left-of-center parties. The fusion of these parties in 1968 almost guranteees that this predominance which began in the early 1930s will characterize Israeli political life for years to come. The political machines set up by the generation of founding fathers have proven so powerful and so self-perpetuating that no liberal-centrist or right-wing opposition is likely to gain power within the foreseeable future.

Second, the *Histadrut* Labor Union, the most powerful creation of the formative years. *Histadrut* controls a socialized medicine system comprising nearly 80 percent of the population. The monopoly of public transport owned by a drivers' cooperative is theoretically controlled by *Histadrut*. The so-called socialist sector of the economy, a vast complex of light, heavy, and service industries, construction and investment companies, mines, banks, credit institutions, export and import agencies, comprises some 40 percent of the total. In theory it is all owned by the "Commonwealth of Labor" represented by *Histadrut*; in reality it is now controlled by government which in turn is closely linked to *Histadrut* and by its own, rather innate bureaucracy.

Third, the collective *kibbutz* and the cooperative *moshav*. These two forms of settlement today represent over two-thirds of the farm population, the biggest part of the country's agricultural output as well as a growing share of the country's manufactured product, especially in the future-oriented cybernetics-controlled industries.

Some of these institutions have since ossified; some have changed; others have lost their original meaning. But their position seems so deeply rooted in habit and social structure, still so reinforced by the lingering power of the founding fathers' original ideology, that they will probably mark Israeli society for a long time to come. The political personality of Israel as we know it today is the product of ideology and circumstance. In Israel, as in other developing countries, ideology was a fusion of nationalism and socialism, and in few places has the latter been characterized by streaks of Utopia as strongly pronounced as here. Dr. Allan Arian of Tel Aviv University, a shrewd observer of the Israeli scene, has remarked that "removing ideology from Israeli politics would be more than depriving the traveler of his map; it would mean divesting him of most of the landscape and much of his vehicle as well. . . . Higher living standards and well-trained techno-crats are not likely to alter characteristics which are such a basic part of modern Israel's heritage."

7

INNOCENTS AT HOME

But there are Arabs in Palestine! I did not know . . . !

—Attributed to Max Nordau, 1897

Two important phenomena of a similar nature and yet opposed, at present manifest themselves in Asian Turkey. These are the awakening Arab nation and the latest efforts of the Jews to reconstitute on a very large scale the ancient kingdom of Israel. The two movements are destined to combat one another continuously until one is beaten by the other.

—Naguib Azuri
Le Réveil de la Nation Arab, 1908

Go and tell the Jews how strong we are, and that they are lost.

—Arab Guerrilla
to Manya Shochat in 1948

Even those with only a rudimentary knowledge of events ahead will have noticed a curious omission in this strange story. So far there has been little mention of the indigenous Arab population.

The reason is a simple one. For the first two or three decades of settlement the pioneers were hardly aware of the Arabs as the source of a possible conflict. The political imagination, like the imagination of the explorer, often invents its own geography. The settlers did not, of course, consider the country "empty," as did some Zionists abroad. What they saw with their own eyes contradicted the ludicrous dictum attributed to Israel Zangwill, "The land without people—for the people without land," which was current in Zionist circles abroad at least until 1903, and to a lesser extent until as late as 1917. Yet even if there were people living in the country, the settlers saw that it was populated only sparsely. They believed they were operating in a political void; and not until the end of World War I were they fully cured of this naive illusion. Hindsight may make all this sound unbelievable today. The fact is that Arab nationalism was clandestine before 1908; it came to the surface only after the Young Turks' revolution. Before 1908 few of the settlers and none of the Zionist leaders in Palestine and abroad ever contemplated the possibility that Arabs and Jews would one day clash in bloody battle over the same stretch of soil, as the Germans and French over Alsace, or the Turks and Greeks over Thrace.

This does not mean that they considered themselves completely unchallenged in Palestine. To the contrary, many early pioneers were obsessed by grave fears of losing the country to adversaries. But these adversaries were European, "imperialist" forces, not Arabs. They saw them looming dangerously in the West, in France or Prussia; and in the East, in Czarist Russia which they had left behind. A *Poale Zion* announcement published in 1908 in Brody (Galicia) urged all young "Workers and Pioneers" to go to Palestine as soon as possible. Otherwise "masses of non-Jews will stream there; before we wake up Palestine will be in other people's hands."

A brief *shock* of recognition that Palestine was now an Arab country struck Ben Yehuda, father of modern Hebrew, upon his arrival in the country in 1882. To judge by the written records, Ben Yehuda's shock was unique among the early settlers. He had had no doubts before; but disembarking at Jaffa Ben Yehuda experienced a sudden crisis of conscience. He saw himself as coming "to this country as a proselyte, a stranger, the son of a foreign country and a foreign people; in this, the land of my forefathers, I have no political and no civil right. I am a foreigner. . . . I suddenly broke. Something like remorse rose in the depths of my soul. . . . My feet stood on the holy ground the land of the forefathers, and in my heart there was no joy. . . . I did not embrace the rocks. . . . I stood shocked. Dread! Dread!" It is not clear from Ben Yehuda's memoirs how he overcame the dreadful "doubt [which] tortured my heart." But his spirit was quickly restored by a Jewish innkeeper's warm hospitality and by the satisfaction he, as a linguist, derived from the fluent Hebrew of a Jewish moneychanger in Jaffa port.

Fifteen years later, early in his career as a Zionist, Max Nordau is said to have come running to Herzl exclaiming, "But there are Arabs in Palestine! I did not know that! We are committing an injustice!" Herzl's response is unknown. The story may be apocryphal, yet it sums up, as such stories often do, the central facts of the case. At any rate, Nordau's fear, if genuine, was as isolated and eccentric a sentiment as the fear that electricity might be immoral because sometimes there are people who are electrocuted and die. For the Zionists, Zionism was tantamount with progress.

The ancient Hebrews, as they were leaving the house of Egyptian bondage, were warned that the Promised Land was occupied by tall, ferocious men, even "giants." The nineteenth-century prophets of Zionism overlooked the possibility of native opposition. Hess, Lilienblum, Pinsker, and Herzl ignored the Arabs. If their presence in and around Palestine was acknowledged, there was always the implied or expressed assumption that Jewish settlement would benefit the Arabs greatly. For this reason the Arabs themselves were considered potential Zionists; they were expected to welcome the Jews as a matter of course. For the prophets of Zionism this was so self-evident that they never even considered another possibility.

It took a non-Jew, a perfect outsider, the Irish nationalist leader Michael Davitt, to appraise the situation more realistically at this early stage. In a book published in New York in 1903, which few if any of the early pioneers had read, he predicted that the Arabs would make war to prevent the coming of the Jews. But, as a "convinced believer in the remedy of Zionism," to which he had been converted after investigating the Russian pogroms, Davitt felt that such Arab opposition need not deter the Zionists. The Arabs, he wrote, can be trusted to "show no more savage propensities toward their Israelitish kindred than Russian seminarists or Rumanian Christians have done in recent years." At the same time, two or three millions of Jews in Palestine would soon develop a national sentiment, Davitt wrote. The new nationalism would nourish a spirit of patriotism capable of defending them from possible Arab aggression. "The Jews of the world would be their foreign friends and allies, while the civilized nations, inhabited by the scattered Hebrews, could not in reason neglect to take a sympathetic interest in [their] protection and welfare. . . ."

David Ben Gurion wrote in 1967 that "none of the great thinkers who dreamed and wrote of our people's revival in its ancient cradle ever envisaged that this revival would be met, from the first day on, by military attack; and that Israel's independence would be achieved only through military victory over the Arabs." Ben Gurion was a latecomer; yet he should have included himself in this assembly of blindfolded dreamers. Like most Zionists, at first he also took Arab acquiescence for granted. His mind was both quick and perceptive. Yet his imagination, otherwise so broad, was curiously selective on this score.

A typical incident took place in 1909. Ben Gurion, Ben Zvi, and the rest of the *Poale Zion* leadership were attending a regional party conference in the Galilee at Segera, a little settlement at the foot of Mount Tabor. The land had been purchased a few years earlier at a very high price from an absentee Arab landlord in Beirut. The transaction led to serious clashes with dispossessed Arab serfs, who had not been compensated by the seller. At a later stage, the Jewish buyers paid the former serfs additional sums over and above the legal purchase price, in order to facilitate better neighborhood relations. But by then the problem was already overshadowed by the politics of nationalism. Rashid Bey, the Turkish Governor General who resided in Beirut and apparently did not care whether Arab, German, or Jewish settlers were living in the Galilee, had approved the transaction. At one point he even sent troops to enforce it. But his deputy in Tiberias, Amin Arsalan, the scion of a well-known local Druse family, was already caught up by nascent Syrian-Arab nationalism. Arsalan sided with the serfs. A feudal landowner himself, his reasoning was neither social nor humanitarian, but nationalistic. He told Chaim Kalvarisky, Rothschild's agent in the Galilee, that he was opposed to Jewish settlement because he objected to the "de-nationalization of the Galilee."

When *Poale Zion* met for its regional conference in a wooden toolshed in Segera in 1909, tension was again running high. Some delegates—there must have been about fifty—attended the deliberations armed to defend themselves with guns, pistols, and sticks. One had been assaulted on his way to Segera and stripped of a camera with which he had planned to photograph the gathering. In defending himself he had fatally wounded one of his attackers. The next day Israel Korngold, one of the settlers, was shot to death, and a second settler was killed in another skirmish.

And yet there is nothing in the record to indicate that the possibility of a political or even military conflict between Arabs and Jews was so much as mentioned by Ben Gurion and the others in the week of party deliberations that followed. The incident was dismissed as a case of armed robbery that turned into a blood feud, so common in the Levant. There were long lectures at the conference on the "agrarian problem," including elaborate discussions on class warfare on the village level. There was much give and take on a project to set up a trade union of (Jewish) agricultural workers in the Galilee. Ben Zvi at one point vaguely touched upon the nationalist character inherent in what he called "medium-sized capitalists" among the Arabs; this was contrasted to the inherent "internationalism" of "Big Capital."

The conference adopted a number of resolutions. One was to found a party printing press; another called for the establishment of a party fund to finance trips of *Poale Zion* delegates to the forthcoming Seventh Zionist Congress in Hamburg. No resolution touched the issue which during the conference had caused the death of two men.

We reach here one of the strangest most baffling aspects of our theme. The Zionists were fervently, and at great human sacrifice, pursuing a national and social renaissance in their ancient homeland. They were blind to the possibility that the Arabs of Palestine might entertain similar hopes for themselves. More responsive than most people of their time to the compelling force of ideas, they ignored the power of related ideas on their adversaries. It was explained in later years that at the time "there was little evidence" of Arab nationalism, and this was true. But was there much more evidence of Jewish nationalism? Zionism was still rejected by a majority of Jews in the Diaspora. Both national movements were taking their first steps. There was in fact a curious parallelism between the two developing nationalisms. Both started as cultural movements in the second half of the nineteenth century. Both grew out of the activities of literary societies; both were closely linked with a renaissance of language. For a long time both movements were served by small, relatively obscure magazines.

The Zionists of course were considerably better organized; one of their main advantages was the presence of a dedicated, although small, advance guard of pioneers, an army without uniform serving the idea with total personal commitment and dedicated to constructive work in a way rarely evinced on the other side. Nevertheless, in 1881, the year when the first Lovers of Zion were forming clandestine clubs in Russia, when Leo Pinsker was at his desk writing *Auto-Emancipation* and Levontin traveled to Palestine as a scout for prospective settlers, in that same year secret societies of Arab nationalists in Beirut and Damascus were distributing illegal pamphlets and revolutionary placards requesting home rule for the Arabs of Syria, Lebanon, and Palestine. As for the Zionists, in 1881 a pamphlet was circulating in Rumania presenting Palestine as a virtually deserted wasteland.

When the first settlers arrived at Rishon le-Zion in 1882, both national movements were still extraordinarily weak; if one was more impotent than the other, it was mainly a question of degree. In all branches of the Lovers of Zion movement in Russia, there were no more than 525 members. In Beirut and Damascus, the number of active Arab nationalists was probably even lower and Arab nationalists were being subjected to serious repressive measures by the Turks. But their movement was already being borne slowly to its destiny through the influence of European ideas, in secret and semi-secret societies and on the wings of a renascent literature.

Both movements developed in spasms, rather than on a plan of sustained effort; both were marked by vivid outbursts with longish lulls between. In 1905 the pioneers of the second wave were just beginning to arrive in Palestine when Naguib Azuri, a Christian Arab and former Ottoman official in Jerusalem, founded a society in Paris known as the *Ligue de la Patrie Arab*. The *Ligue* was destined to play a leading role in the development of Arab nationalism. Azuri published a book entitled *Le Réveil de la Nation Arab*. It contained an attack on Zionism, but at the time few of the men of the Second *Aliya* apparently read it. In 1908 the Hebrew magazine *Ha'shiloach* reprinted some excerpts which were widely ignored. Azuri, alone among most Arabs and Jews, was endowed with a prescience of remarkable accuracy: "Two important phenomena of a similar nature and yet opposed, at present manifest themselves in Asian Turkey. These are the awakening Arab nation and the latent effort of the Jews to reconstitute on a very large scale the ancient kingdom of Israel. The two movements are destined to combat one another continuously until one is beaten by the other." Jews and Arabs represent "two contradictory principles." Azuri went as far as to proclaim that upon the outcome of the struggle between them "will depend the fate of the entire world."

Few Zionists took notice of Azuri's book. If this was a convenient oversight it was an easy one, because of the relative obscurity of Arab nationalism. George Antonius, the eminent Arab historian, admits the great difficulties that even he encountered in tracing the beginning of modern Arabism. In his classic, *The Arab Awakening*, written in the mid-1930s, he relates his futile search for some of the basic texts that emanated from secret Arab societies in the nineteenth century. It was only by accident that he finally found what he was looking for, not in the Near East, but in the secret archives of the British Foreign Office. A minor diplomatic official had included them in a long-forgotten dispatch.

In the beginning, Arabs were even more ignorant of their future adversary than the Jews were of them. This was partly the result of a lower level of political awareness; it was also due to their historical image of the Jew. Traditionally the Arab world knew the Jews only as a docile minority, grateful for the special protection it received at various times under the Arab rulers. It took the Arabs nearly one hundred years to overcome this notion. Even today, after three crushing defeats at the hands of the Jews, Arabs still frequently decry Jews as cowardly misfits shivering with fear at the approach of one valiant Arab fighter. History has taught them to treat the Christian world seriously but not the Jews, who were doomed by the Koran to subjugation. Thus in the beginning, both Jews and Arabs belittled each other. It is extremely hard for one man to understand the nationalism of another.

In an interview more than half a century after the event, Ben Gurion recounted how he had *first become* aware of anti-Zionist nationalism among the Palestinian Arabs. It happened, he said, in 1915, ten years after his first arrival in the country. He had been seized by the Turkish authorities as a Zionist agitator and alleged advocate of Palestinian secession from the Ottoman Empire. He was held in semi-arrest in the fortified compound of the Turkish military headquarters in Jerusalem, and faced "expulsion in perpetuity" from the country. As he walked back and forth in the courtyard, waiting for the result of a last-minute appeal to Djemel Ahmed Pasha, the Turkish Governor General, he met a young Arab acquaintance, son of a wealthy Jerusalem family. Only a few months earlier the two had been law students together at the University of Istanbul, "quite close and friendly, even though we never discussed politics." Seeing Ben Gurion under guard, inside the Turkish military fortress, the young Arab anxiously inquired what on earth had happened, and if he could be of any help.

"I told him I was under arrest as a Zionist, that the Turks wanted to expel me from the country. He looked me up and down silently. 'As your friend,' he said, 'I am deeply sorry. But as an Arab I am pleased.'

"It came down on me like a blow," Ben Gurion recollected. "I said to myself, 'so there is an Arab national movement here' (and not just in Lebanon and Syria). It hit me like a bomb. I was completely confounded. . . ."

There is a curious fascination in this story, in its implied naivete and disillusioned innocence, wistful candor, guile, and apparent ingenuousness. It was recounted by the old Ben Gurion more than half a century after the event. As with most recollections of this kind, made after the lapse of so much time, the facts are probably right. The dramatic embellishment and perhaps the interpretation may be retrospective. If the sudden discovery of a nationalist mood among natives, bitterly opposed to Zionist settlement, had shocked Ben Gurion and confounded him, as he later claimed, he seems to have remained strangely quiet about it.

Ben Gurion was not imprisoned alone in the Turkish fortress. He was in the constant company of friends and fellow detainees; some of them, including Ben Zvi, the future President, published their diaries and memoirs. There was a constant stream of visitors from the outside, mostly fellow members of Ben Zvi and Ben Gurion's *Poale Zion* party. The party's central committee held meetings within the walls of the fortress. Its members crouched together in a corner, sipped tiny cups of Turkish coffee brought in from a nearby Arab coffeehouse, and discussed political events. Yet in the many volumes of memoirs and of published and unpublished party records, there is not a single reference to Ben Gurion's discovery. It may have been a passing thought; or one quickly suppressed and pushed back into the darker corners of the mind, like sex or sweat in Victorian novels.

Actually, despite the "bombshell" of 1915, Ben Gurion continued to dismiss the Palestinian Arabs as politically nonexistent. In December 1917 he made the astounding suggestion that in "historical and moral sense" Palestine was a country "without inhabitants." The blinding effects of national egocentricity could hardly be greater. What he meant in effect was that only the Jews really felt *at home* in Palestine; all other inhabitants were merely the ethnic remains of various waves of conquerors. Ben Gurion was most anxious to accord them civil rights as individuals, but as a nation they had none. Ben Gurion did not want to harm anybody; he went to great lengths to make this especially clear. "According to my moral judgment," wrote Ben Gurion in 1924, "we have no right whatsoever to deprive a single Arab child even if through such deprivation we shall realize our aims."

In view of subsequent events, this statement may appear hypocritical. Thousands of Arab children died or became permanently homeless as a result of the Arab-Israeli conflict. But seen against the prevailing temper of the time, the public and private personality of the writer, his principles and ideals at that early stage, there is little doubt that he fully meant what he said. It was before the rise of Nazism. Ben Gurion did not envisage a full-scale Arab attack. It was still deemed possible to proceed slowly without arousing too much antagonism. We all create mental blocks to prevent us from being deflected in our course. The psychologist will find nothing unusal in men responding as powerfully to fictions as to realities. Newton wrote the *Principia* but also a topography of hell.

The Zionist leaders were frightened men seized by the vision of a world that could be both better and infinitely worse. An almost uncanny clarity of vision in one field—the coming apocalypse in Europe—came at the price of myopia in another. Like most visionaries their eyes were hung with monumental blinkers. At first it hardly penetrated their minds that the country they wished to resettle was not as underpopulated, desolate, or ruined as they thought. They did not imagine that the Arabs who had been living there for centuries could possibly object to becoming a minority—a fully respected minority that would live in more comfort and wealth under the most liberal of regimes—through the advent of massive Jewish immigration from abroad. Later on a defensive mechanism of great complexity would be employed to protect this naive innocence from being contradicted by facts. For decades it was well served by arguments such as: "Only the reactionary Arab feudalists are opposed; the masses of people will soon realize their true advantage; objectively they are allies." Or, typically, "Arab feudalists fan and exploit anti-Zionist feelings in order to dampen popular dissatisfaction with their miserable rule."

It is easy today to dismiss such claims. Yet many people believed in them implicitly because at the time they contained a measure of truth. The young radicals from Eastern Europe inevitably expected that the coming to power of "progressive socialist forces in the Arab world" would lead to Arab acquiescence to their cause.* Later, British duplicity was often blamed for the growing tension: "British colonialism" was accused of inciting Arabs against Jews according to the so-called "divide and rule" principle. Again, if this was a fallacy, it gained so much credence because it contained some truth. In the main, however, such claims gave comfort to those who could not contemplate the resentment, the bitterness, and hatred implanted in the Arab soul through the intrusion of the Jews. There are few things as egocentric as a revivalist movement. For decades the Zionist leaders moved in a strange twilight zone, seeing the Arabs and at the same time not seeing them. Their attitude was a combination of blindspots and naivete, of wishful thinking, paternalistic benevolence, and that ignorance which is often a factor in international events, and sometimes their cause.

It may very well be that without this ignorance most Zionist leaders would not have ventured on their task in the first place. There were exceptions of course, like Vladimir Jabotinsky, the romanticist of power, whom Weizmann disparagingly called "our own D'Annunzio." Jabotinsky preached the conquest of Palestine through the sword.

* In effect they virtually prayed for a Gamal Abdel Nasser. As recently as 1952, when Naguib and Nasser seized power in Egypt, their success was greeted by Israelis with enthusiasm. Ben Gurion "publicly extended" his hand and welcomed the hope of a "free, independent progressive Egypt."

He advocated the forced resettlement of Arabs in the neighboring countries. But a majority of Zionist leaders, from Herzl through Weizmann to Ben Gurion, and the ideologists of settlement, the pacifist A. D. Gordon and the moralist Berl Katzenelson, were made of different stuff. They were humanists, liberals, and social democrats with an instinctive abhorrence of all violence. All were proven wrong in the end; in the beginning they were all so firmly committed to the ideal of liberal justice that they would have laughed at anyone who would have suggested in 1924, or even as late as 1931, that their success might even indirectly cause a terrible tragedy for the Arabs. It was before the holocaust of European Jewry had changed their basic terms of reference. Engaged in organizing an unprecedented "return," they went one step further to Utopia and believed they were capable of realizing their dream by pacific means. The inexorable logic of events later caught up with them; but we know enough about their antecedents, their principles and beliefs, to state with some assurance that had they known, as we do today, that the price of Jewish re-establishment in Palestine would be the displacement of the Arabs, they might have revised their scheme, or even have withdrawn from action in good time. "I am disturbed by the thought that victims of one disaster did not foresee the coming of another," Yehoshafat Harkabi, an Israeli historian of the younger, post-Zionist generation, wrote in 1967. At the root of the Zionists' ultimate success lay a basic misapprehension.

In large measure, this lack of foresight reflected the spirit of the time. In the ninteenth century even left-wing radicals shared some of the optical illusions of the imperialists. Marx endorsed European colonialism as a necessary step toward the victory of socialism everywhere. In the *Communist Manifesto* he called the peoples of Asia and Africa "barbarians." Engels in 1848 hailed the conquest of Algeria by the French as "an important and fortunate fact in the progress of civilization." Marx believed that Africa and Asia, even India have "no history at all. . . ."

The non-European East was a "vacant" territory. Arabs were often considered to be mere nomads. Disraeli called them "Jews on horseback." Some Zionists innocently believed that the "nomads" could be entreated, for a generous consideration, to make more room for the newcomers by "folding their tents" and moving fifty or sixty or a hundred miles inland. Such fallacies were soon followed by more intelligent misapprehensions: the natives would prefer the benefits of sound rule to the mere prestige of independent sovereignty; social progress under the Jews would be better for the Arabs than cynical misrule by their own extortionist chieftains.

Herzl was not committed to Palestine. He would have settled for another territory had his East European disciples, many of whom were radical left-wingers, only let him. But when he considered Palestine as a possible area for the realization of his scheme, in his mind's eye he saw an empty land waiting for the redeeming hand of the Jewish settler. He visited Palestine in 1898; in his report on the trip there is not a single word about the Arab population. There must have been over 500,000 Palestinian Arabs at the time.

Even in his extensive private diary Herzl ignored the Arabs. They vanish before his eyes as in their own Arabian nights. And yet at the same time he perceived things elsewhere in the Middle East more clearly than many others. In Cairo he was struck by the blindness of the British to the rising force of native nationalism. Observing a group of restive young Egyptian intellectuals he noted in his diary: "These are the coming masters [of the country]. It is a wonder that the English do not see this. They think they will be dealing with *felahin* forever." It is a wonder that Herzl did not see that the Zionists would not be dealing forever with Palestinian *felahin*, either.

In 1899 the Chief Rabbi of Paris, Zadok Kahn, passed on to Herzl a letter he had received from Yussuf Ziah el-Khaldi, a former mayor of Jerusalem who was now an Arab member of the Ottoman parliament. El-Khaldi was a man of mature judgment, liberal and tolerant. He readily acknowledged "the rights of the Jews for Palestine. My God, historically it certainly is your country." Yet as a "sacred duty of conscience" he admonished Kahn to take into account the "brutal force" of reality. He advised the Zionists to look for another territory. For, whatever the rights of the Jews, Palestine was now inhabited by Arabs. Arab opposition would make Zionism "unrealizable" there. Therefore, "in the name of God, let Palestine be left alone."

Zadok Kahn decided that Herzl should answer el-Khaldi directly. Herzl did so on March 11, 1899. The exchange can be seen as the first, but not the last, futile contact between leaders of the two camps.

Herzl assured el-Khaldi that his concerns were groundless. There should be no difficulty with the non-Jewish population of Palestine. For,

> who wishes to remove them from there? Their well-being and private wealth will increase through the importation of ours. Do you believe that an Arab who owns land in Palestine, or a house worth three or four thousand francs, will be sorry to see their value rise five and tenfold? But this will most certainly happen with the coming of the Jews. If one looks at the matter from this point of view, and it is the correct view, one inevitably becomes a friend of Zionism.

With supreme self-confidence, Herzl went on to say that if the Zionist proposals should not be accepted (by the Turkish Sultan), "we shall search for—and, believe me, we will find—what we need in another place. But then Turkey will lose forever her last chance to improve her finances."

We have here, for the first time ever, an authoritative Zionist leader expounding on the fact of the Palestinian Arabs. Even within the sharply different context of this early period, the innocence of his reasoning is striking in its naivete. Why should the Arab dignitary from Jerusalem care to improve the Sultan's finances? And, at a time, moreover, when educated Arabs were beginning to assert their own cause against their insensitive and corrupt Turkish overlords?

Herzl assumed that the Arabs would trade their own right of national self-determination for a sizable increase in the standard of living. As a native of Austria-Hungary, with all its warring nationalities, he must have known that there was hardly a precedent anywhere for a people to trade what they considered "national rights" for a sizable increase in the value of their houses and lands.

He had an aristocrat's disdain for the feelings of common people. His proposed Jewish state was to be governed liberally, but by a Venetian style *doge*. Of the Near East he wrote: "Everybody in the Orient is frightened of everyone else. The people are like a raging animal, which can be released, but can also be directed and led in any direction." Herzl never for one moment contemplated the use of violence. He was serious when he warned el-Khaldi that the Jews would look for another country if there were objections to their coming. He was sure that it was possible by purely pacific means to

introduce the Jews as a second nation into a country already populated by another. He expected too much; but unless we place ourselves
in Herzl's frame of mind we shall not understand why. He was a
liberal conservative idealist of the nineteenth century. Only the absolutely fantastic, he wrote, is capable of "seizing people"; its "flag" is a
faith in miracles. Ludwig Gumplowicz, a professor of law at the
University of Graz, better known as one of the founders of modern
sociology, warned Herzl that he was pursuing a mirage. He advised
him to return to literature. "You are endowed with a political naivete
such as one can pardon only in poets," Gumplowicz wrote to Herzl in
1899. "You want to found a state without bloodshed? Where have
you ever seen such a thing? Without force or cunning? Just like that,
open and honest—by easy instalments?"

Herzl's answer, of course, was "yes." In his last book, *Altneuland*,
he drew a rosy picture of the future Jewish commonwealth. Herzl
contemplated a New Society *outside* the accepted framework of the
national state. He envisaged an open, scientifically designed society,
based on cooperative forms of association. "We are not a state . . . we
are simply a *Genossenschaft*" (association). The new commonwealth
would naturally be tolerant of all minorities, religions, and races. Its
motto would be: "Man, thou art my brother." *Altneuland* takes the
form of a utopian political novel. A central passage deals with the
Arab population of the new Zion:

Mr. Kingscourt, the ex-Prussian nobleman, tours the new polity
during the election campaign. He challenges Rashid Bey, a leader of
the local Arabs:

> "You are very curious, you Mohammedans! Don't you consider
> these Jews as intruders?"
> "Christian, how strange is your talk?" answered the friendly Rashid.
> "Would you consider him a robber who takes nothing away from you
> but gives you something? The Jews have made us rich. Why should
> we be angry with them?"

So much for literature. In Palestine itself the actual experience of
the settlers at first confirmed Oscar Wilde's aphorism that life tends
to imitate art. Jewish settlement indeed economically benefited the
Arabs. There were as yet no visible signs of Arab nationalism. The
early settlers generalized greatly on the basis of limited encounters

with individual Arabs. "The Arabs are a calm people, submissive and respectful toward Europeans," S. D. Levontin, the founder of Rishon le-Zion, told his mandatories, the Russian Lovers of Zion in his first report to them, dated March 1882. As the German settlers in Palestine had not encountered any difficulties, Levontin observed, there was no reason to believe that the Jews would. Moreover, if the Germans became "masters of Poland by acquiring the best estates in Poland . . . why could not the children of Israel, this wise and reasonable people, purchase fields and estates in Palestine and thus acquire the country?" Levontin was certain that this was absolutely feasible.

The tendency to generalize on the basis of limited encounters lasted for a considerable length of time. In 1908, Yitzchak Ben Zvi, the future President, and his wife Rachel befriended a young Arab carpenter who told them that he wished to emigrate to America. To judge by their memoirs he seems to have been the only local Arab with whom the Ben Zvi's at that time maintained a close personal relationship. Rachel quickly generalized: "*Their* heart is for emigration; *our* heart is for immigration. They do not have behind them a black Diaspora and no past of their own in ancient Palestine."

Arab notables of Jerusalem demanded as early as 1891 that Russian Jews be prohibited entry into the country and prevented from purchasing land. But, at least in a few cases, the same people who protested in public would sell land to the Jews privately, often at exorbitant prices. This quickly fed an assumption which was prevalent anyway, that the protests were merely devices to raise prices even further.

"We are brothers with our neighbors, the Children of Israel, from time immemorial," the arch elders of Sarafand, a village close to Rishon le-Zion, told the first settlers in 1883. "As brothers we shall live with them." Other Arab notables announced publicly that there were hints in the Koran to the effect that the Jews shall return to their land; it was even obligatory for all true believers to aid them in realizing this divine will. When Levontin made his first tour of the country in the spring of 1882 he was offered land for sale everywhere, in Galilee, in the hills of Jerusalem, and around Gaza; even in the Negev Bedouin chieftains offered him vast stretches of desert land for purchase and settlement by Jews.

During almost every period of settlement, much more land was offered for sale than the Jews could afford to buy. In the first two or three decades they could probably have bought up more than half of all land east and west of the River Jordan. They did not have the money; nor were there ever enough pioneers available for settlement.

Following the revolution of the Young Turks in 1908, Arab nationalism for the first time came out into the open. Between 1908 and 1914 Zionist emissaries in Constantinople, Damascus, Cairo, and Beirut received offers of Arab-Zionist collaboration against the common French or Turkish enemy. Such offers were invariably vague; some were blatantly insincere, others, from all we know, were based upon a series of mutual miscomprehensions. Some Arab leaders apparently were sure that it was in the power of the Jews to marshal such vast forces of international public opinion in favor of Arab independence that Ottoman opposition must surely crumble in the wake. In return for such service they hinted at special concessions for Jewish immigrants to Palestine, which they viewed as a part of Greater Syria.*

It was all left very vague. The two sides never revealed to one another their full intentions. They were moving about uneasily like two wrestlers sizing one another up as they shake hands prior to throwing themselves at each other's throat. It is doubtful whether the Arabs fully understood what was at stake. The European-based Zionist leadership, insensitive as most Europeans of the time to the potential force of Arab nationalism, never pursued these contacts to any clear conclusion. They could hardly do otherwise, for they certainly could not afford at this stage to annoy the Turks who were deeply suspicious of Arab nationalism. At the same time, such contacts as took place between Arabs and Jews invariably confirmed the Zionists in their belief that Arab nationalists, who were staking a claim for vast territories in and beyond the Ottoman Empire, could probably be induced to forgo their claims to so tiny a territory as Palestine with its mere half-million or so of non-Jews.

Such faith was strengthened by the periodic reappearance of mysterious Arab emissaries who offered the Zionists fantastic deals. Some of the emissaries were strongly reminiscent of Rashid Bey in Herzl's utopian last novel. In 1919, Naguib Saphir, an Arab notable of Beirut,

---

* A Zionist observer who attended the Congress of Arab Nationalists in Paris in 1913 interviewed Abd el Hamil Zaharoui, President of the Congress. The Jews "are our brethren in race," Zaharoui stated. "We see them as Syrians who have been forced to leave [Syria] but their hearts always beat together with ours."

offered Weizmann a deal: Lebanon for the Christians, Syria for the Moslems, Palestine for the Jews. It was not the last offer of its kind. Some Arab leaders completely overestimated their own power to negotiate on behalf of their aroused brethren. Prince Faisal of Arabia (later King of Iraq) concluded a famous treaty of "collaboration" with Weizmann in 1918. The treaty, "mindful of the racial kinship and ancient bonds between the Arabs and the Jewish people," confirmed "the good understanding" between Faisal and the Zionists. It stipulated the creation of an "Arab state" separate from "Palestine." Faisal agreed that the latter be open to Jewish immigration "on a large scale." The treaty was never put into effect. In later years it was announced that King Faisal had denied "having written anything of that kind with his knowledge."

Thirty-one years after the Faisal-Weizmann agreement, Faisal's younger brother, King Abdullah of Jordan, was ready to negotiate a peace treaty with Israel and was promptly assassinated. Other offers periodically were proffered by various intermediaries; not a few were adventurers, even shady characters, their real influence nil. If this was less evident at the time, still these negotiations tended to reconfirm the Zionists in their faith that it was possible to reach a peaceful accord. Under its aegis all parties would co-exist like so many lambs and sheep.

The pioneers themselves were not engaged in any surreptitious negotiations but were busy tilling the land in remote villages and farms. Absorbed in their work, which was hard, they lived for their dream, which was brilliant and as yet untarnished by bloody conflict. Before they had come from the Diaspora the pioneers had sung:

> There in the marvelous land of the forefathers,
> All our hopes shall be fulfilled.
> There we'll live, and there we'll work,
> A life that is free, a life that is pure.

It was a total experience, shielded from distracting outside effects. The pioneers moved almost exclusively within the circle of their political organization. In the port town of Jaffa there were at the time two Jewish inns, simple establishments where one could get a bed, usually bug-ridden, or a mat in the corner, for a few coins. Each catered almost exclusively to members of one of the two main political groups, *Poale Zion* (the party of Ben Gurion and Ben Zvi), or its opposition, *Ha'poel Ha'tzair*. Disembarking, sympathizers of the first party would head directly for Chaim Baruch's inn; those of the second would put up in Mr. Spektor's competitive establishment. Within a few days, most of the new arrivals moved to one of the colonies or farms, passed on, as it were, from hand to Jewish hand, with little or no contact with the native population.

In time, of course, such contacts took place. Many young newcomers at first tended to see the Arab *felahin* in the almost biblical simplicity of their lives, as direct descendants of the ancient Hebrews. They saw them as kinsmen, forced by Moslem conquerors to adopt their faith, but—so they hoped—lost to Judaism only temporarily through the changing travails of history. Shlomo Lavie, a leading pioneer of the Second *Aliya*, visited in 1906 two Arab villages in the neighborhood of Jerusalem, the Moslem Colonia and the Christian Ein Karem. "It is certain that their inhabitants are descendants of the ancient Jews," he noted. "With the return of the Jews to settle among and around them, they will remember their true but forgotten ancestry and come back to Judaism."

It seems almost certain that the "return" to Judaism was not meant in a religious sense. Nothing was probably further from the minds of the settlers than a mass conversion of the Arabs to the Jewish faith. Most pioneers were anti-religious or indifferent. But there was hope that cooperation was possible on the rediscovered common ethno-national basis. Of all the fantastic ideas prevalent at that time among the colonists it certainly was not the most incredible. The assumption of common ancestry was quite common at the time; apart from pleasantly satisfying the young pioneers' spirit of romanticism, it was also supported by the best available scholarship. The celebrated Colonel Conder of the Palestine Exploration Fund had recently found Aramaic and Hebrew traces in the language of the Arab *felah*. Some 25 percent of all Arab villages in Palestine were still called by their Hebrew or biblical names. If the Arabs were expected to welcome the return of the Jews because of the implied economic, social, and cultural benefits, would they not be even more ready to assimilate with the Jews as kinsmen?

Such notions were indirectly supported by the leading Marxist ideologist of Zionism, Ber Borochov, the teacher of both Ben Zvi and, to a lesser extent, Ben Gurion. His thoughts on the subject are well worth mentioning as the case history of a man who set too much store by his elaborate dogmatism.

A taste for elaboration has always been a part of Jewish psychology; in Borochov it combined with Marxist casuistry to produce an intellectual construction, which, with all its laborious artificiality, exercised a considerable influence in its time. Borochov formulated an ideology, couched in Marxist terms, which tended to confirm and reinforce the prevailing illusion that the presence of Arabs in Palestine in no way hindered the return of the Jews.

Borochov was no romantic. He mocked Ben Zvi for seeking the lost tribes of Jewish Bedouin in the Arabian deserts. Lavie's sentimentality would have left him cold. Borochov believed not in sentiments or historic memories, but in the "inevitability" of objective forces, propelled by material interests and by the class struggle. In his view, the same "inevitable" social forces that made life untenable for the Jews in the Diaspora would push them through an equally "inevitable" process of "proletarization" on new territory. Palestine, he felt, was ideally suited for this purpose. Not so much because it was the Jews' ancient homeland, but rather because it was so poor in resources. Therefore "international capitalism" was not interested in Palestine, but would leave it to the Jews for settlement. The Arabs did not figure in this equation as a political force of any consequence.

What makes Borochov so puzzling to a modern reader is that he, who had fathered the celebrated Zionist synthesis of nationalism and Marxism, considered it unlikely that the Arabs might develop a national movement of their own. For Borochov it was out of the question that the Arabs would seriously object to the coming of the Jews. His doctrinal reasons for this ruling were simple. Since, in his view, the Arabs were devoid of an "economic and cultural character of their own" they could not be a nation; since they were not a nation they were unfit for organized opposition to external influence. In his eyes, the Arabs could not develop a nationalism of their own. This was "inevitable" like almost everything else in Borochov's theories. As long as the new territory was safe from the evil schemes of international capitalism, no harm could come to its Jewish settlers. The Arabs would assimilate and become like Jews.

Living in Russia, he never even visited Palestine. Oblivious to local conditions, ignorant of Arab affairs, books, newspapers, and the language, Borochov disposed of the centralized Ottoman Empire from a distance. He proposed its dismemberment into a large multi-national federation that could include the newly constituted Jewish territory.

Borochov's writings were followed avidly by his Palestinian disciples. He drew up a list of five conditions essential for the success of the proposed Jewish territory. The five conditions fitted Palestine perfectly:

1. The territory must not possess a developed capitalist economy;
2. Its present government must not be in the hands of one of the main (imperialist) powers;
3. It must already have beginnings of a Jewish community "willing to undergo a process of proletarization";
4. It must not be too close to one of the main centers of high capitalism;
5. Psychologically and racially, the native population must bear some resemblance to the Jews so that "under effective management" the natives would easily adapt to the newcomers' "higher spiritual culture."

He admitted that the Ottoman Sultan might not at first welcome the arrival in Palestine of Jewish revolutionary socialists; but those countries that wanted to be rid of their revolutionaries "will break his opposition." As for the present inhabitants of Palestine, "only laymen consider [them] as being Arabs or Turks. In reality they have nothing in common with Arabs or Turks ... they have no reason to meet us immediately with hostility. On the contrary, they think that by right the country belongs to the Jews and they themselves call it *ara iehuna*."* Elsewhere he wrote that "a part of the Galilean population has absorbed Russian culture within a few decades, under the influence of a few dozen Russian missionary schools ... the natives of Palestine will assimilate economically and culturally with those who will establish order in the country and develop its resources."

For those pioneers who gave the "Arab problem" any thought, there often was an understandable temptation to see it through the reassuring optics of Borochov's ideology. The Marxists of *Poale Zion*

---

* It is not clear where Borochov got his information. There is no such Arab expression. Perhaps he meant *ard jahud* (land of the Jews), which is also unknown as a colloquial Arab reference to Palestine.

were naturally attracted by a theoretical construction which fitted their concepts of class struggle and their faith in the inevitable victory of what they called the international proletariat. Although by 1906, Borochov's influence on other issues was already on the wane among his Palestinian disciples, there is little evidence that his theorizing on the Arabs was seriously put in doubt before 1920.

The second labor party, *Ha'poel Ha'tzair*, was non-Marxist. Its members were equally certain that in the long run there was no conflict of interests between the two nations. Leading European socialists of the time assumed that war was becoming improbable because workers of one nation would refuse to shoot at workers of another. There is little surprise that many of the young worker-pioneers in Palestine—less sophisticated, less experienced than the intellectuals of Paris, Brussels, Amsterdam, Vienna, and Berlin—refused to see any real conflict emerging between their own "proletarian enterprise" and the indigenous population, whose peasants and workers were being exploited by a corrupt upper class of feudal landowners, and who, they felt sure, must soon awaken to a sense of solidarity with them. For the pioneers, whether Marxist or not, there was no such thing as an irresolvable problem. If indeed there was an Arab problem, they felt sure that they had found a practical and just solution for it.

Their solution was, naturally, an economic one; it tied in with the mysticism of physical work so prevalent among the pioneers. It was called *Avoda Ivrit* (Hebrew Labor) or the "conquest of labor" by the Jews. After some hesitation, the men and women of *Poale Zion* concurred. The plan in effect aimed at the establishment of a completely separate economic sector for the newcomers. Native labor must not be "exploited" in the reconstruction of the country by the Jews. Jews must do everything themselves. The natives would continue to benefit indirectly from the general improvement and economic upsurge, particularly in trade. But henceforth Jews must try to be self-sufficient and do all the physical work with their own hands, including the most difficult, the least paying, and the most menial. If there was no "exploitation" of Arab labor, Arab laborers could not "objectively" be opposed to the Zionists.

It was realized that such self-sufficiency must raise the human and economic cost of settlement; for this reason most of the earlier "bourgeois" settlers were violently opposed to *Avoda Ivrit*. Public and private funds were severely limited. Some feared that *Avoda Ivrit* might delay further expansion of the Zionist enterprise. But in the eyes of the newly arrived young radicals from Eastern Europe this was a small price to pay for the kind of moral renewal they were striving for. Also, the newcomers needed these jobs desperately for their own daily bread.

Different people agreed to the *Avoda Ivrit* scheme for different reasons. Marxists of *Poale Zion* assumed that since all national enmity had its roots in economic factors, as long as there was no economic exploitation of Arabs by Jews there could not be any lasting nationalist antagonism between the two. It took decades and much bloodshed before some of the pioneers outgrew this faith. We must not judge them more harshly than we judge other Marxists of that time. Together they were looking forward assuredly to the coming abolishment of politics and to the withering away in socialism of all state coercion through the dismantlement of all those authoritarian structures that cause alienation between people.

The men of *Ha'poel Ha'tzair*, non-Marxist but under the powerful spell of Tolstoyanism, concurred in this view and fought even harder for *Avoda Ivrit*. In their eyes a "moral" right to any country could be acquired only through manual work of the kind most Jewish planters were only too eager to leave to illiterate Arab farmhands. They were convinced that if they were taking the unusual step of claiming a country occupied by others, history would exonerate them of all guilt, not only because they had no desire to displace anybody, but above all, because they were evidently *re-earning* their historic birthright through the bitter sweat of their brows.

Those who slave in the sun with their own hands to make a desert bloom could not be considered conquistadores. Only work "creates an inner right for the country," Eliezer Shochat wrote in 1910. Only work "breeds the deep relationship that exists between an artist and his painting; not the superficial legal one that prevails between a purchaser and the painting he has bought." A. D. Gordon held a similar view. What is so puzzling in all this theorizing is that apparently it never occurred to Shochat or to Gordon that by their own definition of "right through labor" the vast majority of Arabs in the country were daily proving their own claim to it.

The policy of *Avoda Ivrit* was never fully implemented until the Arabs themselves, through violence that led to mutual self-segregation, enforced its near-total application during the Arab rebellion of 1936–1939. In retrospect, even its partial application appears as the most critical of all Zionist measures in the pre-Independence period. *Avoda Ivrit* was predicated in part upon a doctrinaire illusion; it was rampant with intellectual inconsistencies. In effect, it created a subculture, free from the demands of the larger society, not parasitic upon it, and above all enjoying that kind of immunity from "reality" —whether Turkish, British, or Arab—that permitted its members to indulge in their dreams.

The policy and practice of *Avoda Ivrit* left an indelible mark upon Israel's national character. Few measures affected as deeply the Israelis' image of themselves in history. By avoiding the typical pattern of colonial settlers elsewhere, the policy of *Avoda Ivrit* bred in their hearts a deeply felt, and totally sincere, sense of moral superiority over other colonialists. If this be a fallacy, it gained ground, again, because there was some truth to it. There was never a sense of "colonial vocation" among the Zionist settlers. There was a cultural arrogance here as elsewhere; but individual motivation was sharply different. Elsewhere, a colonial career frequently meant social and professional advancement. In Palestine the opposite was true. Elsewhere, those who failed to attain bourgeois status at home often found it in the colonies; again, here the opposite happened. The settlers were not looking for individual material benefits but aimed at achieving a collective goal.

A sense of high adventure certainly played a role, more than was admitted at the time. But there was little, if any, of that general ennui as expressed, for example, by the frustrated European in Flaubert's *Sentimental Education* which has been seen as one key to the Frenchman's colonial vocation: "I feel like running off to live among the cannibals."

O. Mannoni, in *Prospero and Caliban*, one of the few detailed studies of colonial psychology, has suggested that colonial settlers from highly competitive societies tended to compensate their European-bred sense of social or personal inferiority by living as white masters among more primitive, native weak. To the spirit conceived in its own inferiority the services and homage of dependents is balm and honey. The humiliations of anti-Semitism were so obviously a prime factor in Zionism that one would have expected widespread and rather ugly compensatory reactions in the behavior of Jewish settlers toward the primitive Arab natives who worked for them. There were such "compensatory reactions," of course, especially during the earliest period, but neither widespread nor for very long. The first settlers in the Rothschild colonies occasionally behaved despotically toward their Arab employees, for which they were invariably berated by visiting Zionist intellectuals from abroad. The arrival of the young socialist radicals of the Second *Aliya* after 1905 precipitated a marked change of atmosphere.

The young pioneers who were now arriving in the country rarely looked down upon the natives. They were competing with Arab *fela-hin* for jobs on the Jewish plantations. As a rule they admired the Arab *felah* because he was so marvelously "rooted" in labor and agriculture, which the pioneers considered sacrosanct. The new pioneer emulated the *felah* by voluntarily renouncing the minimal living standards of a European. Shmuel Dayan, father of the future general, described his work with Arabs on a plantation: "I saw myself surrounded by strange foreign people; they were mocking me in a strange language. I took courage and worked with unestimable drive, without exactly knowing the job. I drank swamp water from a kerosene tin." At the end of the day he felt deliriously happy for having dug a trench as long and as well as most of his Arab co-workers.

Avoda Ivrit is a key, not only to the Israelis' historic self-image but also to much that happened later on. The separate economic sector implied in *Avoda Ivrit* was the beginning of the Zionist state within a state, which by 1933 had already become a major political factor. The inexorable logic of *Avoda Ivrit* led from a deliberate partition of the economy to the indeliberate partition of the country in bloodshed. There is a deep and tragic irony in the fact that the policy of *Avoda Ivrit* was in its time seen as a means to avoid or allay conflict between the two nations. In some ways it made the conflict worse. It might have given Jewish colonists a sense of moral superiority over colonial settlers elsewhere; at the same time it compounded the future tragedy by causing the deliberate exclusion of the natives from the New Society. It prevented the establishment of a joint basis upon which, *perhaps*, in the fullness of time, a bi-national polity, open to all, might have been tried; or perhaps the commonwealth of *Altneuland*, which Herzl had recommended, with the proviso: "If you will it, it is no fairy tale."

After settlement had begun and before World War I there were only a few isolated voices warning the settlers that they might be treading a path more dangerous than appeared through the tinted spectacles of ideology. Achad Ha'am, the writer, in 1891 protested the view that the "Arabs are wild men of the desert, an ignorant people who did not see and do not understand what is going on around them . . . in time, when our people in Palestine shall have developed to such an extent that they will begin more or less to push aside the natives, the latter will not easily give way." This was probably the darkest warning sounded at the time: but Achad Ha'am did not follow it up with any practical conclusions.

The young pioneers after 1905, who adored Achad Ha'am, took his words as another reason for fully implementing the policy of *Avoda Ivrit*. A Palestinian settler, the teacher and writer Yitzchak Epstein, attended the Seventh Zionist Congress of 1905 in Basel. In a lecture to delegates he complained that the "Zionists were completely ignorant" of the Arab problem upon whose correct resolution so much depended. "In its true form there is no trace of it in the literature of the movement." Epstein proposed an "Arab-Jewish alliance"; he made little impact upon the delegates who were harassed by inner splits and squabbles and by a power vacuum left by the recent death of the founder, Theodor Herzl.

When the first anti-Jewish riots broke out in the mixed port city of Jaffa in 1908, Ben Zvi simply equated them with the anti-Semitic outbursts in his native Russia. Incapable of conceiving a possibly different cause, he immediately classified them as "anti-Semitic pogroms." His wife later testified in her memoirs that Ben Zvi was even convinced that the riots had been instigated by the Czarist consul ". . . the consul hinted to the rioters that if his Jewish subjects are attacked, he will not interfere." In 1920, after a particularly bloody outburst of Arab violence, Ben Zvi accused the new British authorities of having indirectly caused, by their hesitation, this "genuine pogrom, reminiscent in all its details" of a "pogrom in Romanol, Russia." He hinted at a similarity between Sir Ronald Storrs, the British Governor of

Jerusalem, and the notorious anti-Semitic Czarist Minister of Interior, Von Plehve.

In 1908 the Young Turks abolished press censorship. Almost immediately a number of Arab nationalist newspapers and magazines began a series of vicious attacks on the Jewish settlers. Attacks came mainly from members of the higher-developed Christian Arab community. A number of Jewish settlers rashly suspected crude anti-Semitic prejudice, implanted in the hearts of Christian Arabs by their co-religionists in Europe. Ben Zvi spoke of the "new anti-Semites" of the East. An editorial in the *Poale Zion* party magazine, *Ha'achdut*, possibly written by Ben Gurion, stated that "the Christian priests and teachers of Nazareth—that international center of Christianity and anti-Semitism —are enticing the people to revolt against the Jews, to take their land, loot their property and to kill them." A century of "Jesuit activity in Syria and Lebanon ... [cannot] of course remain without results. The hatred of Jews comes to Christian Arab natives with their mothers' milk."

In the first stages of their open conflict with the Arab nationalists, Zionists could not tear themselves loose from European stereotypes. Their lumping together of Arab opposition to Jewish settlement with the cruder forms of European anti-Semitism was simplistic. Perhaps it was all too human, but we rarely bother with the reasoning of those whose motivations we think we can so easily explain away.

The first Zionists deeply disturbed about future relations with the Arabs were liberal English Jews, who worked with Weizmann during his negotiations with the British Foreign Office. Harry Sacher, one of Weizmann's close friends and a former editorial writer on the *Guardian*, wrote on June 14, 1917: "Even if all our political schemings turn out in the way we desire, the Arabs will remain our most tremendous problem." This was four and one-half months before the Balfour Declaration was issued. Sacher's forebodings were still as rare in that overly optimistic period as they were ominously prophetic. Sacher was equally afraid not only of what the Arabs might do to the Jews, but what the Jews might do to the Arabs; for he concluded his admonition with a warning against the poisonous effect of Jewish chauvinism. His alarm was not heeded at the time, except, perhaps, by Weizmann.

It took the Palestinian settlers at least three or four more years to realize the severity of their conflict with the Arabs. During the first years of the British Mandate they slowly awoke to what was at stake. Arab opposition to Jewish settlement now took the form of protestations and indiscriminate violence. Beginning in 1919, gangs of armed Arabs periodically attacked the colonies. In the mixed towns of Jerusalem, Hebron, and Jaffa, Arab mobs ran amok and brutally massacred Jewish women, children, and helpless old men. Most Zionist leaders still underestimated the potential gravity of these outbursts; it was not seen at the time that they tended to eliminate whatever slim chances there still were for an adjustment between the two parties. Civil war is rarely a breeding ground for reconciliation among members of the same nationality or religion; it almost never is between two nations claiming the same stretch of land.

In 1921 the German Zionist leader, Georg Landauer, warned the Twelfth Zionist Congress that *all-out war* with the Arabs was inevitable unless the Zionists made urgent efforts to reach an amicable accommodation with the Palestinians. In such a war, he said, the Jews would lose. Vladimir Jabotinsky, the right-wing extremist, retorted by ironically asking whether during the colonization of America or Australia anyone had bothered to beg the natives for permission. But the majority of Zionist leaders dismissed both Landauer's warning and Jabotinsky's retort. Reading the minutes of these long-forgotten discussions, one is amazed to see how many Zionists at that time still felt that it was entirely feasible to satisfy the demands of Zionism without unduly annoying the Arabs.

Unshaken in their rosy optimism, leading Zionists still considered the conflict as being resolvable by political means, by economic improvement, social change, education, maneuvering, patience, and occasional negotiation. The importance of the Balfour Declaration was generally overestimated; there was a natural tendency to view it as a final, binding document. But history is more often made by men than by abstract phrases in highly controversial documents. When the Balfour Declaration was issued, its vague, moderate wording was immediately interpreted by the Arabs in the most extreme possible context. The declaration's key term was: "*a national home* for the Jewish people." The various non-Arabic translations—the French *foyer*, the German *Heimstätte*, the Hebrew *bayit*—had the intimate, not necessarily political, connotation of a cozy corner; according to Harkabi

the first and final Arabic translation was *Watan Qaumi*, a decidedly
political term, not at all cozy, which stands for "national fatherland."

At the time, Zionist leaders did not notice the difference. Ben Zvi
in 1921 was still arguing against the "fantastic and false" impression
that the Arab movement against Zionism had a solid popular basis. He
maintained that the so-called "national" links between *felah* and *effendi* were fictional; wherever they existed they deserved to be dismissed as "socially reactionary." Sir Reginald Wingate, British High
Commissioner of Egypt, met the first delegation of European Zionists
who had come out to Palestine immediately after the Balfour Declaration; he wrote to Lord Harding that they were sensible people, but
entirely unaware of conditions in the Arab countries.

Menachem Ussishkin, a veteran Russian Zionist leader of the old
guard, arrogantly dismissed the Arabs as a "negligible quantity." He
said: "Everywhere in the world there is a Jewish problem. And what
are people doing about it? Here there is an Arab problem. *Ma Yesh
Laasot?* [So what can we do?]"

Others were slowly beginning to see things more clearly. Chief and
foremost among them was Chaim Weizmann. Like most people
Weizmann had overlooked the Arabs prior to 1916. Unlike most
Zionist leaders, Weizmann, between 1916 and 1921, came to know
some of the leading figures in the Arab world. With his great charm
and gift of persuasion he set about relentlessly assuaging Arab fears,
preaching the idea of Arab-Zionist cooperation, and winning to it
Arab friends. He did not lose sight of Arab national aspirations. But
he assumed that the national sentiments of the Arabs would focus on
Baghdad, Mecca, or Damascus; they would find their "natural and
complete satisfaction" in a proposed Arab kingdom centered around
these historic sites. At the time, this was less improbable than it
would be today. After all, Faisal had signed a formal agreement with
Weizmann and had made it contingent upon the establishment of
just such a kingdom. And Kamel Effendi, the Grand Mufti of Jerusalem, had warmly welcomed Weizmann in Jerusalem in 1918, by quoting a *hadith*, a tradition of the Prophet: "Our rights are your rights,
and your duties our duties."

But Faisal's Arab kingdom came to naught; the Near East was
carved up by the powers victorious in the Great War. The British
appointed a new Grand Mufti in Jerusalem, the violent nationalist

Haj Amin el Husseini, the instigator of past and future riots and bloodshed. The growing vehemence of Arab opposition, the riots and massacres, the second thoughts which the British were having with regard to the viability of "a national home," caused Weizmann to re-examine his original position. In the early 1920s he came to see the Arab problem in a new light.

Weizmann's original aim in securing the Balfour Declaration had been that Palestine should ultimately be as Jewish as England was English. He now began to look for new, interim formulas short of a Jewish state, which he realized was unacceptable to the Arabs. "In Palestine there is a people which resists our coming," he told an American Jewish gathering, which was prone to overlook this fact, in 1923. With this people, "we must arrange ourselves in a serious way." But how?

If Weizmann had any clear ideas on how such an accommodation could be brought about, he did not spell them out. Perhaps he was thinking of a bi-national state. Perhaps he wanted to assuage Arab fears by limiting Jewish immigration to a mutually agreed formula, in the hope that Jewish growth and expansion in Palestine would henceforth be a process so slow as to be almost inconspicuous. But if this might still have been acceptable to the Arabs at the time, the rise of Nazism in Europe would in a few years make any restriction as totally unacceptable to his fellow Jews as bi-nationalism was to the Arabs. In 1931 Weizmann openly opposed the idea of proclaiming a Jewish state as the aim of Zionism. In that same year at the Seventeenth Zionist Congress, meeting in Basel, Weizmann found himself in a minority "with only Ben Gurion's* laborites and a few of the general Zionists understanding me." He resigned as President of the World Zionist Organization, ostensibly for health reasons, and was not re-elected until four years later, when the situation had already changed beyond recognition.

It was the supreme tragedy of Weizmann's leadership that his own people, aroused by Arab violence and by the storm clouds gathering over European Jewry, never permitted him to fully explore avenues of possible compromise. Perhaps there were none; we shall never know.

* At the Zionist Congress of 1925 Ben Gurion had voiced a passionate plea that the Zionists seek agreement with the Arabs. Whereupon he was attacked by Jabotinsky's right-wingers as a doctrinaire socialist and deracinated cosmopolitan.

By 1935 the rescue of refugees already figured more prominently than the need for finding a compromise with the Arabs. For the refugees, as Weizmann told a British inquiry commission, the world was divided into two: countries where they could not stay and countries which would not permit them entry. With an uncanny premonition he spoke of "six millions" who were ready to go. If allowing Jews into Palestine was an injustice to Arabs, not allowing them in was an even greater injustice to Jews. If two rights were clashing in Palestine, Weizmann said, surely the satisfaction of Jewish rights involved a smaller measure of suffering and injustice.

The early innocence of Zionism came to an end with the rise of Hitler in Germany. Few men reflected this change as clearly and sharply as Arthur Ruppin. We met him earlier in this story. A native of Germany, he settled in Palestine in 1907 and ran the first Zionist office in Jaffa. He was instrumental in the founding of the *Kvutza*, the forerunner of the *kibbutz*. After World War I Ruppin played a leading role in Palestinian and Zionist affairs. He headed the main office of colonization—as a kind of "minister" of agriculture and development in the increasingly autonomous Jewish state within a state.

Ruppin was a true representative of humanist Zionism. He had not come to Palestine to assist in the creation of just another nation-state. A rationalist, he shared none of the bizarre metaphysics of Ben Gurion and his fellow Marxists-turned-nationalists. But as a man of action ("for the Jews of Europe Zionism is religion; for me it is deed") and seeing himself in the early 1930s increasingly surrounded by a world of brutal realities, he could not retrace his steps except at the price of abandoning his life's work—settlement, reconstruction, and rescue. To follow his thinking as it developed over the years we have the benefit of his private diaries. He went through four distinct stages.

At first, like most of his colleagues, he overlooked the national aspirations of the Arabs. He assumed that they could be appeased through economic benefits. But earlier than most he realized the short-sightedness of this approach. By 1921 he was already bitterly reproaching his fellow settlers for wrongly aiming at the establishment of a nation-state ("another Montenegro") while at the same time ignoring the existence of an Arab problem. The Balfour Declaration, he felt, was a paper privilege. "Without a better understanding with the Arabs we shall face such tremendous difficulties as will be almost unsurmountable," he noted on January 21, 1921. But "our Arab policy is less than non-existent." What could such a policy be?

It would be necessary to transcend the more vulgar notions of nationalism that were still rampant in Europe despite the horrible lessons of the last war. Ruppin turned against what he called "political Zionism." "A Jewish state of one million or even a few million (after fifty years!) will be nothing but a new Montenegro or Lithuania. There are enough states in the world," he noted on April 29, 1923. The Jews must merge with their blood-brothers, the Arabs and the Armenians. They must build a new "civilized community" of free men to raise the level of human culture throughout the Near East. Therein he saw the only possible "justification" for Zionism. In a characteristic entry a few months later he stated that he would have to quit his work for the Zionist movement unless it redefined its antiquated aims. "Herzl's concept of a Jewish state was possible only because he ignored the presence of the Arabs. He believed he could make *Weltgeschichte* through the diplomatic methods of the Quai d'Orsay. Zionism has not yet discarded this diplomatic and imperialist approach."

The Zionists were in no mood to endorse Ruppin's view. Nor was the Arab reaction—it became more hostile and more violent every day —likely to encourage Ruppin's hope for a new supra-national "civilized community" of Arabs and Jews based upon common racial and linguistic links. Ruppin quit his post as head of the department of colonization, and joining the faculty of the newly founded Hebrew University in Jerusalem, devoted most of his time to the study of contemporary Jewry.

But within a year or two Ruppin reappraised his dream. In this third stage we see him advocating a bi-national state in Palestine. Jews and Arabs should maintain their separate nationalities. A bi-national constitution would guarantee that neither nation dominate the other whatever might be the numerical proportion between the two. To propagate his plan, Ruppin founded in 1926 the society of *Brit Shalom* (Covenant of Peace). He was joined by leading Jewish intellectuals and men of the Hebrew University. Weizmann wrote that his own views were close to those of *Brit Shalom* but that it would take a long period of education "before the Zionists settle down to realities."

In July 1929 Ruppin told the Sixteenth Zionist Congress in Zurich: "We wish to free ourselves of the error which has reigned in Europe for a century, and which has brought about the World War; that in one state only one nation can reign. . . . We wish to overcome in ourselves the chauvinism we despise in others."

The bi-national state was rejected by most Jews as it was by practically all Arabs. *Brit Shalom* never secured the collaboration of a single influential Arab. In December 1931 Ruppin was beginning to doubt his own scheme. "What we can get from the Arabs (the status of a suffered minority as in Eastern Europe) we do not need; what we need (political equality, right of immigration) we cannot get. . . . Although I always recognized the importance of solving the Arab question I never expected Arab power to mount so quickly, or such bitter hostility between them and the Jews." But when Jewish extremists rudely broke up a lecture ("Jerusalem, City of Peace") given at the Hebrew University by Professor Norman Bentwich, one of his colleagues in *Brit Shalom*, Ruppin confided to his diary: "It seems that the whole world is mentally sick, much more so, we Jews. People who have spent their youth in the war and in its aftermath must be handled like the insane." Ruppin's diary at this stage reflects the vacillations of this remarkable man between ethical considerations for Arab rights and a commitment to work for the reconstruction of persecuted Jewry in Palestine. It will hardly come as a surprise to those familiar with the future course of events that he never succeeded in squaring the circle.

The fourth stage in his thinking coincides with the rising tide of fascism in Europe, the collapse of civilization in Nazi Germany, the civil war in Spain, and new outbursts of Arab violence in Palestine, the greatest and bloodiest so far. Rescue was of prime importance now and Ruppin was at the center of Zionist efforts to save what could be saved, he was in charge of absorbing immigrants from Germany and Central Europe. At the moment, he feared, there was nothing that could induce the Arabs to cooperate, not economic benefits nor political guarantees. Ruppin resigned from *Brit Shalom*. He began to believe in blind forces. Ruppin who before could not square his circle now closed it. He who had long reproached his colleagues for ignoring the Arabs, now dismissed negotiations with the Arabs as useless. He came to believe that only the weight of irrevocable facts could lead to a lessening of tension. Such facts were more Jews with more power.

In April 1936 a savage Arab attack on Jewish residents and passers-by in Jaffa resulted in the death of sixteen Jews and three Arabs. It was the beginning of the Arab rebellions of 1936–1939, which were in part supported by the Axis powers. "I find myself these days in a state of supreme calm and cool-headedness," Ruppin noted a week later.

> I have developed a theory for myself. It is in the nature of things that Arab opposition from time to time must find an outlet in such outbursts. We are doomed to live in a state of permanent belligerency with the Arabs and there is no way to avoid bloody sacrifices. This may not be a desirable state of affairs. But such is reality. If we wish to continue our work in Palestine against the wishes of the Arabs we will have to take such sacrifices into account.

Ruppin had come a long way. Fifteen years earlier he had threatened to resign his office if the Zionist settlers pursued a "policy of force." But times had drastically changed. In Europe the lights were once more going out. In December 1937 he was a guest at Government House in Jerusalem, dining with Sir Arthur Wauchope, the British High Commissioner. After dinner the two men, closeted in Sir Arthur's study and facing the magnificent view of nocturnal Jerusalem unfolding below, sadly agreed that "the ideals of the nineteenth century were no longer valid."

For others, too, the circle now closed, never to reopen again. Such exchanges as were still taking place, however rarely, between leaders of Palestinian Jews and Palestinian Arabs, were dialogues of the mute and the deaf. They set a pattern, which, in its utter hopelessness, would hardly change in the course of the next thirty-five years at least. Ben Gurion's brief rounds of negotiations with Arab leaders in 1936 are a case in point. As he put it in later years, there were two kinds of Arab leaders in Palestine: "those who could, and those who could not be bought." Early in his administration of Jewish affairs in Palestine* he resolved not to have any dealings with the first, but to negotiate with proud, incorruptible Arab nationalists only. By the same token he announced that the only Jews who were fit to negotiate with Arabs were those who (1) considered "maximalist Zionism" an absolute

---

* Ben Gurion's labor party had secured a majority in 1933; he was now Chairman of the Jewish Agency for Palestine.

minimum for Jewry and who (2) respected Arab nationalism and were capable of seeing things through Arab eyes. It is puzzling that Ben Gurion imagined that one mortal could combine two such qualities at the same time. Like most new administrators Ben Gurion must have hoped that by the sheer weight of his personality he could succeed where others before him had failed. Dr. Yeuda Leib Magnes, who led *Brit Shalom* after Ruppin's resignation, brought the two sides together.

A series of meetings took place. Ben Gurion negotiated with, among others, Mussa Alami, a moderate Arab nationalist; later he met with George Antonius, the historian and leading theoretician of Arabism in his time. There were language problems and it was rough going from the start. Ben Gurion, who had taken great pains to study Turkish and English, and later even learned Greek and Sanskrit, could speak no Arabic. The Arabs knew no Hebrew, so the talks were conducted in English. Ben Gurion told Alami that the Jews would come and settle in Palestine whether there was agreement or not, but that he would prefer agreement. He proposed a Jewish autonomy within a larger federation of independent Arab states. In return for their acquiescence Ben Gurion offered large-scale economic assistance to the Arabs of Palestine. Mussa Alami, according to Ben Gurion, bluntly dismissed such aid as unacceptable. "I prefer the country to remain desolate for another one hundred years until we Arabs are capable of developing it ourselves." (Remembering this talk many years after, Ben Gurion claimed that already then he had felt in his own heart that "if I were an Arab I would say the same.")

A last attempt with Antonius took place in April 1936, on the eve of the Arab rebellion. Antonius said he understood the arguments of the Zionists; yet the Arabs had no alternative but to oppose the "flooding" of the country by the Jews, as this would undermine the Arab position in Palestine. There was no possibility of reconciling Arab and Jewish claims, said Antonius.

Ben Gurion objected; the contradiction was not that inevitable, he said. Arab culture could develop and Arab independence was still possible elsewhere in the vast Arab world, even if Palestine became "predominantly" Jewish.

It is not by caprice that we return to this country. For us it is a question of existence, of life and death. We have come here and shall come here whether there will or will not be Arab-Jewish understanding. Riots will not stop us. If we have the choice between riots in Germany, Poland or in any other country, and riots in Palestine, we prefer riots in Palestine. Still, I ask what is better for both our sides— to fight or to help one another?

A Jewish autonomous area within the Arab federation, Ben Gurion suggested, would render large-scale assistance to its neighbors. Antonius, with some reluctance, agreed to explore this thought. It is not clear from the record whether he agreed to a *politically* autonomous Jewish area in Palestine; he was mostly thinking of a small Jewish canton along the coastal plain. He insisted that even here there must be a limit to Jewish immigration. This was passionately rejected by Ben Gurion. Jewish immigration could not be limited beforehand, he said. Its dimensions were beyond the control of the Zionists and depended largely upon the extent of suffering and persecution. He was ready to accept only one limitation—a limitation of the territory open to Jewish settlement. According to Ben Gurion, the following exchange now took place:

"What is the territory?" Antonius asked.

"The territory is *Eretz Israel*," I answered.

"What are the borders of *Eretz Israel*?" Antonius asked.

"The borders of *Eretz Israel* are known from history," I answered.

"Borders are artificial things," Antonius remarked. "They are here today and there tomorrow. . . ." He asked again what the territory was.

I answered: "It is the country between the Mediterranean in the west, and the desert in the east, between Sinai in the south and the source of the Jordan in the north."

"You are including Transjordan?" Antonius asked with more surprise.

"Of course," I answered. "Is the Jordan river the border of *Eretz Israel*? It is an *Eretz Israeli* river. . . ."

"Well," said Antonius, "you suggest that what England has not granted you, you will get from us? This is an Arab country and we have a right to full sovereignty."

"In Syria, yes," I said. "In *Eretz Israel* we have been before you. We return to our own country."

An historical discussion ensued.

Ben Gurion published this conversation himself more than thirty years later without any comment. He never explained how he could ever have hoped to reach agreement on such a basis. His flights of rhetoric must not be taken too literally except as an indication of his fierce temperament, and, perhaps, of his inadequacy as a diplomat. In Zionist politics, maximalist rhetorics often served as thin cover for concrete policies infinitely more moderate. In the internal debates among the Zionists, Ben Gurion remained a moderate. If at this stage the Jews had been offered a tiny independent state (comprising the coastal plain and parts of Galilee—smaller even than Antonius's canton), Ben Gurion would have agreed, though reluctantly.

In supporting partition Ben Gurion may have secretly harbored vague hopes for future expansion after the establishment of a firm power base in one part of the country. This suspicion was always uppermost in Arab minds. However, in 1949 Ben Gurion rejected all offers of expansion and declared himself fully content with a state of Israel in only one part of the country. After the 1967 war, he was ready to hand back the occupied areas in return for a peace treaty. But in 1937, perhaps because too small a part of Palestine was offered the Jews, Ben Gurion seemed to have been of a different mind. He hinted as much in a speech in Zurich. A Jewish state, he said, was being offered in a small part of Palestine. Such a state will not "solve the Jewish question." Nevertheless, he was in favor of accepting it. For it was likely "to be a decisive stage *on the road toward the realization of Great Zionism* [Ben Gurion's italics]. It will establish within the shortest time the real Jewish force which will lead us to our historic destination."

The growing estrangement between Ben Gurion and Weizmann can be seen in a comparison of the two men's reason for supporting partition at that time. "I know," Weizmann said with characteristic irony, "that God promised all of Palestine to the children of Israel. But I do not know what borders He set. I believe that they were wider than the ones proposed. If God will keep His promise to His people in His own time, our business as poor humans who live in a difficult age is to save as much as we can of the remnants of [the people of] Israel. By adopting this project we can save more (Jews), etc. etc."

The sins of the Zionists, as J. L. Talmon has written, call for censure, but also for compassion. They were committed in an apocalyptic atmosphere by bewildered men and on the eve of the greatest disaster that any group in modern history has experienced. In the late

1930s, of course, no one could envisage the very worst that finally came to pass, in the gas chambers and crematoria of Auschwitz and Maidanek. But even short of such premonition, what was feared or felt at the time was bad enough, powerful enough to arouse the awareness of a desperate race with time. It imbued the Zionist settlers with the relentless drive of drowning men who force their way on to a life raft large enough to hold both them and those who are already on it. If they were deaf to the legal protestations of the latter, it was not only because they considered the raft as a birthright, not only because they knew that the raft could hold more people than it did, but because they were swept in a storm so ferocious that conventional legality inevitably appeared in their eyes as a travesty and mockery of higher justice.

Friends and enemies of Israel alike frequently overstress the element of premeditation which led to the Zionist state; there is still too little regard for the emotional component of the movement to war between the Arabs and the Jews.

If before 1936 even Ben Gurion had thought that not enough was being done to arrive at a working agreement with the Arabs, in later years he became convinced that there was nothing at all to do. The conflict could not be resolved; perhaps it would eventually be forgotten. Now he would often say that he "understood" the Arabs, their wound was too deep; or even that were he an Arab he would be as opposed as they were to the coming of the Jews. The older Ben Gurion, as though overcompensating for an earlier lack of empathy and for the oversights of his own enthusiastic youth, went to the other extreme. Under the impact of disappointment he grew wiser and perhaps more cynical.

Many others did not. A typical incident occurred during one of the first skirmishes of the Arab-Israeli war of 1948. Manya Shochat, a prominent pioneer woman of the Second *Aliya*, then in her late sixties, found herself accidentally trapped in an Arab-held quarter of Jerusalem. She was seized in the street by Arab irregular fighters, who took her to their chief for trial and possible execution.

Manya Shochat was a truly unusual woman, a figure of extreme complexity who might have come out of a nineteenth-century Russian novel. In her life's story we find a full enactment—rare in one person—of the main qualities, some of them contradictory, which played such a prominent role in the history of Zionism. She was incredibly tough and unbelievably charitable; sentimental and fearless; a fanatic Zionist and a fanatic socialist; a co-founder of *Ha'shomer* (an armed organization of settlers whose motto was: "In blood and fire Judea fell; in blood and fire she shall rise again!"), and at the same time a leading member of the left-wing anti-nationalist League for Arab-Jewish Understanding. She was fully convinced that Arab acquiescence to Zionism could be achieved through the raising of Arab standards of living; and yet on lecture tours abroad on behalf of *Poale Zion* and her *kibbutz*, she passionately admonished the wealthier Jews of America that high living standards were meaningless, only national dignity counted. Already before her arrival in the country, in January 1904, she had achieved some notoriety in Russian revolutionary circles by running arms for the anarchists and participating in clandestine plots and agitation. Once, as a twenty-year-old anarchist in Russia, she shot a Czarist spy to death, dismembered his corpse, placed the pieces in a suitcase, and sent it off by rail to a nonexistent address in Siberia.

She was an outstanding example of the overlapping of Zionism and Russian revolutionism. Her conversion to Zionism was almost an accident. Her worried family invented a sick brother in Palestine and in 1904 induced the twenty-five-year-old firebrand to pay him a short visit. Dismayed at discovering the ruse upon her arrival, she was nevertheless induced to remain in Palestine. She played a prominent role in the early pioneer society. A veteran of one of the first *kibbutzim* and "Labor Brigades," she became a central figure in *Histadrut* and a leader of the *kibbutz* movement. Few had done more in a lifetime to make Zionist settlement in Palestine a success; none had exerted himself more. She was one of the Founding Mothers par excellence, the *La Pasionaria* of Zionism who saw herself a Florence Nightingale.

Seized by the Arabs she was blindfolded and led to an Arab military headquarters. There she stood, unknown to her captors, an old lady of sixty-nine, of small stature, dressed in a long black Russian-style *Sarafan* dress, a short-cut bob, with blazing eyes and chin thrust forward, facing a fierce-looking Arab guerrilla in a time of total war.

"We will kill you," the Arab commander said.

"Kill me? But why?" she asked.

"Don't you know that we kill Jews?"

"You won't kill me!" Manya Shochat said.

"Why not?" asked the Arab.

"Because," she said, "I haven't done anything to you."

It was a perfectly innocent reply and even perfectly reasonable if seen through Manya Shochat's eyes. Unafraid, strong in her ignorance, courageous in her innocence, she echoed almost an entire generation.

In the end the Arabs let the little old lady walk back to the Jewish lines. "Go and tell the Jews how strong we are, and that they are lost."

PART TWO

Sons

8

AN OPEN WOUND

They had to forge themselves an art of
living in times of catastrophe in order to
be reborn, and then fight openly against the
death instinct at work in our history.

—ALBERT CAMUS

Nobel Prize acceptance speech, 1957

Lord you saved me from Ur-Germany as I
 fled
Mother's and father's threshold, and arrived
 whole
In body but with my soul torn, within it the
 lake-of-weeping
Now I live on in my mourning.

—URI ZVI GREENBERG

South of Ashkelon, alongside the Mediterranean Sea, the narrow
coastal road winds through enclosed orange groves and open cotton
fields toward the town of Gaza and the old Egyptian frontier. There
are vineyards and banana plantations; the open fields are dotted by
beehives and plastic-covered hothouses. Scattered along the narrow
road, shaded by fast-growing eucalyptus trees, sycamores, mulberries,
and bohinias, are two dozen or so new villages and *kibbutzim*. A few
of the *kibbutzim* date back to 1943, the time of the British mandate;
the rest are more recent. Most were established after Independence
(1948), at the beginning of mass immigration (1949–1956).

Some of the villages are now settled by a majority of Jewish refugees from the Arab countries. Others are settled by Eastern European survivors of the Nazi holocaust, still others by second-generation Israelis, youngsters from older towns and settlements in the north. A number of canning factories have sprung up in the area and produce jams and fruit juices from the local crops. Some settlements have built themselves processing plants for vegetables and cotton, theaters for live performances, regional schools, and sport centers. Everywhere there are huge cowsheds and chicken farms, orchards and vegetable beds. The area, which prior to 1948 had been only partly suitable for farming and then only on exhausted grayish-brown loams and scarcely fertile dusty steppes, is now largely under artificial irrigation. Part of the water is pumped up from artificial wells; part flows down to this southern region from the north, through the pipes and open channels of the Jordan River Project, completed in 1963.

Few Israeli landscapes reflect the changes of the past quarter-century as visibly and dramatically as this coastal strip. Ashkelon is a new city of gleaming white houses; two-thirds of its population are immigrants from Morocco, Tunisia, and Iraq. Founded in 1953, the new town stands on what had been a barren sand dune littered with occasional tufts of shrub or a scattering of archeological remains. In antiquity Ashkelon had been one of the five strongholds of the Philistines; successively Greek, Roman, Byzantine, Arab, and Crusader, it was destroyed and abandoned in 1270.

Further south along the coastal road, a few hundred yards in front of the old Egyptian-Israeli border at the Gaza strip, the traveler will notice a ruined water tower tipped over on its side, surrounded by luxuriant gardens, with benches under flowering oleander trees next to a little artificial pool. The pastoral scene is dominated by the ruined tower, a gray mass of broken, dirty concrete, its rusty steel beams protruding. A remnant of the first Egyptian-Israeli war of 1948, it is riddled by cannon shells. Nearby the giant bronze statue of a man rises above the treetops, a rough-cut figure in shirtsleeves and baggy pants. The right hand clutches what looks like a hand grenade; the head is slightly turned and looks over the left shoulder out to the sand dunes and the sea beyond. It is not the best statuary. Like most heroic poses it does not appeal to all tastes but its meaning goes beyond such argument. The bronze statue represents Mordechai Anilevicz, the twenty-two-year-old commander of the desperate Warsaw Ghetto uprising of 1943.

The nearby *kibbutz* is named after the dead hero: Yad Mordechai. Its little houses, clustered around a pleasant communal dining room, are set in a wide expanse of tree-shaded lawn. Yad Mordechai was founded in 1943 by one of the last groups of Zionist pioneers which managed to escape Poland on the eve of World War II. They belonged to the ultra left-wing Zionist youth movement *Ha'shomer Ha'tzair*. Anilevicz had also belonged to this movement but was unable to get out of Poland in time. In 1946–1947 the men and women of Yad Mordechai were joined by survivors of the holocaust who had made their way to Palestine as illegal immigrants aboard the ramshackle and overcrowded little boats that ran the British blockade.

Yad Mordechai, with all its pleasant exterior of pastoral calm, is overburdened with heavy memories. It commemorates Mordechai Anilevicz and the Warsaw Ghetto uprising of 1943. Yad Mordechai also played a crucial role in the War of Independence. The combination of both produces an essential key to an understanding of the modern Israeli temper.

In November 1947 the United Nations General Assembly decided to partition Palestine into an Arab and a Jewish state. The basic premise underlying the decision was that two intense nationalisms had clashed over Palestine. Both possessed validity and yet were totally irreconcilable. Regardless of the historical origins of the conflict, the rights and wrongs of the promises and counter-promises, the basic fact was the presence in the country of 650,000 Jews and 1,220,000 Arabs.

If left to themselves, a modus vivendi might have developed between the two sides. There still might have been clashes between the two states of partitioned Palestine; yet they might have at least worked out a bearable "solution." In the beginning, hatred and suspicion would have overshadowed everything. But gradually, the two sides may have evolved a kind of grudging co-existence.

The crucial point is that they were not left alone. On May 15, the day British rule formally came to an end (it had collapsed months earlier), the regular armies of five neighboring Arab states invaded Palestine. We now know that they expected a military walkover, an easy mopping-up operation that would last a few days only. We also know, at least in the case of Egypt and Syria, that their chief aim was not to safeguard the rights of Palestinian Arabs, but to carve out for themselves sizable chunks of territory in a country suddenly abandoned by British power. The Jews of Palestine stood in their way. Employing a style of genocidal rhetoric that would become more and more common in the years ahead, the Egyptian statesman and secretary general of the Arab League, Azzam Pasha, threatened the Jews of Palestine with a bloodbath in the manner of Genghis Khan and Tamerlane.

The invading Egyptian force comprised a number of infantry brigades, roughly totaling 10,000 men. Their infantry was supported by a small air force, heavy artillery, tank and armored units. The fledgling Jewish state, barely a few days old, was as yet unequipped with anything but the most primitive weapons.* Israel was hardly prepared to meet an invasion which some Jewish leaders had considered unlikely until a few days earlier. The Egyptians, relying upon their vast superiority in manpower and equipment, hoped—not without reason—to reach Tel Aviv within a few days.

Yad Mordechai, at the Gaza end of the main highway to Tel Aviv, was one of the first Jewish settlements to bear the full brunt of Egyptian attack. Like all Jewish settlements in the northern Negev (there were twenty-two at the time) Yad Mordechai had prepared some fortifications: a barbed-wire fence, trenches, a few dug-in concrete positions. These were not designed to withstand an attack by regular forces supported by tanks and artillery; nor had Yad Mordechai seriously contemplated such an attack. Only a few weeks before the war the men of Yad Mordechai had been told by an emissary from Tel Aviv that Egypt was not planning an invasion. "You will have to hold out only against bands of Arab irregulars and armed villagers from the immediate neighborhood."

Even at this late stage, as in the preceding sixty-six years of colonization, the Jews, in their incurable myopia, were still underestimating their adversary. But even had they suddenly broken the pattern set throughout six decades, there was little they could now do about it.

---

* The total strength of the invading Arab armies has been estimated at 23,500 men. They were amply equipped with British and French-made tanks, airplanes, heavy artillery, spare parts, and ammunition. Their four-pronged invasion was uncoordinated but simultaneous. The Israelis at this stage had some 3,000 "regulars" under arms and 14,000 inadequately-trained recruits; only 10,000 rifles with 50 rounds of ammunition each, no tanks, four ancient cannons smuggled in from Mexico, 3,600 submachine guns.

When, contrary to expectations, the Egyptian column advanced toward Tel Aviv, Yad Mordechai became the scene of battle. It was neither the longest nor even the bloodiest battle in that short and awful war. Yet it was in all likelihood one of the most decisive.

There were barely over a hundred men at Yad Mordechai, including boys of fourteen years; only about seventy-five or eighty men and boys were capable fighters. Armed only with rifles, some of them antiquated, 3,000 rounds of ammunition, 400 hand grenades, two machine guns, two two-inch mortars with 50 shells, the defenders of Yad Mordechai effectively blocked the advance of a whole Egyptian brigade for a full six days.* The water tower was blown up on the second day. Teen-agers with homemade Molotov bottles threw themselves upon Egyptian tanks and armored vehicles. The settlement was surrounded and under constant artillery fire and it was repeatedly bombed from the air. Twenty-four men—nearly one-third of the active defending force—were killed; another thirty were wounded. On May 22, the fourth day of Egyptian attack, Yad Mordechai signaled to the north, "The men's morale is sinking . . . . They approach exhaustion . . . the settlement must be reinforced or abandoned . . . . It is vital that women and wounded be evacuated immediately."

On May 23, the last machine gun had become unserviceable. Late that night the men of Yad Mordechai decided to abandon their burning settlement. Even as they crawled out of their bunkers choking from the nauseating stench of unburied corpses, and even though morale was abysmally low, they argued among themselves over the decision to retreat. Some of them passionately demanded to emulate the Warsaw Ghetto uprising and fight the battle until the last man had died. Fortunately the dissenters were overruled. The survivors managed to infiltrate through the Egyptian lines and reached the neighboring settlement of Gvar Am, a few miles north.

Yad Mordechai was lost. Nevertheless the battle had a profound military and political effect. During the six days that it lasted, Jewish units farther north were able to improvise a rudimentary line of defense. Although this line was intermittently broken by the advancing Egyptians, and although bitter fighting continued for sixteen more

---

* One of the Egyptian commanding officers at Yad Mordechai, Colonel Mohammed Naguib, later headed the 1952 coup d'état that brought a fellow officer, Gamal Abdel Nasser, another veteran of the abortive Palestinian campaign, to power.

days until the United Nations-imposed cease-fire went into effect on June 11, it had become clear that the Egyptians had failed to attain their major objective. They were deep into Palestinian territory, but their advance on Tel Aviv had been arrested; first briefly at Yad Mordechai, next, more permanently, a few miles north of the *kibbutz*, at Negba. The new state had not been destroyed.

When hostilities were resumed a few months later, the tables turned. Yad Mordechai was recaptured and rebuilt nearly from scratch in 1949; only the shattered water tower was left as a reminder. The Egyptians were pushed back to the Gaza strip and to their own frontier, and remained there until 1967.

Writing of Yad Mordechai fifteen years after the battle, Chaim Laskov, a former Israeli general and chief of staff, quoted an anonymous English poet:

> The race is not to him that's got
> the longest legs to run,
> Nor the battle to those people
> That shoot the longest gun.

Today Yad Mordechai is a thriving little community of some 300 adults and 200 children. The commune has an annual turnover of close to four million pounds. Its hothouses produce roses that are exported by air to Europe. The beehives produce up to forty tons of honey each year. Agriculture—citrus groves, dairy farming, cotton, and barley—is fully mechanized, and augmented by a canning plant which manufactures jams and juices. As in all Israeli *kibbutzim*, the austere life of earlier days has given way to a measure of comfort. Some of the bare cement houses, which the Egyptians had destroyed, were at first repaired in order to accommodate the returnees; they have since been replaced by pleasantly built cottages with two-room maisonettes, private kitchens and bathrooms for each family. There is a library of twenty-four thousand volumes.

The land under cultivation today is almost three times that which Yad Mordechai possessed before 1948. Like all the older *kibbutzim* that were established before Independence, Yad Mordechai has inherited the land abandoned in 1948 by inhabitants of the neighboring Arab villages, Deir Suneid, Beth Girga, and Hirbiya. The *kibbutzniks* had been on quite friendly terms with the Arab villagers before the intrusion of war. The villagers' land is now leased to Yad Mordechai by the custodian of abandoned Arab property. The Gaza strip, to where most of the Arab villagers fled, is only a few hundred yards away. From the rooftops of their *kibbutz*, the men and women of Yad Mordechai can see the dismal refugee camps within the strip where most of the villagers and their descendants have lived since 1948. The villagers can clearly watch the men of the *kibbutz* tilling the soil to which they themselves cannot return. The confrontation across a narrow stretch of sand dune is embarrassing; but, because of what they have gone through, it is inevitably less so for the men and women of Yad Mordechai than it would perhaps be for the more detached outsider.

Let us observe the solitary *kibbutznik* of Yad Mordechai from the vantage point of the narrow sand dune which divides him from the former co-occupants of the territory. The view is disturbing, suggesting the massive arbitrariness and the unbridgeable contradictions in the human condition. It reveals the crushing force of circumstance; the despairing frailty of intent. The *kibbutznik* of Yad Mordechai was swept to these shores by the storms and disasters of Europe. The Arab villager was hopelessly, and as tragically, crushed by forces far beyond his control. When Weizmann told the Council of Ten at the Paris Peace Conference of 1919 that Palestine should be as Jewish as England is English, he added that the Zionists would not go into Palestine "like Prussian Junkers"; nor would they drive out other people. Weizmann was utterly sincere; at least until 1947 when they were attacked, the Zionists too lived up to Weizmann's solemn promise.

The *kibbutznik* of Yad Mordechai originally bought land for himself and settled on it. He had no intention to push out his neighbor. He, too, was moved by circumstance not of his own making. The detached outsider might accuse him today of callousness. Such an accusation would ignore the true sequence of events—the Arabs' invasion of 1948, their refusal to make peace, the indefinite prolongation of the war. In every war, superb idealism touches total selfishness. The accusation of selfishness would be just if events always took place on a *tabula rasa*. But there is never a totally new page. History is always inscribed on the old, as on a palimpsest. The conflict was political and psychological, not economic. The allegation would be just were history to evolve as an intelligent debate between happy, secure, relaxed, and enlightened men, without the passions and panics that are always blind, but sometimes also justified, and as often respectable as they are sordid. The happy and secure never went overseas to start a new life.

The men and women at Yad Mordechai who give this subject any serious thought can best be described as living in a mood of deep and tragic fatalism. It is the fatalism of individuals caught in a situation where, morally speaking, no alternative was entirely satisfactory. None could have lead to a full resolution of their moral quandary, but, then, none ever does in real life. The claims of justice by far exceed the abilities of men to satisfy them.

But even the detached observer may find it not entirely futile at this point to weigh a number of pertinent questions against the available alternatives. It is a worthwhile exercise, for the questions and alternatives evoked by the story of Yad Mordechai are relevant in a much wider sense.

Should the men and women of Yad Mordechai have remained in Poland in 1939? Palestine was one of the few countries to which they could go. Even here there were stringent quotas. Many of their friends and relatives who wanted to join them were refused entry and perished in the Nazi holocaust. In 1943 they began to eke out a new existence for themselves at Yad Mordechai. It was a hard and difficult life, but one which held at the time a promise of freedom and security.

During the first artillery barrage in 1948, Egyptian planes dropped leaflets on Yad Mordechai calling upon the *kibbutz* to surrender. "In the name of Allah, the Almighty God who always speaks the truth," the Egyptians announced, "it was not our intention to begin a war. It is your resistance which has caused us to attack you . . . ." Should they have surrendered? If so, where could the Egyptians have sent them? Who would have taken them? What could or should they have done in the years that followed, as Arab belligerency continued and Yad Mordechai became a target for attacks by saboteurs from across the nearby border? In the meantime a new generation was born and was growing up, fully at home on the new lawns of Yad Mordechai.

The raw forces of real life are nowhere so evident as here. Few scenes in the country are likely to evoke a perspective of history, sharpened by a sense of irony and tragedy, as strongly as that elicited by the narrow sand dune that divides Yad Mordechai from the Gaza strip. The irony is deepened by the fact that the men and women of

Yad Mordechai belonged, as they still do, to *Mapam*, the most moderate and conciliatory Israeli political group. *Mapam* had opposed the establishment of a Jewish state and advocated a bi-national solution.

At the foot of a low hill south of the *kibbutz*, where some of the worst fighting took place during the siege of the settlement in 1948, the *kibbutzniks*, aided by military historians, have attempted a careful reconstruction of the battle of Yad Mordechai. Human figures, cast in metal, Egyptian tanks, armored vehicles, and pieces of artillery represent the assaulting force at a particularly difficult moment for the defenders—May 24, a few hours before the retreat. At the top of the hill, the trenches of the defenders have been redug in the sandy soil. A few yards away, the barbed wire fence surrounding the encampment has been broken through at some points, as though by Egyptian tanks. The display gives a good idea of events during the last hours of battle and makes one wonder how the defenders held out as long as they did.

Another display at Yad Mordechai suggests one possible explanation of the drama, and perhaps also a moral of wider application. It merges with the battlefield both visually and thematically. Across a small park and newly planted forest, the people of Yad Mordechai, aided by public funds, have built a small museum. The museum, a stark, ultra-modern structure, recounts recent Israeli history within the wider context of the Jewish tragedy in modern times. In a cavelike entrance hall, a few graphic displays portray the eclipse of Jewish life in Europe under the Nazis:

> In this place—
> Seek and look, for what can be seen no more,
> Hear voices that can be heard no more,
> Understand what is beyond all understanding.

A harrowing image is evoked of Jewish life in Eastern Europe before 1939. Books, charts, and a few well-chosen photographs suggest the general outlines of a rich and ancient civilization still alive only in the memory of the survivors.

Next, in quick succession are rooms commemorating the deportations and extermination camps, the Warsaw Ghetto uprising, and Jewish partisans in the forests of Poland and the Ukraine. There are the yellow stars, Nazi deportation lists, execution orders—while through an elongated large window cut into the bare concrete wall, the visitor looks on the nearby battlefield and the statue of Anilevicz next to the shattered water tower. The haggard faces of survivors, inmates of the Displaced Persons camps after the war, look down from the darkened walls. There are pictures of the great exodus of 1946–1947. Portrayed is the desperate struggle of the DPs to reach these shores by all means available; their disembarkation at night from illegal boats on desolate beaches; the first Jewish settlements in this part of the northern Negev on Jewish-owned land, but in defiance of British restriction. Finally the visitor reaches a semi-circular hall, where models, maps, photographs, and documents convey glimpses of the history, trial, and final triumph of Yad Mordechai itself. Throughout its various compartments the museum is marked by understatement and by a lack of sentimentality that seems almost inhuman but heightens the end effect to a point where it becomes nearly impossible to bear. It is one of the most instructive museums in the country, focusing as it does, sharply and perceptively, upon an essential facet of the modern Israeli temper. The museum is windowless except at three carefully chosen spots where the architects have attempted to convey a sense of continuity between past, present, and future, between a history so distant in space and already receding in time, and the immediate, so pastoral, environment. If there is such a thing as national consciousness or character, the museum at Yad Mordechai powerfully reflects the Jewish-Israeli variety through two of its main aspects.

One is an unspeakable trauma. The other is an existential sense of self-assertion in adversity: desperate, hopeless as in the Warsaw Ghetto uprising, or equally passionate as in Yad Mordechai, but imbued at least with a determination that not all human effort is in vain. J. L. Talmon, the historian, has called this determination "a kind of divine and creative madness which not only stills all fear and hesitation but also makes for clarity of vision in a landscape bathed in a lurid, distorting light." Yehuda Amichai, the poet, has expressed a related thought: "Most people of our time have the face of Lot's wife turned toward the holocaust and yet they are always escaping."

The holocaust remains a basic trauma of Israeli society. It is impossible to exaggerate its effect on the process of nation-building. The growth of nations, Alexis de Tocqueville observed long ago, bears some resemblance to the growth of men. As in the development of men, the circumstances of birth contribute to the development of nations. In the case of Israel, the images cast upon the dark mirror of the mind at a very crucial early stage were those of a veritable Dantean hell. It was a hell that included extermination of one-third of the Jewish people. The Nazi holocaust caused the destruction of that very same Eastern European world against which the early pioneers had staged their original rebellion, but to which, nevertheless, Israel became both outpost and heir. There is a latent hysteria in Israeli life that stems directly from this source.

It accounts for the prevailing sense of loneliness, a main characteristic of the Israeli temper since Independence. It explains the obsessive suspicions, the towering urge for self-reliance at all cost in a world which permitted the disaster to happen. It explains the fears and prejudices, passions, pains, and prides, that spin the plot of public life and will likely affect the nation for a long time to come. The lingering memory of the holocaust makes Arab threats of annihilation sound plausible. But even had there not been any Arabs, or if by some wondrous event their enmity were to disappear overnight, the lingering effect of traumatic memory would probably be almost as marked as it is today. The trauma of the holocaust leaves an indelible mark on the national psychology, the tenor and content of public life, the conduct of foreign affairs, on politics, education, literature, and the arts. It may very well be, as David Pryce-Jones, a sensitive English writer, has pointed out, that the notoriously lively bustle and busyness and seemingly limitless vivacity of Israeli life merely serve as compensatory devices for a morbid melancholy and a vast, permeating sadness. The most casual visitor is not likely to escape this melancholy. It crops up unexpectedly in conversation; it is noticeable in the press, in literature, in the private rituals of the people.

All over the country countless private and public monuments to the grimmest phase in European history perpetuate a memory which lies in all its morbidity at the center of Israel's historic self-image. If, in Israeli eyes, the world at large has tended to forget too soon, Israelis hardly give themselves the chance. The traumatic memory is part of the rhythm and ritual of public life.

I doubt whether as many books, memoirs, historical and anthropological studies of tiny, obscure Eastern European towns have been written in Poland, Lithuania, or in the Ukraine after 1945 as have since been published in Israel by their Jewish survivors, replete with rich illustrations, maps carefully drawn from memory, lists of names, and family trees. And not merely studies of Jewish life and manners in the best-known, greater centers of population and of learning such as Vilna or Cracow or Odessa, but in forsaken hamlets like Ukoliki (pop. 3,600) as well.

In vast afforestation areas many thousands of trees are annually planted and marked in the memory of lost communities and of individual victims. The use of greenery and frequently quite useless architectural structures is not accidental. From the very beginning, when they considered proper means to mourn for their dead, the Israeli Jews instinctively turned to architecture and afforestation. In previous ages, religious ceremony and prayer would have served as mourning, but in Israel, tree planting and building have always been acts of faith.

Yad Va'shem, the great memorial center in Jerusalem, which is dedicated to the impossible task of tracing and registering the name of every single man, woman, and child among the six millions, is an expression of that faith. Surrounded by young trees, Yad Va'shem is a massive building set on a vast paved terrace facing the pink hills of Judea. In the semi-darkness of the interior hall, the names of Nazi death camps, carved in stone, are dimly lit by a single torch. Close by is a research center. In the rituals of government and diplomacy, Yad Va'shem is given a role parallel, and at times equal in its solemnity, to the role of national symbols that extol military glory, sovereignty, and independence. There are great military cemeteries in Israel, but in Israeli protocol, Yad Va'shem occupies the place of tombs of Unknown Soldiers in other countries. It is here that the wreaths are laid.

There is a separate day of mourning set aside for victims of the holocaust; another memorial day commemorates the fallen of the Arab-Israeli wars. The first falls annually on the twenty-seventh of the Hebrew month Adar. At the sound of air-raid sirens—always harrowing in a country perpetually at war—the entire country falls silent for a full two minutes, in the midst of the busiest morning rush hour. Traffic stops; pedestrians freeze in their tracks. Nowadays, most countries observe Memorial Day rites; few do it with such extreme and elaborate solemnity. All places of entertainment, theaters, movie houses, bars, and nightclubs, close for the entire day and night. The larger papers run special supplements and Parliament meets in special session. Year in, year out, radio and television broadcast special commemorative programs; light entertainment is banned from the airwaves. As time passes, it seems that the subject is further than ever away from exhaustion. In the schools, children are told again all that happened at Auschwitz and Treblinka, occasionally in so brutally realistic language as to provoke sharp parental protests. Thousands of people gather at Yad Va'shem and at other memorial centers. In the larger cemeteries symbolic gravestones commemorate lost Eastern European communities whose only remaining trace is a heap of anonymous ash, flown over from the fields of Treblinka and Auschwitz, or a sackful of hair or a few bars of human soap, brought from Poland and buried here. Thousands of people gather at these symbolic graves on every Memorial Day.

Such rites are more than public opportunities to honor and cry for the dead. In the evolving culture of the new state, Holocaust Memorial Day has a positive function, for as it raises deep existential questions of identity, so it dictates the answers. Schools in recent years have developed a custom of "adopting" one of the destroyed Jewish communities of Europe. The "adoption" takes the peculiarly Israeli form of an almost archeological inquiry into a very recent past: the rise and decline, the life and death, of a civilization which flourished and disappeared within the lifetime of the parents. Schoolchildren pick a community—Salonika, Kishinev, Frankfort, Amsterdam, Warsaw. They study its history, its spiritual and material culture, its way of life and death. Children may improvise a play or arrange an exhibit; they write essays. Teams are sent out to interview survivors. Other survivors are invited to address the class and are questioned by teachers and students. For a week or so, a whole school is made to "live" the past.

Some of this—but not all—derives from older tradition. Jewish history has always been filled with disasters; memorializing their misfortunes has always been a ritual and perhaps a trait of character. Benjamin Disraeli said to the Duke of Portland, "I come from a race which never forgives an injury nor forgets a benefit." An important role is played by ancient religious customs, which seem stronger than faith in God himself.

Jewish prayer has always been marked by more lamentation than that of other faiths. Jewish Holy Days reach further back in time than any other living religious ceremony in the civilized world, with the possible exception of China and Japan. For the praying Jew, not only the High Holy Days but every religious festival, indeed every day in the year, has traditionally afforded opportunity to penitentially recall disaster and martyrdom. With all its emphasis on life and on the living, there is in Judaism an atavistic reverence in mourning that has survived the decline of faith. The mourning and burial rites practiced by even modern, non-religious urban Jews are difficult, intensive, and prolonged. Having discarded all or much of religion, modern Israelis, like modern Englishmen and Swedes, partake in the hedonistic pleasures of the welfare state; yet in the face of death even secular Israelis still observe elaborate and strenuous ultra-orthodox ceremonies of mourning. Most non-religious Israelis still hold to the prescribed *Shiva*, a seven-day period of deep mourning for close kin. During these seven days, men will not leave the house. They do not shave and often sit only on low stools, or on the floor in a shirt symbolically rent at the collar. The seven-day period is frequently followed by a year of abstinence from all public entertainment and pursuit of pleasure. Private mourning rites are public; grief is announced in newspaper advertisements. Similarly, expressions of condolence are submitted not only in person or in private correspondence, but publicly through prominent advertisements in the newspapers. The death of a prominent man, or one with an unusually large family or coterie of friends, is frequently accompanied by column upon column of such advertisements.

Thirty days after the funeral it is customary for friends and relatives to gather at the graveside; this often occasions further press obituaries. A similar observance takes place annually upon the anniversary of death. The mourning and sobbing is still there on the tenth or twentieth anniversary, as it was on the day of death itself.

All these rites are deeply rooted in ancient Jewish custom. Like mourning rites everywhere, they serve not only individuals but social purposes as well. They aid the bereaved to reorient himself after the shock of death. But in Israel—more, probably, than in other urban post-religious civilizations—mourning rites continue to powerfully and publicly reassert the viability of the group.

There is a close affinity between traditional Jewish mourning rites which have survived the decline of faith, and the public commemorations for victims of the holocaust. Mass death has provoked a compulsive need to reassert the group and demonstrate its continuing vitality. Between 1939 and 1945 the Jews, as a people, had a rendezvous with death as no other people in the war. After this confrontation with death, Jews everywhere, even those not personally victimized, felt compelled to seek their identity, as individuals and as a group. Israelis are sure that they have found the answer; and yet, as if to reassure themselves, they must go on asking again and again.

There is an obsessive quality in such preoccupation; inevitably some Israelis, at certain times and places, have found it unduly morbid, burdensome, and even contrived. The holocaust sometimes serves as argument in foreign affairs, and not always in good taste; foreigners have on occasion resented it as emotional blackmail. There are instances when such resentment is justified—here as elsewhere the language of politics is debased. But this does not detract from the centrality of the trauma at other times in the national psychology of Israel.

The loudest cries are still the mute ones. Despite the preoccupation of so many in Israel with the subject, it is excruciatingly difficult to speak or to write about it. The reasons are obvious. Language limps; it invariably breaks down under the weight of this subject. For the actual survivors, awareness can never be articulated by others. It resides silently in the private places of the heart. Those brought up in safety should not presume to articulate the unspeakable horror elucidated by events unprecedented in human experience and still incomprehensible to many through a continuing paralysis in the "normal" mind.

We are on safer ground when we leave this level of experience which, as George Steiner has said, "lies outside the normative syntax of human communication, in the explicit domain of the bestial," and concentrate upon political behavior. When we consider the impact of the holocaust upon political thought in Israel, the first thing we must remember is the apparent uniqueness of the holocaust as an experience, or even as a memory, within the history of a living people. Jews, of course, are not the only people who live under the shadow of a traumatic past. The Armenians are perhaps the closest parallel. Their "unremembered genocide," as one Armenian writer has commented bitterly, "was perpetrated almost thirty years before that term was coined." Japanese have been profoundly affected by the experience of Hiroshima; not only the *hibakusha*—the actual survivors of Hiroshima —but the entire Japanese people, even youngsters who cannot remember the war. Nor were the Jews Nazism's only, or most numerable, victim. Millions of Poles and Russians were slaughtered or gassed by the Nazis. But if others were struck by Nazi barbarism, the Jews nevertheless seem different—and not merely in their own eyes—because of all, they alone were singled out for extermination as a people. They were singled out, not because of what they did, or refrained from doing, and not because of faith or politics, but simply because they were there, they existed.

The impact was so overwhelming, that in Israeli eyes it has taken the form of fate. Young Israelis, especially, have come to believe wholeheartedly that the singling out of Jews for extermination was possible only because, of all peoples, only the Jews had no country of their own and thus lacked the minimum means of resistance.

This does not mean that sovereignty alone automatically guarantees security and survival. The daily experience of sovereign Israel would refute such a notion. Sovereignty is meaningless without the will power and capability to fight for it. But sovereignty, and that alone, permits a people to foster such will power as is necessary for survival and to prepare the physical means for its realization in practice.

Six million perished not because of a cataclysm of nature, as is evoked by use of that inadequate term "holocaust"; they died not because they lacked courage, but because they lacked the minimum prerequisites for putting such courage to practice. It is possible to vanquish and exterminate a people even in its own sovereign state. But with the possible exception of nuclear warfare, there is no mass extermination that cannot be opposed by its intended victims. In the eyes of the younger, post-Zionist generation, the holocaust has thus come to confirm one of the basic tenets of classical, nineteenth-century Zionism: without a country of your own you are the scum of the earth, the inevitable prey of beasts.

But behind this surface of purposeful determination, of flexed muscle and wisdom after the event, behind the proud array of newly acquired sovereign power, behind the impressive spectacle of a young, new society of resolute free men, the whole truth is something else. There remains a suspended confusion, a neurotic constriction, a shifting mood of remembrance and rejection that is one of the root causes for the modern Israeli temper. In the words of Uri Zvi Greenberg, a leading poet of the older generation:

> Lord you saved me from Ur-Germany as I fled
> Mother's and father's threshold, and arrived whole
> In body but with my soul torn, within it the lake-of-weeping
> Now I live on in my mourning.

The moral turbulence is compounded by pangs of conscience, guilt, and shame. The frequent inability of the young, native-born Israeli to confront the survivor of the holocaust is powerfully reflected in a number of major Israeli novels. In Hanoch Bartov's *The Brigade* the Israeli protagonist meets his surviving cousin in a Displaced Persons camp after the war. The young Israeli is filled with the "terror of belonging to him." He is seized with "more than shock, more than disgust." At the end of the novel he vows "never to return there . . . but as I spoke, my thoughts turned to pillars of salt."

Sometimes shame has worked the other way round. Shortly after the collapse of Nazi Germany, a little freighter arrived somewhere in the south of Palestine with illegal immigrants. A young Jewish woman stepped off onto the isolated beach. She had escaped the gas chambers by serving in a military whorehouse. Her left arm was branded with the tattooed inscription: *Nur für Offiziere* (For Officers only). As she was carried ashore by a teen-age member of the *Hagana*, she broke into hysterical tears: "Why am I here? What do you want with me? Why should these healthy youngsters risk their lives for me? There is no place for me on earth. I should be dead."

Yitzchak Sade, a veteran *Hagana* commander who described the incident in a short piece entitled *My Sister on the Beach*, added: "I embrace her shoulders and say: 'You have a place, sister. A very special, single place. Here in our country, you will live, sister. Here you have our love.' "

Like all traumatic memories the holocaust has given rise to ambivalent reactions. The urge to forget and suppress runs parallel to the urge to remember in order that suppression shall not cause further pain and agony. Alternating between remembering and forgetting, some Israelis have come to the conclusion that the only way to attain any peace of mind is to succeed in both. But this is more easily said than done. Organized commemoration is akin to organized religion; its drawbacks are obvious and at times they tend to defeat the original purpose. Such has been the inevitable fate of some routines of commemoration, developed and belabored by the public bureaucracy assigned to this task by Israeli law.* The law itself reflects the profound confusion, helplessness, and inadequacy which have marked most organized attempts at commemoration.

The law established the official Memorial Authority, Yad Va'shem. Yad Va'shem is an "incorporated body," supported by tax funds and "entitled to enter into contractual arrangements, to acquire and hold property." The language of the law is vague and convoluted. It clearly aims to soothe an open wound in the Jewish body politic by stressing and restressing that the purpose of Yad Va'shem is not only to commemorate the six million dead but also the heroism and selfless courage of those who fought back in the ghettoes and forests in order to "save the honor of their people." In a corner of the mind, many Israelis know that there was less resistance in the ghettoes and in the forests than would appear from the voluminous speeches delivered on the subject—primarily because under the circumstances resistance was nearly impossible. But, being human, they hold onto an exaggeration that seems essential to their dignity as a group.

The law empowers and calls upon the memorial authority of Yad Va'shem to (1) "establish memorial enterprises" (but does not specify which); (2) "gather, study and publish the *entire* testimony concerning holocaust and heroism"—a patently impossible task—"and endow the nation with its lesson" (it does not say what that lesson is); (3) "*implant* in the country and throughout the Jewish people the day designated by the Knesset as Memorial Day for the holocaust and for the heroism [of the resisters] and foster an atmosphere of unanimity in memory." The latter is an oblique reference to the dissensions among surviving partisan and resistance groups as to which did more in the ghettoes, concentration camps, and forests.

The activities of Yad Va'shem have been handicapped not only by

---

* "Law on the Commemoration of the Holocaust and the Heroism," passed in the Knesset on August 9, 1953.

such vague legislative directives, but by the sheer inadequacy of human imagination to devise meaningful ways and means of commemoration for an event that transcends understanding. This is well illustrated by the very first plans drawn up in the early 1940s by the originator of Yad Va'shem, Mordechai Shenhavi, a member of Kibbutz Mishmar Ha'emek. The Israeli writer Yehuda Kasten, in a historical review of Yad Va'shem, published in 1964, has thrown a fascinating light upon this early period. Shenhavi told Kasten that after the first horrible news started to arrive in 1941, he had had a dream. In this dream he saw huge masses of people passing by him. Each carried a gravestone on his back and looked at him demandingly. Some bore familiar faces of relatives and friends Shenhavi had known in his youth in Poland. As they disappeared into the distance, each person put down his gravestone, until an enormous mountain of stone arose high on the horizon. It became Shenhavi's life obsession to set up "a memorial to the dead, to preserve each man's human uniqueness, the fact that he was not just a mere heap of matter."

But how? Shenhavi's solution was quantitative. Soon after he had had his dream he began to consult architects. Sheer size was considered to best reflect the unfathomable depth of the tragedy. Structural mass was to them the only idiom for communicating an incomprehensible magnitude. As the news came in and the death figures rose from one million to two, three, and then six million, so Shenhavi's plans increased in volume and outlay. Imagination, never an outstanding quality of public bodies, faltered; it would probably have faltered in any case. A Michelangelo may not have been more successful than Shenhavi. Other early proposals included the erection of a huge tower that would emit black smoke and be visible over almost the entire country. Another suggestion called for the dispatch to Israel of a full boatload of human bones and ashes from the fields surrounding Auschwitz, Treblinka, and Svobidor.

It was probably inevitable that Yad Va'shem would be involved in bitter argument and recriminations from its inception. Should it primarily be a monument? Or a scholarly institution? If its "message" was obvious, as some claimed, then perhaps it was not necessary? If necessary, perhaps not obvious? Some asked if Yad Va'shem really ought to draw so bleak a picture. How can human dignity be preserved if such is its message? Was the tragedy "Jewish" or "human"?

Should scholarly research at Yad Va'shem concentrate on the study of anti-Semitism or on totalitarian politics in general?

These questions have never really been resolved. Over the years a macabre worship of death has marked some of the activities at Yad Va'shem. There is a self-defeating element in tea parties held in a Memorial museum to celebrate the publication of yet another book on the holocaust, or in the manufacture of keyrings, bearing the yellow Star of David, that were sold outside the building by private vendors until public outcry put an end to it.

The overemphasis of the subject in school curricula, while powerfully affecting the imagination of children, has not always led to the expected results. Nor could it be otherwise. Trauma cannot be "taught" like chemistry or foreign languages. The profound confusion is evidenced by the fact that some teachers, who will oppose Grimm's fairy tales because of the nightmares likely to result from their alleged cruelty, insist upon giving students a fully realistic picture of what happened in the gas chambers and crematoria. A teacher might be against sex education for the young but will insist upon what is called "courses on the holocaust" for kindergarten children.

More recently there has been added emphasis in these guidelines to tales of resistance and rebellion under the Nazis. The avowed aim—reflecting a widespread neurosis—has been to "avoid shocks likely to push young people into a state of depression and fatalistic apathy," or else—here is the most serious problem—cause them to "distance themselves" in a false sense of shame from those who died such ignoble deaths. Teachers are admonished "first of all to dismiss the vicious allegation leveled against the masses of our people in the Nazi-occupied countries that they 'went like sheep to the slaughter.' " Teachers are advised to underline the tremendous power of the Third Reich, which succeeded within the space of a few months to subdue nearly all of Europe. They must emphasize that millions of non-Jewish civilians were similarly put to death, "including hundreds of thousands of Soviet prisoners-of-war, young men, physically fit and well trained as soldiers but nevertheless as helpless and perhaps even more helpless, than Jewish women, children and old men who were led to the slaughter." But even today the incredulous reaction of some schoolchildren is to ask: "Yes, but why didn't our army come to their rescue?"

The attitudes of younger, native-born Israelis to the holocaust, and to the Jewish Diaspora in general, have always been highly ambivalent, a mixture of compelling awe and of compelling shame. This is at least partly a result of standard Zionist education. A regular textbook on Hebrew syntax—used for many years in Israeli schools—included the following analysis of Bialik's great lament on the pogrom of Kishinev in 1903:

> This poem describes the mean brutality of the assailants and the *disgraceful shame and cowardice* of the Jews of the Diaspora *shtetl*.

"Disgraceful," "shame," and "cowardice" are key terms here that point to the heart of Zionist education in its earlier stages. A repellent new term entered the vernacular of Israeli teen-agers after 1945 with the arrival of the first survivors of the Nazi death camps. The refugees were derogatorily referred to by youngsters as *sabon*, or soap. The term has since become generic for cowardice and weakness. To threaten "to soap" someone is to threaten to ruin him. For many years Israeli schoolchildren were taught that the Diaspora was not only a catastrophe, but a disgraceful shame. In her controversial account of the Eichmann trial, Hannah Arendt suggested that during the Nazi holocaust the Jews—through the passivity of their leaders—cooperated in a sense in their own destruction. There was relatively less turmoil over this accusation among Israelis than among Jews elsewhere, because, rightly or wrongly, it confirmed a Zionist cliché image of Diaspora Jewry.

In the shifting moods of remembrance and rejection, younger Israelis are frequently torn between anger and shame at the very notion of having such an accursed past. Their ways of avoiding the issue are as complicated as their attempts to meet it head on. But this is true also of older people. Some older people are consumed by that sense of guilt which observers have often noticed among the survivors of harrowing accidents and disasters. Psychologists call this "guilt at survival priority." It contains an undercurrent of guilt feelings simply at being alive, when so many others, dear and close, died before their eyes; whereas they themselves survived through blind luck, cunning, a greater physical fitness, or, not infrequently, through cruel disregard for fellow human beings in a world that had completely succumbed to the bestial. For them, history has been a nightmare from which, like Stephen Dedalus in Joyce's *Ulysses*, they have been "trying to awaken."

Others, veteran settlers, prominent in Israeli public life, who spent the war years in Palestine, are sometimes haunted by a fearful anguish, a lingering doubt which can never be resolved that, perhaps, they might have done more than they actually did to diminish, even marginally, the extent of the tragedy. Perhaps they had been too disciplined in their loyalty to the Western allies, to whom, quite naturally, the rescue of Jews had seemed a task subsidiary to the defeat of Hitler's Germany. Perhaps their loyalty had been exaggerated; perhaps they should have been more self-centered. Perhaps they had not been dramatic enough in their pleas to the Western allies to permit rescue operations. Perhaps they themselves had not been exhaustive enough in rescue operations of their own, through Zionist agents in Lisbon, Geneva, and Istanbul. Such questions can never be answered satisfactorily. The very uncertainty has deeply affected the Israeli leadership and colors their thinking to this day.

The political elite has been almost wholly comprised of immigrants, or sons of immigrants of Eastern European origin. Most members of the political elite lost all or part of their families in the holocaust. To understand this inner crisis it must be remembered that while rescue had always been a basic tenet in Zionist ideology, the Zionist leadership during the war was far from able to act independently. The Zionists did not operate in a political vacuum. The exigencies of power politics at times forced the Jewish leaders in Palestine to enter compromises of such tremendous moral implications as to burden their conscience ever since. Rescue was one objective; at the same time, they felt, real rescue depended upon the attainment of national independence. The key to the latter rested with the Western allies. The desire to gain Anglo-American support for Jewish independence restrained Zionist pressure on the allies to do more for rescue; it limited independent Zionist operations as well.

Leaders of the Jewish underground security force, *Hagana*, in one instance developed a plan to parachute hundreds of young Palestinian Jews into occupied Europe. Their aim was to fan resistance among those doomed to die, and to organize underground routes of escape. It was a fantastic plan and might easily have become a suicide mission.

But there was hope that a few parachutists might succeed in blowing up a gas chamber, or at least a railroad track leading to one. The plan was vetoed by the British. The reasons are still unclear, just as it shall forever remain mysterious why the allies never bombed Auschwitz—or the railroads leading to it—from the air, although they twice bombed, in full daylight, a German chemical factory that was only a few miles away from the death camp.* The Zionist leaders have never been sure that they acted rightly in succumbing to such vetoes.

Even short of parachuting *Hagana* men into occupied Poland, there were a number of measures that might have been tried which Palestinian Jews refrained from. They might have tried to infiltrate small commando units into Europe via Turkey and the Balkan countries. They might certainly have protested more strongly and more publicly against allied refusals to take more effective action against the death factories in Poland. There is today no doubt that the resources of the Jewish community of Palestine, meager as they were and divided between volunteering for the British army and maintaining the *Hagana*, were not exhausted in effort to ward off the greatest disaster in the history of the Jewish people. Some Israelis argued in 1945 that, in deference to British sensitivities, these independent resources were hardly used. The question has haunted Israeli politicians ever since. Its moral dimensions are monstrous. The mere raising of the question in a sensational law suit for libel in 1953** caused the downfall of an Israeli cabinet.

---

* At the trial of Adolf Eichmann the text of a letter from the British Foreign office to Dr. Weizmann, preserved in the Weizmann archives, was made public for the first time. In this letter, written on September 1, 1944, the permanent undersecretary of the foreign office referred to Weizmann's urgent plea to the British government to bomb Auschwitz. He assured Weizmann that the matter had been most thoroughly considered by the Air Staff, "but I am sorry to inform you that in view of the very great technical difficulties involved" the Air Staff was unfortunately compelled "to refrain from pursuing the proposal."

The transcript of the trial continues:

Mr. Justice Halevy: "What were the technical difficulties?"

Attorney General Hausner: "Perhaps they are known to the author of the letter. I do not know, Sir. For myself I do not think there were any."

** This was the so-called Kastner case. Dr. Rudolf Kastner was a Jewish Agency official in wartime Budapest in charge of the local Zionist Rescue Committee. Eight years after the war, in an obscure private newsletter, Kastner was accused of having, in effect, been a Nazi collaborator, the indirect murderer of a million Jews. He had allegedly desisted from any rescue work, save for a few hundred well-connected, rich, or promi-

Gideon Hausner, the Attorney General at the trial of Adolf Eichmann in 1962, spoke for many when he said that this question "will continue to plague our national conscience." Dr. Nachum Goldmann, former president of the World Jewish Congress, has publicly admitted that "we are all guilty of not having gone to all lengths." Goldmann himself had pleaded with the American Secretary of State Edward Stettinius in 1944 to respond to a specific German offer. That year the Germans had made their offer of Jewish lives for American or English trucks. Goldmann asked Stettinius to agree to it. Stettinius refused for reasons of military strategy. "We were too impressed," Goldmann later admitted bitterly, "with the argument that the [allied] generals should be left in peace to fight the war."

When Israeli historians reflect upon events prior to and during World War II, they invariably conclude that, during this greatest calamity that has befallen the Jewish people in their long history, few non-Jews and no single sovereign state had actively come to their rescue with a specific intention to save them. It is impossible to exaggerate the impact of such conclusions on the evolving national temper. Hitler once publicly derided the democracies which "ooze sympathy for the poor tormented Jews, but remain hard and obdurate themselves when it comes to helping them." Israelis have generally tended to agree with that statement, citing the general refusal of the democracies, before, during, and after the war, to permit Jewish refugees in significant numbers to enter their territories.

A number of incidents immediately after the war, some of them trivial, tended to reconfirm the bitter lesson in Israeli eyes. Early in 1946, tens of thousands of East European Jews, survivors of the camps, were streaming westward, trying to "get out of Europe"—which to them was a graveyard—and into Palestine where they hoped to assume a new identity. Not only were the gates of Palestine closed to them, but a British general—in a famous interview—chose to de-

---

nent Zionists and members of his own family, whose release he had secured through his apparently amicable relations with the Gestapo. An anxious, but ill-advised government (in 1953 Kastner was a senior government official) sued the editor of the newsletter, Malchiel Gruenwald, for criminal libel. It soon regretted this step. After a long, sensational trial, the case was dismissed. The District Court, after the presentation of a good deal of evidence, in effect endorsed the bulk of Gruenwald's charges. The Supreme Court later overruled this verdict by a 3 to 2 vote, but the cabinet had already fallen.

scribe these refugees as well-fed, healthy, and robust, their pockets
"bulging with money." In London, Ernest Bevin publicly complained
that the Jews were always pushing themselves to the head of the
queue. It is impossible today to convey a sense of the rage that such
statements, coupled with restrictive immigration policies, aroused at
the time. The lingering effects, however, can still be easily noted.
Such statements and policies, coming as they did, at a crucial formative period in the life of a new community, have profoundly affected
the Israeli's picture of himself in the contemporary world. It is, above
all, a picture of utter loneliness.

Arab encirclement and belligerency—whatever their cause in later
years—have only tended to sharpen the general outlines of this picture. Since Independence in 1948, Israelis have lived in a state of
geographic and political isolation unusual in the modern world. Since
World War II almost every country has been linked to others by
military and political pacts or alliances. Most countries today share
common markets, or, at least open borders, a common language, or
religion, with another. Israel has none of these. Apart from its geographic isolation it is probably the only country in the world that is
engaged in constant military conflict and yet has membership in no
military, political, or economic alliance. The frustrating consequences
of this claustrophobic isolation have been considerable. Against the
background of the holocaust and its immediate aftermath, the total
effects of isolation have multiplied and given rise to that pessimism of
encirclement and of being entirely and utterly alone in the world,
which, even today, is a chief characteristic of the Israeli mind.

> When our children under the gallows wept,
> The world its silence kept. . . .

Nathan Altermann wrote in a well-known poem. The feeling is shared
by many. It is a root cause for Israeli attitudes which to the outside
world frequently seem unduly stubborn. Pious admonishments from
outside have very little effect; the most cosmopolitan Israelis will
insulate themselves against foreign criticism to an abnormal degree.
For, in their eyes, since World War II the civilized world has little
moral ground on which to stand when it sermonizes Israel to do this
or to refrain from doing that. In the late 1940s David Ben Gurion

epitomized this in the remark, "It is not important what the *Goyim* are saying but what Jews are doing." Ben Gurion's reputation has assured a long life to what still is a dangerous half-truth. His remark is still oft quoted. It was under the impact of World War II that in the mid-1940s a new breed of Jews started coming out of Palestine: tough, pessimistic, militant, and as far from the idyllic image of the founding fathers as real life is from Utopia. The "new" breed were a tiny minority, of course, and still are; but it is an active minority that has set a tone.

In Elie Wiesel's haunting story, "Dawn," an eighteen-year-old Jewish terrorist is ordered to shoot a British hostage in cold blood as an act of reprisal for the hanging of a fellow terrorist; the story takes place during the anti-British disturbances in Palestine after World War II. The young man is a survivor of Buchenwald. For him terrorism has come to mean that Jews are no more "the only ones who are afraid." Previously he had believed "the mission of the Jews was to represent the trembling of history, rather than the wind which made it tremble." But as he is preparing for his role as executioner he is haunted by the ghosts of his past, and before them he must justify his ghastly act. He kills his man but the expected "Dawn" is not dawn at all but merely another phase of night. "There is night now and there will be night tomorrow and the day the week the century after."

On a different if slightly ludicrous level, the new realism of disillusion and toughness reoccurs in Shabtai Teveth's factual reportage of the 1967 war, *Tanks of Tammuz*. He quotes a fascinating little dialogue between a Colonel Shmuel and a younger officer named Georgie. Colonel Shmuel, scion of an ultra-orthodox Jerusalem family, is a former *bachur yeshiva*, a rabbinical scholar. He became a professional soldier in the late 1940s and has remained one ever since. In the midst of hectic preparation for battle, the rabbinical-scholar-turned-colonel was given to the following historiosophic contemplations:*

> "We cannot even estimate the damage done to us by Hitler. He has destroyed the nation's creative nucleus, the synagogue. It is because of the synagogue that we are a nation, and for no other reason. Sometimes I think that the two pillars of Judaism today are the Israeli army and the rabbinical seminaries in America."

* In the English translation this section is missing.

"The army, sir? The army isn't really the true character of the Jewish people."

"I agree, Georgie. But only in the end of days the wolf shall live with the lamb, and even then I prefer to be the wolf."

"Yes, sir."

The Eichmann trial of 1961–1962 had, in a sense, a deeply cathartic effect upon some Israelis. As the tale of horror evolved daily in the courtroom, it served as a first opportunity for many to squarely face the past, while one of the chief torturers sat in the dock of a Jewish court of law. The trial and the verdict apparently played a role in preparing the ground, emotionally, for the resumption of more normal relations with all things German, including the subsequent exchange of ambassadors with West Germany in 1965.

At the same time, political reactions evoked by the holocaust deepened considerably. After the Eichmann trial Chaim Guri, a poet of the younger generation, wrote that, from now on

> . . . free men will turn from time to time to look at their receding past without freezing into pillars of salt. They will be wiser. They will not evict from their souls this chapter in the chronicles of life but will live it fully, unashamed.
>
> Then they will endow their liberty its truest meaning; that it is not self-evident. . . .

In 1962 a team of social psychologists studied the impact of the Eichmann trial upon students at the Hebrew University of Jerusalem. Their report concluded that the trial had elicited an almost unique case of "high involvement" in a public issue. It had deeply influenced student attitudes; it had led them to adopt a more pessimistic world outlook. While there were differences between students who themselves, or their families, had actually survived, and those "who had neither suffered nor had relatives who had suffered," the holocaust occupied a "central" position in the world outlook of both. "Centrality" was measured in terms of emotional involvement, anxiety, distrust of Gentiles, and feelings of interdependence with all Jews. Interdependence meant that "every Jew should regard himself a survivor of the holocaust."

At the time of their publication these findings were met with some suspicion. Such a high degree of involvement as was claimed by the researchers was, perhaps, of a temporary nature. Public exposure to the trial itself had been constant and unrelenting. For more than a year the newspapers had been filled with it almost daily. A large part of the court proceedings had been broadcast live. A survey of listeners was taken on the first day of the trial; 60 percent of all Israeli Jews over the age of fourteen had listened to at least one of the two sessions; 38 percent had listened to both sessions, most of them for the entire period of the broadcast.

Thus it was argued that the high degree of involvement with the issue would lessen after the highly sensational trial was concluded. But this has not been the case. The effects of the Nazi holocaust upon the national psychology reached a new peak in the weeks preceding the Six Day War of 1967. Israelis, including many young people, were seized by abysmal fears; many were certain that another holocaust was being prepared for them by the rulers of Egypt, whose bloodthirsty statements were resounding hourly on the radio. Many impartial foreign observers have testified to the breadth of such feelings at the time, and how genuine the fears seemed. The available evidence has further been corroborated by soldiers' letters and by interviews with young soldiers immediately after the war. Doubtlessly, some of the statements were rhetorical. But that does not deter from the power of the trauma.

Among younger Israelis, a renewed preoccupation with the so-called "Jewish condition" has been apparent in recent years. The Zionists had originally wanted to reform that condition drastically; and yet in the novel form of Arab belligerency and abysmal hatred it pursues them to this day in the land of their dreams.

War and dangers have put their stamp on Israeli life for many years. At times of war it has not been necessary for young Israelis to be religiously observant, to throw their Zionist education overboard and identify with the historic experience of Judaism. They must not be orthodox traditionalists to feel that sense of existential anguish that had been a distinguishing mark of the Jewish temper in the Diaspora. In times of danger the ghosts of old pogroms hover like clouds over Israel. The upsurge of a certain "intellectual" or propagandistic anti-Semitism among Arabs has acted as a powerful contributory factor.

Arab anti-Semitism is a by-product of the Arab-Israeli wars. In the 1950s when anti-Semitic slogans became a common feature of Arab propaganda, Israelis tended to overlook them, especially since they so blatantly contradicted a central assumption of Zionism, that Israel was the most effective, indeed only, antidote to anti-Semitism. But as the Arab-Israeli conflict grew more bitter and more violent, the repulsive character of at least a part of Arab propaganda became so pronounced that few Israelis could reasonably continue to ignore it.

In a conflict as bitter and total as this—and against the background of the Nazi Holocaust—there is, of course, a natural inclination in Israelis to see the adversaries as representatives of absolute evil. Democracies do not easily go to war; when they do, they tend to view the contest as having a final, apocalyptic quality. But even had there been no such built-in readiness, the tone and imagery of Arab letters and public statements would themselves have sufficed to evoke intense feeling. Arab letters abound with references to the *Protocols of the Elders of Zion*. The *Protocols* have been described as a "secret speech by Herzl at the Zionist Congress." The late president Nasser on one occasion himself recommended the *Protocols* to an Indian visitor. "It is important that you read it. I will give you a copy. It proves beyond all doubt that 300 Zionists, each knowing the others, control the fate of the European continent and elect their successors from among themselves."*

Yehoshofat Harkabi, an Israeli scholar and student of the Arab-Israeli conflict, estimated in 1967 that of 160 recent books in Arabic dealing with Israel, some fifty are either based directly upon the *Protocols* or quote them sympathetically. Viciously anti-Semitic tracts have been issued in recent years not only by state-owned publishing houses in Cairo and Damascus, but in the relative freedom of Beirut as well. Some such tracts have openly justified the Nazi crimes; others have hailed Eichmann, following his execution, as a hero who "fell in the holy war"; still others have resurrected ancient blood accusations ("The Jewish god is not content with animal sacrifices. To placate him human sacrifices are necessary. Hence the Jewish custom to slaughter infants and suck their blood to mix it with unleavened bread at Passover . . .").

All this may very well be a transient form of "war racialism," as one noted Arabist, the French professor, Maxime Rodinson, has claimed.

* In the official collection of President Nasser's speeches and press interviews.

Rodinson has compared this vitriolic outburst to the anti-Prussian phobia of the English during World War I, or to the even more intense hatred between Frenchmen and Germans after the war of 1870. Perhaps Rodinson is correct in assuming that anti-Semitism, not being indigenous, could not be as serious in the Arab countries as in old Russia or Poland where it was rooted in popular myths and religious images.

Rodinson ignores that those with burnt fingers are notoriously more sensitive to fire. Even as "war racialism," Arab hatred of Israel appears fearfully ominous in the eyes of people suffering a memory of historic outrage from personal or first-hand experience. Such hatred is downright frightening when accompanied, as it often is, by harrowing threats of physical and political annihilation. Perhaps such threats will pass. While they last, they powerfully affect the national psychology.

Daily Arab threats continue to obstruct the sense of "normalcy" that had been one of the major, more naive aims, of the early Zionists. But it is not necessary to cultivate a derangement of the senses when reality itself is insane. Precisely because memory of the holocaust is so alive, Arab threats of annihilation arouse in many Israelis what almost amounts to a cultural reflex. The Arabs do not realize that in the Israeli arsenal, this reflex is more powerful a weapon than a mighty armored division. It is an involuntary gift presented to the Israelis by their enemies; it adds resolve, inventiveness, devotion, cohesion, vigor, pluck, and paradoxically, that kind of nervous but fertile "anxiety" which is often said to be a root cause of the traditional Jewish spirit in the Diaspora.

The tragic irony is deepened by a fatal parallel. There is a symmetry between the Israelis' traumatic memory of holocaust and the neurosis of shame and anger, humiliation and white rage, that has been generated among Arabs by Israel's recurrent successes. Both sides are in a sense "possessed." One of the costliest and most persistent tragedies is that people involved in great upheavals seldom realize what is happening to them. Both Arabs and Israelis frequently seem overwhelmed by their own feelings. Psychologically they are related; politically they constitute a vicious circle. Harrowing memory has helped Israelis to gather enough inner strength not only to avoid defeat but to go from one partial victory to another. Conversely, the terrible memory of loss and humiliation has kept alive among Arabs a sense of blind determination, born of abysmal outrage; this so far has prevented them from agreeing to any lasting settlement. The Arabs feel unable to accept the kind of total reconciliation that the Israelis, because of their past, insist upon. Arab refusal is rooted in their own sense of outrage.

The Palestinian Liberation Organization retains in its propaganda and press statements the old Arab place names within Israel. A memorial institute in Beirut republishes old maps of the country, marked with the names of villages which disappeared completely as a result of the 1948 war. Harkabi, bitterly ironic, called this institute "a kind of Arab Yad Va'shem." The loss of Palestine has bred something of an "Arab Zionism." It is almost as prolific in its literary output as the Jewish Zionism of three or four decades ago. Aside from their recurrent calls for vengeance and bloodshed, the tracts of the Palestinian organizations are reminiscent of Zionist pamphlets in the early 1920s. The emblem of the Arab terrorist organization *el Fatah* (two fists, holding two submachine guns crossed over a map of pre-1948 Palestine) is almost a direct copy of the old emblem of the Jewish terrorist organization, *Irgun Zvai Leumi*, which fought the British before 1948 (one fist, one rifle, superimposed upon the same old map).

Arab outrage—just like Israeli memory—is not the only factor, of course. The situation is complicated by inner Arab rivalries and by the clashing interests of outside powers. Sheer outrage is an important factor, though. A prominent Lebanese scholar, Dr. S. Hamady, underlines the importance of "face" among Arabs. She calls Arabs a "shame-society." Among intellectuals, the frustrations bred by the apparent irretrievability of Arab glories of the distant past, are compounded by the failure of modern pan-Arabism, and hurt even more as a result of Israel's establishment and consolidation.

The establishment of Israel in 1948 is commonly referred to by Arabs as a calamity so great that it reflects not only upon their military prowess, but injures, in an almost metaphysical sense, the whole human order of being. Israel is an abominable crime; it is a "cancerous growth," an injection of unspeakable evil.

If judged solely by the vast body of Arab literature relevant to this subject which has sprung up since 1948, the Palestinian calamity appears almost as great in some Arab eyes as the holocaust appears in the eyes of the Jews. The terms used by Arabs in conversation and in writing are *Nakbat Falastin*, the Palestinian disaster, or *Karrissat Falastin*, which is even closer to the word "holocaust" as used by Jews. It denotes terrible group catastrophes, earthquakes and outrages of near cosmic dimension. Constantine Zurayk, a professor of history at the American University of Beirut, coined the first term shortly after the 1948 war, in his now classic *Maana el Nakba* ("Lesson of the Disaster"), a searing analysis of the Arab defeat of 1948. *Nakba* and *Karrissa* have since become common usage among literate Arabs.

As a topic of serious discussion *Ilam el Karrissa* and *Ilam el Nakba* —Science, or Study, of the Holocaust—has occupied a prime place in Arab political literature since 1948. Arab writers have produced hundreds of volumes on the subject. With one or two exceptions, the tone and intent of these volumes has never been conciliatory. Their aim is not to explore possibilities of co-existence. How can there be co-existence with what is seen as a crime against nature? The aim of these volumes has been rather to outline ways and means which will finally enable Arabs to wipe the traces of that crime off the face of the earth. Such ways and means often have included far-reaching social and cultural reforms within the Arab camp, as a precondition for effectively uprooting the Israeli intruders. The argument has not been over the right of Israel to exist, but rather on Arab capabilities to destroy her as an independent political entity. The need for such destruction is almost invariably seen as axiomatic. The most frequently used, non-euphemistic threats, according to Harkabi's account, have been "to massacre," "to destroy," "to liquidate," "to eradicate," "to clean up," "to suffocate," "to execute," "to uproot" "to throw into the sea," "to mop away," "to annihilate."

Euphemistic terms frequently used by the Arabs have been "liberation of the homeland," "re-Arabization of Palestine," "restoration of stolen rights," and "uprooting the source of disaster."*

---

* Harkabi's analysis, although based on a vast collection of authentic Arab statements, including hair-raising threats of genocide, has occasionally been criticized in Israel as unduly alarmist. Such criticism, in face of so much evidence—its authenticity has never been denied—reflects that element of wishful thinking which has always been so strong in Zionist politics. In the first stages of settlement there was an inclination to overlook the Arabs as a possible political factor; later there was a tendency to belittle the psychological impact upon the Arabs of their recurrent defeats. For example, it has been said of Dr. Harkabi's findings that his reading of Arab statements is too literal; that he takes Arab threats and expressions of outrage at face value, in a manner unjustified by

If the articulation of aims is occasionally accompanied in Arab letters by the doubt that they may be unattainable in practice, such doubt always hinges on the author's espousal of this or that vital scheme of political, social, cultural, or religious reform. Upon the implementation of such reform, the most far-reaching targets become obtainable. It can be argued that, after reform, the issues raised by *Nakbat Falastin* may appear less burning and may be gradually forgotten by the Arabs. Ancient resentments lose their poignancy by the eroding effects of time. We no longer weep for Hecuba and the Trojan women. But this can hardly be a consolation for Israelis now. Time, said to be the great healer, until now has deepened the wounds, not cured them.

---

what is called "knowledge" of the "true" Arab character. There is an element of paternalistic condescension in such rejoinders. Their implication is that Arabs do not really mean what they say, that we know them even better than they know themselves. Harkabi's response has quite rightly been that Arab statements must be taken in a literal sense—if only because one must respect one's adversary. "To understand the Arab position the Israeli must imagine what he himself would have done if he were an Arab . . . he must try to estimate in his heart the deep feeling provoked by what the Arabs are convinced was a great outrage. Let him imagine in his heart that he is a Palestinian refugee, uprooted from his environment, where he and his forefathers grew up. . . . Let him try to measure the force of the blow delivered to Arab nationalism (and self-esteem) by Israel's establishment and consolidation."

9

LIVING DANGEROUSLY

My father was four years at their war
And did not hate or love his enemies.
But I know that he, already there,
Formed me daily out of his tranquilities,

They were so very few that he could pick
Between the bombs and smoke
And put them in his tattered sack
With the remains of mother's hardening
cake.

Nameless dead he gathered in his eyes,
Numerous dead he gathered for me so
That I might love them, in his glances
recognized,

And not die like them by terror taken . . .
He filled his eyes with them, he was
mistaken:
To all my battles I must go.

 —Yehuda Amichai

  "Here We Loved" from the sonnet
  sequence

For almost its entire existence Israel has been in a state of war or
semi-war. For almost its entire life it has been under military and
partial political and economic siege. In a previous chapter we have
observed the dominant role of ideology in the history of the Jewish
resettlement of Palestine. We must now extend that observation to

include the presence of violence. Between this ideology and the ensuing violence lies the middle ground of decision wherein some Israelis find themselves constrained, while others find freedom and choice.

Early Zionism was predicated upon faith in peaceful change. The discovery that this was nearly impossible has profoundly affected the Israeli temper. As in other liberation movements, whether social or national, the Zionist mystique of redemption has become powerfully intertwined with a mystique of violence. The resulting dissonance is today a main characteristic of Israel. The two mystiques represent two facets of the Israeli experience—the bright and the somber, the hopeful and the tragic, alternating, overlapping, clashing. Upon the outcome of this confrontation much of the future course and quality of Israeli society depends. In past decades its main features have been war and siege.

In this perennial siege, the bloodiest and most dramatic stage occurred in the years after Independence in 1948. But this was only the culmination of a bitter struggle that had begun much earlier. Jewish resettlement of Palestine, from its earliest antecedents in the last quarter of the nineteenth century, was almost never unopposed. Violently, or non-violently, Jewish settlers clashed with Turkish and British authorities and with the indigenous population of the country. The first serious clash in the history of the resettlement took place as early as 1886. Muslim *felahin*, from Yahudiya, an Arab village a few miles south of Petach Tikva, who could no longer graze their cattle in the swampland, broke into the new colony in broad daylight, when most of the men were out in the fields. Five settlers were injured; one later died of her wounds. It was not a demonstration of political violence but a protest by peasants against the violation of an old custom, which the Jews, by applying legally justified force, had flouted. Had the Jews not been "foreigners," this and similar incidents would have somehow been resolved, as they were in cases involving Arabs only, but the national issue soon compounded the tensions beyond all hope of reasonable and pacific reconciliation. From the earliest days of settlement the settlers struggled for their daily security; at the very least they were on constant alert against what they initially had somewhat naively called "Arab banditry," and only much later "aggression." The struggle has now lasted for almost a whole century and its end is not in sight.

Israelis are fond of saying that in this prolonged entanglement with forces that have often been superior, their main weapon has been an awareness of *ain brera*, there is no choice. *Ain brera* deserves to be inscribed on the currently motto-less national coat of arms. But it is more than a watchword or statement of intent such as *in God we trust, Liberté-égalité-fraternité*, or *honi soit qui mal y pense*. It implies a fatalistic, daily shrugging of the shoulders; it excuses much and explains even more; it also connotes a deep irony. Zionism started out in the nineteenth century fired by a spirit of Messianic utopianism; *ain brera* reflects an inner reconciliation by the former revolutionaries and their heirs with that part of life which seems immune to ideology and change. Rebels against fate have become themselves fatalists.

Israelis often say, "Yes, we live dangerously. *Ain brera!* There is no choice! But we are free!" They rarely pause to think that this may be a contradiction in terms. If freedom implies both the existence of choice and a subjective awareness of the choices—for alternatives often go unnoticed—then Israelis are definitely not free. On the other hand, the contradiction disappears if we endorse the view that freedom implies an acute realization of limits: an awareness of iron rules under which men allow themselves to ignore choice with the apparent blessing of science, or under the aegis of forces commonly called blind, or inexorable. We have seen in a previous chapter how in the earlier stages of Zionism some of the most influential pioneers went out to stage a madly romantic uprising against these very forces; how contrary to all conservative reasoning they revolted against the human condition itself. And yet even in Israel they were not able to escape it. The early pioneers never aimed at the establishment of a fortress state populated by men who would spend much of their adult lives under arms; and yet this is precisely what circumstance has forced them to do. The Zionist dreamers envisaged a safe haven in Israel for persecuted Jews everywhere. But in Israel today, Jews, as Jews, live in greater danger of their lives than anywhere else in the world.

Living dangerously—at war, or for periods under interminable tension—has become a way of life, an apparent routine, a capricious but regular standard, almost a canon of existence. The average native-born Israeli has known nothing else his entire life.

He has been a soldier in and out of uniform since his seventeenth or eighteenth birthday. Para-military training may have begun for him at the age of fourteen or fifteen. If he is forty-five years old, he has most likely been in active service in four full-fledged wars. He was a soldier with the British forces during World War II, and three times a soldier in the Arab-Israeli wars (of 1948, 1956, and 1967). His Israeli service has included—and, for many, still includes—reserve duty of three to eight weeks annually for which all men are liable to be called until they are fifty-four years old. Consequently many of the veterans probably participated as well in one of the numerous, bloody skirmishes that have broken out between the four wars. If a man is over fifty, he is likely to have also seen action in one way or another during the Arab rebellion of 1936–1939—either as a watchman, as a member in one of the Jewish underground defense organizations, or as a youthful message runner. While still in his teens he became accustomed to life in cordoned-off areas; various sections of a city were divided by sandbagged positions and manned by armed volunteers; gunfire at night was as regular as the full moon; inter-urban travel was safe only in daytime and then only in armored buses or car caravans under guard. All this before he reached the age of nineteen in 1939; the rest came afterward.

In the year 1970, nearly 50 percent of all Israelis were native born and fell into these categories in varying degrees. The picture drawn here applies first and foremost to this group, yet the immigrant to Israel can often be included in it as well. If he arrived in the country during the years of pioneering before World War II, his life has been marked by civil strife and war almost as much and sometimes to an even greater degree than the native born. If he came later, from war-torn Europe, it is even more certain that death and destruction had been close companions of his earlier years. There is no point even to attempt to reduce such backgrounds to any common denominator. Happiness is uniform, as Tolstoy wrote, but the story of every unhappy family is different. Let us pick the intensely personal story of one native-born Israeli writer, Moshe Shamir: "My son is named after my brother who fell in the War of Independence," he wrote in 1968.

This was exactly twenty years ago, when the almonds of 1948 were in full bloom. I am named after my father's brother, who fell in the ranks of the Red Army at the gates of Warsaw. This happened in 1920. My father was named after the brother of his father who was murdered in the Ukraine during a pogrom by rampaging peasants. This was in 1891 . . . Are we now still at the beginning of the road? At the middle? At the end? I only know this: in this half-century in which I live and breathe, fear of death has never left our house. . . .

In a nation of harassed refugees and survivors of disasters who have lived in open and violent conflict for so long, one expects to find a kind of feverish tension, a constricting air of constant emergency, of crisis and drama, that would be suffocating in its relentless permanency. Many foreign visitors arrive in Israel with just such expectations. The air, as we have seen in the previous chapter, is burdened by memories of a disastrous past that deeply influences the reactions of people. Yet foreigners often expect more tangible signs of current crisis, which they perhaps derive from a too literate reading of newspapers. More often than not the dangers must be pointed out to them. Unless they travel in certain exposed border regions or in the Arab territories occupied by Israel since the war of 1967, where problems are of a special nature, visitors often search in vain for signs of the human toll incurred by such a life. Faces are not more pallid than elsewhere; looks are not more anguished. Gestures and manners are not more nervous or abrupt.

There are, of course, numerous external aspects of the war that nobody can miss. The front lines on the River Jordan and along the Suez Canal that are likely to erupt in full-scale battles are distant and closed to civilians, but the ominous echoes of artillery fire rumble across a large stretch of seemingly pacific landscape. City streets are dominated by large numbers of young (and some middle-aged) men and women in drab army uniforms. The highways swarm with fully armed soldiers hitchhiking home or back to the front. Air-raid shelters are everywhere. On the main highways, cars must slow down at unexpected roadblocks as the police search for suspect Arabs. (There is almost free travel between Israel and the occupied areas.) At the entrance to movie houses and theaters ladies' handbags and gentlemen's attaché cases are checked for hidden detonants by aging civil defense guards. Evil-looking iron bars, barbed- or meshed-wire fences, enclose the campus of the Hebrew University of Jerusalem, and even the Wailing Wall on High Holy Days, as a protection against saboteurs.

Before 1967 the heaviest burden of war was felt in the border settlements. After 1967 their burden was still the heaviest, but now the dead hand of war often penetrated the interior of the country as well, in the form of sabotage and bombings in centers of civilian life —a supermarket, a student cafeteria, a crowded bus station, a residential boulevard, a movie house, an open street market.

And yet despite such disruptive dangers, the country never seemed more self-confident than in the years after the 1967 war, never on such a steady upsurge in so many vital fields of civilian life. Industry and building boomed; the rate of investment grew; education, tourism, the social services, even the arts, expanded as never before. More books were written and sold. The number of art galleries rose by a third. Never had there been as many night clubs, fancy restaurants, fashionable boutiques, cosmetic salons, boîtes, and discotheques for teen-agers. In Tel Aviv alone there were almost twice as many theaters in 1969 as there had been three years earlier. (Their repertoire was demonstratively pacific.) An ambitious program was launched in Tel Aviv for slum clearance, urban renewal, and beachfront development. A new university—the seventh in the country—was opened in Beersheba; two more were planned for the near future. As Arab saboteurs were making life in Jerusalem even less safe than it had been prior to 1967— when the front line between Israel and Jordan had run through the middle of town—work began on the construction of a vast green belt around the medieval walls and ramparts of the Old City. The battered stones were nightly illuminated in a program of son et lumière, which extolled the history of Jerusalem, City of Peace. The country's economic rate of growth soared from one percent in 1967 to 13 percent in 1968 and 9 percent in 1970. More immigrants were arriving in the country from affluent and "safe" countries than ever before in the history of Israel.

Casualties soared as well. Almost daily newspapers displayed the pictures of boys in their late teens who had fallen in action along the Suez Canal or in the Jordan Valley. But in a curious atmosphere of surface equanimity the country was just about bursting at its seams.

There is, in fact, nothing extraordinary in this equanimity. It is neither unique nor arrogant, mean nor unfeeling, nor particularly heroic. All over the world people have learned to live with danger with an apparent ease that might possibly explain why the world is a vale of tears, and perhaps why, in spite of everything, we are still here.

The islanders on Stromboli build their huts along the edge of a living volcano; when it erupts they take to their boats; as the lava subsides they return to bury their dead and rebuild their houses as though nothing had happened.

We do not really know how this is achieved. Auschwitz and Hiroshima have been endlessly studied and written about because they are said to be a part of our own civilization; observers of Hiroshima still wonder how it is possible for survivors to feel at home, as they apparently do, in this world of ours. By what dreams, by what illusions, have they managed to overcome their memories, fears, and anxieties? The condition of former inmates of Nazi concentration camps cannot have been much different and at least a hundred thousand former inmates of these camps are said to be living in Israel. In Israel their difficulties are compounded by the continuing harassment of near-permanent war, yet generally they have managed to return to a normal life. Not many can be even remotely conscious of the means by which they have achieved this adjustment, or of the psychological price they have paid.

Nor are the real strains incurred by a dangerous life any more palpable among the majority of Israelis whose single exposure to peril has been here, and not in Nazi Europe or in a Jewish ghetto in the heart of a rioting Iraqi or Algerian city. It is customary to talk of such perils, past and present, as a source of high morale. But no one really knows the full human costs—as against the purely budgetary costs—of continually facing up to hazard. We know that it is no small matter to live under a constant threat of annihilation; but such knowledge is invariably vague. Some suspect the price may be high, but no one really knows the exact amount paid by Israelis in psychological entanglements, debilitating repressions, compensations, and illusions, dangerous and otherwise.

Consider, then, a second-generation Israeli, at one of the crucial moments that occur all too frequently in his life, the hour when he is called upon to bid his family good-bye and to forsake his civilian occupation, whatever it may be, in order to rejoin the army. He has already finished his regular, compulsory period of two and one-half or three years' army service. But he remains a reservist until he is fifty-four. Let us assume that he is thirty years old, married, with children.

In such a case it could easily be his seventh or eighth call-up within the past five years.

He was either born in the country or brought to Israel at a young age. He is neither refugee nor immigrant. He is a product of life in the new country. His character and outlook have been fashioned by its peculiar challenges and demands. He was probably carefully brought up by a fretting mother who ran out into the street after her wily offspring with just another banana (for vitamins) or another spoonful of sour cream (for strength). In school—frequently in his youth movement as well—he was nurtured on solemn ideals of social justice, Jewish humanism, voluntarism, tolerance, comradeship, and above all, respect for the sanctity of human life. In school he recited lines by Rachel (Bluwstein), the popular poetess of the Second *Aliya*, herself a pioneer in the Jordan Valley during the early days of settlement before the first World War. She wrote in "My Country":

> I haven't sung thy praise
> Nor glorified thy name
> In tales of valor
> And in wars.
> Only a tree I plant
> On Jordan's bank.
> Only a path my feet have tracked
> Across the fields.

He was probably made to learn these lines by heart; and rightly so, for they reflect the original ethos of this entire enterprise, the extraordinary craving to plant and to build that was such a powerful force in the early days of settlement; it was only marginally "nationalistic," and without it the state of Israel would probably never have come into being. He probably still knows those lines by heart, as well as the words and lively tune of another famous song:

> We have come to the country
> To build and be rebuilt by it.

He remembers them fondly: to build, not to make war. But on the day he is called up again by the army—when he kills as he occasionally must—on such days there occurs and reoccurs in his life a bitter moment of truth. He now senses that somehow, somewhere, he must reorient his outlook. If his previous commitments were superficial, if he is ignorant, or weak, or tired, he simply conforms to the group in which he finds himself, and adopts its norms, which may be brutal or humane. On the other hand, if he has a particular strength of character, if he is especially sensitive, his reorientation will be more personal and will reach deeper. He begins to be more alert to the evasions behind the pathos and Victorian humanism of the early Zionists. He realizes that nothing in life is given; trees planted, paths cut in the fields are not enough. Whatever is his has been paid for with unjust deaths. Such knowledge matures him considerably; he becomes perceptibly sadder. The outsider cannot fully realize the depth and extent of this sadness unless he first considers the time sequence and the toll. He must measure the intensity of effort and the disruption of normal life against the blind hopes and glorious promises perennially attached to them by public and private opinion.

Young men have gone to war three times within less than twenty years. Each war called for near total exertions; each war was fought in the firm belief that it would bring peace within reach, or at least a little closer. None has. On the contrary, year after year, war after war, the basic situation remains static. There are some Israelis, still in their early forties (as there must also be Egyptians), who have three times in their lives fought over the same arid, desolate, God-forsaken wadi in the desert that controls a strategic point along the old Egyptian-Israeli frontier. They have gone from war to war; it has always been the same, dismal, bloody wadi, only a few miles long, yellowish-brown, under a thick dustcloud in the scorching heat of the desert sun. They took it, they left it: they took it again and left it again. They took it once more; nothing changed.

Many thousands must go through life haunted by the harrowing sights, sounds and smells, which have been the recurrent features of their youth and manhood; the groans of wounded and those dying in their arms; the screams of fear more piercing than the thunder of nearby explosions; the sight of uncountable corpses littering vast flat expanses of sand; the wretched refugees walking off into an unknown distance; the machines of war ablaze like huge torches against the darkening desert skies, the stench of burning fuel and incandescent rubber mixing with the reek of roasting human skin and flesh.

"When, my friends, have we last seen peace?" the poet Chaim Guri exclaimed some years ago in a short prose piece. "This soil is insatiable," he wrote bitterly. "How many more graves, how many more coffins are needed until it will cry out—enough, enough!"

One of the few surviving Israeli paratroopers dropped into Nazi-occupied Europe in 1944, herself a near-legendary figure, rose at a public meeting in her Upper Galilee *kibbutz* shortly after the 1967 war. Her interpolation was brief. "There is one question that gives me nightmares and I would like to ask it," she said. "How many wars will our boys fight before they will become animals?" She sat down again and waited for answers.

It is the younger Israeli who must bear on his shoulders and with his nerves the main burden of this seemingly endless emergency. One result has been a growing cult of toughness among younger people. It has led on occasion to bizarre refractions of the mind. In the diary he kept during the Suez-Sinai war of 1956, Moshe Dayan recalled being told that two distinguished paratroop officers had taken to spiritualism and were communicating with their dead comrades on those nights when they were not out on action.

"I could not believe my ears," Dayan wrote. "I cannot imagine more balanced characters than these men. When I told A. this, he answered, to my surprise, without a smile that if I had gone out on action for two years and each week my best friends had fallen right next to me, my sobriety and stubbornness would fail me and the borderline between life and death would become obscured."

There have also been cases of senseless murder and wanton destruction, such as the mass killing in 1956 of peaceful Arab villagers at Kafr Kassem; or the attempted razing, in 1967, of the town of Kalkilya, only a mile across the pre-1967 Jordanian border, for reasons, apparently, of personal vengeance. Before the razing, the population of this unfortunate town had been evacuated and sent off to fend for itself in the hills.

Nevertheless, these have been extreme cases and relatively rare. The killers of Kafr Kassem were court-martialed. A few years later they were amnestied; yet the massacre at Kafr Kassem led to an important decision in the highest Appelate Military Court, which enjoined all soldiers to disobey any manifestly illegal order. Such a principle had not been clearly established before. There is little doubt that the Kafr Kassem verdict had a profound effect on the subsequent behavior of military personnel.

In the case of Kalkilya, while army sappers were still moving through the doomed city, systematically blowing up one house after another, the destruction order was rescinded. In Kafkaesque fashion, the same military authorities who first destroyed, now invited the population back and then financed the complete reconstruction of all that had been heartlessly and senselessly blown up before.

Legendary and still revered by army regulars, youngsters, and by a section of the popular press is the figure of Meir Har-Zion. In an army which is supplanting the *kibbutz* as the "most genuinely Israeli institution," Har-Zion has become a sort of culture hero, the living symbol of a "new," coldblooded, fighting Jew with an armor-plated conscience. In the Israeli army, paratrooper units, much like the cavalry in the early history of America, perform the most arduous tasks and take the heaviest toll. Har-Zion is Israel's most famous paratrooper. He acquired his fame in the mid-1950s, and continues as a hero even though, severely crippled in action, he long ago returned to civilian life. Moshe Dayan has written that Har-Zion's "fighting instinct and courage set an example for the entire Israel Defense Forces." Yet Har-Zion came closest to justifying the fears that a lifetime of waging war and decades of legitimized killing may turn men into animals.

Har-Zion was born a third-generation *sabra* in 1934, in the village of Herzlia a few miles north of Tel Aviv. His father was an agricultural laborer. His mother's father had been brought to the country in 1868, at the age of three. In bringing their son to Palestine, Har-Zion's great-grandparents, orthodox Russian Jews, were fulfilling a pious vow that if God graced them with a son, they would go to live in the Holy City of Jerusalem. Har-Zion's grandfather grew up in the medieval Jewish quarter of Jerusalem. He was one of the first who turned from the religious, "non-productive" life to join the early pioneers in their newly established colonies. He moved to Rishon le-Zion, planted a vineyard and an orange grove, and worked in the fields until he was ninety and died three years later.

His daughter, Har-Zion's mother, was born in Rishon le-Zion. She became a schoolteacher and her modest earnings supplemented her husband's meager wages as an agricultural laborer. Har-Zion had a very trying childhood. The Arab rebellion broke out when he was three years old and the family home, on the outskirts of Herzlia, was subject to all kinds of dangers. His parents separated when he was thirteen. His mother and two sisters moved to Beit Alpha, a *kibbutz* in the Valley of Esdraelon; he and his father went to Ein Harod, another *kibbutz* in the same area. He was a moody and restless teen-ager with an obsessive urge to prove his courage and physical prowess, and often ran off on dangerous adventures.

While he was still a boy, he set out alone on strenuous and highly dangerous foot tours of the southern desert and forbidden border areas. When he was fifteen, seized by curiosity to see the River Jordan where it flows through Arab territory, he took his thirteen-year-old sister Shoshana and crossed the Jordanian border at Beisan. The two children climbed a few barbed-wire fences, successfully maneuvered a mine field, and calmly walked hand-in-hand past a Jordanian police station to the river bank, some five miles away, where they ate their picnic lunch within full view of Arab villagers and soldiers. On this first excursion the two youngsters managed to get away. They were not to be so lucky the next time when two years later they went off to tour the length of the River Jordan north of the Lake of Galilee, a forbidden area where few Israelis had set foot in the past ten years, and fewer had returned alive. Har-Zion and his fifteen-year-old sister were immediately captured by the Syrians, savagely beaten, and thrown into a Damascus jail. They were repatriated some time later through the efforts of the International Red Cross. Other Israeli prisoners in Syria either died under torture or went slowly insane after years in horrible jails.

But even this did not daunt the two youngsters; they continued on their private jaunts. This playful courting of danger, this desire to explore enemy-held territory, was not an isolated phenomenon at the time. There was an irrepressible urge among teen-agers to roam about in Arab-held lands. Some were returned unharmed; some were shot. The sensitive novelist Naomi Fraenkel, a biographer of Har-Zion, has suggested that the craze may have been peculiar to the atmosphere of the first decade of Independence. In 1948, Har-Zion and his contemporaries had been children; they had received a marvelous gift, a whole new country to tour and explore. Yet it was claustrophobically fenced in on all sides; almost everywhere they turned were signs, "Halt!" "Danger! Mines!" Crossing those borders became a tempting challenge.

Har-Zion was eighteen when he joined the army in 1953. To his physical prowess and daredevil courage, tested and refined on his private jaunts as a teen-ager was now added a brutal ruthlessness that soon stamped him for a "special" unit of commando fighters. It was a new unit, in which he was one of the first recruits. The unit is now fortunately extinct. At that time Company 101 served to deter Arab terrorist attacks on Israeli civilians through the staging of retaliatory acts. The then Chief of Staff, General Moshe Dayan, explained the new doctrine of retaliatory strikes against civilian targets across the border: Arab governments would restrain their own irregulars only after it became clear that the "theft of one cow from Ramat Ha-Kovesh will hurt Kalkilya (across the nearby Jordanian border), and that the murder of one Jew at Ruhama will endanger the population of Gaza."

It was not a very far-sighted policy and not especially effective; the difference between act and retaliation blurred quickly in the recurrent pattern of strike and counter-strike, until both became so frequent that they culminated, almost inevitably, in the Sinai war of 1956.

Har-Zion seemed born to his new task; he possessed a natural aura of authority. His courage, in the face of danger, was almost super-human, or—as others will have it—almost animal-like. As a young commando, he took part almost nightly in difficult reprisal actions. Unsparing of himself and of others, he was brutally indiscriminate in inflicting punishment upon his adversaries. He began to personify an Israeli version of the Indian Fighters in the American Wild West. Laconically killing Arab soldiers, peasants, and townspeople in a kind of fury without hatred, he remained cold-blooded and thoroughly efficient, simply doing a job and doing it well, twice or three times a week for months; finally he was put out of action, critically wounded in a raid on a Jordanian police station. His life was saved by an emergency battlefield tracheotomy with a penknife, but he suffered permanent injury to his hands and voice.

His legend stems only partly from his army exploits. He was as well known and admired for his private exploits. It was in these private ventures that he showed himself a man not only capable of daring, but of ruthlessness that served only his own private whims.

One cloudy evening in April 1956, Har-Zion, bored by the inactivity of a short holiday from his unit, decided to make a private foray into enemy territory. He evaded the mines along the Israeli-Jordan border near Jerusalem by jumping from rock to rock. He later declared that he had wanted to have a look at Jericho and the monasteries cut into the rocks of Wadi Kelt. On his way back to Jerusalem on the main highway, he shot and killed an Arab soldier. This killing on a private jaunt did not discolor his by now legendary fame. Some time later his sister was killed by some Bedouin on one of her own illegal trips into enemy territory. Har-Zion took the law into his own hands, killing two Bedouin whom he thought to be among those responsible for his sister's death. This time he was arrested, and could have been charged with murder. At Prime Minister Ben Gurion's personal intervention he was released without trial. The case was closed, but not forgotten.

Today, half crippled, married, with four children, he lives on a lonely farm atop a windy mountain overlooking the Jordan Valley south of the Lake of Galilee. He published his private diaries in 1969 —the laconic account of his youthful exploits:

> Halt! Rolling stones ahead of us. I notice a man roaming in the area. Now we can no longer try to withdraw quietly. He must be liquidated. I raise the tommy-gun. Jibli approaches, crawling. "Har, for God's sake, the knife!" His tightly-pressed teeth glitter in the darkness. . . . I lower the tommy and unsheath my commando knife. We crawl towards the man who is now singing an Arab song to himself. In a moment his song will be a moan of agony. I tremble all tense and ready, it is the first time I use this weapon. Will I fail? We come closer and closer. Here he is, a few meters away. We jump. Jibli gets hold of him. I push the knife into the striped robe covering his back. Blood spurts from the wound. Now there is no time for thinking. We stab. The body before us moans, fights for its life. Slowly, resistance ceases.

General Ariel Sharon, a former commander of the paratroopers, contributed an enthusiastic introduction to this diary. He wrote that Har-Zion was the fighting symbol not only of the paratroopers, but of the entire Israel Defense Forces.

Such legends are likely to grow wherever men, no matter how little they like it, are forced to live by their swords. Popular legends are keys to the coded articulation of a culture. We must read them at our own risk with little confidence in what we presume to have deciphered. Every army to an extent relies on the exploitation of the baser instincts in men. The borderline between so-called "legitimate" and illegitimate brutality is nowhere clear. It is further blurred by war. In such a brutalizing situation it is surprising that relatively few Israelis have gone as far as Har-Zion, and that by and large he remains a notable exception. The legend, though, may be more important than the man himself. Symbols, like caricatures, must exaggerate in order to be effective. How effective are they?

The first thing to note is a spreading cult of toughness. It does not go unopposed; there are frequent protests in the newspapers, by teachers and parents. This cult of toughness is not, as yet, accompanied by a disdain of intellect and of moral qualities. But there are times when it comes close. Teachers, parents, youth leaders, engage in a constant battle against the senseless emulation of military practices and needless rigors in the youth movements and schools.

The para-military youth organization GADNA ("regiments of youth") has been especially prone to this kind of regimentation. GADNA operates in conjunction with the educational authorities in nearly all of the high schools. Senseless tests of endurance under excruciatingly difficult conditions of climate and terrain in the name of a spartan ideal of physical fitness have led to fatal accidents among teen-agers. Almost every summer a number of children die of sunstroke in the desert where they have been made to march for days, or tumble down deep precipices while walking on narrow mountain paths in exercises designed to steel their nerves and train them to unflinching courage.

A spartan rigidity has developed over the years and now marks large segments of the younger adult population. It often spills over from the military life, where it was acquired, to the civilian sphere. Foreigners are often more aware of such characteristics than some of the most critical Israelis. In 1969 a team of young Israeli long-distance walkers participated in an international walking contest in Holland. One of the Dutch organizers asked the Israelis why everything they did was done in military rhythm. "Singing, eating, resting, everything! Why are there never dropouts on the Israeli team? Why does everything with you function as in a well-oiled but inhuman machine? Your teams," said the Dutchman, "remind me of German youth groups during the thirties. . . ." An Israeli newsman who had overheard the remark reported that the Dutchman meant no insult. "He simply wanted to indicate elements of the Israeli character." The newspaperman also reported that when some members of the Israeli team suddenly had felt sick and wanted to drop out, the team captain had announced: "It is better to die than stop walking, and be a disgrace to Israel."

Frequent and prolonged periods of service in the army breeds a stark, intensely introverted, icy matter-of-factness in the young that contrasts sharply with the externalized, rather verbose emotionalism of their elders. Such starkness is partly the natural reaction of the young to a public atmosphere still heavy with the ideological fervor and slogans of a previous age. But it is also a result of the kind of life they lead. The more puritan older settlers often grumble that young people are too selfish, too career-minded, not sufficiently responsive to this or that sacred tenet of traditional Zionist ideology. They voice their fears frequently in the stately columns of the daily newspaper *Davar*, a curious mixture of early *Pravda* and old-style Quakerism, mouthpiece of the ruling labor establishment, and the abode of untiring watchdogs for purity of pioneering manners and ideology. There were times, in the early 1960s, when discotheques, and even espresso coffee shops, were declared corrupt and decadent by some old-timers.

Yet younger Israelis have never shirked their responsibilities in time of danger. The power of ideas to sustain human enterprise, a power that played such a great role in the earlier lives of the founding fathers, has been substituted among younger people by an unreflecting, elemental urge for self-preservation.

The language of younger Israelis is often inordinately stark, divested of all ornament and elegance, without nuance, and delivered in harsh staccato sequences. One reason is that "official" Hebrew is still too formal and lags far behind the needs of daily intercourse; the developing street patois that substitutes for what is missing or inadequate in the dictionary is still raw and unformed. Another reason may be more important. The harsh starkness that marks *sabra* speech and manners stems from many years of deliberate educational efforts to produce "normal," "manly," "free," "new" Jews, unsullied by the shameful weaknesses of exile.

Yael Dayan, the novelist, draws a portrait of the young *sabra* hero in her *Envy the Frightened*. "Do you know what he is afraid of? To be afraid—this is the fear that masters him, until all other fears,

human normal, healthy ones, are pushed aside and stop existing."
Bruno Bettelheim, the psychologist, quotes an Israeli psychoanalyst,
who has devoted much of his professional life to the study of *kibbutznik*. ". . . our children are ashamed to be ashamed, are afraid to be
afraid. They are afraid to love, are afraid to give of themselves. . . . I
am not sure whether it is a deficiency in emotion or a being afraid of
feeling. . . ."

The letters written by young Israelis to their sweethearts are notoriously dry, unimaginative, and frequently oddly impersonal. They are
often so skimpy in exclamations of love, devotion, or longing—indeed
of any feelings whatsoever—that a reader may suspect a near-total lack
of sensitivity and refinement. Or else he may suspect that the young
writers, if they have feelings, are so frightened by them—or so
ashamed and embarrassed—that they have apparently resolved to keep
them permanently concealed. One does not talk of feelings, one rarely
admits that they exist.

The tendency to shy away from feeling, as from some vast unrecon-
noitered enemy territory too dangerous for loquacious traveling, is a
basic trait in the character of the new generation of Israelis. It was
well illustrated in a conversation in New York a few weeks after the
Six Day War of 1967. Elie Wiesel, the Jewish writer, interviewed
Colonel Mordechai Gur, one of the celebrated heroes of the war.
Colonel Gur's brigade, at considerable cost in human lives, had
captured the Old City of Jerusalem. The emotional impact upon
Jews everywhere had been tremendous. During the nineteen years that
intervened between 1948 and 1967, the Wailing Wall, the old Jewish
quarter, the Temple Mount, Absalom's tomb, and all other religious
and national monuments within the ancient city walls had been
closed to Israelis. The following questions and answers ensued between the Jewish writer and the Israeli general:

> Wiesel: . . . you were the first up on the Temple Mount, weren't you?
> Gur: That's right.
> Wiesel: Were you excited?
> Gur: What do you think?
> Wiesel: Did you cry?
> Gur: No, I did not cry.
> Wiesel: Why not?
> Gur: I don't know. I don't like tears.

Wiesel: Did you feel any?

Gur: Of course. Like all the others. But I didn't cry.

Wiesel: What *did* you feel?

Gur: I don't think I can put it into words.

Wiesel: Try.

Gur: No, I don't think people should discuss their feelings.

Wiesel: What should people discuss?

Gur: Who says you've got to discuss anything? You don't have to.

Wiesel: I beg to differ. It's a duty—and a privilege—to talk about this. . . .

Yet out of the same war came an extraordinary document of una-bashed self-revelation in a style that Wiesel would have loved. Shortly after the war a group of young *kibbutzniks*, headed by a former pupil of Martin Buber, went from *kibbutz* to *kibbutz*, asking ex-fighters a number of penetrating, highly personal questions. They tape-recorded a long series of interviews with young soldiers, which were later pub-lished under the title *"Siach Lochamim"* ("Fighters' Talk"). The interviews and dialogues exude an air of unrehearsed spontaneity and represent a long stream-of-consciousness meandering on life and death in the Holy Land today. The young men are talking among them-selves about themselves. They touch upon deeply personal problems with rare candor and lack of reserve, and ponder such controversial subjects as "individual morality" in times of war, the limits of "duty," "patriotism," and "discipline." The reliability of the dialogues has been enhanced by the lucky accident of timing. They were recorded almost immediately after the war; many participants were still in a state of semi-shock, and had not yet closed up emotionally, or frozen intellectually under the crushing impact of political clichés that the continuing crisis would generate.

The picture that emerges from this unusual document is far from uniform. But, like participants in a psychodrama who engaged in group therapy by acting out their innermost problems, some of the speakers in these dialogues seem close to an emotional breakdown from the harrowing blow of a war they had been educated, not in favor of, but rather against. To understand this schizoid anguish, it must be remembered that, in spite of the emphasis on "manly vigor," unsullied by the "weakness of exile," no single group in Israel has been so systematically brought up in a spirit of humanitarian idealism as these young products of *kibbutz* society. Yet, at the same time, no group in the Israeli population has a better fighting record. One youngster in *Siach Lochamim* noted this fighting record and the high casualty rate among *kibbutzniks*. He concluded bitterly that the *kibbutz*, which was meant as a new way of life, was becoming a main reservoir for "specialists in making war"; the new way of life was becoming a new way for the young to die early. "We have always been taught to respect human life above everything else ... and here we are turning living and breathing people into heaps of bones and tortured flesh...."

None of the participants in these dialogues doubted the justice of their cause; they saw it not in terms of ideology but of survival. None rejoiced in victory. Few could forget the scenes of suffering, or overlook the price paid by both victors and vanquished. "What's the point of living?" asked one. "It is a tax we pay," answered another, "like income tax. And we must carry on."

One said: "I came back terribly depressed. Victory meant nothing for me. I couldn't even smile, although people were cheering us when we passed the Mandelbaum Gate [in Jerusalem]. I never want to go back there ... we had to do it, I know. But don't let it happen again. If it never happens again, perhaps it was worth it. Perhaps...."

"I am still trying to run away from it. No, I don't even want to think about it.... I feel like vomiting, an awful feeling of disgust whenever the subject comes up...."

"There it was, the tank, that a short time ago had attacked us. It was hit ... going up in flames ... a figure emerged from it ... all in flames moving towards an Israeli jeep in dazed agony, in flight in the wrong direction ... a moving torch all ablaze ... the men in the jeep killed him ... he may have died anyway ... his death was inevitable. But not to those who shot him. During the day, when they go about their work, they may forget him ... but at night he will be there all right. He'll be there with them when they dream and when they wake...."

"I would go to war willingly if I knew that it was the last war. But I know I am going to die for something which has no end...."

"Maybe we really ought to have a lot of children; to have more and more children," said one.

"Why?" asked another, "so there will be a lot of soldiers?"

"No, so that if one dies he would not be missed so much."

"How can you raise children this way and show them flowers and all sorts of beautiful things and know at the same time that maybe in ten years, they, or their fathers. . . ."

They posed such questions again and again, and, of course, found no answers. But pervading their bitter fatalism was a kind of determination, repeated often in these dialogues, not to let circumstance completely destroy the moral fiber.

One soldier told his interviewers that in one of the battles, after he had shot an Egyptian, he discovered that he had missed. "I had to shoot," he said, "but I was glad that he got away."*

If you are forced to do something bad, or negative, you must "know that you are doing something bad." Can a man rise above the dismal condition of his life? Most participants in the dialogues felt that it was possible, if they could only remain themselves: cool and moderate even when provoked to hate and cruelty by savage, hating, primitive enemies. If, even in the heat of battle, they could retain their critical faculties, if they could scrupulously exercise "normal" moral restraints. Perhaps they would not succeed, but they must continue to try. Although hated, they must not hate. Desperate, they must not lose hope. Victorious in battle, they must still clear their minds of cant. This is perhaps what one young soldier had in mind when he wrote to his wife during the Six Day War.

> . . . we see soldiers and they wave goodby . . . and between those waving, lie others who will never get up on their feet again . . . when you look upon all this senseless destruction, when you look at these gigantic machines of war you feel like asking the human species, "Tell me, have you gone absolutely berserk?"

Intensity of experience is inordinately heightened in Israel by the closeness of everything. Proximity, as it increases cohesion, aggravates the strains of permanent war. The war has been mostly a "limited" one, but in a country as small as Israel even "limited" calamities easily assume an air of sickening abundance. As in a pressure cooker, lower temperatures produce faster results.

* This is a classic Jewish dilemma. When Jacob returned from Haran he was threatened by Esau's army of four hundred men. The Bible says that Jacob was "greatly afraid and distressed" (Genesis 32:7). Rashi, the classic annotator, explained: he was "afraid" of death; he was "distressed" that he might kill.

Distances are short. Much of the country is uninhabited desertland; it is thus even smaller than it appears on most maps, where it is a tiny speck. From a rooftop in Tel Aviv the outskirts of Jerusalem can be seen with the naked eye; Haifa is only an hour's train ride from Tel Aviv. Within this small triangle, close to 80 percent of the population is concentrated in tight, human clusters. Israel is a highly urbanized society, yet it is extremely difficult for individuals to achieve that anonymity, which is both a blessing of life in great urban centers and a cause for some of its pains. Insulation is rare; most Israelis live almost painfully close to each other, in small flats, with little privacy. As in other Mediterranean countries, much of the drama and comedy of daily life happen out of doors in full view and hearing of all. Seven or eight months of the year, people leave their hot, badly insulated living rooms to eat and play on the balconies that attach to all flats as a matter of course. Most Israelis live in small, cooperatively owned apartment houses that are managed (or mismanaged) by tenant committees, or by all of the tenants together. The system, characteristically Israeli, nurtures a degree of neighborliness infinitely more intense than that found in other urban societies. It can sometimes be excruciatingly hard to bear.

Another characteristically Israeli institution is the neighborhood unit of near-identical cooperatively owned apartments, the *shikun*. A product of mass immigration and bureaucratic convenience, it is likely to remain a central feature of Israeli housing for at least another generation. The *shikun* is a planned housing development. It is often built as a housing estate for people who already know each other well: for specific ethnic groups, members of a single profession, or even of a single political party. There are *shikunim* for Zionist veterans, immigrants from Poland, from Iraq, or from the United States, for teachers, needle workers, journalists, and, of course, for demobilized soldiers. Tenant owners can sell their flats to anyone, regardless of the "character" of the *shikun*; yet a tight atmosphere of togetherness remains.

A large part of the Israeli population still lives almost tribally within the confines of a particular ethnic group, or mother tongue. But because Israel is so small and its manners so informal, it is still easier than it would be in bigger, older, or more stratified countries, to know "practically everybody," from the Prime Minister to the latest boxing champion. There is at least, a strong feeling that one knows. Chaim Topol, the young actor, expressed it in a remark in 1969 to the American magazine, *Vogue*: "I know *everyone* of my age in Israel."

This is especially true in the case of *kibbutzniks*, of veteran settlers and their descendants. Insofar as morale is concerned, veteran settlers probably still count the most. They form the political and intellectual elite; judging by the casualty rates, they also bear a highly disproportionate share of the security burden. *Kibbutzniks* are only 4 percent of the population, but 25 percent of the casualties in the 1967 war were *kibbutzniks*.

Under such circumstances, tragedy rarely remains isolated within the narrower confines of family intimacy. It quickly spreads to a widening configuration of overlapping circles. In the *kibbutz*, with its communal dining room and similar collective arrangements for hundreds of members (one large, loose family, really), this is too obvious to require any further elaboration. But it is often true also in the towns where news travels fast and immediately affects apparent strangers. On a hot summer afternoon, it takes but a short while for most people in the *shikun*, or on the street, to know that the red-headed boy from number 5, who was only nineteen, whose mother beats her rug on the balcony too early in the morning, whose father works as a tax collector for the city, was killed this morning by a landmine, or during an artillery barrage on the frontier.

Until the cease fire of 1970 hardly a day has passed without casualties. The names of those killed are broadcast over radio and television. Pictures of the dead are regularly and prominently printed in the newspapers. This is a common procedure in most countries; but here the papers are all national, and so the tragedy is as well. Every fourth or fifth speech by the Minister of Defense, or by the Army Chief of Staff is a funeral eulogy. Death in war has often been as common and as regular in Israel as death in traffic accidents. And yet, each time it strikes, it electrifies the country as though it were the first time. Each death in action draws strangers closer to one another. It is at such moments that one notices in Israel a sense of cohesion so strong it makes the country seem more like a big village than a state.

The mass media powerfully dramatize this state of affairs. Israelis are obsessive listeners to the radio news. It is almost a druglike addiction. Few try to kick the habit; even fewer succeed. Enforced absti-

nence can lead to curious withdrawal symptoms as when, during a
strike of newscasters a few years ago, pharmacists in Jerusalem claimed
that the record quantity of headache pills were sold. The extraordinary strength of this addiction is brought out by international comparisons; yet it is so obvious that audience surveys are not really needed.
No people in the entire world tunes in to the news as often, as
regularly, and with such fervor. Seven or eight times a day, at the
sound of a news beep, most Israelis pause at whatever they are doing,
to hear whether there has been another air battle or artillery exchange
across the Suez Canal or some new act of sabotage by Arab terrorists.
Not infrequently names of the latest casualties are read out. ("My
God, isn't that so-and-so's son?") Modern Israelis turn to their radios
like their ancestors once turned to prayer. The habit of listening to
the news so often goes back to World War II when German forces
under Rommel were approaching Palestine from the southwest.

Israelis are early risers. Most people are at work before half-past
seven in the morning. At six and at seven, the sound of "Here is the
news, read by ..." spreads from window to terrace, echoes through
courtyards and streets from one end of the country to the other.
"Today, in the early hours of the morning, a landmine ... the Minister of Foreign Affairs last night warned that if Egyptian artillery guns
... the body of corporal. ..."

The habit of following the news so often and so closely partly
explains the sudden shifts in the public mood, which can be as sharp
as they are frequent. Israelis easily fall from heights of exhilaration to
dark abysses of gloom; from glowing hope for imminent peace to
bleak depression that the war will never end and that they may be
crushed by it. One morning there is a hopeful report that the Arab
position is softening; a few hours later the morning's hopes are
crushed by a subsequent newscast. Gloom sets in until the next sudden shift in mood. One day the great powers are ready to impose a
settlement; next day they are in disagreement again. One day seven
Syrian MIG fighter planes are shot down by two Israeli Mirages. Next
day an Israeli airliner is blown up at a foreign airport.

Israeli buses are often equipped with radio sets. Theoretically they
must be turned off at the request of a single passenger, but such
requests are rare, and not always effective. The loudspeaker, attached
above the luggage racks, emits mostly pop music, lost in the general

commotion. But every hour on the hour comes the NEWS. It blares out over the noise of traffic, and the entire bus falls silent. There is an eeriness in scenes like this that is characteristically Israeli. The entire country turns, for a few moments, into an intricate system of exposed and interlocking nerves; at such moments it resembles a huge village square teeming with humanity, exhilarated or worried. In restaurants too, in sidewalk cafes, offices, workshops, green grocers (even in some elevators serviced by Musak), the news is switched on a couple of times each day. Men, off to temporary reserve duty with the army, would sooner leave a bottle of brandy behind than part with their handy, Japanese-made transistors. They carry the news with them, even as they make it, wherever they go. It has been estimated that seven out of ten combat soldiers during the 1967 war carried transistors to the front and switched them on as often as possible. At dinner parties or late evening get-togethers, food and conversation are frequently interrupted by "Hold it, the news is on," or by an irritated, "Dammit, we just missed it." More moderate addicts, professing ignorance over this or that latest event, are frequently met with incredulity, admonition, or the somewhat contemptuous cry of *"Ma? Lo shamata chadashot?"* (What? you haven't heard the news?) It is one of the basic stock phrases of everyday conversation. Another is *"Ma nishma?"* (What's happening?) which has become as much an informal greeting as "hello" or "nice to see you."

All this may be part and parcel of what has traditionally been considered the "Jewish" character. It is often said that Jews are congenital worriers. Not only have they always been great newspaper readers, but in many countries they are prominent as journalists and editors. Jews are said to pursue news like others pursue liquor because they are constantly taxed by nervous anxieties. Perhaps this relentless pursuit of the news relieves such anxiety, which in turn is perpetuated by the pain inflicted through the cure. There is an almost masochistic quality in this pursuit. Jews have a wistful tendency to expect a situation to worsen; when it does not, it is regarded as misleading or temporary. Perhaps Jews have been conditioned by their history to regard calamities as a law of nature.

Most observers of the Jewish scene point to the role of humor in this essentially pessimistic attitude toward events. Humor is often described as a weapon in the hands of weak Jews facing superior forces. It is seen as a psychological defense mechanism to preserve the sanity of men in absurd situations. Jewish jokes are only in the narrowest sense about Jews; they are more often little essays in irony. In a classic example, a Jewish refugee running from the Nazis across Europe during World War II finally reaches Portugal. He rushes to the American Embassy and pleads with the visa officer for an entry permit to the United States. The American visa officer checks his list and patiently informs him that he may come back in twelve years when his Polish quota will be due. The refugee thanks him profusely. He withdraws to the door and turns around meekly for one more question. "Yes? What is it?" the Visa Officer inquires, less patiently. "Mr. Consul, I just want to know—when I come back in twelve years, is that in the morning or in the afternoon?"

This kind of *Galgenhumor*, once so dear to the European Jew, has become almost extinct in Israel. One finds it among older people, and then quite rarely. Most traditionally "Jewish" jokes, even those about Israel, are nowadays conceived in New York, in Moscow, or in Warsaw, where, during the Arab-Israeli war of 1967, the few remaining Jews became such a prominent source of sardonic, widely quoted anecdotes, that the irritated pro-Arab authorities issued a special warning against this "counter-revolutionary" activity. Yet foreign-made humor, however successful it is abroad, often sounds flat, contrived, and irrelevant to Israeli ears. *Sabra* humor—not a very developed art as yet—is different. It rarely touches upon the security situation. There are few Israeli-made jokes on the Arab-Israeli conflict. *Sabra* humor hardly excels in the kind of biting, yet humane, self-irony that is the hallmark of traditional Jewish humor. It is cooler, a bit distant, or abstract, in the shaggy-dog style. In his humor, the *sabra* is critical not of himself, but of the high-sounding pathos of the older generation: "At this festive occasion of Herzl's death, let us stand for a moment in his favor."

But while much of the traditional Jewish humor seems gone, much of the perennial fretting remains—the traditionally Jewish routine of complaining and griping that Leo Rosten, in *The Joys of Yiddish*, identifies as essential components of a condition known in Yiddish as *kvetching*. The modern Hebrew equivalent, *ohev tzarot* (a love of trouble), is but a dim echo. Another Yiddish word *kutter* (from the

German *Kater*, or cat) has been for some years a *sabra* expression for whining. It is noteworthy that a Yiddish word fell into the vernacular of youngsters who do not otherwise speak that language, to denote an activity for which there is no lack of authentic Hebrew terms.

Yehiye b'seder (it will be all right), *bli panika* (don't panic), *al tidag* (don't worry), and *lo asson* (it's not tragedy) are four of the most common Hebrew expressions in daily usage. They are employed in more varied ways than similar expressions in another language. The other side of worry is the constant admonition not to worry, that everything will be all right. The sight of a broken-down car on the road, an unhappy expression on someone's face, the news of another border incident, all evoke a quick rejoinder of *al tidag* or *bli panika*. But when a public speaker tells an Israeli audience that "things are not going to be easy. . . ." or "we may soon find ourselves again in great trouble. . ." or "it is going to get very tough. . ." an audible murmur of "I told you so. . ." usually rumbles across the hall.

An irrepressible penchant for pessimistic prophesying can be noticed daily in the Israeli press. The United States is constantly on "the verge" of "selling Israel out"; or buckling under "extremely strong pressure." The Russians are "just about" to land forces in the Near East to join their Arab allies. The French government reportedly has advised Egypt to refuse a peace settlement with Israel. The Egyptians appear "just about" to launch an attack.

It is the Israeli way of screaming *gevalt*,* or "Help! Burglars!" at the slightest noise. There are times when such *gevalts* are backed up by facts, or realistic estimates. In at least as many instances there are no substantiating facts whatsoever; the headlines are just as black and the editorials just as angry. The "well-informed sources" of the newspapers, or their "political observers" are frequently ill-concealed pseudonyms of the writers themselves. They have continually voiced so many unnecessary prophecies of gloom that it is a wonder newspapers are still so avidly read by the general public, unless the public buys them precisely for the gloom they are spreading. Any slight increase in emigration has evoked desperate cries that the country will soon be empty. A few elderly Jewish ladies visiting a Christian clergyman in

---

* *Gevalt* is another well-known Yiddish word, both an expletive and a noun. It denotes fear, shocked amazement, a cry for help, or a desperate expression of protest. According to a Jewish proverb, "man comes into the world with an *oy* and leaves with a *gevalt!*"

Jerusalem can cause a press campaign against the dangerous assaults of proselytizing missionaries. *Gevaltism* is the marked characteristic of the Israeli press.

Israeli newspapers, when they are proven wrong in their dire predictions, do not lose readers. An inner need seems to be satisfied. Israelis are apt to repeat to one another: "The Americans are quiet now, but they will make mince meat of us soon enough if we refuse to agree to their demands. . ." or "Well, prices are stable now, but just wait until after the elections, when you will see everything collapse. I have it on good authority. . . ." There is a built-in hyperbole in such *gevaltism*. During the economic recession of 1966 a favorite anecdote was about a sign at Lod Airport that proclaimed: "Will the last one out [of the country] please switch off the lights."

But while Israelis cheerfully await the worst, they desperately go on hoping for the very best—above all for peace. A survey taken a few years ago showed that Israelis, irrespective of background, sex, age, occupation, and cultural or economic level, had a greater fear of war than of any other possible disaster. Literature imbues these findings with a depth of nuance that statistical figures lack. Much that is written by Israeli-educated or Israeli-born younger writers has as a main theme the experience of war, which has been the central experience in the life of the young generation. I am not aware of a single novel, poem, or play that even remotely extols the so-called virtues of war. In literature—less so in daily journalism—the tone is set by nausea, not by pride or glory. Victories are portrayed as terrible defeats. At its best, new Israeli literature has been marked by an instinctive pacifism and by so compulsive a desire to understand and empathize with the "enemy" that some critics have warned against the "suicidal" tendencies it may reflect.*

The ardent hope for peace that powerfully pervades Israeli literature and public opinion is genuine and sincere. But because this hope belittles the sense of outrage Arabs feel about what they consider a

---

* I have in mind, mainly, the works of Avraham B. Yehoshua, S. Yizhar, Amos Oz, and Yehuda Amichai, whose work is generally regarded to be among the best—and most successful—currently produced in Israel. The list could be considerably extended to include among others, the brothers Matti and Aharon Megged, Dalia Rabikovitz, Yoram Kaniuk, Hanoch Bartov, Benjamin Tammuz, Pinchas Sadeh, Yitzchak Orpaz (see next chapter).

foreign, immoral intrusion, it remains largely a utopian one. Hopes can be self-defeating if they are linked to an ideal that ignores the complicated realities of human life. There is a dreamlike, unrealistic quality in the current Israeli ideal of peace. Under its spell the conditions of peace are set so high that they can hardly be realized. The Israeli ideal of peace is a product of historical experience. It is another reflection, among the many we have already seen, of the original ideology of Zionism that was committed to an idealistic assumption of man's perfectibility; it testifies to the lingering strength of that ideology. In the aftermath of the 1967 war the Israeli ideal of peace occasionally exuded an almost religious, Manichaean air.

It assumes an absolute, immediate, total, almost eternal condition. "Unless we get that," they seem to be saying, "we shall not move an inch. We shall remain firmly where we are." But peace is never absolute, even between allied nations; it can never be *both* immediate *and* complete. In modern times, and in the aftermath of indecisive war, it can be neither. Peace, as Israel demands it, will only come as the result of slow growth. It cannot be attained by a signature. The Israeli call for formal, final peace settlement assumes the attainability in the Near East of conditions which now prevail only in the Scandinavian or Benelux countries. There is a pervading dream of open borders, friendly exchange of embassies, tourism, trade, and cultural relations as between Belgium and Luxembourg. Yet the enviable conditions in the Benelux countries are the result not only of centuries of readjustments, but of the absence of all serious contention. The Israeli ideal of peace is strongly moralistic; like all moralists, Israelis tend to lack historical perspective, and make up for the lack by holding firmly to pious hopes. In the Israeli call for formal, final peace, there lingers a desperate hope that the Arabs will not only refrain from making war, but will finally see the light. Israelis still hope, a hope as old as Zionism, that the Arabs will come round to recognizing that their decades-old opposition to the return of the Jews has been a horrible misunderstanding. It is not very likely the Arabs will ever see it this way.

If "ease is inimical to civilization," as Toynbee claims, adversity has not been without its comforts. Israel vividly illustrates Toynbee's theory on the creative interplay between challenge and response on a national level. There has been no lack of powerful challenges. The vigor of the Israeli response to these challenges can be seen today in every corner of the land. Observe, for example, the tight net of flourishing villages and lively towns which is fast turning wide stretches of the country into one vast, contiguously settled area; or the enormous afforestation schemes that cover the once denuded rocky surface of the mountains. We see the response in the vast irrigation projects that nearly everywhere have turned the neglected, dusty landscape from yellow-brown to many shades of evergreen; parts of the former arid steppes are today hardly different from the best developed farmlands in the south of France, or in northern Italy. The response can be seen in the cities and industrial complexes that have sprung up in the desert, from Eilat (where the bare, mountainous nothingness of 1949 has been turned into an important oil port and an amusing tourist center) to Arad (a desert city of 15,000 inhabitants, where there was only rock and sand as recently as 1959) to Beersheba (which will soon be one of the country's university centers). The Israeli landscape bespeaks an epic of achievement that has probably not been equaled anywhere in such a short period.

Similarly, what Toynbee calls the *stimulus of hard countries* has also been in ample supply during Israel's period of growth. Though hardened by the cold winters of Russia, Poland, and Rumania, the pioneers took to the Palestinian climate only with great difficulty. Unaccustomed to the hardships of the land, as they were to physical labor, they responded through personal exertions of such magnitude that they not only persevered but were subsequently rewarded by the gradual decline of the original challenges themselves.

The human environment has not been less challenging than the physical. It is not necessary to recount the continuous pressure exerted for decades by the Arabs in order to underline *their* role as a powerful, challenging stimulant. The knowledge that he might be hanged tomorrow concentrates a man's mind wonderfully. The unrelenting antagonism of the Arabs has kept Israelis, as it were, on their toes long after the initial "heroic" period of pioneering enthusiasm waned, and throughout the arrival of huge masses of "non-ideological" immigrants. Arab enmity has helped the Zionists to maintain what too often disappears in other revolutionary regimes—an atmosphere of "permanent revolution."

Above all, Arab antagonism has helped to foster the sense of shared social purpose, unity, and cohesion that continues to prevail among a people notorious for their quarrelsomeness. There are times in the lives of communities when an enemy renders a service that even a friend cannot match. Few things are as difficult, or dependent on pure chance, as the forging together of a great amorphic mass of people. It is no little matter to gather such peoples, speaking tens of different languages, of vastly different cultural backgrounds, into a working social mechanism capable of effective communal action. Moreover, to do so without excessive coercion, within the legal framework of a parliamentary democracy, acutely sensitive to individual rights, is a feat that is as difficult as it is rare. In this respect, Arab antagonism has been a great help to Israel. The early Zionists had envisaged it differently; but events have borne out Freud who said that it is easy to tie men together with bonds of love if there are enough other men on whom to release aggressions.

Serious social and cultural dissensions have threatened the stability of Israel in the two decades of its existence. The pressures of mass immigration have been considerable; there have been grave tensions between Oriental "dark-skinned" and European "white" immigrants; such tensions have been potentially further aggravated by the fact that the "white" old-timers are usually better off economically than "dark-skinned" immigrants who arrived in the country more recently; moreover, immigrants from Europe, because of their education and more valuable skills, usually advance more quickly up the social-economic ladder.

The serious conflict between religious Israelis and secular Israelis over the separation of synagogue and state continues to be a highly explosive issue. It has not been resolved but merely shelved. It has been impossible even to reach widespread agreement in the Jewish state over the most basic question of "who is a Jew?"

State intervention in the economy, often needlessly heavyhanded and doctrinaire, has been another source of conflict which under other circumstances could divide Israelis into two opposing camps. Furthermore, the widening generational gap between "ideology-oriented" old-timers and "pragmatic" sabras has caused a near breakdown in communication between the ruling political elite—probably the oldest in the world—and younger people.

These are grave conflicts that could have seriously abraded the delicate tissues of a new society, but the thrust of Arab enmity has greatly helped to minimize their effect. Arab enmity has made the search for "consensus" the overriding rule in public affairs.

As in Samson's riddle, "out of the strong came forth sweetness" (Judges 14:14); the benefits, of course, are largely communal and are not blindly and indiscriminately accepted. Israelis are often neurotically sensitive to the more dangerous implications. Chief among these has been the threat of "militarization" in civilian life.

Even as the elemental instinct of self-preservation has given rise to much social discipline, there remains a widespread, almost compulsive resentment of all regimentation. The result is a peculiarly Israeli mixture of self-reliant individualism and readiness to cooperative effort. The latter largely depends on flexibility and free play for the former. Israel is a fortress, but not a garrison state. It is very far from being a military society. Between his frequent army call-ups, the average Israeli remains a fanatic civilian. An Israeli chief of staff once raised a public storm when he announced that Israelis were reservists on leave. He would have been closer to the truth had he said that the army is a body of civilians temporarily donning uniforms.

The average Israeli youngster matures in an atmosphere of almost riotous liberty. Endowed with an antimilitarist tradition, he normally tries to make the army an image of himself. The brutality of war takes its toll on him, of course, as we have seen earlier. But there is a positive influence as well. Although the army has become a highly professional body, with no lack of discipline, the Israeli soldier is perforce trained by example and language, not by order and punishment. In combat units the rotation for home leave is often determined by drawing lots among the men, not by orders from commanding officers.

The army is not an aristocratic institution, as it continues to be in some democratic countries. There is no deliberate attempt to break the will of recruits.* It is a citizen army, and the gap between officers and men is minimal. There are few privileges of rank. The Israeli

* So great was the fear of a standing army during the first years of independence that the original law of conscription stipulated that young men would serve only one year in the army proper, and follow this with another year of compulsory public service in an agricultural settlement. Only gradually, and after a good deal of debate and hesitation, and under the compelling pressure of a deteriorating security situation, the Knesset empowered the Defense Minister to cancel or curtail the agricultural period, and substitute instead further military service.

military code bluntly states that officers have no privileges whatsoever, only duties. Officers are usually addressed by their first names. *Adoni* (Sir) or *Ha'mefaked* (*mon commandant*) are rarely used, except toward senior officers from the rank of colonel upward, and then sometimes ironically. Soldiering has traditionally seemed ridiculous and chimerical to Jews.* A deep resentment of "military forms" has remained an essential element of the Jewish makeup. There are no fancy uniforms, except for officers going abroad on representative missions; and no decorations except battle ribbons, distributed to all who have served in any capacity during a period of war. Military titles are used in writing, but only sporadically in verbal address. The use of such titles in civilian life, after retirement, is frowned upon.

Job turnover among officers in the army is unusually rapid and the army is almost never a lifelong occupation. Most senior officers are weeded out soon after they reach forty. This practice has helped to prevent the establishment of a military class. Army officers must readapt to civilian customs in order to survive in whatever profession they choose upon retirement. They are usually hired by industry, banks, investment firms, or government-owned development companies, mainly for their administrative skills, which they are often forced to develop further and refine by returning to a university for a year or two after retirement.

Years of soldiering in war have only marginally enhanced the so-called martial virtues. A proposal to create high school military academies for boys planning an army career was vetoed out of fear that such academies might encourage undesirable "militarist" tendencies among young cadets. A compromise was reached. Within a number of existing secondary schools, subsidiary courses, supervised by the schools themselves, were introduced for boys interested in a military career.

Much of the character of Israeli public life has been shaped by the fact of war. But there remains an obsessive fear of militarism, a talismanic regard for civilian controls. Experience has shown repeatedly that the more security is threatened, the stronger the respect for civilian controls.

The military of course has wielded and continues to wield enormous influence. But this influence—with few exceptions—has never

---

* *Goyim-nachess*, in Yiddish: the silly games of Gentiles.

been decisive. Although war has come to be Israel's main business, there are as yet no recognizable war lords, either within the military bureaucracy nor in the vast industrial complex that has sprung up to produce the implements of war. "Militarism" remains one of the nastiest words in the political dictionary; it has a highly derogatory connotation in professional army circles as well.

Military heroes enjoy an aura of glamorous prestige that few civilian politicians could possibly muster. But until recently Israelis have preferred to be governed by tottering old men in their sixties or seventies, or by a grand old lady whose chief public appeal has been a motherly, old-fashioned Jewish, and slightly teary-eyed sentimentality. They have preferred such government to glamorous, undisputedly efficient and competent war gods. Moshe Dayan has been the single major figure in public life who built his political career solely upon his fame as a military hero; it is doubtful whether he, or any other military hero, would resort to plebiscitarian rule were he to become Prime Minister some day.*

Much of the future character and quality of Israeli life depends on the continuing strength of the pioneer tradition of human rights and human dignity. Can it survive? In the aftermath of the 1967 war, the tradition itself became the subject of bitter political argument. For as a result of 1967, the familiar landscape that had given birth to this tradition was swept away; its contours changed beyond recognition. The early pioneers envisaged a life in peace, not one of perpetual war; they imagined a society of free men, not a regime of conquest that would control hostile aliens in occupied territories. Few events in the tragic history of Zionism were as potentially decisive as that war; none were so full with unforeseen difficulties and contradictions.

The new, vastly expanded cease-fire lines that resulted from the war considerably improved Israel's strategic security. But for the first time

---

* Yigal Allon, one of Dayan's main competitors for the premiership, is another former general. But his military career, which ended in 1950, is hardly a part of his public image, nor a main factor in his ascendancy, as in the case of Dayan. Allon did not catapult suddenly from one power pyramid to another, but rose through the party apparatus. General Ezer Weizmann, a nephew of the late President, resigned from the army in 1969 and was appointed overnight, to a *Gahal* seat in the cabinet (transportation). He is the first military leader whose appointment to a high political office was not preceded by a period of apprenticeship within a party. Yet his tenure lasted only a few months.

in Israeli history, the quality of political life and the very fabric of society were in serious jeopardy. The occupied territories held over one million Arabs, at best passively hostile, at worst engaged in terrorist activities. The absence of any formal peace discussions excluded Israeli withdrawal. What will be the fate of these million Arabs? And what lies in store for the increasingly disillusioned heirs of Zionist idealism who now find themselves in the unaccustomed role of hated occupiers?

As Thomas Jefferson once said of America, Israel holds the wolf by his ears, and can neither hold him down nor safely let him go. Grave moral and existential questions are left hanging. There are no clear answers, for this is no abstract dichotomy, equitable as in mathematics, but a conflict among humans, who in their fear and fury have irrevocably resorted to tragic choices. At the root is a disastrous struggle between two rights, a clash between two irresistible compulsions, the very essence of high tragedy. It is through tragedy that we recognize the glory and the degradation in human affairs, and sense the defects and excesses of some of our most cherished values. In the words of Reinhold Niebuhr, "Tragedy elicits admiration as well as pity, because it combines nobility with guilt."

In Camus' *La Peste*, Tarrou tells Dr. Rhien that there are on this earth whips and victims. In choosing between them one must try not to be on the side of the whips. Yet, he adds, there is a third possibility. A third way that may lead to the cure, to peace among men. After a long silence Rhien asks Tarrou if he has any notion of what that way might be which one must take to arrive at peace.

"Yes," answers Tarrou. "Yes, compassion."

10

FATHERS AND SONS

> . . . the discovery of the reconciling formula
> is always left to future generations in which
> passion has cooled into curiosity and
> agonies of peoples have become the exercise
> in the schools. The devil who builds bridges
> does not span such chasms till much that is
> precious to mankind has vanished down
> them forever.
>
> —R. H. TAWNEY

In the shorthand language of cartoonists, Israel is often represented by two familiar images. Both are immediately recognizable, even abroad, and are easily identified with at home. One is the slightly haggard, stooped figure of an elderly man. He wears a dark, dust-stained, somewhat old-fashioned suit. His walk is a bit furtive. His brow is furrowed to a wizened look, suggesting at once energy and fatigue, the resolve and worldly weariness of an eternal contemporary who has seen and remembered everything. The other is the puckish figure of an eager teen-ager in khaki shorts and open sandals. The little fellow, a kind of overgrown Dennis the Menace, exudes an air of infantile naivete, combined with childish cunning; charming innocence mixes with blunt artlessness and the bridling of untutored strength. His low forehead is covered by the so-called *kova tembel*,* a triangular, inverted sailor's hat, that is so popular in Israel.

---

* Literally, "foolscap." *Tembel* is Hebrew slang for fool, buffoon. Of recent origin, *tembel* possibly derives from the English slang word, dumbbell.

The first character represents *Grandfather Israel*—the wandering, persecuted Jew finally come home. Within the context of history and traditional Zionist ideology, *Grandfather Israel* stands for the original force behind the movement that led the Jews out of the lands of their dispersion back to Palestine, where they hoped to find safety and rest. *Grandfather Israel* represents a past, an inherited sensibility of great depth but of uncertain future.

The second figure is in some ways a response to the first. It represents the *sabra*—ignorant of the past, or indifferent to it, a race cast solely into the present, avidly living every moment, keen, practical, "uncomplicated"—an Israeli "icon" par excellence.

Our two figures communicate, in sharply oversimplified symbols, a psychograph of modern Israel that suggests basic forces of sustenance and inner conflict. Let us observe them both at closer range, always bearing in mind the pitfalls of all simplifications of this kind. Symbolic images, like the shadows cast by distant mountains, are likely to be gross exaggerations of reality. But let us not shut our eyes to them altogether; they are likely, at times, to reflect a dimension of reality that one might otherwise miss. Perhaps they even convey a number of truths that transcend the preoccupations and overt political passions of the moment.

Both figures live in the hazy landscape of an all-pervasive Present, in the gap between Past and Future that is powerfully challenged by both. The Past is Jewish; it harks back to the persecutions of the Diaspora, and the desperate passions generated by them. The Future is Near Eastern; it heralds tomorrow's confrontation between Israel and the resentful, hostile Arab peoples around, and (since 1967) in Israel's very midst.

It is a sad landscape, even though everywhere one sees the marks of an enormously successful effort at human and physical reconstruction. For one sees not only flourishing new cities, universities, fertile fields, forests, and irrigation works, but also the icebergs of hate, the bruises of continuous war, and the scars of another people's agony. Our two archetypes, the elderly Jews and the naive *sabra*, move about uneasily. There is the sun, the marvelous sea, the flowers, the desert; but there are also treacherous crevices and crags. In the older man's tradition, otherwise so rich, there is little to guide him safely through. The young fellow is even more on his own; his mind wanders in obscurity. There is an inherent tension, a basic polarity, between the two types. Each treats the other with a mixture of suspicious piety and condescending admiration.

There is nothing unique in the ill-concealed exasperation of the young with the old, nor in the bafflement of the old with the young. Generational conflict is rampant everywhere, nowhere so intensive as in countries populated by immigrants. For some years sociologists have insisted that the generational gap in Israel delves so deeply that one must speak of two distinct sub-cultures. Again, this is not an Israeli peculiarity but, at least since the youth rebellions of the 1960s, a phenomenon common to most industrial societies of the West, including the most settled and homogenous. Compared to other Western societies, the generational conflict in Israel may even appear relatively mild and non-violent on the surface. Nevertheless it remains a reality. Its latent force was seen in the late 1950s and early 1960s, during the political demise of David Ben Gurion, "father of the Jewish state." His resignation and subsequent defeat in the elections of 1965 were greeted by a large number of younger Israelis with relief, even a wistful joy. Ben Gurion's rejection by his own party has been compared to the tribal killing of the divine king described by Frazer in *The Golden Bough*.

The generational conflict in Israel is muffled by the fact of war, the common mortal danger shared by all. Yet the war itself may very well be a main cause of conflict; the apparent impossibility, so frustrating to so many, to put an end to it. The frustration was illustrated in the mid-1960s by the youthful reaction to an absurd, though appealing, incident.

A Tel Aviv maverick, Abie Nathan, mortgaged his small cafe and flew a monoplane, *Shalom I*, to Egypt, on a one-man peace mission. The Egyptians turned him back; the Israelis in turn prosecuted him for illegally leaving the country. The enormous outpouring of popular sympathy for Nathan reflected the younger Israelis' weariness with an old leadership that was talking and talking peace but not achieving it. For a brief moment in 1966, the unconventional gesture of a naive cafe owner epitomized the deep uneasiness of an entire generation. When Shulamit Aloni, one of the few members of parliament under forty, publicly kissed Nathan upon his return, she was scolded by her uncomprehending party leader, the elderly Golda Meir, who saw in

Nathan no more than a misguided meddler.

With this in mind, let us return to our two images. *Grandfather Israel* is a forbidding father figure. He stands for authority and experience. He frequently preaches the ascetic puritanism of the pioneering age and sternly offers irrefutable lessons of the past. He sees that past through the spectacles of a more or less dogmatic historicism. His memory is notoriously long; indeed, there are times when he seems perfectly overwhelmed by it. Yet there are other times when his memory makes a more selective use of the past—as when he views the history of Judaism solely as the tale of one prolonged and bloody pogrom; or when he sees the establishment of Israel, or its aggrandizement, as one gigantic act of retaliation against Jewry's historic debasement in the Diaspora. *Grandfather Israel* is on his way out.

The young fellow in his *kova tembel* is on his way in. The silly headgear is an important part of this figure's image. The hat is not accidental; nor is his facial expression, which is normally a little naive or vague. It is clearly the older generation's image of the young. The young fellow is much less touched by "ideas" or historical considerations than the older man. This could be merely a result of his youth; his raw strength is as yet untutored by experience. Yet clearly there are deeper reasons. His main characteristic is a keen avidity; it is of a kind that often marks ascension to sudden wealth without a certain future. His biography makes him less likely to be fired by the sense of outrage, or by that hope for a better world, which kindled the imagination of his elders. He senses that they were marvelous dreamers in their times and he acknowledges, a bit grudgingly, their daring. But he finds it difficult to follow their logic to its ultimate conclusions. Face-to-face with the Arabs he is both more extreme and more moderate than his elders. He might be more ruthless in action, but at the same time he is more flexible. He is pragmatic where his elders were more likely to have been doctrinaire. Confronted by the Arabs in Palestine, who resented their arrival, older Israelis either averted their eyes or resorted to wishful thinking, or blatantly misinterpreted Arab opposition by making sterile comparisons with European pogroms. Younger Israelis are not so burdened.

Moshe Dayan pointed out this difference between the older and younger generations in a talk to a Tel Aviv audience in 1969.

"In my youth," he said, "I traveled a good deal with my late father, through the Valley of Esdraelon. We used to meet Arabs. At that time, especially in the winter, Arabs wrapped their faces in a *keffiye* until only their nose and eyes remained exposed. My father was not born in this country; he came from Russia when he was seventeen. He would say: 'Look, they have the eyes of murderers.' But these Arabs were not murderers ... it only seemed to my father that in the eyes which peered through the *keffiye*'s folds he saw the same look that he remembered from his Russian *shtetl*. But this did not make these Arabs into murderers."

Older Israelis were baffled and frightened by the Arabs. Younger Israelis are at once more rational and more honest with themselves. Older Israelis often fell prey to an act of grandiose, pious self-delusion. Younger Israelis are more inclined to look squarely at the facts. They were born into a situation they did not themselves create. They are, of course, deeply involved in it; yet they are also less compelled to moralize their own, personal biographies.

It is easier for young Israelis to empathize with the Arabs, to see their point of view. This makes them more formidable, more dangerous opponents for the Arabs; it also makes them more apt to compromise on principles hitherto sacrosanct in Zionism. Public opinion polls have shown a preponderance of young people among the "doves," whereas older people tend to be "hawks." In the second and third generation the urge to survive and prevail is sometimes ennobled by a flash of historical guilt. Such instances would undoubtedly be more widespread if Arab enmity were not so abysmally total. That they exist at all is a measure of Israel's growing maturity as a nation.

The old pioneers pursued essence; the younger generation's approach is existential. The former lived under the spell of ideas; the main life impulse of the latter is what the French call *le dur désir de durer*. It is a largely unreflected urge. The former were oriented to a future perfect; the latter are living intensely in the here and now. "What we have to ask ourselves is not 'What will be?' but 'What is?' Now is now."*

They find themselves locked in a desperate struggle which seems endless. They did not initiate that struggle; they inherited it. Yet they see themselves inextricably entangled in its snares. They struggle well;

---

* Moshe Dayan, in a talk to army reserve officers, August 1969.

they hold their own. There is something about them of the absurd hero—they are forever running at great speed toward a destination they never seem to reach; they leap high but are pulled back by gravity to a shaking ground that does not support their weight.

A minority among them cannot escape a certain feeling of moral vertigo. The certainties of one age are the doubts of the next. Young Israelis are able to judge their elders from the facile vantage point of hindsight. They may on occasion confront them with bothersome, unpleasant questions: How did they actually imagine their resettlement in this part of the world? Did they not foresee the Arabs' bitter hostility? How could they have ignored it so? Alternatively, members of the younger generation are asked by their own growing children questions more difficult to answer than those on sex: "Why the Arabs?" "Why we?" "How did it start?" and, most difficult of all, "How will it all end?" It is impossible for such parents to offer answers that echo the simple and well-rounded arguments and symmetrical half-truths of the older generation. One young parent wrote in 1969 that doing this would be almost as if, when "asked by my daughter how children are born I would send her to my grandmother to hear the tale of the stork."

A word of caution is necessary. To discuss a feeling of moral vertigo among the young is not to describe a mass phenomenon. The malaise is restricted to a sensitive, small, but not uninfluential, minority. However, a likelihood exists that it may spread and increase within the foreseeable future. Moral vertigo may spread as a result of battle fatigue. As the toll of casualties mounts so does the recurrent question, "*Ma yehiye ha' sof?*" (What will be the end?) which moreover is a very Jewish question, imbedded in a susceptibility that for Jews is almost second nature.

A feeling of moral vertigo is even more likely to grow and spread as a result of recurring, if inconclusive, successes. The liberal conscience is often a function of success, not failure. It does not grow of insecurity and weakness, which are more likely to produce a callous fanaticism, but of self-assurance and strength. Doolittle, in Bernard Shaw's *Pygmalion*, tells Pickering that he cannot afford to have any morals and adds: "*But Governor, neither could you if you was as poor as me.*" The liberal conscience often begins as a luxury of the secure. It rarely strikes a society before that society has arrived.

This was illustrated in the aftermath of the war of 1967. Not surprisingly, the war had a twofold effect on public opinion. It fanned extremist sentiments and archaic religion-nationalistic myths in one part of the population; in another part it awakened a crisis of conscience. Soul-searching debates are nothing new to Zionism. This time, however, the crisis was of unprecedented proportions. When it hit, it hit mostly younger people. In the aftermath of war a nagging realization began to grow, that by drawing the Arabs' teeth Israel had assumed at least a measure of moral responsibility for their future.

There were impassioned appeals to make an immediate, unilateral effort to resettle Arab refugees, who were now, for the first time since 1948, under Israeli jurisdiction; demands were also voiced to encourage the establishment of an independent Arab state in the occupied areas. This would underline the principle that Jewish claims for Palestine were not exclusive, but equal in value, morally and politically, to those of the vanquished Arabs. Nothing came of these suggestions, mainly because there was no significant reciprocity on the part of the Arabs, and partly because the Israeli cabinet, exhausted by success, paralyzed by the effects of internal dissension, sanctimoniously shut itself to new ideas and fresh approaches.

The crisis of conscience that appeared in the aftermath of the war was rooted in a number of causes. There was, first and foremost, the added sense of strength and security afforded by an astounding victory in the field, which led to new strategic borders but not, most frustratingly, to a resolution of the conflict. Equally important was the sudden opportunity for younger Israelis to face the mass of vanquished Arabs in the occupied towns and villages of the West Bank and the dismal refugee camps of the Gaza strip. For younger Israelis this was the first opportunity of its kind.

The attitude of most Israelis to the tragic problem of the Arab refugees has always been involved and contradictory. Themselves a nation of refugees and children of refugees, Israelis often thought of themselves as sympathetic to the plight of the Arab refugees. But as a nation besieged, threatened, and at war, such sympathy necessarily had its limits; Israelis never really understood the full tragedy of those who had lost their ancestral homes as a result of Israel's re-establishment. In the 1967 war some of the worst refugee camps were overrun by the advancing Israeli forces. Because threats and war continued after 1967, there was no material change in Israel's official attitude to the refugees. But at least some younger Israelis were struck by the sudden confrontation with so much misery. Statistics and abstract slogans suddenly took on human forms. The wretchedness was too heartbreaking, at least in the eyes of a sensitive minority, to be easily dismissed by the accepted political cliches.

"I had a terrible feeling during the meeting with the civilian population [in the occupied territories]," a young *kibbutznik* soldier is quoted in *Siach Lochamin*.

> "I just couldn't. I had a terrible feeling. Kids, three or four years old, already knew how to raise their arms, to walk about town with raised arms. For me this was awful. Kids the age of my son walk with their arms above their heads. I remember that old men and women came to implore. It was an awful feeling, awful. It's a horrible feeling to have to explain to these women that nobody intends to kill their husbands. Horrible, and I can't free myself from it."

The soldier was relating an intensely personal reaction to an incident probably witnessed by many, perhaps indifferently; yet his description comes as a cultural shock to most Israelis, who immediately transfer the image to the photograph, well-known to every schoolboy, of a terrified Jewish child in Poland, with his arms raised high above his head, on his way to a concentration camp. The two situations are, of course, different and incomparable, but the associative reflex is less discriminating.

In a previous chapter I described the traumatic impact of the Nazi holocaust upon the national psychology of Israel, especially during times of war, increased tensions, or danger. The effects of the trauma are complex. It leads to exertion in war, but also to pangs of conscience in victory. If it leads to resolve, it holds, at the same time, a potential of compassion and empathy for the wretched loser. The moving confession of another young soldier quoted in *Siach Lochamim* illustrates this point. In the early days of confusion following the war, masses of civilian Arabs fled the territories suddenly occupied by Israel. The young soldier, remembering this terrible exodus, testified to his sense of personal identification:

> "If I had [in this war] a clear association with the . . . holocaust, it was in a certain moment, when I was going up the Jericho-Jerusalem

road and the refugees were streaming down (towards the River Jordan) . . . I felt directly identified with them. When I saw those children carried in their parents' arms, I almost saw myself carried by my father . . . [my] identification was precisely with the other side, with our enemies." Still another soldier bitterly admitted that when he entered an Arab refugee camp in order to put down a disorder, he felt "like a Gestapo man . . . I thought of home, I thought my parents were being led away . . ."

Many Israeli soldiers were surprised, and some were deeply disturbed, to discover among the refugees a form of "Arab Zionism": the living memory of a lost homeland, to which they were passionately attached as the Jews had remained attached to Zion in the lands of their dispersion. The education of these young soldiers—some were born after the establishment of Israel—little prepared them for a discovery such as this. Upon entering a refugee camp one young soldier discovered that the inmates were still organized into and dwelled as small clans or neighborhood units according to the village, town, and even the street they had lived in prior to their dispersion in 1948, villages and towns that were now thoroughly Israeli: Beersheba, Zarnuga, Ramla, Lod, Jaffa, Rehovoth. He described his confused reaction in *Siach Lochamim*:

> "I remember it made me boil," he said at first.
> *Question:* "Why?"
> *Answer:* "I remember I couldn't grasp it. [After all] nineteen years had passed. . . . How dare you say that you are from Beersheba . . . that you are from Rehovoth. [At first] it made my blood boil."
> *Question:* "And now?"
> *Answer:* "Now I think I understand. First and foremost they have preserved some glimmer of hope to return. I think this war was a result of this hope . . . I can [no longer] be angry with them . . . I can only pity them. In reality, for them these nineteen years have been a waste of time . . . nineteen lost years, in inhuman conditions, for a hope that will not come true."
> *Question:* "You didn't have some respect for people who remained loyal to their homes, to the place where their forebears were born? After all there is the same element in us. 'Our hope is not yet lost, to return to the land of our forefathers.'* We were also

---

* First line of the Israeli national anthem, *Ha'tikva* ("The Hope").

educated on loyalty to place, home, soil and to a lost country. The myth of the lost country is really our own myth. Didn't you connect these things?"

Answer: "When I try to clarify these things to myself today, I say that . . . it's clear, their tragedy is a real one . . . and in my view today there does not seem to be anything more to prevent them from living alongside us . . . Again I don't know if . . . that's already a political problem, the more basic problem of how to establish links among people, between two nations. But I see no reason, even today . . . yes, why shouldn't there [again] be Arabs in Zarnuga and Beersheba . . . and let them say they are Zarnugians and Beershebans."

Let us take a closer look at this uneasiness, despite the fact that it clearly concerns only a minority. We find this minority in a number of key focal points, in the arts, in the *kibbutzim*, in the universities, to some extent even in the upper echelons of the army. Because we are dealing here with a changing mood, it is difficult to assess its real force and its potential. It is as easy to exaggerate its importance as a wave of the future as it is to dismiss its significance as the spiritual malaise of a marginal few. As an intellectual mood it probably embodies a measure of fashionable posture.

Israel is too much part of the Western intellectual world to escape the contagious effect of a currently widespread tone in political ethics. Here, as elsewhere, there are those who think they are being rigorously moral, when actually they are feeling only vaguely uncomfortable. But if the malaise does partly reflect a half-baked infatuation with general moral principles, characteristic of young people everywhere in today's Western world, it is not sheer irresponsible emotionalism either as some critics claim. Nor is it the thoughtless preaching of those who in a kind of vicarious masochism need not face the full consequence of their pious sermons. It is true that in their empathy with the Arabs, those afflicted with the malaise occasionally find themselves in a moral cul-de-sac. Bound as they are to moral principles, they are unable—because of the ferocity of Arab opposition and the absence of any significant reciprocity—to put those principles into practice. Yet they show a patient tenacity, somewhat surprising under the circumstances. In a world where ideals and reality are unequally mated, men must be judged by their aims, not only by their ability to achieve them.

The malaise is a second- and third-generation phenomenon. It has never been widespread. Where it hits, it often strikes the very nerve center of culture. It rises and ebbs, depending upon circumstances, but it rarely is absent altogether. Some observers have claimed that it marks the transition from "Jew" to "Israeli." But the intellectual roots of this phenomenon are older than the sovereign state of Israel. They are clearly embedded in a sensibility often identified with the "Jewish" temperament.

Jews are said to have a deep penchant for doubt, an irresistible tendency to exorcise current intellectual fixities, their own routine persuasions as well as those of others. This restless quest antedates Israel; it is older than Zionism. Zionism itself was an iconoclastic uprising against the routine and inertia of Jewish life in the latter part of the nineteenth century. The emergence of a traditionally Jewish moral zeal, a disturbed uneasiness in Zionism, among second- and third-generation Israelis, is one of the profound ironies of our theme. It reflects the highly ambivalent attitude of the Zionist pioneers themselves toward their Jewish past:

"Our teachers had a little bag, and in it things of all sorts gathered from here and there, for past and future use, for left and right," S. Yizhar, a leading Israeli writer of the second generation, writes in *Days of Ziklag*, generally considered the representative war novel of the post-Independence generation.

. . . We have always been the product of a clever compromise. . . . We grew up on experimental food. . . . One [teacher] sought to emulate [pagan] heroes and valiant hunters, Nimrod and Ismael and Esau and Joab and Abner while another teacher sought to reincarnate his grandfather, and the renowned Rabbi Eliyahu and the glory of Rabbi Nachman of Brazlav. . . . Too educated to be simple farmers, too ignorant to carry the magnificent heritage . . . what wonder is it that we are at once attracted by the opposites.

The roots of the problem are, of course, more varied than this. The uneasiness probably also stems from the irate reaction of youngsters educated to *admire*, but never really to *emulate* an official educational ideal. The ideal type they are taught to worship and admire is the heroic image of their iconoclastic parents: the Zionist pioneers, filled with revolutionary zeal, rejecting all automatic fixations of purpose

and disposition. Yet the conduct prescribed by their parents to Israeli
youngsters precluded the possibility of a similar non-conformism in
their own lives. Israeli education has long been bedeviled by this
contradiction.

The uneasiness, which rose to the surface in the aftermath of the
1967 war, had in some measure been there in the years before. There
has always been a gnawing, if limited, guilt feeling among a small
minority of Israelis, that some of their best lands were those from
which the Arabs had in one way or another been forced out. The Arab
exodus of 1948 had left behind a vast amount of rural and urban
property, officially specified as abandoned. A small number of Israelis
have consistently refused, as a matter of principle, to rent, buy, or live
in any such abandoned property. Among some intellectuals, university
people, and artists, a vague if persistent predilection for self-censure
has survived the vicissitudes of war and threats of annihilation from
the Arab side.

For some years now this moral crisis has been reflected with ever-increasing intensity in contemporary Israeli literature. Poets are sometimes better guides to the sensibility of an era than are politicians or
journalists. Works of imagination serve as tentative guidelines to lev-
els of reality more shadowy and yet deeper than those reflected in
political programs and Gallup polls. Let us examine the works of some
outstanding young authors, not as an exercise in literary criticism,
which would transgress the limited scope of this inquiry; but rather as
an investigation into a culture and a society.*

The works of these younger authors contrast sharply with Israel's
surface image of self-righteousness. They are at variance with the
official Zionist view which regards the Arab-Israeli dispute as a war

* Obviously, only a limited selection of authors can be discussed here, those whose
work touches upon and illustrates our theme. The list could be extended considerably.
Significantly, a full list would include nearly all the better-known younger writers who
made their debut in the period after Independence. The works discussed are, of course,
in no way representative of the total scope of these authors. It must also be remembered that a number of highly regarded authors of the *older* generation—notably three
of Israel's finest poets, Uri Zvi Greenberg, Nathan Altermann, and Jonathan Ratosh—
display in their works an unhesitant, aggressive nationalism, sharply divergent from the
uneasy self-consciousness, the perplexed, tormented ambiguities of the younger generation.

between the sons of light and the sons of darkness, the plowland and the wasteland, or, as in American Wild West films, between the good guys and the bad guys. When openly political, their writing leans to a tormenting sense of guilt, which in extreme cases takes the form of a gnawing complex of legitimacy.

Guilt and legitimacy are powerfully evoked in a hauntingly suggestive novella entitled *Facing the Forests* by Avraham B. Yehoshua. The moral or existential anguish elicited by the paradox and contradictions inherent in the Zionist enterprise frequently dominate the tone and content of modern Israeli letters; but few writers have tread this dangerous ground with as much literary competence and human compassion as Yehoshua. Barely twenty-six years old when he published *Facing the Forests* in 1963, Yehoshua has since been widely acclaimed as one of the most gifted writers of the younger generation. Resented by some critics as "subversive," "suicidal," "masochistically identifying with the enemy," Yehoshua has nevertheless been particularly successful with younger readers.

Facing the Forests relates the slow development of a "subversive" crime: a case of political arson in a national forest. The forest, financed by Jewish contributions from abroad, was planted atop the remains of an abandoned Arab village. Yehoshua's nameless protagonist is a drifting, badly blocked, balding history student, about thirty years old. Sick of his studies, "bored by his dreams," tired "even of his own words and certainly the words of others," his "defective eyesight" placing "many things in doubt," he decides to seek complete solitude in order to finally write his thesis on the Crusades. An elderly, idealistic official in charge of land drainage and afforestation at the Jewish National Fund reluctantly offers him a job as fire watchman in a forest. The history student accepts, and moves himself and his books and papers to a lonely ranger station in the middle of the forest. Totally isolated, his single connection with the outside world is a pair of binoculars and a telephone linked to a distant fire department.

The reader can scarcely ignore the allegorical character of the basic setting. Few things are as evocatively symbolic of the Zionist dream and rationale as a Jewish National Fund forest, and few point more markedly to the human tragedy inherent in its achievement than the ruins of an Arab village, abandoned by its inhabitants during the 1948 war, on which the forest is planted. Moreover, the Crusader theme—

subject of the student's dissertation—has often been used by Arab propagandists against Israel. Israeli writers, too, have been compulsively obsessed by it.

Yehoshua's protagonist seeks total solitude. However, he is not to be entirely alone. One of the former villagers, an old mute Arab ("it isn't clear who cut out his tongue, we or they") has remained behind and is employed as a caretaker. With him is a little Arab girl. The forest, an eerie landscape of young trees and plaques with the names of distant contributors and honoratoria ("Louis Schwartz of Chicago," "The King of Burundi and his People"), is visited by official delegations, tourists, and local hikers. Their loud wild singing reaches the watchman, diverts him from his studies. One group of hikers makes its way to his outpost:

> They simply wanted to ask him a question. They have argued, made bets, and he will be their judge. Where exactly was the Arab village that is marked on the map? There should be an abandoned village in this area. Here—they even know its name, something like. . . . The watchman regards them with tired eyes. A village? He wonders . . . no, there is no village here. The map is probably wrong. The hand of the surveyors must have trembled. . . .

At the beginning, the student-watchman strains day and night to detect signs of fire in the forest. He experiments with his alarm system; he keeps a wary eye on every movement by the old Arab, for he suspects that the mute caretaker harbors plans of revenge. The student's former mistress pays him an unexpected visit. Toward the end of a long, derisively non-communicative day, he manages to make love to her on his narrow cot, upstairs in the ranger station. His binoculars

> . . . are still dangling on his chest, crushed between them. From time to time he coldly interrupts his embraces, raises his binoculars to his eyes and peers into the forest. "Duty," he whispers in apology.

Yet it gradually becomes clear that the watchman really wants the fire to break out. Once or twice he actually tries himself to put the forest to the torch. He uses the kerosene collected for this purpose by the Arab caretaker, but he fails, much to his own and the Arab's dismay. From this moment on, the two are inseparably linked. He lectures the old man on the history of the Crusades. The mute man stammers wild sounds, gesticulates his answers.

> He wants to say that here is his house; that there was also a village here; they simply hid everything, buried it. . . . What is it that perturbs the Arab so much? Apparently his wives were murdered here as well. Obviously, a dark affair.

When the mute Arab finally does set the wood on fire, the student, exhilarated and relieved, does not sound the alarm. Another man calls the fire brigade, but it is too late. At dawn the protagonist stumbles in the smoldering remains through a "sad nakedness, the nakedness of lost wars and vainly shed blood." His eyes drift over the smoking hills. He lowers his brows and—

> there, from within the smoke and fog, arises before him the small village, reborn in a few basic lines, as in an abstract drawing, like every sunken past.

His thin smile is interrupted by the appearance of his aghast boss, the elderly director of the Department of Forests. Impertinently he asks his employer to "find a solution" for the little girl left behind by the arrested arsonist. Only now the elderly director (portrayed in a grotesque caricature of the early pioneers) senses what has really happened.

> He suddenly assaults the watchman . . . with his clenched and heated fists he strikes. He is restrained with difficulty by the policemen. Clearly, he accuses only him. Yes, this one with the books, with the foggy spectacles, with this learned cynicism of his.

Facing the Forests can also be read as an abstract, Kafkaesque parable, of course. It can be seen as a very contemporary, bleak, pessimistic portrait of modern man, balking at the repressive constraint of manmade civilization, who secretly longs for Dionysiac release in the fires of a chaotic cataclysm. Such an interpretation is valid and perhaps it explains Yehoshua's more universal appeal. But *Facing the Forests* must first and foremost be taken for what it avowedly, unhesitatingly is, an arrangement of mirrors through which the author inspects the Israeli political and cultural reality; it is a medium of self-knowledge.

Yehoshua once said of himself that he could write a story about

Hong Kong but the same motifs that interest him would again occur. In this novella, the new forest is clearly symbolic of the new Israeli society that has been established. upon the ruins of another. The implied masochism, of which he has been accused, is not at all vicarious. If he is not a "patriot" in the accepted sense, it must be remembered that Yehoshua—a fifth-generation Sabra—is as committed as the next Israeli to Israel's survival. Nor can Yehoshua be called an angry young man, an esoteric outsider, furiously kicking the pillars of establishment. He is Dean of Students at Haifa University.

Darkly suggestive, as in a mythic drama, the symbolic transmutation of guilt and claustrophobic anguish is even more evident in the work of Amos Oz. Born in Jerusalem in 1939 of a distinguished family of early settlers and right-wing, militant Zionists, Oz graduated from Hebrew University and has lived most of his adult life in a *kibbutz*. He has published two full length novels (*Another Place* and *Michael Mine*) and a score of short stories. His novels and short stories are set in a nightmarish landscape of permanent siege, bathed in the lurid, distorted light of impending disaster.

His best-known, most controversial work to date has been the novel *Michael Mine*, published in 1968. The manuscript was finished a few weeks before the Six Day War of 1967. If *Michael Mine* has scandalized some reviewers, it has elicited just as warm praise from others. The former dismissed it as a literary failure, or as politically dangerous and subversive; the latter regarded *Michael Mine* as a rare achievement in contemporary Hebrew letters. One distinguished critic, Gershon Shaked, while criticizing it on other points, called it an educational novel in the grand tradition of the nineteenth-century Hebrew enlightenment. The heated controversy would suggest that Oz touched an open nerve.

Among Israeli readers Oz has enjoyed a spectacular success. *Michael Mine* was the best-selling novel of the 1968–1969 period; close to 40,000 copies were sold in the first eighteen months after publication. (A similar per capita rate would mean a total sale of 3.3 million copies in the United States.) A true comparative figure would probably exceed this by one-third, since the number of Israeli readers whose Hebrew is sufficient to read a novel, hardly exceeds two-thirds of the adult population.

There is some significance in this extraordinary success, which goes beyond pure literary merit. Second to reading books that please and flatter us most, we tend to eagerly swallow those that stir the deepest wounds. *Michael Mine* is the story of Hannah, the young wife of Michael Gonen, a loving, good-natured, but very dull geologist in Jerusalem. Michael is a native of Holon, a new Israeli city founded in the mid-1930s on empty sand dunes along the coastal plain. Hannah, like Oz himself, is a native of Jerusalem.

There is something deliberate in the contrast Oz draws between the new, seemingly alien, ahistorical Holon and the ancient, Arab-Jewish (later partitioned between the two) city of Jerusalem. The oppressive air of constant strife has always been much stronger in Jerusalem than elsewhere in the country. In Oz's novel, with its strong autobiographical features, the unique atmosphere of Jerusalem—admirably drawn —supplants the tensions and complexities of Hannah's inner realm of fantasies. We meet her trapped in the dead monotony of a normal bourgeois existence. The security of her life sharply clashes with the dread and violence latent in the surrounding Jerusalem landscape: a city divided, its "Europeanized" Israeli sector surrounded on three sides by an ever-present menace, the deadly hostile Arab natives:*

> Dark mountains loom at dusk beyond the defiles of the streets in Jerusalem, mountains growing in obscurity, as though waiting for the darkness to fall upon the drawn-in city. . . . Nebi Samuel, a lone tower, stands on a high hilltop in the north, stands motionless beyond the borderline and watches day and night the old lady [as she plays the piano in the Israeli sector] . . . erect with her back to the open window. At night the tower grins, grins slim and tall, grins as if whispering to itself: "Chopin and Schubert. . . ." At dawn the [Arab] twins train at [throwing] hand grenades among the cliffs of the Judean desert southeast of Jericho.

The Arab "twins" Halil and Azis are key figures in Oz's narrative, and haunt Hannah's dreams. They dominate her suppressed desires,

---

* Oz wrote *Michael Mine* before the 1967 war and the ensuing annexation of Arab East Jerusalem by Israel. Circumstances have since changed; less so the quality of existential nightmare expressed by Oz. Reunited under Israeli rule, an invisible line continues to divide the two sectors, and will likely do so for a long time to come. "You look in vain now for the barbed wires," the poet Amichai wrote in 1967, but "you know well that such things don't really disappear." The Israeli sector, no longer surrounded by enemy troops but instead by occupied territories, remains an island cast in a sea of Arabs, in many ways a microcosm of the larger Arab-Israeli dichotomy.

her memories, her increasingly lunatic fantasy life. The twins are part
of the "natural," i.e., Arab, surroundings, upset by the Jewish intruder.
Hannah is more attracted than frightened by them. In fact, she adores
the "twins" and applauds their anti-Israeli violence. In desperation she
clings to her uncomprehending husband's body "as Emma Bovary
grasped at Rodolphe and Leon." (Robert Alter) But Hannah's ecstatic desire to break loose of the trap of existence is infinitely
stronger.

It would be misleading, of course, and unfair to Oz as an artist, to
interpret his imagery solely from a strictly political viewpoint. The
"twins" are meta-political symbols of primeval vitality, yet they are
also, clearly, representative of an immediate, painful reality. To ignore
that reality would be as false as would be a purely aesthetic approach
to the work of Yehoshua. In an interview in 1968, Oz
stated that in Israel's founding fathers he discovered a "human complexity and sometimes a schism that fascinate me." The generation of
founding fathers was, he said, both "marvelous and appalling"; it
awakened in him a "will for indirect *confession*, confession by way
of indirection . . . ." It is not difficult to detect both the marvel and
the horror. "If writers did not employ indirect, camouflaged means to
express their basic emotion, their work would be one long howl, one
perpetual lamentation, and then of course the critics would voice
much heavier objections . . ." The artist's function is to transfigure his
experience, not to revel in it. Oz knows that no experience can be
transfigured unless it is first understood.

In *Michael Mine*, Hannah imagines: ". . . the twins at dawn train at
hand grenades . . . they do not use words. Their bodies are mated.
Submachine gun on shoulder. Drab commando uniforms, smeared
with lubricant from the guns." Halil and Aziz had been Hannah's
playmates as a little girl, now, as Arab guerrillas, they are harbingers of
Arab revenge on the Jewish intruders. Their development in Hannah's
fantasy life reaches its climax toward the end of the book, in the
description of a successful guerrilla attack. In Oz's narrative the attack
coincides with and heralds Hannah's reconciliation with herself
through a cathartic fantasy of destruction:

> The concrete water-pool will rest on great pillars . . . four strong hands
> will flex. Mated as in a dance. As in love. . . . A delayed action mech-

anism . . . a detonant . . . bodies will wail against the slope . . . then suddenly and not suddenly a dim explosion will bark. . . . And the outbreak of flowing laughter. Bold and sweeping and making one tremble. A brief linking of fingers . . . first words. A scream of joy. Slumber. The night's color is violet. Heavy dews, all over the valley. A star. Opaque lumps of mountains . . . over the wide spaces will descend a cold calm.

Clearly, then, the appearance and success of Amos Oz and A. B. Yehoshua at this particular time raise more questions than can be safely answered without courting the danger of wild, unsubstantiated speculation. The observer of Israeli life stands perplexed at this outburst of bleak, depressive pessimism amidst a new, achievement-oriented society largely predicated on a brilliant dream. It might be said of Israel, as Scott Fitzgerald said of America, that it was a willingness of the heart. An observer is challenged to decide whether the nightmarish anguish that permeates the work of Oz and Yehoshua is merely the local reflection of a more universal "modern temper" in Western culture; or whether it marks, above all, the spiritual vacuum created by the receding future of the classic Zionist dream, a vacuum that cannot satisfactorily be filled by feats of arms.

Beyond speculation is the *freedom of awareness* among young artists and their public that is remarkable at a time when siege and war, terror and repression, dominate all communications between Israel and her enemies. The future of this freedom is not certain, of course. It could erode in continuous crisis. It might be crushed in the Spartan garrison state that remains a distant, but not altogether unthinkable, possibility. Conversely, this freedom of awareness is itself an important guarantee against just such a devolution of the Zionist state.

Oz and Yehoshua are, in a sense, "new" writers. Their expressionist or symbolic mode has generally been treated as a departure in modern Israeli letters. With few exceptions, the leading younger novelists and poets of the post-Independence period practiced a rather drab and sometimes didactic genre of social (or socialist) realism. Shamir, Shacham, Bartov, Guri, Meged, S. Yizhar, to mention only a few of the best-known authors, belong to the generation that fought in the War of Independence in 1948. The fiction of this group was deeply concerned with the nation's destiny. The treatment and possible resolution of social problems (the absorption of immigrants, the transformation of "selfish careerists" into dedicated *kibbutzniks*) was as important for these writers as were the lives of their leading characters who were often submerged in the text as two-dimensional protagonists of a specific ideology. Yet already in this early period, a passionate, unrelenting moral motivation is discernible, a deep concern, overriding all others, for the preservation of human values in brutal times.

As spokesmen of generational change, as articulators of the complex of Zionist guilt—in this strictly limited sense—some of the earlier writers were clearly precursors of Oz and Yehoshua. A reader of these books, twenty years later, is struck by a curious quality of almost premature old age that marks some works of the then twenty-two- or twenty-four-year-old writers in a newly born, enthusiastic, forward-looking nation. One never saw such young bodies carrying such old heads. S. Yizhar, perhaps the best and most representative writer of the post-Independence generation that went through the war of 1948, is a good case in point. In his shorter period stories, and his mammoth war novel, *Days of Ziklag*, Yizhar has portrayed his heroes (mostly teen-aged soldiers of the 1948 war) as harassed by debilitating doubts and morose moral agony.

The abjuration of sacred Zionist causes is a frequent theme in Yizhar's work. He mocks the "proud flag"; "homeland" is a word that says everything and nothing. His heroes complain that the heavy weight of Zionist rhetoric is "like a millstone around your neck." In Yizhar's work the ultimate purpose of Zionism—national existence—is scrutinized by a deeply conscientious mind refusing to be a mere handmaiden of necessity. A committee of literary mandarins refused Yizhar Israel's most coveted literary award (the Bialik Prize) in 1958 because, they said, in *Ziklag*, he "tears down more than he builds up." Nevertheless, he was given a safe seat in the parliament by the labor party.

Some Israeli critics have seen Yizhar's *Days of Ziklag* as a kind of Israeli *Naked and the Dead*. In *Days of Ziklag*, Yizhar described seven days on a sandy hilltop along the Egyptian front in 1948. The fighting is brutal; the hill repeatedly changes hands. Yizhar slowly develops his characters and achieves what has often been called the collective portrait of an entire generation.

War novels tend to be overpowered by exterior forces; character and human plausibility often remain subsidiary to external happenings. The dramatic events described in Yizhar's *Days of Ziklag* only rarely overshadow the rich inner lives of his main characters. Like Adolph in Strindberg's *Creditors*, Yizhar's young heroes feel not guilty, but inextricably responsible. They are marked and nearly destroyed by the sudden collapse, in war, of the Zionist-Socialist-humanist values on which they had been raised:

"Am I on fever? It is too hot to breathe," Yizhar's hero says in the heat of battle on the last day of *Ziklag*.

> When they come, you won't shoot at them? You'll pull away? Raise a white flag? Scream at them, "Tolstoy, Tolstoy, Gandhi, Gandhi!" No, no. You are this sort of creature that shoots, that takes precise aim to strike, and prays at the same time not to hit. Right. But how? Either don't shoot them or don't pray! Right. What's right?

Yizhar examines his hero's attitude to Zionism, through a repeated sifting of the ends and means employed to achieve it, of war, innocence, and death. In the explicit language, which he uses well, Yizhar has etched the portrait of a generation of native-born youngsters, whose thoughts are at war with their actions. "The hill is ours," he writes on the last page of *Ziklag*, and so are "the fields, the wide expanses, the country. Have we *finished?*"

The question remains open as a wound, as do so many other questions raised by Yizhar's miserable, guilt-ridden protagonists. Yizhar's work is essentially an exploration of young men placed in crucial situations not of their making. They are pursued by terrible doubts; they are despairingly aware of how incapable they are of changing things through their own will power. "Whatever hits a man is his choice. Choice, stupid word, woe that it was made to tick under your skull."

Yet it does tick. In *Tale of Khirbat Khisa*, written shortly after the 1948 war, which saw the creation of the Arab refugee problem, Yizhar was the first to sharply focus on a theme that in the following years was to disturb the conscience of many Israeli writers: Israel's deep moral responsibility for the fate of these refugees. *Khirbat Khisa* is an Arab village, easily taken, without battle, by Israeli forces in the War of Independence. In a harrowing narrative, heavily interspersed with bitter reflections—perhaps the most conscience-stricken, deliberately guilt-ridden piece of contemporary Israeli literature—Yizhar describes the coldblooded, systematic expulsion of the Arab villagers from their homes, and their dispatch, like cattle, to the "other side":

"What will they do there?"

"Let them ask their charming leaders," answered Yehuda [who had earlier compared the villagers to animals].

"What will they eat and drink? They had to think of that before they started."

*"Started what?"** I asked.

"Don't you play the righteous one," Yehuda said angrily, "now *we* are making order in this area."

A few pages later, a fellow soldier attempts to console the young hero with visions of *Khirbat Khisa*'s brilliant future as an exemplary, modern Israeli settlement:

"They'll take this land in hand and work it. It will be nice here."

"Sure, what else? How didn't I guess that before? *Our Khirbat Khisa.* Housing and absorption problems. Hurrah, we house and absorb. We'll open a co-op grocery, a school, perhaps a synagogue. There'll be political parties. They'll discuss lots of things. The fields will be plowed and sown and reaped, and great feats will be accomplished. Bravo, Hebrew *Khisa!* Who'll remember that there was once a *Khirbat Khisa* which we drove out and inherited. *We came, shot, burned, blew up, repelled, pushed and exiled. What the hell are we doing here!?"***

A little later he asks:

Will the walls not scream in the ears of those who will live in this village? The sights, the wails that were heard and not heard, the frightened innocence of a muzzled herd, the surrender of the weak, and their valor, the one valor of the weak who don't know what to do and can't, the feebled mute, will they not put the air astir with shadows, sounds and looks? . . . I felt within me a stupefying collapse."***

---

* Author's italics.
** Author's italics.
*** On the subject of Arab refugees, consider, for example, *To Remember and Forget* by Dahn Ben Amotz, a novel about the love of an Israeli for a young German woman, published in 1968. In a number of dialogues between the two, Ben Amotz endeavors to puncture the common Israeli attitude of total righteousness by making a favorable comparison between the attitude of the West German government to Jewish refugees,

Yizhar's guilt-ridden hero reappears in "The Captive," a terse self-examination by a young soldier, deeply perturbed by his own behavior yet ultimately impotent to follow the dictates of his conscience. The title of the story is darkly indicative of the wider theme: "The Captive" immediately suggests a "captive" country, taken and "imprisoned" by the Jews. This is one of Yizhar's best-known, most controversial short stories. When it first appeared in 1949 as a companion piece of *Khirbat Khisa*, the military authorities made a brief, unsuccessful attempt to ban its circulation under the military censorship act.

Khirbat Khisa was written in the first person singular (strongly suggesting that the protagonist was expressing Yizhar's own, innermost conflict). "The Captive" was written as a dialogue between the perplexed hero and the author, who addresses and admonishes the protagonist in the imperative. The story bears a resemblance to Albert Camus' "The Guest." Like Daru, the French-Algerian schoolteacher ordered by the gendarme to escort an arrested Arab to the next town where he would be tried and punished for an offense under a law that is not his own and which he cannot understand, Yizhar's hero is ordered to escort a captured Arab shepherd, who is vaguely suspected of espionage, to rear headquarters, apparently for summary execution. Camus' Daru sets his prisoner free, only to be rewarded, upon his return, with threats by the Arab's compatriots: "You handed over our brother. You will pay for this."

Yizhar's protagonist also wants to let his Arab go; yet weak and hesitant, he never brings himself to do it. He feels sure the man is innocent by Arab standards, and probably by his own as well. As they travel by jeep to the rear, he knows that he ought to let him go, to return to his life, his family, and children. Letting him go would be "simple," "fair," and "humane." He realizes, in shock, that here in his hands, a matter is being decided that could be otherwise called "fate."

> Give life to an oppressed man. Think of it. To obey your heart. To go by your love, your own truth, by what is greater than all greatness—the liberation of man.

and the attitude of the Israeli government to Arab refugees. The treatment of Arab refugees in *To Remember and Forget* is of special interest in view of the extraordinary Israeli touchiness on everything German.

Release.
Be a man.
Release!

Yet the prisoner is not released; the story reaches an ambiguous conclusion. A deep sadness remains, a lingering admonition, a despair. It "will remain here, among us, unfinished."*

The art of Oz, Yehoshua, or Yizhar cannot be viewed in isolation. It must be seen within the general frame of their lives—perpetual siege and endless war, with all the concomitant brutality, fear, tyranny, and dehumanization, the somnambulant politicians, the ambivalence of abstract rights and claims, the basic will to survive, the doubts inherent in sheer physical survival, the banality of death. At the same time we must not forget that it is easier to evaluate the injustice suffered by the Arabs than it is to devise means of correction that would not only be acceptable to Arabs but would also preclude an even greater human tragedy. In Israel, as in most countries, men of letters do not exercise political power. As mediums of self-examination, they are, as Thomas Mann once said of his craft, not a power, but a consolation. But at least in Israel, a younger generation of writers is preparing the ground for the emotional détente and the ideological disarmament for any future settlement.

The uneasiness reflected in literature stems not only from the Arab dispute. It harks back, of course, to Israel's earliest beginnings. Because Israel, as a nation-state, originated in an act of self-consciousness, Israelis are continually fascinated and disturbed by themselves. They are exalted by their achievements, and worried by them. A perturbed self-consciousness seems to be endemic of all self-created, "artificial" states. Yet there is probably no other country where people

---

* The Arab "captive" reoccurs as the theme of at least two more works by younger Israeli writers, in "The Swimming Contest" by Benjamin Tammuz and "On the Point of a Bullet" by Yitzchak Orpaz. Both writers make deeply suggestive use of the captive as a literary and quasi-political symbol. Both writers cause their "captive" to die an ignoble, unnecessary death; both are guilt-ridden; both picture themselves as the truly vanquished, whereas their defeated, dead Arab captives emerge, ultimately, as victors. A fourth, somewhat different example, is Yoram Kaniuk's description of the brutal, senseless murder of a captive Arab family, in *The Acrophile*. Kaniuk's hero, numb with fear, takes part in the ghastly act to prove something to himself. Nothing is proven except his own remorse and the beginning of his own disintegration.

are as concerned with "defining themselves": "Who are we?" "Why are we here?" "What is an Israeli?"

It is intriguing in this context to observe the extraordinary appeal of archeology as a popular pastime and science in Israel. The millennia-spanning mixture of ancient and modern history, coupled with notions of "controversial" legitimacy, combine to produce this peculiarly Israeli syndrome. Archeological finds have inspired nearly all Israeli national symbols, from the State Seal, to emblems, coins, medals, and postage stamps. For the disquieted Israeli, the moral comforts of archeology are considerable. In the political culture of Israel, the symbolic role of archeology is immediately evident. Israeli archeologists, professionals and amateurs, are not merely digging for knowledge and *objects*, but for the reassurance of roots, which they find in the ancient Israelite remains scattered throughout the country.

Archeology in Israel is a popular movement. It is almost a national sport. Not a passive spectator sport but the thrilling, active pastime of many thousands of people, as perhaps fishing in the Canadian lake country or hunting in the French *Massif Central*. Israel, of course, easily lends itself to such a national sport. The country is a treasure house of antiquities. "Archeology thrives on wars and on the dead, like the hyena or the hawk," the poet Yehuda Amichai has written. The plains and mountain passes of Israel are a veritable outdoor Louvre of the art of warfare.

There is an easy attraction in archeology, it combines adventure with bookish toil. In the long and arid summer months one picks potsherds and oriental glass fragments like flowers and mushrooms. But mere excitement and great amounts of antique remains do not fully explain the syndrome, which in this form is unknown in other countries. From time to time the government has made half-hearted attempts to curtail private digging in the interest of science and the public museums. Such attempts have run up against the apparently irresistible enthusiasm of the public. Some of the daily newspapers employ regular archeology columnists. Archeological finds, relevant to the country's ancient Jewish past, are likely to be heralded as major news events. An appeal for volunteers to work an important archeological excavation will elicit thousands of applications. Professor Yigael Yadin's bi-monthly, rather highbrow quiz on archeology ran for two years as a popular television program. There are important archeological collections and semi-private museums in the most unlikely places—in dozens of *kibbutzim*, in remote villages and towns, all assembled by enthusiastic amateurs with little, if any, outside assistance.

Not surprisingly, perhaps, the best known amateur is General Moshe Dayan. His long pursuit of archeology as a bloodless field sport has brought him into occasional conflict with the law and once, in 1968, to a close brush with death. (See Chapter 1, p. 17) Dayan's private home holds one of the major archeological collections in the country. Shortly after his accident he told an interviewer what he was so obsessively looking for in his archeological diggings. He was in search, he said, of

> the ancient Land of Israel. Everything that ancient *Eretz-Israel* was; those who lived here then, their way of life. You sometimes feel that you can literally enter their presence. They are dead to be sure. But you can enter the homes of silenced people and sometimes feel more than when you enter the homes of the living. *I like to stick my head into a hole in which the people of Bnei Brak lived* 6,000 *years ago** . . . to have a look at their kitchen, to *finger* the ashes left there from long ago, to *feel* the fingerprints which that ancient potter left on the vessel.

Israel's outstanding professional archeologist, Professor Yigael Yadin, like Dayan is a former general and chief of staff. Professor Yadin has said that for young Israelis, a "belief in history" has come to be a substitute for religious faith. "Through archeology they discover their 'religious values.' In archeology they find their religion. They learn that their forefathers were in this country 3,000 years ago. This is a value. By this they fight and by this they live. . . ."

Having run most of the questions to earth it remains for the patriotic archeologist to dig them up. He does so by directing his efforts to the exploration of the country's Israelite past, often to the exclusion of other rich and fascinating periods, Hellenistic, Roman, Byzantine, Moslem, and Crusader. Existing Nabatean and Crusader ruins have indeed been lovingly, impressively restored at great cost by the Israeli government, but this has been done primarily to promote the tourist industry. Archeological *excavation*, as opposed to the restoration of

---

* Author's italics.

existing sites, has largely been restricted to Jewish objects.

There are undoubtedly deep psychological reasons that lend Israeli archeology its distinctive political, even chauvinistic, air. Freud compared the techniques of psychoanalysis to those of archeology. The student of nationalism and archeology will be tempted to take note of the apparent cathartic effects of both disciplines. It is possible to observe in the pursuit of patriotic archeology, as of faith or of Freudian analysis, the achievement of a kind of cure; men overcome their doubts and fears and feel rejuvenated through the exposure of real, or assumed, but always hidden origins.

New nations, paradoxically, resemble senile old men in their insistent search for the fountains of their youth; and the more distant the roots the greater the feeling of rejuvenation. This is sometimes achieved by myth-faking, as when archeology is used to produce symbols of a false, "unbroken" past, a political continuity uninterrupted through the centuries. It is well known in Ireland and in some of the central American countries. Israel has not escaped such myth-faking. Fake myths of the past can produce a fake, and sometimes dangerous, present. The insistent search for authentic roots into the distant history of the country at times ignores three thousand years of subsequent Jewish history and ethics by reaching back directly to the barbaric Hebrew tribes of ancient times.

In Europe the birth of archeology as a science coincided with the rise of nationalism. There has been a growing interaction between archeology and nationalism in many cultures, from Henry VIII's appointment of an Antiquary of the Realm, to the considerable support in manpower and equipment given to Professor Yadin by the Israeli army and air force.

Archeology often converged with nationalism in the new nation-states created in Europe after 1918. In Estonia and in Finland, in Czechoslovakia under Masaryk, and in Poland, the resources of archeology were used politically to provide material symbols of unbroken historical continuity. This was done through the discovery, and occasional fabrication of "national" features in the distant pre-history of Poland, Czechoslovakia, Finland, or Estonia. In Israel today, the uses of archeology are psychologically comforting. Even more than proving things to others, archeology serves political men to prove something to themselves.

In modern Hebrew it is customary to speak of an Israeli *bulmus* for archeology. *Bulmus* is an old talmudic term, derived from the Greek *boulimos*. It denotes a ravenous hunger, a faintness resulting from prolonged fasting, an exaggerated eagerness, a fit, a rage, a mania.*

The present *bulmus* for archeology is of relatively recent origin. The early Zionists had no more than a passing interest in archeology. Herzl was not at all attracted by it. On one occasion, according to his diary, his attention was briefly drawn to a plan by Colonel Henning Melander, a Swedish army officer and world traveler, who proposed to dig up the Temple Mount in Jerusalem. Melander announced his intention to uncover the Holy Tabernacle, much as Schliemann had uncovered the crown of Agamemnon at Troy. Herzl notes (September 3, 1889) that he discussed this romantic project with the Grand Duke of Baden, his powerful friend and supporter at the imperial court of Germany. The Grand Duke told Herzl that the Kaiser was planning to intervene with the Sultan of Turkey on Melander's behalf, for the Kaiser was "greatly interested" in the project. Herzl apparently was not, for he never mentions the subject again.

In the same way as he was ready to establish his proposed Jewish state in another territory, so he was unmoved by the symbolism inherent in the Palestinian monuments of antiquity. Characteristically he remained impassive even at the Wailing Wall, which he visited during his brief stay in Jerusalem during the fall of 1898. In his written plans for the new Jerusalem there is nothing on archeology. His aim is rather to thoroughly "clean up" Jerusalem, "remove everything that is not sacred" to one of the three religions, "empty the dirty hovels, burn down the non-sacred ruins," transplant the ancient bazaars and construct a "modern clean, well-ventilated" town around the holy places.

The early pioneers were hardly more moved by the charm of antique sites. Although the First and Second *Aliya* (1882–1914) coincided with the first Palestinian excavations on a grand scale by Petrie, Macalister, Sellin, and others, the settlers apparently took little notice of them. It seems likely, of course, that their hard struggles in the present left them little leisure to bestow upon the past. Even more

---

* "He who is seized by *bulmus* (on the Day of Atonement) is to be given food even if it be unclean" (Yoma, 8:6). "A *bulmus* of incest" (Midrash b'Reshit, 51).

important was their strong orientation toward the future. Whatever free time they had was devoted to their plans for a brilliant tomorrow. They were true believers, with little need for the buried proofs of yesteryear.

In the vast literature of the early pioneers there are remarkably few references to the subject. In 1904 the German archeologist Dr. Benzinger delivered a lecture in Jerusalem on his recent excavations at Tel el Mutasselem. The young Aaron Aaronsohn, who would soon be an outstanding figure in the community of early settlers,* was present at the lecture. He confided to his diary that archeological excavations meant nothing to him. For this reason "I do not mind when I see the *goyim* dealing with them."

Ben Zvi, the future President, was fascinated, not by archeology, but by ethnology. He searched the deserts for lost tribes of Jewish bedouins. He was scarcely as moved by antiquities as he was by the discovery of a few authentic Jewish *felahin*, obscure Hebrew Arabs in the Galilean village of Pekiin. This was living—not stone-dead—proof of a continued Jewish presence in the country.**

The present *bulmus* for archeology has grown with the second and third generation of settlers. In 1920 men of the famous Labor Brigade were employed as earth diggers at the excavation of Hammat-Tiberias. But the anarcho-syndicalists of the Brigade seem to have approached their task with much less respect than they did the building of roads and the draining of swamps. Digging up the past was not building the future.

The first real outbreak of excitement occurred in December 1928. It was a time of low morale and distress, generated by Zionist difficulties with the British government, by economic crisis, and mounting Arab

---

* Aaronsohn (1876–1919) was the son of a pioneer family from Rumania that settled in Zichron Yaakov in 1882. A brilliant scholar of unusual versatility, a botanist, agronomist, geologist, and geographer, he achieved international fame through his discovery in 1906 of the single-grained wild wheat (triticum dicoccoides), the earliest-known prototype of bread-producing grain, a discovery of some consequence not only for agronomists but for historians of civilization as well. In World War I, Aaronsohn headed a Jewish spy ring in Palestine that supplied British intelligence with vital information prior to General Allenby's conquest of the country.

** Ben Zvi's little book on the Jews of Pekiin, first published in 1922, opens on a characteristically euphoric note: "Like a saga of olden times, like an echo that rises from the depth of past centuries, the news of remnants of Jewish *felahin* in Pekiin rings in our ears."

opposition to Zionist settlement. Sudden euphoria spread among the left-wing, non-observant, anti-religious *kibbutzniks* of Beit Alpha, when they accidentally discovered a sixth-century synagogue on their ground. The *kibbutzniks* hit the mosaic floor of the synagogue during the digging of an irrigation ditch. The discovery was considered to be of "national importance," and so it was at first kept secret from the (British) regional inspector of archeology. A Jewish archeologist, E. L. Sukenik (father of Yigael Yadin), was summoned by the *kibbutzniks* from Jerusalem. An excavation was arranged under "Zionist" auspices. For weeks, excited *kibbutzniks* from the entire region volunteered their labor.

This unprecedented enthusiasm heralded the fervor of future years. By 1947 it was fully developed. In the summer of that year a Bedouin shepherd boy, pursuing a runaway goat along the cliffs that rim the Dead Sea, accidentally came upon an unknown cave. He threw a stone into the cave and heard the sound of breaking clay. It was thus that Israel was supplied with its most important archeological relic to date—the Dead Sea Scrolls.

For Israelis, the scrolls have since assumed a hallowed air. In the eyes of some, the scrolls are almost titles of real estate, like deeds of possession to a contested country.

The seven Dead Sea scrolls that were purchased by the government of Israel prior to 1967 are now enshrined in Jerusalem like the bones of a saint—in a specially built sanctuary appropriately called the *Shrine of the Book.** The building is part of the larger complex of the Israel National Museum and faces the Knesset building. Together with the Knesset building, the *Shrine of the Book* serves as a station identification mark of Israeli television. The *Shrine* has been designed to symbolically dramatize its content. An onion-shaped dome of blaz-

---

* These scrolls were bought from Arab dealers through various intermediaries. Their acquisition was proclaimed, an act of state by the Prime Minister in a solemn announcement in parliament. They include a first-century manuscript of the Book of Isaiah older by at least a thousand years than any previously known Hebrew copy of the Old Testament; the so-called War Scroll, the Manual of Discipline; the Thanksgiving Hymns; the Genesis Apocryphon; a Habakkuk commentary; and other scrolls. More scrolls from the caves of Qumran (the so-called Temple Scroll and other fragments) were seized by the Israelis during the war of 1967, and are kept at the Rockefeller Museum in East Jerusalem.

ing white sits upon a low base of basalt. White surfaces sharply contrast against sheer black. This, we are told, represents the Forces of Light contrasting against the Forces of Darkness—the mystic subject of one of the better-known scrolls. Within the dome, the upward phallic thrust of an enormous, clublike structure is said to represent the national will to persist. This, the heart of the shrine, is reached through a dramatically unbalanced, off-center arched tunnel, narrowed by tilted walls of rough stone. At the end of this passageway, which is dark and cavernous and can only remind one of the fallopian tubes leading to the womb, is the domed rotunda on which the scrolls are displayed behind plated glass.

The rotunda evokes a chapel. In the middle, on an elevated pedestal shaped like a round altar, the entire length of the scroll of Isaiah is displayed in a great circular glass case. High above it is an opening to the sky, originally designed to jettison a thin spray of water out from the dome. Upon second thought this idea was abandoned. The shrine was planned by an American architectural firm, headed by the sculptor-architect, J. F. Kiesler. Consciously or not, Kiesler absorbed to a remarkable degree local feelings toward the scrolls, in all their complexity. No building in Israel is as clearly based upon the exploitation of anatomical shapes and erotic symbols. In the Shrine of the Book, archeology and nationalism are mated as in an ancient rejuvenation and fertility rite.

The highest pitch of emotional involvement in archeological symbols was reached in 1963, upon the excavation and painstaking restoration of the ancient Zealot fortress of Masada. The psycho-political role of archeology in Israeli culture is nowhere as blatant as in the cult of the scrolls and the patriotic ceremonials of Masada.

Masada was originally built by Herod the Great as a military citadel and as a pleasure palace for himself. It is dramatically perched on a butte-like cliff top thirteen hundred feet above the Dead Sea in the waterless wilderness of Judea. After the fall of Jerusalem in A.D. 70, a group of Jewish zealots withdrew to Masada, where they made a last stand against the infidel conquerors. The intensely emotional story of the siege of Masada by the Romans, the mass suicide of its defenders, of the men, women, and children who drew lots and slew one another rather than fall prisoner to the Romans, is well known. It has been preserved by Josephus Flavius, the Jewish Roman historian, who also quoted the last speech of Eleazar Ben Yair, the Zealots' general:

. . . long ago we resolved never to be servants to the Romans nor to any other than God himself. . . . We were the first to revolt against them and we are the last that will still fight them. I cannot but esteem it as a favor that God has granted us that it is still in our power to die bravely and in a state of freedom, unlike others who were conquered unexpectedly. It is very plain that we shall be taken in a day's time; but it is still an eligible thing to die after a glorious manner together with our dearest friends . . . Let us then save our wives before they are abused and our children before they have tasted of slavery; and after we have slain them let us bestow that glorious benefit upon one another mutually, and preserve ourselves in freedom as an excellent funeral monument for us.

Masada was excavated by Professor Yadin in the years 1963–1965. He was assisted by thousands of Israeli and foreign volunteers, who were all seized by a kind of holy zeal. Yadin's account of the Israeli volunteers is filled with descriptions of their enthusiasm. His otherwise restrained text is marked by enraptured exclamations:

It was an unforgettable moment. Suddenly a bridge was thrown across two thousand years. . . .
How great was their satisfaction, and ours, when they—the young generation of the independent State of Israel—uncovered with their own hands the remains of the last defenders of Masada. . . .

As a social phenomenon, Yadin's excavations at Masada illustrated an interesting, and probably unique, feature of Israeli life and manners. Unpaid work at archeological excavations is the single social task, other than volunteering for dangerous tasks in army crack units and for service in exposed border settlements, that Israelis volunteer for in large numbers. The great excavation at Masada has barely exhausted the fund of available mass enthusiasm.

A young volunteer at the excavation next to the Wailing Wall in 1969 told the story of an encounter in the Arab quarter of the old city of Jerusalem as he walked home tired and dusty after a long day's work. "One puzzled Arab asked me: 'For what do you work, if not for money?' I answered, 'Inspiration,' and he said, 'Where do I find that? There is none in my life.' I told him I must be lucky."

Yadin's excavations at Masada uncovered Herod's luxurious castle villa. They also confirmed in general outlines the story of Masada as told by Josephus. Among many other period items, a potsherd was found bearing the name Ben Yair, quite possibly the lot cast by the zealot-general in the suicide agreement.

Masada has since been restored and partly reconstructed by the National Parks Authority. It is now fairly easy to reach and is visited annually by a great mass of tourists. The patriotic ceremonies that regularly take place at the top of Masada exemplify the convergence of politics and archeology in modern Israeli culture. Even before the excavation youth movements of all political shades staged emotional pageants at Masada. Select units of the Israeli army were marched up to the fortress not long after induction. Recruits to the armored corps gave their oaths of allegiance on Masada. The rites took place in nocturnal ceremonies lit by hundreds of blazing torches. A characteristic remark by Professor Yadin, made during a speech at one such ceremony in the summer of 1963, has often been quoted:

> When Napoleon stood among his troops next to the pyramids of Egypt, he declared: "Four thousand years of history look down upon you." But what would he not have given to be able to say to his men: "Four thousand years of *your own* history look down upon you. . . ." The echo of your oath this night will resound throughout the encampments of our foes! Its significance is not less powerful than all our armaments!

A bizarre, and sometimes strangely pagan, air prevails at such ceremonies, staged by secular moderns over the graves of ancient religious zealots. The zealots of Masada would no doubt have opposed modern Israel's Westernized and secular character just as they opposed the Romanized Jews of their time. They would undoubtedly have resented today's non-kosher food, Israel's arts, sports, and politics as passionately as they opposed the Roman infidels.

The tenacity of the ancient Hebrews, in their drawn-out struggle with the Romans, today inspires Israeli patriotism. It lends an added dimension of time, of ancient myth, and historical tradition to what would otherwise be a struggle by settlers for new lands overseas. Yet there remains a deep irony, which even the Israeli nationalist cannot afford to ignore. The zealots of Masada were unique, but there is a disconcerting parallel between the ancient Hebrews and the Palestinian Arabs who opposed—and still oppose—the return of the Jews with as much zeal and fanatic passion (and with as little success) as the ancient Hebrews, who, upon these same historic hills, opposed the encroachment of Philistine settlers and the conquests of technologically superior Roman armies.

The zealots resented the tolerance and humanism of the Romans as fiercely as they resented their paganism. They did not mind being exploited and tyrannized by their own high priests and military leaders, so long as the priests did not succumb to the pleasures and temptations of Roman civilization.

In this last respect, at least, the apparent historical continuity is intriguing. The vaguest comparison between the Hebrews and the Palestinian Arabs will, of course, immediately sound frivolous to most Israeli ears. Naturally it is a little farfetched; the Zionist settlers were not Roman legionnaires. The Palestinian Arabs have not committed suicide although they have preferred rule by their own retrogressive leaders to that of the Zionists, which promised to be more civilized and progressive by contemporary standards. And yet, with all the obvious differences, the comparison should not be immediately dismissed as altogether preposterous. It may offer a point of view from which to look and compare and investigate the terrain for possible avenues of reconciliation. Victors often believe that only they are rational. They are prone to dismiss the dogged determination of the vanquished as the blind, irrational fanaticism of the politically primitive. Wise victors learn from their own history that yesterday's irrational fanatic may be hailed tomorrow for his perseverance.

11

THE POLITICAL STYLE

We converted the human dust which gathered here from all the corners of the earth, we converted them into a sovereign state which occupies an honorable place in the family of nations.

—DAVID BEN GURION, 1967

Israelis endlessly complain that they are a misgoverned people. They continually call for abler, stronger, more effective government. And yet, at the same time, few peoples are so suspicious of authority, so abusive in their attitude to power, and so adept in the ancient art of circumventing it. This dual, and often paradoxical, approach to power is a main characteristic of the Israeli political style.

To expect too much from the mere fact of sovereignty is a common feature of most new nations. If, like the Jews, they waited long for their sovereignty, and eventually fought for it, an impetuous people will naturally be keyed up with high expectations. They will sometimes expect a government to perform miracles. The Israelis' demands of their government are often exorbitantly high. The government is expected to achieve—short of turning men into women and women into men—practically everything else from peace, prosperity, and the pursuit of happiness to high wages, low prices, comfort, liberty, order, good theater, efficient schools, public cleanliness, even love, especially from the foreign press.

Great as these expectations are, the Israelis' willingness to grant their government decisive powers has been continually checked by robust distrust and healthy suspicions. They are a new nation and they are an old nation. Their attitude to power remains ambivalent in the extreme; the reasons are partly historical and partly spiritual or religious.

Israelis prefer their government to reflect not one party but the consensus of at least half a dozen; they prefer not to follow the policy of one but to accept the lowest common denominator of many. Israeli voters, as a rule, disperse power to a relatively larger spectrum of competitive, mutually restricting, parties, than do the voters in most other parliamentary democracies. The tendency to spread the vote widely has become an integral part of the established political system. Even the issue of national security invariably proves insufficient to rally a simple majority behind one leader, or even behind a group of leaders within a single political group.

Israel is not governed by one elite, but by a plurality of elites. This has been so since Independence, indeed since the early days of settlement. The elites are confederated; for, with so much dissension, the state could not have functioned otherwise. Yet the confederated elites remain extremely jealous of one another. Their past quarrels and debates have been so bitterly ferocious, so marked by frequent splits and schisms, so absolute in their respective claims, as to suggest religious sects engaged in argument over sacred tenets of this or that divine revelation. The word *arachim* ("values") has always had an important place in the internal debate. It connotes near-absolute ideological and moral fixities. Values are always "basic": "Jewish values," "socialist values," "Zionist values," "moral values," "national values," "pioneering values," "cooperative values."

Parliamentary records are filled with anxious debates over sacred "values," to support or oppose purely technical or administrative measures. To the uninitiated outsider, traffic control, air pollution, foreign travel, or television would seem to lie beyond the scope of formal ideology; less so to those who debate such questions in the Knesset. Not infrequently ideology is camouflage for baser interests that are obscured by elaborate political ritual. The thick cloud of ideological dissension over "values" often screens a naked power struggle. The ostensibly pious pursuit of "values" sometimes obscures greed and personal ambition. Yet it is also true that in the past eighty years of Zionist history, abstract ideas have wielded such enormous power over the minds of men that unless one takes them seriously, no rational explanation of events is even remotely possible. Even today it would be a grave mistake to underestimate the continuing role of ideology in Israeli current political affairs.

The various Israeli interest groups and ideologies have at times been represented by up to twenty-five different political parties. In the pre-state period, there were election campaigns in which as many parties actually competed for the favor of the voters. The past ten or fifteen years have seen a gradual consolidation of the many parties. But the proliferation of power remains a prominent factor; the change has only been in degree. The most important power factions now contain six major and at least four minor parties. The major parties are in fact coalitions of at least six smaller subdivisions within them.

The present political elites, as represented by the parties, are often compared to a confederate league of semi-autonomous feudal principalities. Three or four elites are presently "united"—but most uneasily—within the "Alignment of Labor parties." They represent a cross-section of so-called labor interests (urban workers and unions, *kibbutzim*, cooperatives, technocrats, union-owned industries). Two or three additional elites, or parties, represent the religious-orthodox establishment. At least two more stand for the so-called "bourgeois" interests of the urban middle class, the liberal professions, shopkeepers and private entrepreneurs, and the non-socialist urban proletariat. Each elite is aided by and in turn itself helps party-controlled financial enterprises. Each gets a slice of public funds; each has a share in the state bureaucracy and in the economy. Each elite, or party, has its own mass-basis or "public," tightly organized by well-run political machines.

The politics of consensus are deeply rooted in the history of the pre-state period. They bear witness to the lingering strength of the institutions and procedures established early in this century by the founding fathers. The politics of 1909, or even 1921, affected a few hundred Zionist settlers only; their procedures survived the age of mass democracy. The ruling parties of today preceded the state, and not vice versa, they even preceded colonization. With the exception of a few splinter groups, the settlers' parties were founded in Eastern Europe as Zionist clubs.

Each party not only acted as a travel agency for prospective immigrants but soon also established its own agricultural settlements, investment firm, urban housing scheme, bank, trade union, labor exchange, kindergarten and schools, publishing house, newspaper, and sick fund. At one time or another several of the parties even maintained private underground armies.

In the pre-state period, an immigrant's first stop upon arrival would often be his local party branch headquarters. He lived in a party-affiliated, or party-sponsored block of flats. He found employment through the party labor exchange. His children were educated in party-controlled schools. He read the party newspaper. When sick, he lay in a party-dominated hospital, and recuperated in a party convalescent home. He played football on the party soccer team.

Much of this extreme partisanship withered away with the establishment of the state. Schools, labor exchanges, immigrant absorption, and the bulk of public housing are now nationalized. But Israel remains a state of many parties. Some parties have retained a measure of their pre-state role of independent economic and cultural entrepreneur, as banker, builder, publisher, and Tammany Hall-style purveyor of welfare. The sick funds are still party dominated, as are some of the housing projects. Agricultural settlements remain "affiliated" to this or that party. Certain rural sections still are, in effect, one-party enclaves; in such areas most *kibbutzim* and adjacent cooperative settlements are tied to the same party.

From what we have seen so far it would seem that the politics of consensus are mainly a result of the limitations imposed by a mushrooming multi-party system. Yet there seem to be deep cultural reasons as well. First and foremost among them is the Israelis' "instinctive attitude" to power.

Political independence has come to Israelis at great human cost. In the flush of achieving it, against so much external opposition (and some internal doubts as well), a cult of "the state" was born in 1948; its high priest was Ben Gurion. In one form or another the cult continues to this day. It finds expression in the postulate of *mamlachtiut*—approximately, "statism"—a shibboleth of Israeli politics. *Mamlachtiut* is a modern Hebrew coinage, and stands for a particular matter-of-fact attitude to public affairs. A man of *mamlachtiut* will judge issues on merit only, and will look above party politics, personal prestige, and the interests of selfish, sectarian pressure groups.

As we have seen in an earlier chapter, a form of anarchosyndicalism marked the development of the Zionist pioneer society from its inception. *Mamlachtiut* is often its negation. It calls for the state to be the chief regulator curtailing, even substituting for, the free play of semi-autonomous social and political bodies. There is an irony here which has marked many other post-revolutionary situations. Few factors contributed to the re-establishment of the Jews in Palestine as heavily as their unbridled individualism, their excessive partisanship, their spontaneous distrust of power; few instruments were more effective than the autonomous social and economic institutions, the counter-agencies through which the Zionist settlers achieved a degree of independent home rule long before the formal establishment of Israeli sovereignty in 1948. In Israel today, nearly everybody pays homage to *mamlachtiut*. Its promulgation in practice (with the exception of the army) is sometimes a different matter.

"Unity" is another shibboleth of new nations, especially embattled ones. In Israel, the governed and their governors repeatedly evoke the overriding need for unity. "Factionalism" is condemned. Yet it seems that to most Israelis the taste of factionalism in real life is less bitter than the idea; they partake of it constantly. In their constant demands for "unity," Israelis recall the chorus men in an operetta, staunchly singing *avanti* in unison, while remaining glued to the same spot.

The Israeli political system has evolved from the voluntary Zionist institutions and settlers' organizations of the pre-state period. As a system it has been remarkably stable. But all Israeli governments have perforce been unstable, easily shaken, often tottering, coalitions of warring political factions representing six or seven major confederated elites who traditionally share the government among themselves. No call has been voiced longer or more insistently than the recurring call for fusion among the dissenters. But when, in August 1969, an unprecedented pre-election merger of four labor parties finally achieved a close majority in the outgoing parliament (63 seats of 120), the electorate reacted as if it were duty bound to avert a mortal danger: within a matter of weeks it promptly reduced the new party to a minority status again. In the ensuing election it was returned with only 56 seats.

From time to time many Israelis will plead: "What we need is a strong leader." Yet when it comes to casting votes, they normally display a deep distrust of powerful men. Some of their leaders have been of the so-called charismatic type. Yet the popularity of such men (as expressed by public opinion polls) rarely affects the fortunes of their parties at the voting booths. Ben Gurion was the "father of the state," and as charismatic a leader as there ever was. He never received more than 38.2 percent of the vote (1959). Most of the time he had to be comforted with less: 35.5 percent in the first elections of 1949; 37.5 percent in 1951; 32.2 percent in 1955; 34.7 percent in 1961. In 1960, the list headed by Ben Gurion received only 7.9 percent of the vote.

Israelis are quick to criticize their leaders—for indecisiveness, doctrinal dissension, or outrageously buckling under to special interest or splinter groups. The system, as it is, lends greater leverage to small, even minuscule factions and interest groups. In consequence, much horse trading has taken place among the parties, a good deal of it quite ignoble. Such deals often result in "undemocratic" concessions to religious splinter groups, who hold the balance between the main political blocks. The concessions have led to blue Sabbath laws, laws prohibiting the raising and selling of pork, and the lack of civil marriage and divorce. The secular majority normally resents such concessions to a religious minority which has never polled more than 15.4 percent of the popular vote. Yet it seems to resent the alternative even more.

Such in-fighting is favored, of course, by the prevailing system of proportionate elections. The present electoral system, like the parties themselves, originated in the pre-state period. Its model was the election system in the short-lived Kerensky regime in Russia, which in the eyes of the pioneers appeared as the acme of democracy. The proliferation of smallish parties—each incapable of gaining a majority—is encouraged by an electoral system which treats the entire country as a single constituency.

Electoral reform is often spoken of. By introducing twenty or more constituencies, it is hoped that the number of splinter groups will be reduced and individual candidates will be responsible to the voters, not simply to the party machine which placed them on a list. But even reform is not likely to evolve a two- or three-party system. After reform, five, six, or even more parties will undoubtedly remain, and coalitions will in all likelihood be as necessary as before.

The diffusion of authority is a major characteristic of the Israeli political style. It explains some of the more perplexing aspects of

Israeli public life: the paradox of conservative immobilism in the midst of a dynamic society, the amazing longevity of some of the institutions of the early pioneering era, the excruciatingly slow process of legislation, the immense difficulties of reform in almost any field, the irremovability of politicians whom neither mistake nor old age nor senility can displace from office. It is also one of the reasons why Israel, despite general conditions conducive to the growth of authoritarian, oppressive rule, is still a free country. We have touched upon this aspect earlier. Let us now go into it in greater detail.

At least six factors have militated for absolutism. First and foremost, the permanancy of war. Second, the high regard accorded to military leaders; the "efficiency" and selfless dedication of the military are often contrasted in the public mind with the apparent muddlemindedness and excessive partisanship of the politicians. Third, the absence of a constitution to limit the prerogatives of the legislature, which remain in theory, unlimited. Fourth, the prevalence of a "state ideology" (Zionism, to a lesser degree Zionist socialism). Fifth, the prevalence of arrogant power elites who believe more in "*educating*" the people than in "*serving*" it. Sixth, an electorate partly seized by traumatic fears and partly "Oriental" with little prior experience of Western-style democracy. The effect of these six factors has so far been remarkably limited.

Consider, for example, the impact of "state ideology," or constant war. Israel is a self-created state with all the self-conscious uneasiness that normally accompanies such self-creations among reasonably civilized people. But it is also a state with a missionary sense of purpose: from the creation of an "ideal" society (fashioned on socialist or biblical models, or on an amalgam of both) to the strictures imposed upon individuals by the policy of the "ingathering of the exiles," to the demands of victory in a "just war" which is often pictured as a struggle between the children of light and the children of darkness. Wherever a single purpose is made the supreme goal of a state, that state is in danger of becoming absolute, at least temporarily. Other countries, engaged in shorter wars, or similarly addicted to official state ideologies, became sterile and dreary tyrannies, seats of perverse, oppressive regimes.

Israel's longstanding and single-minded pursuit of Zionism as an official state ideology and its pursuit more recently of one overriding goal

—survival in the face of continuing external threats—often breeds a conformity of outlook which in foreign, and some local, eyes occasionally appears quite stifling. But appearances are often misleading. Israel, Janus-faced, often presents one image inward and another to the outsider. The latter image is controlled by a provincial determination not to let the skeletons out; it is governed by ancient strictures "to tell it not in Gath and publish it not in the streets of Askelon." The outsider in search of truth must penetrate through heavy curtains of apologetic phraseology. Behind it he is likely to perceive a different picture.

There is remarkably little unanimity in Israel on almost any subject. Whatever national discipline exists is restricted to matters pertaining to defense, and even here discipline assumes a peculiar form. It is almost never the result of any general philosophy of obedience; rather it appears as a concession made temporarily, on an *ad hoc* basis, for clearly pragmatic reasons. In all other fields, there remains an almost religious addiction to an extreme form of self-reliant, sometimes wildly anti-social individualism.

If, as is often said, the atmosphere of a "nation in arms" enhances militarism, Israel has had near-ideal conditions to ensure the supremacy of the army over all civilian authorities. But such supremacy has been successfully averted. In fact, for most of the time, the army has actively participated in the creation of an intensely civilian culture. The army's comparative informality, the forced retirement of officers at an early age, have helped to preserve to a considerable degree the voluntary spirit of the old militias. Israel's military ideal remains the embattled farmer, the armed civilian, the unprofessional soldier, an ideal which harks back to the earliest days of settlement: Cincinnatus, reluctantly abandoning the plow to pick up the sword, not Caesar.

The percentage of military personnel within the population is one of the highest in the entire world, perhaps the highest with the exception of North Vietnam, North Korea, or Taiwan. But the influence of the army leadership upon political decisions is small. There have been bitter personal clashes over military and political decisions between army leaders and their civilian chiefs, during the Ben Gurion and Eshkol administrations. The army leadership invariably bowed to the final verdict of the civilians. Public opinion has always been alert to the potential danger of militarism and the political elites have echoed and nearly always amplified this concern. It could be said that next to constantly guarding themselves against the Arab threat, Israelis more consciously guard themselves against the potential danger of militarism than against any other danger.

Where continentals refer to an "art" and Americans to a "business" of government, Israelis speak of a "craft." The Israelis' "craft of government" is akin, in some ways, to the Americans' "business." Government as a "craft" portends a certain sobriety, a measure of reserve and a lack of mystification. "Art" calls for worship. The exercise of power as a "craft" implies a smaller amount of reverence and often a good deal of disparagement.

The attitude of Jews to authority—all authority, including their own —has traditionally been highly skeptical. It still is, to a considerable degree. Jews rarely took the need for government for granted; society was always seen as superior and more permanent than the state. For Jews, the nineteen centuries of their dispersion have served as a constant training course, a unique school in self-discipline as well as in the civic art of treating authority with disdain. In the Jewish tradition, power is evil; the mere striving for it is objectionable.

A strong measure of this ambivalent demur and hesitation survives in the Israeli political style to this day. Indeed, it would have been astonishing if a tradition of political behavior, so ancient and so deeply ingrained and so thoroughly tested, disappeared immediately simply by fiat of newly acquired sovereignty. Perhaps one day it shall; there are few indications as yet. Civic indiscipline has been portrayed in Zionist mythology as a "diasporic" quality, an attribute of *luftmenschen* and rootless intellectuals. Nevertheless, although offensive to the idea of *mamlachtiut*, a basic disrespect of authority remains one of the most marked characteristics of Israeli Jews. As regards the Israeli mind, which is our theme, there is a certain unity in this respect, which is not difficult to trace, a fairly regular psychological pattern, a complex of sardonic loyalties and half-hearted suspicions, sensitivities, ironies, and conceits, which if not common to all, are still common enough to generalize about.

The ethnic humor of the Jews has always reflected their basic disrespect for authority. The traditional humor of the Jews—with all its biting self-irony—is by and large dying out among Israelis; it remains a lively art in one area only—government and politics. The main thrust of Israeli political humor remains the destruction of the "hero ideal." In a classic anecdote, a man rings the Prime Minister's office shortly after Ben Gurion has resigned.

"May I speak to Premier Ben Gurion?"

The operator tells him that Ben Gurion is no longer in office.

"Oh," says the man, "thank you." A few minutes later he rings again and again asks to speak with Premier Ben Gurion. Again, he receives the same answer. The third time, the operator begins to get annoyed.

"We've told you three times that Ben Gurion is no longer in office. Stop calling."

"I am terribly sorry to bother you," says the man, "but I can't hear the news often enough."

There are endless examples of this sort.

With all their professed attachment to *mamlachtiut*, and while managing their public affairs with tolerable success, the Israelis' distrust of authority sometimes stops just short of anarchism. Anarchism, in a positive sense—the robust, self-reliance of free individuals, a philosophy of extreme, even naive democracy, equality, voluntarism, reciprocity, and spontaneous cooperation—has been a characteristic of many immigrant societies. Where it has survived, as in America, it has been a cause of disorder, but also one of the guarantees of liberty. The anarchist strain that runs through Israeli life flows from several sources. It echoes the classic susceptibility of the outsider in society, the hostility of the Jew to the (Czarist) tax collectors. Intertwined with this are the two intellectual trends which strongly influenced the early Zionist pioneer movement: libertarianism in the anarchist style of nineteenth-century, prerevolutionary Russia, and syndicalism fashioned after related French or Italian models.

The socialist pioneers derived their ideas from both Marxist and pre-Marxist sources, the so-called "utopian" varieties of socialism, with all their emphasis on anarcho-syndicalist features. There were times in the early 1920s when some of the most influential new settlers seriously hoped that the Jewish National Home would develop into a harmonious community of free villages (not unlike those Kropotkin had advocated). They conceived of the entire country as a network of cooperative or collective agricultural and industrial associations with a minimum of coercion and a maximum of voluntary, reciprocal engagement by free, yet committed individuals.

Although the Golden Age of justice and liberty did not materialize, the cult of egalitarianism continues. If it is weaker today than in 1924, it is nevertheless strong enough to preserve and maintain a degree of egalitarianism higher than in most countries.* There is a continuing emphasis in Israeli life on *hitnadvut* ("voluntarism") as opposed to legal coercion, and on social authority as opposed to state organization. The tradition of *hitnadvut* is evident in the preferential regard accorded to the *kibbutz* and cooperative movements, a result not only of their disproportionate political power but of the lingering strength of the pioneer ethos. It can be seen in the dominant public position of the Histadrut trade unions and their subsidiaries. The Israeli unions did not grow out of the national economy, but actively shared in its creation through the establishment of "labor-owned" firms. Like the parties, they preceded the state.

It will come as no surprise to students of utopian ventures that within ostensibly voluntary social organizations, the pressures for conformity and compliance can occasionally be greater than in state organizations based on legal coercion. The saving grace of Israeli society and of Israeli politics has been the vast proliferation of these voluntary social bodies and the resultant dissipation of central power. The bureaucracy of "voluntary" organizations in many cases has made *hitnadvut* an empty phrase. It is still easier, nevertheless, for the individual to persevere by maneuvering through a great number of small, frequently competitive bureaucratic tyrannies than to be entwined within the wheels of an omnipotent state machine.

Few words are heard in Israel as often as *le'histader*. Although it is the reflexive verb of *seder* ("order"), it means quite the opposite of formal order. In the vernacular, the meaning of *le'histader* is "to take care of oneself," "to fix oneself up," to steer through life by bending the rule to one's purpose, to organize oneself as best one can. A close equivalent is the French *s'arranger*. In Israel, as in Italy (where it is called *arrangarsi*), *le'histader* is a vital element to the art of living. It

---

* According to the *World Handbook of Political and Social Indicators* (1961) the percentage of income gained by the top 10 percent of the Israeli population was one of the lowest in the world: 24 percent. Comparative percentages elsewhere were: Australia, 28 percent; New Zealand and Sweden, 30 percent; United Kingdom, 31 percent; Italy, 34 percent. The so-called *Gini* index of inequality listed Israel, after Australia, as the country with the least amount of inequality: Australia, .347; Israel, .352; New Zealand, .357; U.K. .366; U.S.A., .397; Sweden, .399; Italy, .403.

is the Israeli's password through the maze of authority, the thicket of law, the confines of impersonal regulations. Regulations are "objective" and thus theoretically just; but the needs of the individual, his private concepts of right and wrong, are superior. The average Israeli recognizes few regulations of universal applicability. In his dealings with the authorities he invariably demands, firmly and loudly, exceptional treatment. His demands are frequently accompanied by an emotionalism so intense that a public official, if his heart is not wholly stone, will be hard put to resist.

There are many ways to "take care of oneself," *le'histader*: the intimate phone call to a friend, or a friend of a friend; the help of one's political party. This latter is the easiest aid a single individual can marshal effectively. In dealings with the Israeli bureaucracy, few measures are as effective—and as widely practiced in seeking a special, individual kind of justice—as an imperious pounding of official tables, a high tone of outrage, a demanding wail. The ultimate weapon is the sitdown strike; it has rarely been used without effect.

The average Israeli's first reaction, upon finding himself in conflict with the law, is to negotiate with its representative. Passionate debates, rich in gesticulation and argument, between policemen and trespassers, are a common feature of the Israeli street scene. There are occasional cases of police harshness, in rare instances, even brutality, but the timidity of Israeli policemen, especially toward minor trespassers, is proverbial. Some say it reflects a degree of uneasiness in practicing a traditionally "un-Jewish" profession. Few Israelis respond to police orders in the streets without prolonged argument. Few will docilely accept a traffic ticket for jay-walking, speeding, or driving through a red light, without an intense effort to dissuade the issuing officer from writing out his form, or without, at least, an attempt to bargain over the paragraph he has chosen to describe the contravention, which may call for a higher fine than another paragraph on his list. Bribes are rare and are likely to be ineffective; persistent argument, whether reasonable or not, is more often crowned with success.

Foreign professors teaching at Israeli universities have noted this tendency in students as well. The number of Israeli students who demand to be exempted from entrance examinations, or who fail at examinations but firmly appeal the results, is said to be considerably higher than elsewhere. There can be any number of convincing reasons to demand all sorts of waivers; she was pregnant and should not be "punished" for that; he is a new immigrant; he was recently divorced; he must work outside; there was a death in the family; he lives in a distant suburb; his wife was sick, his flat too small, his children too numerous; he may miss a great professional opportunity, and so forth. Some visiting professors find the response to such appeals excessively lenient. This leniency may be one reason, among many, why Israeli universities have been spared the unrest that has plagued more rigid academic institutions on the continent.

The lenient response to demands to flout this or that established regulation is by no means restricted to the universities. It can be met in almost any public body, in the way that municipal building ordinances are enforced (or not enforced), or customs collected (or not collected) at the ports, how licenses are issued, taxes levied, and concessions granted. There are firm regulations that restrict the height of buildings or prohibit the closing in of terraces, or regulate peddling in the streets or the opening of shops in residential areas. The appearance of Israeli towns, frequently an affront to the eye, indicates that there are apparently many ways of getting around such rules or of evading punishment for disregarding them.

Yet such irregularities must be weighed against the advantages of living in a society, which continues to maintain a remarkably low level of coercive discipline without disintegrating into sheer chaos. It is not that the authorities, whoever they may be, arc flagrantly negligent in the exercise of their tasks. But it is possible at times to observe in the manner in which authorities go about their duties, a kind of mischievous gentlemen's agreement with the governed, which allows a relatively high but still tolerable amount of disorder, and a violation of civil discipline in the interests of the mannerism, selfishness, eccentricity, custom, or anomaly of the individual. There is a baroque quality in the elaborate ritual through which this is achieved, in the histrionics of both enforcers of the law and the enforced, the appellants and the appellees. In fact, though not in theory, Israel is a permissive society. Notwithstanding the pressures for change, in the name of order and efficiency, it has continued so long because it apparently agrees with one of the deepest national traits.

This libertarian multiplicity, this Whitmanesque enthusiasm for variety, this commitment to the decentralization of power within a network of interlocking but autonomous social, political, and economic institutions—the *kibbutzim*, the unions, the socialist sector of the economy, the direct-action political parties, the self-reliance of the individual, the professional groups—all this animated contrariness and diffusion sometimes overshadows an important consolidating factor, which adds refinement and complexity to our theme.

The Israeli political scene, often raucous and noisy with the clatter of endless disagreement, can be acerbated, stifled, and maimed by tremendous personal rivalries, hatreds, antagonisms, and fanatic loyalties. Yet within it there is often a strong quality of theatrical drama. For the duration of the show the actors assault and poison each other; at the same time they are animated by a common desire to make the show succeed and hold the public in its spell for long after.

The several veto groups and power elites that dominate the Israeli public scene share a remarkably high number of common traits, biases, and interests. Not the least of these common interests is the preservation of power by the veteran leadership of each group. In the realization of this interest the various oligarchies will sometimes lend one another considerable assistance, as though united by a common desire to maintain their traditional strongholds against the pressing onslaught of the ambitious young. The elites that dominate the Israeli public scene share a common suspicion of the young, the ambitious newcomers, the innovators, the impatient who call for reforms in the social and political structures established during the pioneering age.

The common traits shared by the various elites are not always obvious. The observer of Israeli life even at close range—during short periods, especially at election times—may easily be overwhelmed by the great variety of forces, causes, and interests, each draped in the distinct colors of its own ideology. Such a narrow-focus view of Israeli affairs might move an observer to wonder how it is possible for the system to function at all, much less with tolerable success. A wider-focus view over a longer period of time offers at least one answer to this puzzle. The wider-focus view brings out the existence of a Mandarin class, erratic but effective, locked and united within what can loosely be called the Israeli political establishment.*

The Israeli Establishment is said to comprise at the most a few

---

* Few English words have enjoyed a more spectacular international success in recent years than "establishment," in its present pejorative context. The word first entered Israeli usage in its unadulterated English form, but was soon rendered into Hebrew as *mimsad* (a derivative of *mosad*, "institution").

hundred men and perhaps a dozen women. Its firmest pillar is the long-standing personal intimacy of its members. Their main instrument of contact is the direct telephone line, the unlisted number. The password into their council chambers is "consensus." The operations of the Israeli Establishment are deliberately shrouded in darkness, the rites and unwritten rules are mysterious and carefully disguised behind an elaborate edifice of conflicting ideological platforms and formal or informal committees, both within the government and without. In the national economy the main function of the Establishment is to preside over the distribution of resources received from local taxes and from the funds contributed by Jews abroad. In political life, the Establishment controls the assignment of top jobs within the state hierarchy, and in many other areas as well. Among insiders this occupation is known as "distributing the dumplings."

Characteristically, the very existence of an Establishment is still hotly denied by many prominent Israelis of the older generation. Veteran Israelis, powerful in politics, managers of the economy or distinguished in the upper echelons of official "society," who helped to create the Establishment, easily grow indignant when reminded of it. The mere mention of the term "Establishment" is sometimes considered blasphemous, an unjustified insinuation, an attack on sacrosanct "values" to which the veterans claim they have devoted their entire lives.

Pontificating on this issue, the editor in chief of *Davar*, the daily organ of the leading labor party and himself as clearly "established" as an English duke, once called the Establishment a "conventional lie." Such touchiness is rooted in the lingering strength of the Zionist Dream; its rationale can be found in some of the founding fathers' most cherished articles of faith. A few weeks before his final resignation in 1963—after an almost uninterrupted tenure of thirty years in the highest public office,* Ben Gurion was asked by an interviewer how long he thought he would still remain "in power." His reaction was characteristically irate. He did not like this term, "power," there was no such thing in Israel. He was not "in power," he said. He was Prime Minister, all right, but that was not being "in power."

The present Establishment is made up of the leaderships of the

* As Chairman of the Jewish Agency for Palestine, 1934–1948, and Prime Minister and Minister of Defense, 1948–1954; 1956–1963.

several elites that emerged in the pioneering period and still dominate the public scene. Who qualifies for the Establishment? Who belongs to it? Theoretically, everybody qualifies, whether young or old, of European or Afro-Asian origin, the native born as well as the more recent immigrant. In reality, the Establishment is made up largely by men in their sixties and seventies. Establishment men in their fifties are scarce, in their forties a real rarity. In 1970 only three out of twenty-four cabinet ministers were under fifty, and just barely; the average age was sixty-three. Although Israel is a "young" country, the present Establishment has been remarkably suspicious of younger men. A prominent labor party leader in 1967 wanted to curtail the number of officeholders under a certain age, in order to prevent the "undesirable" intrusion into positions of power of men under fifty. His advice, fortunately, was not taken. But in the Israeli system, a forty-five- or fifty-year-old man aspiring to office is still regarded as a "Young Turk" and classed among the "ambitious young." What sociologists call "upward mobility" is in Israel a difficult and painful process. For example, in the first Israeli parliament (1949) the average age of members was forty-three. The average age in the sixth parliament (1969) was sixty-three. In the intervening twenty years the average age of members had risen by exactly twenty years.

As a group the Establishment is still largely made up of veteran settlers from Eastern Europe who arrived in the country before Independence, although in a few exceptional cases veteran Zionist leaders from abroad have qualified for membership immediately upon arrival in the country.

The mandarins lead remarkably similar lives. If they are cabinet ministers they occupy relatively modest "official" apartments in Jerusalem. Their salaries are rarely higher than that of the average high school teacher. The mandarins enjoy certain privileges, of course, in lieu of money. They do not pay their private telephone bills from their own pockets; they have the free use of a car—which they usually drive themselves; they frequently enjoy a free trip abroad, when they may take the opportunity to replenish their modest wardrobes. Although there now is more personal wealth in Israel than is apparent, wealth and power still rarely coincide.

Just as the older mandarins lead remarkably similar lives in the present, so there are many similarities in their personal pasts. The majority have come from Jewish middle-class or lower-middle-class homes in Poland, or, to a lesser extent, Russia. In fact, a circle drawn on a map of Russia at a distance of 500 miles from Minsk would probably include the birthplaces of at least two thirds of the present *mandarins*. Their formal education has usually been irregular; either they interrupted high school or dropped out of the university without a degree in order to serve the cause of Zion as pioneers in Palestine. Some were active in Zionist politics abroad; more participated in the training abroad of young pioneers for manual labor on Palestinian farms. Whether they are now associated with one of the labor parties, or with the "bourgeois" right-of-center, many mandarins can point to a role they played in the "heroic period" of settlement. With the possible exception of the orthodox-religious Establishment, most older mandarins at one time or another actually worked as manual laborers—draining swamps, building roads, planting vegetables and orange groves, driving a tractor, or the like.

The few younger mandarins were undoubtedly involved in one or another dangerous underground operation prior to the establishment of the state. Some were members of the terrorist *Irgun Zvai Leumi*; others worked for the more moderate *Hagana*, ran arms and illegal immigrants from Europe into Palestine, or carried out dangerous missions in the Arab countries.

Members of the Knesset do not automatically belong to the Establishment, just as there are important members of the Establishment who never belong to parliament. Nevertheless there are enough mandarins in the Knesset to consider its composition as a reflection of the Establishment. The ethnic composition of parliament is one of the measurable indices of what appears to be a general rule. Under the Israeli electoral system, the candidacy of at least 100 of the 120 members is tightly controlled by the Establishment. The marked predominance in parliament of Eastern European pioneers and their offspring reflects the Establishment even more than it reflects the electorate.

Of the 277 Jewish members of parliament between 1949 and 1970, 74 percent were born in Eastern Europe, or in Central Europe of Eastern Europe parents; 68 percent would boast of a past in the "heroic" age of pioneering or underground activity. Despite vast changes in the ethnic composition of the Jewish-Israeli population, the predominance of Eastern Europeans in the sixth and seventh

Knesset of 1965 and 1969 was almost as marked as it had been in the Knessets elected in 1961, 1959, 1955, 1951, and 1949.

Out of thirty-three new members elected in 1965, twenty-two were of Eastern European origin. Of thirty-five new members elected in 1969, nineteen were immigrants from Eastern Europe, and ten were born in Israel of Eastern European parents. Twelve of the newly elected thirty-five had the usual "heroic" background. Although the population has more than quadrupled since 1948—largely through immigration—only two were immigrants who arrived after that date.

In the 1969–1974 parliament, 80 percent of Jewish members were either Eastern European immigrants or sabras of Eastern European parents. The significance of these figures becomes apparent if we remember that in 1970 roughly half the Jewish population of Israel was of "Oriental" (Afro-Asian) origin.

This is not to say that "Oriental" Jews are disenfranchised, or "powerless." A considerable number of "Oriental" newcomers have succeeded in recent years in gaining important positions in the town halls and local party machines of the labor party. But the number of "Oriental" Jews, immigrant or native born, who have reached positions of real power on the national level, remains extremely small. Those who have visibly reached top positions have done so less by virtue of their personal renown or capabilities (which may or may not be considerable) than as a result of being patronizingly co-opted into office by an Establishment of mandarins anxious to alter an image of Eastern European ethnocentricity, without really changing the makeup of the Establishment. In the army there has not been a single officer of "Oriental" origin who reached the two top ranks of general.

The predominance of Eastern European veteran settlers within the Establishment is not surprising. The veterans maintain a firm hold upon the institutions and instruments of power partly because they themselves have created them. In Israel, as in Mexico or India, the "revolutionary party" tends to remain in power long after the revolution is over. It remains in power through popular "gratitude"; and through the adept manipulation of the institutions which the veterans created in the first place, for themselves. Like well-tailored suits, they fit their measurements perfectly.

It is not difficult, then, to sense a dialectic counterpart behind the turbulence and libertarianism of Israeli life. The dissension and disorder of the public scene obscure the existence of an elderly Establishment of frustrated authoritarians who are exceedingly paternalistic.

The paternalism of the mandarins can partly be explained as the natural reaction of former revolutionaries who have themselves attained power. The founding fathers brought with them from their miserable lives in Russia an intense suspicion of authority; subsequently much of the drawn out struggle between the Zionist settlers and the Turkish or British rulers of Palestine consisted of Jewish attempts to circumvent their authority. Some of the veteran leaders boast in their memoirs of successes in this regard: how they misled the Turks and the British, evaded their immigration restrictions, avoided their taxes, and stole their property—for the benefit of the *kibbutzim*, Histadrut-owned industries, and the clandestine Jewish militia.

Hillel Dan, in his book *Be'derech lo Slula* proudly relates how, during World War II. his Histadrut-owned supply and construction company (the multi-million-pound *Solel Boneh*) unhesitatingly harmed the British war effort by stealing British army equipment and raw materials in great quantities. As one of the biggest army suppliers in the Near East, the Histadrut-owned company was ideally placed for this purpose. Hillel Dan notes that to the best of his knowledge nothing was ever stolen by his men for personal gain. The stolen goods were all transferred to *Solel Boneh* warehouses. "I always saw *Solel Boneh* as the carrier of a national mission," Dan wrote. "As the son of a persecuted people . . . I felt that we were entitled to demand that the non-Jewish world materially contribute to the increase of the Jewish potential.*

Individually and as a group, few men could have been more adept in undermining authority as the leaders of Palestinian Jewry prior to 1948. When they themselves in turn became the authority, they became obsessed with the idea that every citizen was, by definition, untrustworthy. The immediate consequence after 1948 was a shatter-

* This remarkable man, one of the great pioneers of Israeli industry, who built an economic empire, was himself a union employee. His monthly salary hardly exceeded that of a first-class welder in the steel mills he had helped to build. When he was dismissed from his job in 1958, by a Histadrut leadership suspicious of his power and anxious to decentralize his growing economic empire, his severance pay—after almost three decades of employment—was £60,000 ($26,000). Dan invested this sum; within four years he was to declare a profit of over half a million Israeli pounds.

ing system of restrictions and controls in almost every area of life.

Within two years an enormous bureaucracy was assembled, as labyrinthine, heavy, and distrustful of any one man's intentions as the bureaucracy of a centuries-old, decaying empire. Israelis were put at the mercy of a maddeningly confused machine, which issued inscrutable decrees without warning (some of them retroactive), and which was soon drowning in a sea of papers that even the most assiduous bureaucrat could not work his way through in a twenty-four-hour day. The State Archives in Jerusalem holds a collection of official forms designed in the early 1950s for public use; the collection might well serve as field material for psychology students exploring the so-called authoritarian personality.*

Some of the early restrictions were lifted in the mid-1950s. The bureaucracy has since considerably improved. With all their commitment to abstract ideologies, the founding fathers were endowed with a precious gift of adaptability. This explains why they were ultimately successful; and why the society they created escaped the brutalities that accompanied other attempts to institutionalize Messianic visions in everyday life. When the reality contradicted the doctrine, the founding fathers often, though grudgingly, resorted to improvisation. The improvisations contradicted theory, but they worked. The gradual abandonment after 1950 of plans for a largely socialized economy is one case in point. The introduction of hired labor into the *kibbutzim* is a second. The abolition of the earlier system of harsh bureaucratic restrictions is a third example.

Yet vestiges of the old style have remained. The paternalism of the veteran leaders is as distinctly a characteristic of the Israeli political style as is the libertarianism of the masses. In 1965 a study of bureaucratic manners at *Amidar*, a state-owned public housing agency, produced some fascinating figures. Of those officials with public contact, 60.2 percent did not believe in greeting their visitor, nor would they answer his greeting, 63.7 percent would keep a visitor standing and would not offer him a chair. Some of the most distinguished of the veteran leaders regard themselves less as servants of the people than as their benefactors, and expect to be treated accordingly. Their tours of

* Example: "To the Collector of Customs, Jaffa Harbor. Honored Sir: I hereby *beg* to be *permitted* to pay you the customs due for the importation of my car, Number —, etc., and thanking you in advance, etc. . . ."

inspection through the countryside—surrounded by bevies of anxious-
to-please underlings—sometimes resemble the nineteenth-century pro-
cessions of Victorian philanthropists through the orphanages, old-age
homes, and poorhouses of their time. When referring to citizens,
whether newcomers or old-timers, they often employ the strangely
brutal term *chomer enoshi* ("human material").

A common admonition of veteran politicians to newcomers, even
when they are justly grumbling, is *Shma, k'sh'bati* ("Now listen here,
when *I* came ..."). "When I myself came to the country," veteran
politicians will tell new settlers in remote and difficult regions,
"When I myself came to the country forty years ago, conditions were
worse, very much worse. We really suffered but we did not complain.
Now you mustn't complain either, but work hard as we have done and
don't mind if you suffer a little bit." Some add: "Remember what we
have done for you."

The semi-official biography of Golda Meir by her close friend and
admirer, Marie Syrkin, cites a revealing little incident which took
place in the early 1950s, when Mrs. Meir was Minister of Labor, and
throws light upon a common trait among veteran politicians. Marie
Syrkin describes an inspection trip to a recently completed housing
development for new immigrants.

> Golda was surrounded by disgruntled new immigrants from Eastern
> Europe, who, disdaining preliminary courtesies besieged her with angry
> complaints about the houses, the climate, the scarcity of work for
> professionals, the neighbors. . . . *"Not one word of gratitude,"* said
> Golda bitterly to a companion as she left.

To appreciate the rigidity of this patronizing remark, it must be
considered in the context of its time. The incident took place at a
particularly difficult period. There was massive unemployment, public
housing for immigrants was still inordinately austere, unbelievably
ugly, maddeningly monotonous, and devoid of all but the barest comforts. Moreover, the incident involved a group of confused refugees
undergoing an extremely difficult process of adjustment, who had
been forced to change their professions, to learn a new language, even
a new alphabet.

Ben Gurion has on occasion spoken in a similar vein. In 1967 he
summed up what he thought were the greatest achievements of the

state which he had helped to establish. His choice of words was self-revealing and bespoke a common attitude among veteran leaders. He referred to the immigrants who had come to Israel after independence as "human dust":

> We converted the human dust which gathered here from all the corners of the earth, we converted them into a sovereign nation which occupies an honorable place in the family of nations . . .

Ben Gurion went on to describe the language the immigrants were speaking on arrival (presumably Yiddish). He borrowed a term commonly used by chicken farmers to describe animal mash—*blilei saffa*, literally, a "mishmash" of language. "We gave hundreds of thousands [speaking] a 'mishmash' of language . . . their national tongue."

The paternalism of the veterans grew naturally from their role as a self-proclaimed pioneer elite. Like many former revolutionaries who have grown old in office, they came to believe not only in their own irreplaceability, but in the infallibility of their judgment as well. Veteran Israeli leaders still habitually display an aristocratic contempt for what they disdainfully call the "masses" or the "man in the street." The socialists among them are often more disdainful of "the street" than the non-socialists, for the early idealism of the former has been corroded by their many years in office. Their political experience has taught them that only organized power matters. They are notoriously insensitive to public opinion that is not formalized as an ideology, as a political party, or as an organized pressure group. Hence the habitual contempt of the aging mandarins to the results of public opinion polls.

The insensitivity of the Establishment to public opinion is so deeply ingrained that it often applies not only to "ideological" or national, but to local, politically neutral, aesthetic issues as well. Such issues, dividing public opinion and a resolutely adamant Establishment which thinks it knows better—and usually wins—often arise in the field of city zoning. An argument might revolve around the sale of a public park to private enterprise; or to the routing of noisy public buses through a quiet residential street, against the will of its inhabitants. The public nearly always loses. When a few dozen residents of Haifa protested the stench and smoke of a municipal garbage disposal plant by staging a peaceful demonstration outside the mayor's home a few years ago, the mayor not only refused to accept a signed petition but called the police to remove the demonstrators from his front yard.

Perhaps the best-known case in recent years was the building in 1968 of a giant power station in the heart of residential Tel Aviv. The smokestack of this power station now dominates the city skyline. It was erected against the urgent warnings of nearly all local air pollution and town planning experts, and against widespread, but politically unorganized, public opposition.

The Israeli economy, as it grows more sophisticated, has been considerably liberalized in recent years. Yet it is still probably the most directed and controlled industrial economy outside the Soviet bloc. The private sector of the economy, theoretically free, is still largely influenced by a few ministries, through a tight network of restrictions, permits, production schedules, defense orders, monetary measures, and the like. In a country with a strong sense of national purpose (with government as chief articulator of that purpose), the power of informal controls is often as great as—and sometimes greater than— the power of formal controls.

The paternalism of the Establishment has been diminishing in recent years. The veteran mandarins are physically exhausted and generational change must have its way. A new managerial class of technocrats, less "committed" to an ideology, has come into being. Yet generations do not drastically succeed one another like the acts of a drama, but merge gradually like images cast upon the screen. Traces of the old-style paternalism were still very much in evidence in the late 1960s and early 1970s. The introduction of television was delayed until as late as 1968, mainly because mandarin opinion considered television "uncivilized," what Russian commissars call *nyet kulturnye*.

The paternalism of the Establishment can still assume grotesque forms. It is still not unusual for the mandarins to prescribe to Israeli mothers the number of babies they ought to have. (The public response to such suggestions has, of course, been somewhat disappointing.) After the elections of 1969, which cost the alignment of labor parties its brief majority in the Knesset, leading labor mandarins publicly voiced their deep "disappointment" in the people. In large newspaper advertisements the public was berated by the mandarins;

if everything should not turn out as favorable as it had been before, or might have been in the future, the public would have only itself to blame.

A labor Minister of Transport once announced in all seriousness that people ought not to own private cars. In his view, citizens should travel by bus or train, although the crowded and uncomfortable Israeli trains do not offer pullman car service for those ready to pay more for comfort or privacy, and the introduction of a two-class system on the trains is banned as an anti-egalitarian measure.

The English Beatles are immensely popular in Israel; their songs are played daily on the radio, are heard everywhere, hummed, danced to, and even translated into Hebrew. Yet in 1966 an inter-Ministerial committee of mandarins decided to withhold the foreign currency permit necessary to enable the Beatles to perform in Israel because they lacked the "sufficient artistic and cultural standard." The decision was approved "with great satisfaction" by the permanent parliamentary Committee for Culture and Education.

Kibbutzniks are still prominent within the Israeli Establishment. This has been so for almost half a century. Until at least the early 1950s, merely to be a member of a *kibbutz* amounted to potential membership in the ruling elite. A disproportionate number of *kibbutzniks* have played a role in politics, in the upper echelons of the state bureaucracy, in the diplomatic service, in the army, in the trade unions, in Histadrut-owned industries and investment companies. The large number of *kibbutzniks* in government—unlike the similar plethora of lawers in the governments of other countries—has not been the result of any special training. *Kibbutzniks* within the Establishment have been, and still are, inspired generalists; they are amateurs, not professionals, of government. Until a very short time ago higher education was frowned upon by the *kibbutz* as a form of bourgeois affectation.

At the peak of *kibbutz* power, in the early 1950s, the proportion of *kibbutzniks* in positions of power was estimated to be at least seven times their proportion in the population as a whole. Their proportion has declined in recent years. It is still four or five times their share of the population. In 1969, the *kibbutz* population was slightly more than 90,000, or 3.4 percent of the total population. Roughly 15 percent of the top political positions in the country were held by *kibbutz-*

niks. Kibbutzniks and former *kibbutznik*s held some 30 percent of all seats in parliament.

The political initiative of *kibbutznik*s stems from a deeply ingrained, passionate interest in public affairs. The personal involvement of *kibbutznik*s in the politics of the country has always been stronger, more intense, more sustained, and usually better organized than any other single group within the community of Zionist settlers. In most cases, *kibbutz* membership followed a logical path, from membership in the political organization with which that *kibbutz* was affiliated, to more active participation in the life of a party. If and when that party split, its *kibbutzim* were also torn asunder. The effect of party splits on *kibbutz* life was so personal that adherents of one faction could no longer live in the same village with supporters of another. The adherents of one group were forced to move away—they and their families —to other *kibbutzim*, where they would be surrounded only by likeminded men and women. The *kibbutzim* were, by nature, one-party enclaves. They still are, to a considerable extent, politically monolithic.

Most *kibbutzim* are still affiliated, formally or informally, with three of the four main components of the present alignment of labor parties (Mapai, Mapam, Achdut, Ha'avoda). Others are separately linked to the two religious parties (National Religious and Agudat Israel), or to the Independent Liberal Party.

Until a few years ago, the most extremely collectivist Mapam-affiliated *kibbutzim* adhered to a principle of "ideological collectivism." This semi-religious rule meant that the minority must not only comply with the majority decisions, but had to embrace majority opinion and ideas as well. The principle of "ideological collectivism" has tacitly been abandoned in recent years, but even in the more moderate, non-Mapam *kibbutzim*, the prevailing pressures for conformity are still so great that at least 90 percent of the vote cast at each *kibbutz* goes to the party with which that *kibbutz* is affiliated.

The political prominence of *kibbutznik*s also stems from Israel's historic self-image as a nation of pioneers. This was an important reason for their predominance in the public affairs of pre-Independence Israel. For a considerable length of time, *kibbutznik*s constituted a kind of "natural" elite within the community of settlers, an elite of both "value" and "function." *Kibbutznik*s more than any other group were implicitly accepted by a majority of the settlers as the virtual personification of highest Zionist purposes. The personal life-style of *kibbutzniks* was a projection—in dramatic magnification—of libertarian ideas and ideals of social justice with which even outsiders liked to identify vicariously. The ideal of *kibbutz* life was often worshiped, at least verbally, by those personally unprepared to live by it.

Value elites are often rewarded by high esteem; functional elites, by power. *Kibbutzniks* were amply rewarded by both. As a group, *kibbutzniks* grew to accept the moral legitimacy of their highly disproportionate share in power with sanguine self-confidence. For them it was the most natural thing in the world. They accepted their supremacy as unhesitatingly as did the aristocracy before the French Revolution. Their prominence in the governing bodies before and after the establishment of the state was rarely challenged by others.

In the Israeli political system, the cabinet is appointed by the Prime Minister and confirmed by the parliament. The proportion of *kibbutzniks* in the cabinets from 1948 through 1969 was on the average even higher than in parliament. Between the years 1949 and 1967, about one third of all cabinet ministers were *kibbutzniks*. In the last cabinet before the appointment of the first Grand National Coalition (on the eve of the 1967 war) there were seven *kibbutzniks* (including Premier Eshkol, nominally a member of Kibbutz Degania). In the second Grand National Coalition, as re-formed after the elections of 1969, four (or 16.5 percent of the twenty-four cabinet ministers) were active *kibbutzniks*, whereas the *kibbutz* population was now 3.5 percent. An additional six cabinet ministers were former *kibbutz* members, still actively representing *kibbutz* interests. This would mean that in a broad cabinet of politicians representing over 90 percent of the popular vote, no single segment of society, no single sector of the economy, was as powerfully represented as the *kibbutz*. In the 1969–1973 parliament, 15 of 120 members were *kibbutzniks*. At least 30 more were former *kibbutzniks*, or closely associated with the *kibbutz* movement and its interests. Two of the three main *kibbutz* movements were more strongly represented in the *Knesset* than were the labor party's branches in Tel Aviv, Haifa, and Jerusalem.*

---

* The *kibbutz* population (1969) broke down as follows: *Ichud Ha'kvutzot V'hakibbutzim*, 31,064; *Ha'kibbutz Ha'meuchad*, 25,960; *Ha'kibbutz Ha'artzi*, 31,860; *Ha'kibbutz Ha'dati*, 4,100; *Kibbutz Ha'oved Ha'Zioni*, 1,200; *Kibbutz Agudat Israel*, 640; others, 965. Total: 95,789, or 3.4 percent of the Israeli population as a whole.

The relative weight of *kibbutzniks* within the Establishment is now steadily declining. This is not always immediately obvious at first glance. At political conventions and official state ceremonies veteran *kibbutzniks* from the Jordan Valley or Upper Galilee still stand out as the Barons of the marches that once appeared in Westminister. But although they are still strongly represented everywhere, there are now fewer *kibbutzniks* than ever before in the top echelons of the army, in the state bureaucracy, in the administration of Histadrut unions and Histadrut-owned enterprises.

With growing affluence and diminishing (but still considerable) political power, the *kibbutzniks* remain a kind of rural aristocracy, privileged, influential, retaining the spirit and values of a former era within well-defined, carefully protected enclaves. *Kibbutzniks* retain a predilection for traditionally "aristocratic" vocations: farming, army, government, welfare, and diplomacy. As a group, *kibbutzniks* preserve a strict social and cultural distinctiveness. The *kibbutz* is not a closed society; it remains open to outsiders who wish to join. Its exclusivity remains a fact, since so few outsiders actually join nowadays. The *kibbutz* is divorced economically from its immediate rural or semi-rural environment. *Kibbutzim* do not market their produce through non-*kibbutz* intermediaries in the area, nor do they buy their personal necessities in the shops of neighboring villages and towns.

Kibbutz children commonly are in touch only with the children of other *kibbutzim*. Their contacts with children of the immediate non-*kibbutz* environment are rare. Such children are often of "Oriental" background and live on a considerably lower cultural and economic standard. *Kibbutz* boys usually marry *kibbutz* girls and vice versa. "Inter-marriage" with non-*kibbutzniks* often ends up in town.

As a politically privileged group, *kibbutzniks* preserve a fully developed sense of their own importance as an elite. They are still seriously and conscientiously trying to remain a serving elite. Although nowadays there is a growing reluctance among *kibbutzniks* to exchange the pastoral life for another, *kibbutzniks* are still deeply committed to the *kibbutz* tradition of distinguished amateur public service. In *kibbutz* parlance this is called being on *shlichut* (on "mission"). Choice "missions" are the army and the foreign service. Young *kibbutzniks* still volunteer for extended periods of badly paid service as field officers in certain crack units, such as the tank corps, air force, paratroopers and frogmen, which offer a measure of excitement and adventure, but also call for a great deal of personal effort, unusual dedication, and frequent sacrifice. Older men often serve in an embassy or in the administration of technical aid to developing countries. In 1970, *kibbutzniks* occupied leading Israeli foreign aid posts in a dozen African countries, in Latin America (including Cuba), and in Asia.

After a few years "on mission," *kibbutzniks* usually retire to their old lives. The modern *kibbutz* is a highly diversified, sophisticated agro-technical enterprise. It displays a remarkable capacity to reabsorb former jet pilots, navy captains, ambassadors, generals, ministers, directors of aid programs, administrators of gigantic national enterprises. Nowadays at least 70 percent "go home" to the *kibbutz* from the various outside jobs they had held for interim periods of varying length. They return to their old lives, although not to the old menial work. They will advance to more managerial jobs within the *kibbutz* —as heads of tractor stations, or *kibbutz* factories, as coordinators of inter-*kibbutz* committees, as teachers or research analysts. A number of prominent *kibbutzniks* have remained "on mission" for ten, fifteen, and even twenty years while retaining their *kibbutz* membership.

When a *kibbutznik* becomes a cabinet minister, he, too, occupies an official residence in Jerusalem, though his family often remains on the *kibbutz*. In the past ten years, some cabinet ministers and lower-ranking officeholders have treated their *kibbutzim* as "country places" to which they return for weekends and recess periods, or to entertain visiting foreign dignitaries. Not a few such officeholders are said to have become economic burdens to their *kibbutzim*. The burden is probably offset by various advantages that accrue to a *kibbutz* through intervention by an office-holding member: government loans, lease of valuable public land, public concessions, and the like.

The general public no longer regards *kibbutzniks* as glamorous supermen personifying the highest national ideals. The public is now more impressed by victorious generals and war heroes. The old glamour of the *kibbutznik* pales in an increasingly sophisticated economy geared to science-based industries. The new glamour boys are high-powered technologists, scientists, management consultants, and the like. Young urbanites now often consider *kibbutzniks* as tied to an obsolete ideal of agrarian bliss.

Yet among many *kibbutzniks* the elitarian notions of the past have remained quite strong. Still powerful is the old sense of unabashed self-assertion. This is a unique phenomenon in some ways, for most elites in today's world are notoriously embarrassed and self-conscious. *Kibbutzniks* justify their political prominence by proclaiming it right and proper. Some cite their past and present achievements in the public interest. Others maintain that their prominence guarantees what they call the "hegemony" in present-day Israel of the "laboring man." Ironically, the old self-image of *kibbutzniks*—as paragons of labor—is now also changing. Many *kibbutzniks* no longer see themselves as "workers," nor even as the "vanguard" of the proletariat. A few years ago, a team of researchers asked a number of *kibbutzniks* to what social class they thought they belonged. A third replied, the "middle class."

Despite the fact that *kibbutzniks* now have to compete with scientists, technologists, management consultants, etc., as national heroes in the public eye, their way of life is still that of a favored elite. They lead healthy, open-air lives in clean, modern, and frequently beautiful surroundings, engulfed by what are probably the largest, greenest, best-tended lawns and flower gardens in the country. *Kibbutzniks* breathe clean air while the average urban Israeli lives in polluted overcrowded cities that are already crumbling from within through fast-growing slums, neglect, mismanagement, and urban decay. Most of the older *kibbutzim* now provide recreational facilities comparable to those of an average American country club. Lavishly equipped gymnasiums, swimming pools (sometimes olympic size), and tennis courts are available exclusively for residents of *kibbutz* communities that number no more than 1,200 souls. These are luxuries that most urban Israelis could not possibly afford. Even if they can pay the price, comparable recreational facilities are simply unavailable in the main Israeli towns. In Tel Aviv, for example, only one or two prohibitively expensive luxury hotels—and a single country club—offer a severely limited number of well-to-do club members the use of recreational facilities of the kind now fairly common in *kibbutzim*.

The average middle- and upper-class apartment in Tel Aviv, Haifa, or Jerusalem is certainly more spacious than individual living quarters in the *kibbutz*, which are still austere and modest by any standard. Urban apartments are better appointed with amenities of modern living, central heating, air conditioning, comfortable and tasteful furniture, and the like. Yet, in the *kibbutzim*, too, living conditions are now greatly improving. Many *kibbutzim* now offer each married couple, instead of the old small room in a dreary row house, an attractive two-room apartment, surrounded by a parklike environment.

Private quarters, of course, are only one element in the comparison of life-styles. The disadvantages of *kibbutz* life in private comforts must be weighed against its advantages in public amenities of all sorts. The average *kibbutz* child now grows up in a culture-conscious environment of such intensity as can be matched by only a tiny minority of urban middle-class families. Not a few *kibbutzim* now maintain their own museums and art collections. The participation of *kibbutz* children in the growth of such institutions and in their routine operation is considerably more active, more personal, more direct, than the participation of urban children in the cultural life of the richer but more diffuse cities. Nearly all *kibbutzim* now boast sizable libraries, their own small drama groups, choirs, orchestras; many offer well-attended art courses. The *kibbutz* of today is often referred to as an "island of culture." *Kibbutzniks* still have the time and patience to read serious books and Israeli writers often discover their most avid, most interested, and most critical readers within the *kibbutzim*. Research has shown that *kibbutzniks* read more books, more newspaper and magazine articles, than any other single group in the population. The *kibbutz* community of less than 100,000 souls publishes nearly 200 periodicals on a regular basis, apart from the weekly "diary" published separately by every *kibbutz*. The periodicals range in subject matter from cattle breeding to economics, from sociology, education, politics, and religion to literature and music.

The education and welfare of their young has been a fetish with most *kibbutzim* since the early days of settlement. *Kibbutz* children are now perhaps the best-brought-up children in the country. The investment and current expenditure on *kibbutz* education is higher on a per pupil basis than anywhere in the country, including the richest areas and fanciest urban suburbs.

Non-*kibbutz* schools are overcrowded and usually understaffed. Classes of fifty pupils are not unusual in the larger towns. The average urban schoolclass numbered thirty-nine pupils in 1968. In the *kibbutzim* there are rarely more than eighteen pupils to a class; in many there are fewer.

The public school system for non-*kibbutz* children is plagued by an acute shortage of qualified and experienced teachers. Mass immigrations as well as the increasing reluctance of gifted youngsters to teach in elementary schools have led to a general lowering of academic standards since the pre-state period. Whereas many urban teachers are young girls who consider teaching an interim job before marriage, *kibbutz* schools are still taught by a relatively larger number of male teachers. The average *kibbutz* teacher is more mature, has been longer on the job, and his training has been more extensive. *Kibbutz* children are the natural beneficiaries.

12

IN A SMALL COUNTRY

> Where are the new times? This country
> seems to grow twin-like days, parched,
> drought-ridden and turning in the circle of
> a single fate. Every soul is called upon to
> undergo penance and seek an interpretation
> in them.
>
> —YITZCHAK SHENHAR
> *Perason (An Unwalled City)*

We approach the conclusion of this survey. The reader is now in possession of many useful clues that enable him to recognize in the living and petrified aspects of Israeli life some of the main forces at work. At some points we have studied minute details, sifting the shadings and subtleties. At other times, we have examined our theme from a distance, as one observes the rough charcoal lines and inchoate blots of color in a drawing, to catch the atmosphere, feeling, and tension of a scene in perpetual movement and change.

We have seen that what men thought was true was often more important than the truth itself. The origins of Israel bear witness to the power wielded by ideas over the minds of men. Feeling and sensory experience have been no less important as mainsprings of the Israeli motivation. For this level of political reality we sometimes consulted poets; in the long run, their evidence may well prove more reliable than that of historians, social scientists, or journalists.

The reader will discern, first and foremost, the heavy shadow of the past that lurks behind the modern facade of an ostensibly brand-new nation. The new technology, the demands of total and perpetual war, the smooth efficiency of the military machine, science-based industry and urbanization—all are significant ingredients of the life and temper of the country. A new breed of hard-boiled, "pragmatic" politicians is succeeding generations of True Believers and octogenarian founders. The past is a lengthening shadow that diffuses as the years go by; yet it continues to cast a spell which few Israelis ignore. In this sense, Israel remains one of the least "synchronized" countries on earth. Its several clocks strike different hours. Israel resembles a man racing ahead with his eyes turned back in a gaze transfixed by a landscape that constantly recedes into the distance. Memory, a main source of inspiration of Zionism, remains one of Israel's major emotional resources today. Israel is more "future oriented" than most countries. But it is also badly orchestrated, like a band simultaneously playing an old Hassidic tune, a Wagnerian march, the "Internationale," and an atonal symphony by Schoenberg.

This is why Israelis and outsiders have such contradictory attitudes about the country and its people. Schopenhauer said that every nation ridicules the others, and that all are right. The conflicting images are further entangled with stereotypes that seem unusually powerful. Israelis are probably the only predominantly Western people whose birth as a nation has been accompanied by—and whose formative years suffered from—a near-total exposure to modern mass media. The process of history making has been so encumbered by the manufacture of images that it is often difficult, for foreigners and Israelis alike, to disentangle fact from fiction. Jews have often inspired stereotypes. The Israelis have not escaped this peculiarly Jewish predicament. As "objects of display" at fund-raising dinners, Israelis have fared unusually well. But the well-worn adjective "fearless" is as trite and often as misleading as the old stereotype of the "scheming Jew." Israelis are viewed by too many as people who dance the *hora* when they are not planting trees in the desert; or who busy themselves asking for money when they are not off fighting the Arabs. The girl soldier with a submachine gun in one hand and a volume of Kierkegaard in the other is a trite cliché, although less harmful than the "crooked nosed businessman" of old. Conflicting stereotypes of the Israeli as the "underdog" or the "ruthless oppressor" of peace-loving Arabs co-exist in the public mind. It is dangerous for a country to rely so much on stereotypes; stereotypes replace one another almost overnight, and reality is never as simple, as decisive, as the stereotype would have us believe.

This is why so much in the foregoing chapters may seem to the cursory reader a catalogue of peculiar eccentricities, a mass of anomalies; taken together they constitute the spirit of place and add up to what we loosely call the character of a people. The combination of the rational and the irrational in Israeli affairs frequently appears confusing, sometimes tragic, always pathetically human. The various findings often cancel out one another, as in the debit and credit columns of a balance sheet. The reader has been exposed to the contradictory ideas and passions that influence the behavior of Israelis as individuals; and the habits that govern them as a people. We observed the archaic loyalties and utopian yearnings; the robust individualism and the tribal attachments; the fears generated by present difficulties magnified in the lurid and sometimes distorting light of past recollections; the pious, perhaps naive hopes sustained by what has essentially been a Messianic movement, an offshoot of nineteenth-century populism; the disillusioned toughness bred in the hangover atmosphere of the "morning after," the feverish heyday and the Thermidor of the Zionist revolution.

We saw how men fired by a Messianic idea of redemption ended up by "playing the game of the world." We observed the change in the order of priorities, which occurred in the early 1930s; the emergence of a new nationalism, more self-centered, considerably less lofty, than that envisaged by the early Zionist idealists. It may be, as an English wit once remarked, that the power an idea wields over human life is directly proportionate to the degree of error it contains. An experience of recent Palestinian, Jewish, and Israeli history certainly increases belief in the blind forces of history. The change of priorities that came about in the early 1930s was certainly "justified" by later events in Eastern and Central Europe. But what was desperately urgent and just in the eyes of the Jews was equally unjust in the eyes of the Arabs. The Arabs rightly suspected that by supporting the Zionists, the Europeans and Americans were evading their own responsibilities at the expense of the Arabs.

An irresistible force collided with an immovable body. Historians will argue endlessly whether the collision was unavoidable; the argument will be wisdom after the event. The Arabs bore no responsibility for the breakdown of civilization in Europe. Yet their opposition to Zionism grew so ferocious, their insensitivity to Jewish sentiments so great, their refusal of all compromise so absolute, their violence so indiscriminate, and their policies, finally, so genocidal—that the original imbalance between right and wrong was lost. In time it was almost entirely superseded by fresh concerns, by a new balance of rights and wrongs within the framework of an entirely new *existential* situation. There is an unexpected element of irony in the fact that the Israeli Jews, who owe their existence as a nation to their extraordinary memory of past history, should now be forced to rely on the Arabs forgetting theirs.

The Arab-Israeli collision profoundly affected the evolution of Israel as a nation. Today it colors the attitude of Israel to the outside world; and the attitude of the outside world to Israel. With all their addiction to "modern" causes, Israelis have been obliged by the collision to remain attached to habits of mind which sometimes appear anachronistic to the young American and European. The explosive mixture of nationalism and religion that goes into the making of Israeli patriotism might have been easily comprehensible to a nineteenth-century Irish nationalist. It would have been entirely comprehensible to a nineteenth-century Eastern European nationalist, for the nationalism of Poles and Russians often came intertwined with Catholicism or Orthodoxy. The Israeli mixture of nationalism and religion today confuses, disturbs, and often repels many non-religious Israelis, especially the younger generation. It appeals even less to many young Europeans and Americans living in a post-nationalist, secular age. Yet Israeli nationalism—which is now so self-centered because of the threat to Israelis both as individuals and as a nation—is not static but an evolving sensibility. It first flowered in the hothouse atmosphere of repression and war, and like every human sensibility, it is open to change. Peace with the Arabs, even some kind of semi-permanent border settlement, could alter attitudes beyond present recognition.

There is among Israelis today an elemental, almost tribal sense of sticking together which sometimes confounds outsiders from the fragmented societies of the West. The passions engendered by the Nazi holocaust in Jews old enough to remember it, the fierce loyalties generated among Israelis by the state of permanent siege, are not easily understood by a great number of young Europeans and Americans. But the outsider is often mistaken when he applies to the Israeli scene the standards of his own, vastly different condition. He must look for the turbulence beneath a surface which is only seemingly smooth. He may misjudge unless he remembers the different time sequence and the order of prior events. He deals not in abstractions, but with living people and the fateful interaction within them of ideas and events.

The future of Israel depends upon the future of the Arab-Israeli conflict: the political system, the law, the economy, the arts, the makeup of society, the quality of life. Yet even if that conflict is resolved—and whatever the future territorial arrangements may be— Israel will always remain a very small country. However close its future links with world Jewry, the Israeli nation will always be a very small one.

The smallness of Israel as a country and as a nation is another key to the future. The narrow strip of land can be crossed by car from Tel Aviv to Jerusalem in less than an hour. It takes less than eight hours by car and forty-five minutes by plane to travel the entire length of Israel along its longest, most narrow axis from the Red Sea port of Eilat to the Lebanese border in the north. From a low flying helicop-ter, Israelis in less than three hours can crisscross the elongated scrap of land for which they, and others, have fought so hard, for so long. In a brief afternoon, between lunch and tea, one can glance at almost all of it, its fields and gullies, shelves and crags, deserts and mountains, its dried-up brooks, its mire and its rocks, its rivers and its farms. A certain sense of spaciousness is retained by the stupendous contrast of desert and fertility, and by the anomaly of a country bordered by the Mediterranean Sea in the west and the rugged mountains of the east. But this, too, is relative. The extreme smallness of the country en-hances the insularity of Israeli life, an insularity which is likely to persevere even in the event of peace.

The population, in relation to that of other countries, is similarly insignificant. In 1970 there were slightly more than two and one-half million Israeli Jews. According to the most optimistic estimates, the Jewish population is not likely to exceed six million by the year 2000. It might be considerably less.

Israel's size poses great challenges, promising and dangerous. The Messianism of the founders, their boundless pretensions and high-sounding language, have lost much of their charm for more sober-minded, pragmatic generations of younger Israelis. "It will be up to you," Martin Buber pronounced in 1921, "whether Palestine will be the center of humanity or a Jewish Albania; the salvation of peoples or a game of the great powers."

In a similar vein, Ben Gurion characteristically proclaimed early in his rule that Israel must be *Ner La'Goyim*, a light to the nations of the earth, "a model for the redemption of the human race." Younger Israelis set their sights much lower and many will be content if Israel will simply be a pleasant place in which to live.

The very smallness of Israel could well enhance the pleasure of living in it. This will be especially so at a time when elsewhere sheer mass or magnitude threatens the individual. Participatory democracy stands a better chance in a community of three, four, or five million than within the lonely crowds of fifty or eighty million. Small countries are slightly more immune to the social diseases afflicting contemporary mankind everywhere. The practice of free, relatively small political communities enchances pride of citizenship, it mates solidarity with robust individualism. As it facilitates administrative controls, it also breeds a kind of civic courage which in the long run is a better safeguard to liberty than the best-formulated constitution. But to succeed, Israel must remain receptive to, and in a sense part of, the larger culture of man. Such participation is today no idle dream, even in small and distant countries. It is possible only if, aided by the advances of technology in travel and communication, the openness and tolerance of the liberal tradition are maintained.

For a country to be a pleasant place in which to live, more than liberty is needed. In this respect Israel has had considerable luck. The institutions and social patterns of a relatively egalitarian welfare state were set by the generations of founders. Many of their pious expectations and predictions never materialized; but Herzl was right, generally speaking, when he predicted that in the future Jewish state the individual would neither be crushed between the millstones of capitalism nor beheaded by the leveling pressure of socialism. Israel has not evolved as the Utopia envisaged by the early pioneers. The pioneers' dream of a free *Commonwealth of Labor* has not materialized beyond a mixed economy of state, "social," corporate, and private initiative. The ideal of university men ploughing fields and workers discussing philosophy was defeated by the demands of a modern, differentiated economy. Yet much of the libertarianism of the earlier days has successfully withstood the test of time and the pressing constraints of permanent war.

The austere look of gray shabbiness which characterized the society of pioneers—and which was sometimes mistaken as the hallmark of equality—has disappeared. Small pockets of new urban wealth now contrast sharply with larger pockets of poverty on the edges of the cities and in the countryside. But if we take as our standard of comparison the year 1952—a time when over 100,000 new immigrants were living in canvas tents or shacks of corrugated iron—the conclusion must be that the social contrasts in 1970 were considerably less blatant than those of eighteen years before.

Stripped of the pretensions of an earlier age, divorced from the inflated rhetoric with which the founders endowed the institutions they built, the foundations nevertheless remain for younger Israelis to build upon. The next installment may well be even more revolutionary than the last. In Israel, as elsewhere, the scientific revolutions of the second half of the twentieth century are likely to precipitate such radical changes as are today contemplated primarily by science fiction novelists. With the second highest per capita rate of university students in the world, with already more doctors per capita than any other country on earth, with additional universities and research centers to those already in existence, with advanced agricultural techniques to realize the full potential of climate and soil, and with a rapidly growing economy that is increasingly sustained by scientific industries, Israel could well become one archetype for the development of small nations in a modern world. Israel will always be a mere speck on the map. To be at all noticed, it will have to sparkle.

Will it? The dangers of smallness are at least as grave as the corroding effects of continuous war. Smallness also begets provincialism; provincialism breeds arrogance; arrogance leads to ethnocentricity; ethnocentricity comes at the risk of prejudice and cultural isolation. The possible effects of ethnocentricity upon the quality of Israeli life must not be underestimated. It comes to a head in the problem of religion. Since Israel is officially defined as a "Jewish state," the issue revolves around the crucial question "Who is a Jew?" No other issue has divided Israelis as sharply, and the controversy is still far from resolved.

What makes a man a Jew? Nationality? Race? Birthright? Religion? Free will? Castigation by "others"? A combination of all or some of these factors? If Jewishness is a nationality, can there be a Christian or a Moslem Jew? If it is a community of race, is this a border that cannot be surmounted by the decision of an individual to opt in or out of it? If it is free will, is Jewishness a daily plebiscite? If it is religion, does this preclude free thinkers who could thus be only incomplete Jews? and Israelis? Does it preclude Christians and Moslems who tie their fate to that of the Jews by marrying a Jew? If religion determines the Jew, which faction within the religion makes the determination? For, as a faith, Judaism is splintered, and lacks a central authority. Who, then, is a Jew?

Steeped in the liberal tradition of nineteenth-century nationalism, most of the early Zionist thinkers clearly envisaged a thoroughly secularized state. Lilienblum, Pinsker, Ben Yehuda, and Herzl clashed with the orthodox rabbis and endeavored to neutralize their influence. In *Altneuland*, Herzl's blueprint for his proposed polity, the leading character, David Litwak, proclaims: "The New Society is based upon the ideas that are a common product of all civilized people." In Herzl's text, Litwak's words were immediately applauded warmly by "the aged Rabbi Samuel." We now know, that on this score, too, Herzl's optimism was unfounded.

He proposed to settle his commonwealth mainly with Jews, but also with "Christians, Mohammedans, Buddhists, and Brahmans." "... Next to our temples" Litwak observed, "you find [their] houses of divine worship ... [but] my comrades and I [make] no distinction between people. *We ask for no one's religion or race.* Let him be a Man, that is enough for us." Elsewhere, in a "testament" to this people, Herzl wrote: "Arrange your state so that aliens will feel well in it."

Herzl, like most of his colleagues, *underestimated* not only the nationalism of the Arabs, but also the latent forces of ethnocentricity released by the Zionist revival; and he *overestimated* the liberalism of the Jews in an age of universal selfishness which—although of an apocalyptic turn of mind—he could not foresee in all its fearful brutality.

The early pioneers often attacked Herzl's blueprint as too devoid of

"Jewish characteristics." But they as well generally applied to Zionism the secular principles of the Russian socialist radicals. Many early pioneers were even more anti-clerical than Herzl. The young men and women who went to Palestine as pioneers in the first decade of the century slammed the door shut not only on the inequities of Czarist Russia but also on the medievalism of Jewish orthodoxy. They envisaged a thoroughly secular *Commonwealth of Labor*, with free intermarriage between Jews and Gentiles; religion, whether Jewish, Christian, or Moslem, would not be an affair of state. The new *Commonwealth*, to be sure, would be a haven for persecuted Jews: this, after all, was its *raison d'être*. At the same time it would be an open society based upon separation between the state and the synagogues, churches and mosques within it. The founders were not opposed to religious observance, but regarded it as a private matter. They saw the Bible mainly as a historical record testifying to their ancient nationhood in Palestine. Otherwise, the only binding, or inspirational, aspect of the Bible was the social ethos of the prophets, which fused with the expressed desire of the pioneers to establish a socialist state based upon justice and love.

Their behavior was often demonstratively and sometimes foolishly anti-rabbinical. In the early 1920s a group of young atheistic pioneers is said to have marched to the Wailing Wall on the Day of Atonement munching ham sandwiches. Ben Gurion married his wife in a civil ceremony in New York; he later refused, *on principle*, to undergo a religious ceremony as well. Histadrut-owned workers' restaurants refused for a long time to maintain kosher kitchens, again on principle. Many pioneers refused to be "Jewish" in any but a national sense. A special nomenclature came into being, to re-emphasize the distinction between Judaism as a closed religion and Judaism as a nationality —open, presumably, to members of different faiths. The pioneers often called themselves "Hebrews," not Jews. The pioneer was a *Poel Ivri* (*Hebrew* worker). His union was the *Histadrut Ha'ovdim Ha'Ivriim B'Eretz Israel* (Confederation of *Hebrew* Workers in Eretz Israel). In the 1930s and early 1940s most settlers still campaigned not for a Jewish, but for a "Hebrew" state. Thousands of middle-aged sabras remember marching through the streets in anti-British demonstrations chanting the slogan, *Aliya Chofshit! Medina Ivrit!* (Free Immigration! A Hebrew State!)

Only after the holocaust did the appellation "Jewish" slowly creep back into daily usage. It was still mainly a national, not a religious, term. Jews were men and women of Jewish extraction and identity who had suffered; it did not apply solely to the formal adherents of a faith practicing rites prescribed by ecclesiastical authorities. As late as 1948, the idea of God was still a source of considerable embarrassment. It perturbed and divided the delegates to the first ("provisional") Constituent State Council, which drafted and passed the Israeli Declaration of Independence. A proposed explicit reference to God was deleted from the draft. Instead, the signers of the Declaration put their "trust in the Rock of Israel." The oblique reference was open to more than one interpretation.*

The personal behavior of many early pioneers was deeply influenced by the ideas they held, which were frequently atheistic. But, like Herzl, they too underestimated the power of innate forces, as well as their own propensity for change under the influence of age and the impact of future events. Young men are influenced by ideas; older men by circumstance. The secular religion of reason was followed by a reconciliation with the rabbis; the demonstrative Godlessness of the early pioneers was followed by the gradual adoption of orthodox rabbinical rules into the body of universally binding state law. Orthodox Judaism is not (yet?) the established religion of Israel. Yet in an important sense the prevailing state of affairs is already more stultifying and illiberal than that in countries with an officially established church. Israeli law distinguishes between "Jewish" and other nationals ("Arab," "Druze," and sometimes *nochri*, or "alien"). Since March 1970, the question of who is a Jewish national is determined by orthodox rabbinical rule.

Prime Minister Golda Meir, herself a lifelong secularist and non-observant Jew, urged the Israeli parliament to incorporate the talmudic definition of Jew into the secular state law: "In the twentieth century," she said in 1970, "we shall not throw away the prayer shawl and the philacteries." She explained her position by saying that the state must not encourage "mixed" marriages between Jews and Gentiles. Her reasoning was not "religious" but "national." Mixed marriages

---

* Most foreign translations of the Declaration are incorrect in translating "Rock of Israel" as "God the Almighty."

between Jews and Gentiles were endangering the future existence of the Jewish people.

Earlier Zionists had bluntly dismissed the possibility of a theocracy, for as Herzl wrote in *Der Judenstaat*, "if faith keeps us united, science makes us free." In a famous paragraph in the same book, Herzl promised to keep the theocrats "in their temples, just as we shall confine our professional soldiers to their barracks." As in other fields, reality proved stronger than the dream. The avowed theocrats of Israel, who consistently demand the imposition of talmudic rule as the binding law of the state, now wield considerable political power, Although the religious parties never received more than 16 percent of the effective popular vote, their power within the various coalition governments has always been much greater than that warranted by the election returns.

The power of the theocrats has been enhanced in recent years by the revival among secular politicians, socialists, and liberals, of a curious quasi-religious piety. A kind of sentimental religiosity has seized the former rebels against orthodox religion and talmudic observance. They do not necessarily return to the orthodox fold. On the contrary, they often remain flagrantly non-observant; most Israeli politicians never, or rarely, go to synagogue, nor do they keep a kosher home. They will often eat pork, violate the Sabbath, and give their children a secular education. Their newly found religiosity is of an atavistic, sentimental, almost mystic character. It probably reflects the deep psychological crisis of an aging power elite, and in some cases borders on chauvinism and racism. The combination of orthodox piety among the secular political elite and the direct political power of the clericalist parties has dominated the Israeli legislature in recent years and has caused the erosion of principles formerly held by the secular majority.

The Israeli Declaration of Independence stipulated full equality for all citizens, "irrespective of religion, race, and sex." It prescribed not only freedom of "religion" but also—at the insistence of liberals and secularists—freedom of "conscience." This part of the Declaration of Independence is not now regarded by the courts as binding, but merely as expressing the "credo and vision of the people," which carries no constitutional authority.

It may be possible for a sculptor to copy an antique statue, but the legislator cannot reproduce an ancient state of mind. This nostalgia for Jewish tradition which has seized Israelis in recent years facilitates the incorporation into state law of ancient talmudic rules. Yet the nostalgia cannot re-enact the ancient state of mind which gave birth to talmudic law. Without that state of mind the laws enacted will either be short-lived, ignored, or so stultifying as to sooner or later cause a social explosion.

The ban on public transportation on the Sabbath is mainly a burden on the poor, for the well-to-do drive their own cars which cannot be banned from the roads. The ban on smoking on the Sabbath in the lounges or restaurants of major hotels is a nuisance; so is the prohibition to deliver telegrams on the Sabbath, or the stopping of public escalators on main street intersections, or the impossibility of booking airline reservations, or the Sabbath closing of public W.C.s. The ban on civil marriage is a more serious burden, especially on those who cannot marry at all because of the antiquated strictures of religious law. Among the latter are not only partners in "mixed" marriages, but also Jewish divorcees who would like to marry Jewish men with the surname of Cohen; all Cohens are held by the rabbinical courts to be descendants of the ancient Hebrew priests, for whom such misalliances were forbidden. Among those who cannot marry are widows who have not been "released" by the brother of their late husband; the latter is enjoined by religious rule to assume the marital status of the deceased.

In the case of "mixed" marriages, simplified conversion procedures might have meant some relief from undue burden. But easy conversion procedures run counter to the age-old Jewish aversion to proselytizing. Conversions merely to facilitate marriages between Jews and Gentiles are not approved; only after irrefutable proof of exceptional piety and meticulous ritual observance is a candidate accepted into Judaism. Hence the paradox that born Jews who eat pork have their marriages easily approved by the Rabbinate; but Gentiles who would like to convert in order to become a Jewish marriage partner must first "prove" they never touch pork or smoke a cigarette on the Sabbath. Moreover, the Tel Aviv Rabbinate has in recent years performed conversions only after first checking the police for "security clearances"; the implication is that non-Jews, even if they are Israeli citizens, might be security risks. Even if the process of conversion is facilitated in the future—a doubtful possibility, in view of the longstanding orthodox practice on such matters—conversion as the price of marriage is insupportable in a liberal society which does not offer the alternative of civil marriage.

The religious conflict is, of course, another aspect of the problem of identity which bedevils modern Israelis. The problem is a new one, especially for Jews. It was unknown in previous ages. It never bothered Josephus Flavius although he became, consecutively, a Jewish rebel leader and a Roman nobleman. Spinoza never speculated on it. The question of Jewish identity first arose with Jewish emancipation from the European ghetto early in the nineteenth century. The early Zionists never even dreamed that it would bedevil the Israelis long after their attainment of national independence, which was meant to take care of the problems of identity.

Other countries, too, have been torn by grave State-Church conflicts, which sometimes lasted centuries before they were resolved; in some places the conflict between the secularists and religionists continues to this day. Its resolution in Israel could not have been expected in the brief time that has passed since Israel's inception as a state. The important thing to note, however, is that the trend, in recent years, has generally been retrogressive. The orthodox religious establishment has tended to interfere more and more in the secular affairs of state; it now often lends its weight to the forces of national intransigence, xenophobia and chauvinism that are the inevitable outgrowth of siege and perpetual war.

In the aftermath of the 1967 war, a formal religious ruling was issued by the Sephardic Chief Rabbi of Israel, Yitzchak Nissim, prohibiting the evacuation of areas occupied by Israel in that war. The "prohibition" was issued as a *psak halacha*, which in Judaism is comparable to a papal bull or encyclical. The Chief Rabbi's *psak halacha* enjoined all Jews as individuals, as well as the Israeli government, to refrain from "even contemplating" the return of any territory that was included in God's promise to His People. Luckily only a small minority of Israelis have recognized the Rabbis' authority to make such an intervention.

The clash between secularists and religionists is likely to intensify in the foreseeable future. It would be foolish to make any predictions as to its outcome. But it seems clear that if Zionism was destined ultimately to merely bring about the establishment of another national theocracy, combining medieval orthodoxy with modern chauvinism, both Jews and Arabs will have paid too high a price for it.

Everything is still fluid. The 1967 war, as it fused in some hearts the intransigence of aroused nationalism with the archaisms of an ancient religious faith, so it produced powerful antidotes within a nation which has come of age, in a spreading re-evaluation of values. The belief in progress which Henry Adams, speaking of America, called "doubtful and even improbable principle" is still very much alive among Israelis; it remains the founders' main bequest to the young. Had Israel been established in quieter times, had it been able to develop more slowly in the calm and sunny peace of its green plains and rugged mountains, it is possible its people might sooner have come to share with other, happier nations the traditions of civility and the same subdued tone, instead of assuming the tense, exclamatory voice it now strains so often.

A harassed people has come into its own under convulsive circumstances that had not been imagined by anyone. What was planned as an orderly exodus came as a desperate escape. A people who strove above all to flee their historic fate—utter dependence upon the shifting moods of tolerance—were denied their aim. Instead of calm and rest there is unending and unnerving conflict. Instead of peace there is war with no end in sight.

Little wonder it is, then, that issues which might have been more satisfactorily resolved in calmer times still loom in the country's future like storm clouds which can bring either spring showers or late winter hail. In their fight for physical survival, the Israelis' determination to persevere seems undiminished. But as they come of age as a nation they are torn by conflicting forces, contending for their character as a people.

Let us close by quoting three famous slogans that have inspired the return of the Jews to their ancient patrimony:

If I am not for myself, who then is for me?

We came to build the land and to be rebuilt by it. . . .

If you will it, it is no fairy tale.

The first is an old talmudic saying; it requires no further explanation. The second, a song of the early pioneers, reflects their lofty
vision of human reconstruction within the good society. The third was
coined by Herzl; it gives an indication that the tale is not yet done.

Notes and Bibliography

The last forty years have produced a large number of books relevant to the main themes treated in this survey, but an updated History of Zionism, from its inception in the early 1880s until the establishment of the independent state of Israel in 1948, is not yet available. Adolph Boehm's monumental *Die Zionistiche Bewegung* (Berlin, 1935), covers only the first half of this period; it is, furthermore, far too apologetic and uncritical to appeal to the modern reader.

Nor has the history of Palestine in the past hundred years been made the subject of any full-length scholarly study. There are many books on particular periods and isolated events. But no Israeli or foreign scholar has yet attempted to treat the subject as a whole. This may seem surprising in view of the universal interest in the Arab-Israeli conflict, an interest which seems to grow in direct relationship to the growth of despair in the conflict ever being resolved. Actually there are good reasons for the lack of full-length studies. The issues are still too emotional and controversial to serve as subjects for detached observations. Too, there is the scarcity of reliable source material. Zionist and Israeli state archives are still partially closed, including those containing documents pertaining to the period prior to World War II. The archives are entirely closed for the crucial pre- and post-independence period that begins in 1946. There is also a scarcity of personal memoirs and published diaries for the period after 1936.

It is for these reasons that this bibliography deals mainly with the earlier period. Following is a list of works upon which I have relied in the writing of this book. It indicates above all the heavy debt I owe to the efforts of others. It is not a complete bibliography of any aspect of the subject; nor does it include a list of all the works consulted, or the names of all the living personalities I interviewed.

The bibliography is arranged according to the grouping of topics in the book. In each case I include those works that I have mainly relied upon, or have quoted; following those is a list of other books which may help the reader to further pursue some of the topics discussed.

Professor Walter Laqueur and Dan Bavly, old friends and critics, have read the manuscript and I am deeply grateful to them for their invaluable suggestions and efforts to pick out mistakes. I am equally grateful to another old friend and mentor, Meyer W. Weisgal, former President of the Weizmann Institute for his critical support and encouragement; and to my editor Thomas C. Wallace who skillfully reduced this book to more manageable proportions. The responsibility for results is, of course, entirely my own.

1.

For the events leading up to the Six Day War of 1967, see Walter Laqueur: *The Road to Jerusalem*, New York, 1968; and Theodore Draper: *Israel and World Politics. Roots of the Third Arab Israeli War*, New York, 1968. For the war itself, see Randolf S. and Winston S. Churchill: *The Six Day War*, London, 1967.

For biographical details of Israel's aging power elite see the following: On Shazar, his own, charmingly written memoir, Zalman Shazar: *Morning Stars*, London, 1968. On Eshkol, Terrance Prittie: *Eshkol*, London, 1969. On Dayan, Arieh Hashavya: *Ayin Achat le 'Mars (One Eye to Mars)*, Tel Aviv, 1969; Moshe Dayan: *Diary of the Sinai Campaign*, New York, 1967; Naphtali Lau-Lavie: *Moshe Dayan, a Biography*, London, 1968; Moshe Dayan: *Mapa Chadasha, Yachasim Acherim (A New Map, New Relations)*, Tel Aviv, 1969. On Golda Meir, Marie Syrkin: *Golda Meir*, New York, 1969. On Shmuel Dayan, Shmuel Dayan: *B'yemei Chason u'Matzor (Days of Siege and Vision)*, Tel Aviv, 1953; and an anthology of his works in English translation, *The Promised Land*. On Kadish Luz, Kadish Luz: *Avnei Derech (Milestones)*, Tel Aviv, 1962; and Echad: *Mi'shneim-Assar (One of Twelve)*, Tel Aviv, 1970. There is a personal memoir by the late President Ben Zvi's widow, Rachel; Rachel Yanait Ben Zvi: *Anu Olim (We Ascend)*, Tel Aviv, 1957.

On Ben Gurion, there are mainly his own recollections in the two volumes of David Ben Gurion: *Medinat Israel Ha'mechudeshet (The Restored State of Israel)*, Tel Aviv, 1969; and Moshe Pearlman: *Ben Gurion Looks Back (Talks with the Author)*, London, 1965; as well as the biographies by Robert St. John: *Ben Gurion*, New York, 1959; and Michael Bar Zohar: *The Armed Prophet*, London, 1969.

On the "price of Zionism," see George Antonius: *The Arab Awakening*, London, 1938; Jean Paul Sartre (ed.): *Le Conflit Israel Arab, Les Temps Modernes*, Paris, 1967. The best-written, best-reasoned presentation of the Arab case is by the French-Jewish scholar Maxime Rodinson:

Israel and the Arabs, London, 1968. The bitter fate of the Palestine refugees has been chronicled by Don Peretz: *Israel and the Palestine Arabs*, Washington, D.C., 1958.

The new species of anti-Semitism, generated in the Arab countries by their war with Israel, has been documented in great detail by Yehoshafat Harkabi: *Emdat Ha'Aravim b'Sichsuch Israel-Arav (The Arabs' Position in Their Conflict with Israel)*, Tel Aviv, 1968.

I have also relied upon and cited Abdullah, King of Jordan: *Memoirs*, London, 1950; Jacob Talmon: *The Unique and the Universal* (essays), London, 1968, and *Israel Among the Nations*, The Six Day War in Historical Perspective, London 1970; Shlomo Avinery: *Mechir Ha'tzionut (The Price of Zionism)*, in *Mooznaim*, Tel Aviv, 1966. (An Interview with Ehud ben Ezer.)

2 and 3.

For the Eastern European Jewish background, I have relied mainly upon Simon Dubnov: *History of the Jews in Russia and Poland*, Philadelphia, 1946; Elizabeth Herzog and Mark Zborowski: *Life is with People*, New York, 1952; Maurice Samuel: *The World of Scholem Aleichem* and *Prince of the Ghetto*, New York, 1942 and 1943; Louis Greenberg: *The Jews in Russia*, New Haven, 1944; Louis Ginzberg: *Students, Scholars and Saints*, Philadelphia, 1928. Thomas Masaryk's masterful *The Spirit of Russia*, New York, 1919, delineates the anti-Semitism of Czarist Russia and indirectly casts light on the mind of the Russian-Jewish intelligentsia. The roots of modern Jewish nationalism have been traced in Benjamin Halpern: *The Idea of a Jewish State*, Cambridge, 1961. A good source for early Zionist stirrings in Russia and Rumania is A. Druyanov: *Ktavim L'toldot Chibat Zion (Historical Writings on the Lovers of Zion Movement)*, Tel Aviv, 1938.

See also, Chaim Weizmann: *Trial and Error*, London, 1949; Meyer Weisgal and Joel Carmichael (eds.): *Chaim Weizmann: A Biography by Several Hands*, New York, 1964; Shmaryahu Levin: *Childhood in Exile*, New York, 1929; A. U. Kovner: *Die Beichte eines Juden in Briefen an Dostoewski (Dostoevsky's Correspondence with a Russian Jew)*, Munich, 1927; Eliezer Ben Yehuda: *He'chalom V'shivro (Dream and Awakening)*, Jerusalem, 1942.

Shalom Spiegel: *Hebrew Reborn*, New York, 1962, recapitulates the revival of modern Hebrew and introduces the main heroes of this nineteenth-century drama. Zalman Shnëur, *Chezionot*, Berlin, 1923, one of the great Hebrew poets of the Diaspora, has lauded the Jewish *shtetl* in

Vilna, my famed grandmother, city and mother in Israel
Jerusalem of the Exile, you have comforted an Eastern people
    banished to the north.

See also, Y. L. Gordon: *Kitvei Y. L. Gordon* (*Collected Works of Y. L. Gordon*), Tel Aviv, 1928.

There are hundreds of detailed descriptions by Jewish writers and by others of the anti-Semitic riots (pogroms) in Russia after 1880. A vivid description of the pogroms by a non-Jewish outsider will be found in Michael Davitt's *In the Pale*, New York, 1903. An English translation of Chaim N. Bialik's poems of wrath, which were the battle cry of the Zionists, is included in S. Y. Pnueli (ed.), *Modern Hebrew Poetry*, Vol. I, Jerusalem, 1966.

4.

The interrelationship between the Jews of Russia and the revolutionary movements is reflected in Adam B. Ulam: *The Bolsheviks*, New York, 1968, p. 190; Masaryk (*op. cit.*), Vol. I., p. 123; Bertram D. Wolfe: *Those Who Made a Revolution*, New York, 1935. The relationship is analyzed in L. Dennen: *The Jew in the Russian Revolution*, Menorah Journal, New York, Summer, 1932. See also Leon Trotsky: *My Life*, New York, 1969, and his *History of the Russian Revolution*, New York, 1932; also William Henry Chamberlain: *The Russian Revolution*, New York, Vol. II, p. 92.

The ideologists of modern Jewish nationalism, acting primarily under the impact of Central, Southern, and Eastern European nationalist movements are described by Theodor Herzl: *The Jewish State*, New York, 1904; Moses Hess: *Rome and Jerusalem*, Leipzig, 1882. For Hess, see Isaiah Berlin: *The Life and Opinions of Moses Hess*, Cambridge, 1959; Zvi H. Kalischer: *Derishat Zion* (*Seeking Zion*), Thorn, 1866; Leo Pinsker: *Auto-emancipation: An Appeal to His People by a Russian Jew* (English translations by Arthur Hertzberg will be found in his *The Zionist Idea*, New York, 1959).

The impact of German romanticism upon Zionist thought is described by Hans Kohn: *Living in a World Revolution*, New York, 1964.

For the development of Jewish and Zionist socialist movements, see A. Tartakover: *Toldot Tnuat Ha'avoda Ha'yehudit* (Hebrew, *History of the Jewish Labor Movement*), Warsaw, 1929, and Z. Even-Shoshan: *Toldot Tnuat Poalim Be'Eretz Israel* (*History of the Labor Movement in Israel*), Tel Aviv, 1968; A. Levinson: *B'reshit Ha'tnuah* (*At the Beginning* of the Movement), Tel Aviv, 1947; Zvi Gershuni: Zichronot (Memoirs 1870–1903), Jaffa, 1919; D. Ber Borochov: Ha'leumiut U'milchemet Ha'maamadot ([Jewish] Nationalism and the Class Struggle), Tel Aviv, 1932, and Ktavim (Collected Works), Tel Aviv, 1955; Nachman Syrkin: Essays on Socialist Zionism, New York, 1935; Yitzhak Ben Zvi: Zichronot V'reshumot (Memoirs), Tel Aviv, 1936; Nachum Nir Reflex: Pirkei Chaim (Memoirs),Tel Aviv, 1955; Stepniak (Sergei Kravchinsky): The Career of a Nihilist, New York, 1889, quoted in Greenberg: The Jews in Russia. For Mazzini ("without a country you are the bastards of humanity"), see Duties of Man and Other Essays, London, 1915. For Ferdinand Lassalle, as a precursor of Zionism, see his Tagebuch, Vienna, 1911; M. Z. Feierberg: Le'an, Tel Aviv, 1944.

The best anthology in English translation of the early Zionist writers and ideologists is Arthur Hertzberg: The Zionist Idea, New York, 1959. See this excellent annotated collection for selected texts of Moses Hess, Moses L. Lilienblum, Leo Pinsker, Eliezer Ben Yehuda, Theodor Herzl, Ber Borochov, and others.

Theodor Herzl's Der Judenstaat appeared in English translation of Jacob D. Haas, New York, 1904; Altneuland, New York, 1902; Herzl's Diaries (ed. R. Patai), New York, 1960.

5 and 6.

For conflicting impressions of the landscape, see Herman Melville: Journal of a Visit to Europe and the Levant; Vivien Nooks: Edward Lear, the Life of a Wanderer; London, 1968; Pierre Loti: Jerusalem and La Galilee, Oeuvres Complètes, 7 vols., Paris, 1894. A sardonic criticism of contemporary travelogues will be found in Mark Twain's Innocents Abroad.

See also, Ludwig August Frankl: Nach Jerusalem, Ein Reisebericht, Berlin, 1935; M. A. Ginzburg (ed.): Devir: Michtavei Ha'doktor Levi (Dr. Louis Loewe's Letters from Jerusalem), Warsaw, 1883; Laurence Oliphant: Land of Gilead, London, 1881, and Haifa, Life in Modern Palestine, London, 1885. More reliable than many literary texts are photographs in the Bavarian War Archives included in Gustaf Dalman: Hundert deutsche Fliegerbilder aus Palestina (One Hundred Air Photos Taken by the German Air Force Before and During World War I), Gutersloh, 1925.

For the settlers' view see A. G. Kressel (ed.): Sefer Petach Tikva (The Book of Petach Tikva), Petach Tikva, 1952; D. Judelevich (ed.): Sefer Rishon Le-Zion (The Book of Rishon Le-Zion), Rishon Le-Zion,

1941; A. Samsonov (ed.): *Sefer Zichron Yaakov* (*The Book of Zichron Yaakov*), Tel Aviv, 1943; B. Chabas (ed.): *Sefer Ha'Aliya Ha'Shniya* (*The Book of the Second Aliya*), Tel Aviv, 1949.

For the early days of settlement, I have relied mainly upon Alex Bein: *Toldot Ha'hityashvut Ha'tzionit* (*History of the Zionist Colonization*), Tel Aviv, 1945; Shmuel Yavnieli: *Tkufot Chibat Zion* (*The Era of the Lovers of Zion*), Tel Aviv; *Leket Teudot Le'toldot Vaad Ha'lashon V'ha'akademia 1890–1970* (*Documents on the History of the Hebrew Language Academy*), Jerusalem, 1970; Eliezer Ben Yehuda: *Ha'chalom V'shivro* (*Dream and Reality*), Jerusalem, 1941; I. Kollat: *Ideologia U'Metziut B'tnuot Ha'avoda B'Eretz Israel 1905–1919* (*Ideology and Reality in the Labor Movement in Eretz Israel*), Doctoral thesis, submitted to the Hebrew University, Jerusalem; Yaari-Poleskin: *Cholemim V'lochamim* (*Dreamers and Fighters*), Tel Aviv, 1931 (English abridgement; *The Saintly Heritage*).

Berl Katzenelson: *Darki La'Aretz* (*My Path to Israel*), Tel Aviv, 1948, contains the Histadrut leader's personal reminiscences. Katzenelson was more conscious than were other writers of the strange characters attracted to the Palestinian settlements. He wrote in 1912 that Palestine shall be restored to the Jews only through the efforts of madmen and sworn nonconformists. The same type of men "created the settlements of America and Australia" and have given the world new social forms. "From the days of the Anglo-Saxon pioneers in America to the Dukhobars of Russia." *Ketavim* (*Works*), Vol. I., p. 14, Tel Aviv, 1946.

Much of the flavor of the times is reflected in personal memoirs, the most important of which are: S. D. Levontin: *Le'Eretz Avoteinu* (*To the Land of Our Forefathers*), Tel Aviv, 1924; Shlomo Zemach: *Shana Rishona* (*First Year in Palestine*), Tel Aviv, 1956; Itamar Ben Avi: *Im Shachar Atzmauten* (*The Dawn of our Independence*), memoirs of the first child raised in the Hebrew language, Tel Aviv, 1962; Menashe Mairowitz: *Zichronot Acharon Ha'Biluim* (*Memoirs of the Last of the Biluim*), Jerusalem, 1946; Zvi Shimshi: *Zichronot* (*Memoirs, by the Father of Ben Zvi*), Jerusalem, 1938; Shimon Kushnir: *Netivo shel Naar Oved* (*A Working Boy's Path in the Second Aliya*), Tel Aviv, 1955; Yitzchak Ben Zvi: *Zichronot V'reshumot Me Ha'neurim ad 1920* (*Memoirs and Notes up until 1920*), edited by Rachel Y. Ben Zvi, Jerusalem, 1956; Zvi Nadav: *Kach Hitchalnu* (*So We Began*), Tel Aviv, 1957; Joseph Eliash: *Zichronot Tzioni Me'Russia* (*Memoirs of a Russian Zionist*), Jerusalem, 1955; Arthur Ruppin: *Pirkei Chaim* (*Memoirs and Diaries*), 3 vols., Tel Aviv, 1968; and Shlomo Lavie's memoirs: *Aliyato shel Shalom Laish* (*The Advent of Shalom Laish*), Tel Aviv, 1964.

I have also relied upon Aaron David Gordon: *Kitvei* (Collected Works), 6 vols., Tel Aviv, 1930; J. C. Brenner: *Kol Kitvei* (*The Collected Works*), edited by M. Posnanski, Tel Aviv, 1955; J. C. Brenner: *Igrot* (*Letters*), Tel Aviv, 1941; M. Singer: *Im Brenner Le'Eretz Israel* (*With Brenner on the Way to Eretz Israel*), Haifa, 1969; S. Kushnir *Anshei Nevo* (*Men of Nebo*), Tel Aviv, 1968; David Horowitz: *Ha'etmol Sheli* (*My Yesterday*), memoirs of the former communard who later became Governor of the Bank of Israel, Tel Aviv, 1970; Hillel Dan: *Be'derech lo Slula* (*On Unpaved Roads*), the memoirs of another former communard who later became an industrial and financial tycoon, Tel Aviv, 1963; David Ben Gurion: *Michtavim le'Paula V'la'yeledim* (*Letters to Paula and the Children*), Tel Aviv, 1968; Allan Arian: *Ideological Change in Israel*, Cleveland, 1966.

For further reading on the Labor Brigade, see *Gedud Ha'avoda* (*The Labor Brigade*), a collection of documents and memoirs, Tel Aviv, 1932. The records of Bittania were published in *Kehilateinu, Liveteihem u'maavajehem shel Chalutzim Rishonim* (*Our Community: Dreams and Hesitations of the Early Pioneers*), Beth-Alpha, 1964. Horowitz (*op. cit.*) is the only known critical treatment of this bizarre commune; even Horowitz, aware of the remaining sensitivities, delayed publication of his memoirs (written in the late 1950s) until the eve of his retirement from public service in 1970. See also Arthur Koestler: *Arrow in the Blue* for a description of the author's life in the early 1920s in one of the Palestinian communes; and Samuel Kurland: *Cooperative Palestine*, New York, 1947.

7.

The parts in this chapter dealing with Ben Gurion's first "discovery" of an Arab problem are based primarily upon a taped interview with the former premier.

The Herzl-Nordau incident is cited by Professor Zvi Werblowski in J. P. Sartre's dossier: *Le Conflict Israel Arab*, p. 391.

Most of the documents reflecting the early exchanges between Arabs and Zionists are now kept in the Central Zionist Archives, Jerusalem, and I wish to express my gratitude for permission to consult their records.

I have also relied upon, and am deeply grateful to, Neville J. Mandel: *Turks, Arabs and Jewish Immigration into Palestine* (a thesis submitted to Oxford University, 1965). This is the most thorough examination thus far of British, Zionists, and Ottoman documents of the 1881–1914 period. The great importance of Mandel's work is in his proof, convincing in view of the evidence he supplies, that, by 1913, the Arabs of Palestine were fully aware of—and vehemently opposed to—the Zionist enterprise; and that, far from originating in the wake of British imperialist policy, or in the non-consummation of the abortive Weizmann-Faisal pact, the Arabs and the Jews were set on their collision course as early as 1913.

Two other important studies of the same subject are P. Elsberg: *Ha'sheela Ha'Aravit B'mediniut Ha'hanhala Ha'tzionit Lifnei 1914* (*The Arab Question and Official Zionist Policy before 1914*), in *Shivat Zion*, No. 4, Jerusalem, 1956; and Yaacov Roi: *Ha'emda Ha'tzionit Klapei Ha'Araviim 1908–1914* (*The Zionist Position Toward the Arabs 1908–1914*), in *Keshet*, Nos. 42–43, Tel Aviv, 1969.

From an Irish nationalist and an Arab nationalist exile in Paris come two of the first realistic estimates of the Arab-Jewish situation. See Michael Davitt: *Within the Pale*, New York, 1903, pp. 243–244; and Naguib Azouri: *Le Réveil de la Nation Arab*, p. V., Paris, 1905.

Other works consulted: Richard Lichtheim: *Shaar Yashuv* (Memoirs). Lichtheim represented the Zionist executive in Constantinople prior to 1914 and led some of the earliest exchanges with Arab nationalists in the Ottoman parliament. David Ben Gurion: *Anachnu U'shcheneinu* (*We and Our Neighbors*), Tel Aviv, 1931. The record of Ben Gurion's futile talks with Arab nationalists in the 1930s is in David Ben Gurion: *Pegishot im Manhigim Araviim* (*Meetings with Arab Leaders*), Tel Aviv, 1967. In this memoir Ben Gurion mocks his own naiveté toward the Arabs, as expressed in his earlier book of 1931: "The accepted assumption of the Zionists of that time was that our work greatly benefits the Arabs . . . [therefore] the Arabs will receive us with open arms." (*Pegishot*, p. 10)

See also, Moshe Sharett: *Yoman Medini* (*Diary, 1936–1937*), Tel Aviv, 1968; Arthur Ruppin: *Pirkei Chayai* (*Memoirs and Diaries*), Tel Aviv, 1968; Chaim Arlosoroff: *Yoman Yerushalaim* (*Jerusalem Diary, 1931–1932*), Tel Aviv, 1949.

Ber Borochov's theories on the Arabs will be found in *Le'sheelot Zion V'territoria* (*Zion and the Territorial Question*), *Ketavim*, Vol. I, p. 147, and *Ha'platforma Shelanu* (*Our Program*), p. 282. Borochov's limited, Europe-centered view is typical of that of most socialists of the time. For Engels' and Marx's Eurocentrism, which today is overlooked by most Marxists, see Shlomo Avinery (ed.): *Karl Marx on Colonialism and Modernization*. His dispatches and other writings on Africa, India, etc., New York, 1969, pp. 47, 132.

The *Poale Zion* announcement of Brody, in Galicia, 1908, is cited by Mendel Singer: *Im Brenner Le'Eretz Israel*, Haifa, 1969.

Herzl's official report on his Palestinian tour is in the Central Zionist Archives. For Herzl's remarkable oversight of the Arabs, his Diaries are especially useful. (See entries dated March 3, 1903, and during his Palestinian tour of 1898). The utopian streak in Herzl's Arab program is apparent in *Altneuland*. Yussuf Ziah el-Khaldi's letter to Herzl (March 1, 1899) is in the Central Zionist Archives, File H III d.14. Herzl's answer is in *Igrot Herzl* (*Herzl's Letters*), Jerusalem, p. 310.

O. Mannoni: *Prospero and Caliban*, New York, 1964, is one of the few detailed studies of colonial psychology. I have used it as a contrast to the Zionist pioneers' unique frame of mind. Achad Ha'am's warnings of 1901 are in *Emet Me'Eretz Israel* (*Truth from Israel*), *Al Parashat Drachim*, Vol. I. Harry Sacher's prophetic warning of 1917 is cited by Leonard Stein: *The Balfour Declaration*, London, 1961, p. 622. Israel Zangwill's advice to the Arabs to "fold their tents and quietly get out" is cited by Joseph Nedava: *Israel Zangwill and the Arab Problem*, *Ha'uma* Quarterly, No. 14, Tel Aviv, October, 1965.

I have also relied upon references to the Arabs in the personal memoirs of the pioneers, cited in the notes to previous chapters, especially Levontin, Zemach, Ben Yehuda, Ben Zvi, A. D. Gordon, Shlomo Lavie; also Gad Frumkin: *Derech Shofet B'Yerushalaim* (*A Judge's Life in Jerusalem*), Tel Aviv, 1954 (especially in reference to Ussishkin's arrogance), and M. Kalvarisky in *Sheifoteinu*, Vol. II, pp. 53–54. Gumplowitz's letter to Herzl is contained in the *Herzl Yearbook*, New York, 1958.

Weizmann's and Ben Gurion's reasons for accepting the 1936 partition plan are outlined in Ben Gurion: *Ba'maaracha*, Vol. I, p. 128, and in Weizmann: *Trial and Error*, London, 1949, p. 474.

For more on Manya Shochat, see her biography by Shlomo Shva: *Shevet Ha'noazim* (*The Daring Tribe*), Tel Aviv, 1949; and *Sefer Ha'shomer*, Tel Aviv, 1957, p. 385.

8.

An English version of Uri Zvi Greenberg's poem appears in *Modern Hebrew Poetry*, a bi-lingual anthology edited and translated by Ruth Finer Mintz, Berkeley and Los Angeles, 1966.

See also, Yitzhak Sade: *Achoti al Ha'chof* (*My Sister on the Beach*), in *Pirkei Mikra*, Yad Va'shem Publications, 1968. Yehuda Kasten's review is in *Ha'aretz*, 1964; Hanoch Bartov: *Wounds of Maturity*, New York, 1968; Elie Wiesel: *Dawn*, New York, 1961. On the Eichmann trial see Gideon Hausner: *Justice in Jerusalem*, New York, 1966.

Other works consulted: Robert Fulton (ed): *Death and Identity*, New York, 1965, on the social function of burial and mourning rites in primitive societies; and Christopher Sykes: *Crossroads to Israel*, London,

1965. This is the best history of Palestine under the British mandate. It is especially useful in its masterful description of the desperate mood of the Palestinian Jews after the rise of Nazism in Europe. For the history of the 1948 Arab-Israeli war I relied upon Netanial Lorch: *Edge of the Sword*, New York, 1961. Details of the battle of Yad Mordechai can be found in M. Larkin: *The Six Days of Yad Mordechai*, Tel Aviv, 1965. George Steiner is quoted from *Language and Silence*, Essays, 1958–1966, London, 1967.

The Kastner case has been described fully and rather passionately in at least one English language book, Ben Hecht: *Perfidy*, New York, 1961.

See also, Shabtai Teveth: *Chasufim B'tzariach* (*Exposed in the Turret*), Tel Aviv, 1968. The section quoted is from the Hebrew original, which was deleted in the English translation, *Tanks of Tammuz*, London, 1968. Teveth cites the case of another high-ranking officer in the Israeli armored corps, a lieutenant colonel who in his youth had been one of the living corpses found by the Russians in Auschwitz at liberation. He told Teveth that as a sixteen-year-old boy he and other inmates of the concentration camp had exchanged views on what they would do if they should ever get out alive. He remembered saying: "When I get out I want a big loaf of black bread, and to eat as much of it as I like. But I'll also have a rifle with a bayonet, so that people will be afraid of me." He used to tell his subordinates that he still believed in what he had said twenty years before. "Bread and a gun equals survival." (*Tanks of Tammuz*, London, 1968, p. 257.)

For the impact of the Eichmann trial on public opinion see Chaim Guri: *Multa Ha'Zechuchit* (*Facing the Glass Cage*), Tel Aviv, 1962; S. N. Herman, Y. Peres, and E. Yuchtman: *Reactions to the Eichmann Trial in Israel: a Study in High Involvement*, in Scripta Hierosolymitana, Vol. 14, Jerusalem, 1965.

The source of recent Arab anti-Semitic utterances is Y. Harkabi: *Emdat Ha'Aravim* (*op. cit.*), Tel Aviv, 1968. The view of Arab society as a "shame society" is from Dr. S. Hamady: *Temperament and Character of the Arabs*, New York, 1960.

Constantine Zurayk: *Maana el Nakbu* (*Lesson of the Disaster*), is available in the English translation of R. Winder: *The Meaning of Disaster*, Beirut, 1956.

9.

The English translation of Yehuda Amichai's poem is by Ruth Finer Mintz (*op. cit.*).

Moshe Shamir: *Chayai im Yishmael* (*My Life with Ishmael*), Tel Aviv, 1968; Moshe Dayan: *Yoman Maarechet Sinai* (*Sinai Campaign Diary*), Tel Aviv, 1965.

Meir Har Zion's story has been told in his own words, *Pirkei Yoman* (*Chapters of a Diary*), edited by Noemi Fraenkel, Tel Aviv, 1969.

Bruno Bettelheim's testimony on the cult of toughness among *kibbutz* children is in *The Children of the Dream*, Macmillan, 1967, pp. 255–256. The opposite phenomenon is recorded in *Siach Lochamim* (*Fighters' Talk*), which contains fragments of observations and conversations, issued by young members of the *kibbutz* movement, Tel Aviv, 1968. There is an abridged English version; Henry Near (ed.): *The Seventh Day*, Soldiers' talk about the Six Day War, London, 1970.

On Jewish wit, I have consulted Salcia Landmann: *Der Judische Witz*, Breisgan, 1960; Leo Rosten: *The Joys of Yiddish*, New York, 1968; Theodore Reik: *Jewish Wit*, New York, 1962.

Arnold Toynbee's theories on the comforts of adversity are in his *A Study of History*, Abridgements Vols. I–VI, London, 1946 (Chap. II: "The Challenge of the Environment"). Freud expresses a similar thought in *Civilization and Its Discontents*: it is easy to tie a great many people with bonds of love as long as there remain others to receive their expressions of aggression.

For an analysis of the relationship between the civil power and the army in Israel, see Amos Perlmutter: *Military and Politics in Israel*, London, 1969; B. Halpern: *The Role of the Military in Israel*, in J. J. Johnson (ed.): *The Role of the Military in Underdeveloped Countries*. I have also relied upon Yehuda Bauer: *Diplomatia U'machteret* (*Diplomacy and Underground*), Merchavia, 1966—on the relations between the underground *Hagana* and the Zionist executive in the pre-state periods.

For life in perpetual conflict, see also: *Childhood Under Fire* (in Hebrew) edited by Abba Kovner, Tel Aviv, 1968, a collection of children's reactions to war.

10.

For Moshe Dayan's talk, see Moshe Dayan: *Mapa Chadasha, Yachassim Chadashim* (*op. cit.*); the full text of Dayan's "Now is Now" was translated into English, *Jerusalem Post*, September 12, 1969. For a good description of the siege atmosphere see Chaim Guri: *Dapim Yerushalaim* (*Jerusalem Pages*), Tel Aviv, 1968.

For further reading on the *sabra*, see M. E. Spiro: *The Sabra and Zionism*, a study in personality and ideology, in *Social Problems* (Fall,

1957); Bruno Bettelheim (*op. cit.*); Georges Friedmann: *The End of the Jewish People?* London, 1961; Ferynand Zweig: *Israel, the Sword and the Harp*, London, 1969. Zweig is particularly incisive on the *sabra* figure, which he sees torn between the two main mystiques of modern Israel, "the mystique of violence" and "the mystique of redemption."

Literary works quoted and/or consulted: S. Yizhar: *Yemei Ziklag* (*Days of Ziklag*), Tel Aviv, 1958; by the same author: "Khirbat Khisa" ("The Ruin of Khisa") and "Ha'shavui" ("The Captive"), in *Arbaa Sipurim* (*Four Stories*), Tel Aviv, 1966; A. B. Yehoshua: *Mul Ha'yaarot* (*Facing the Forests*), Tel Aviv, 1968; Yitzchak Orpaz: *Al Chudo shel Kadur* (*On the Point of a Bullet*), in *Essev Pere*, Tel Aviv, 1959, *Nemalim* (*Ants*), Tel Aviv, 1968, and *Massa Daniel* (*Daniel's Journey*), Tel Aviv, 1969; Dahn Ben Amotz: *Liskor V'lishkoach* (*To Remember and to Forget*), Tel Aviv, 1968; Amos Oz: *Arzot Ha'tan* (*Lands of the Jackal*), Tel Aviv, 1965; *Makom Acher* (*Another Place*), Tel Aviv, 1966, and *Michael Sheli* (*Michael Mine*), Tel Aviv, 1968; Yariv Ben Aharon: *Ha'krav* (*The Battle*), Tel Aviv, 1966; Binyamin Tammuz: "Tacharut Sechiya" ("Swimming Contest") in the collection of short stories by this author, Tel Aviv, 1964; Yehuda Amichai: *Shirim* (*Poems*, 1948–1962), Tel Aviv, 1964, and *Achshav B'raash* (*Now Noisily*), Poems, 1963–1968, Tel Aviv, 1968; Yoram Kaniuk: *Ha'yored Le'maala* (*The Acrophile*), Tel Aviv, 1961, *Himmo, Melech Yerushalaim* (*Himmo, King of Jerusalem*), and *Adam ben Kelev* (*Son of a Dog*), Tel Aviv, 1969. English translations of *Acrophile* and *Himmo*, New York, 1961 and 1969.

See also, Aharon Megged: *Ha'matmon* (*The Treasure*), Tel Aviv, 1963; Matti Megged: *Sofo Ha'mar shel D.* (*The Bitter End of D.*), in *Lamerchav*, December 14 and 21, 1956; Pinchas Sadeh: *Al Matzavo shel Ha'adam* (*On the Condition of Man*), Tel Aviv, 1967, and *Ha'chaim Ke'mashal* (*Life as a Parable*), Tel Aviv, 1968.

For Dayan's remarks on archeology, see *Jerusalem Post*, October 6, 1968. For Sigmund Freud's remarks on archeology, see *A Disturbance of Memory on the Acropolis*, in *Character and Culture*, New York, 1963, p. 311, and *Letters*, to his fiancee, December 1883, London, 1960. I have also relied upon Suzanne Cassirer Bernfeld: *Freud and Archeology*, The American Imago, Vol. 8, 1943. The political functions of archeology in newly established nation-states have been described in Graham Clark: *Archeology and Society*, London, 1947, p. 191.

Aaron Aaronsohn's oblivion of archeology is shown in E. Livneh: *Aaronsohn, Ha'ish U'zmano* (*His Life and Times*), Tel Aviv, 1969. Shlomo Sharon: *Shorashim V'chassifatam* (*Exposing Roots*), in *Mooznaim*, March, 1967, explores the psychoanalytical implications of the

Israeli archeology craze. In his view, the visible exposure of past roots and layers—including the study of the Nazi holocaust—leads to a cathartic effect.

See also, Ben Zvi's book on Peki'in: *Ha'yishuv Ha'yehudi B'Kfar Peki'in* (*The Jewish Population in the Village of Peki'in*), Tel Aviv, 1922, p. 3. For Eliezer Ben Yair's speech, see Josephus Flavius: *Wars of the Jews*, Vol. VI, Chap. VIII.

The full text of Yadin's 1963 speech is in Benno Rothenberg: *Masada*, Levin-Epstein, Tel Aviv, no date.

11.

For further reading in English, on the Israeli political system, see Leonard Fein: *Politics in Israel*, Boston, 1967. This is a most comprehensive study, rich in insights, unusually sensitive to crucial detail and easily the best written book in its field. Allan Arian: *Ideological Change in Israel*, Cleveland, 1968, underlines—rightly, I think—the lingering strength of ideology in Israeli politics. The multi-party system is scrutinized in Emanuel Gutmann: *Politics and Parties in Israel*, Akademon Press, Jerusalem, 1961. See also, Lester G. Seligman: *Leadership in a New Nation: Political Development in Israel*, New York, 1964; Amitai Etzioni: *Alternative Ways to Democracy—The Example of Israel*, Political Science Quarterly, No. 74, 1959.

The comparison of jokes to dreams is by David Riesman: *Individualism Reconsidered*, Glencoe, 1954, p. 349.

Hillel Dan is quoted from his memoir, *B'derech lo Slula* (*On Unpaved Roads*), Tel Aviv, 1963, pp. 160–161.

The incident between Golda Meir and the immigrants is cited by Marie Syrkin (*op. cit.*), p. 264.

Index

FOR THE BEST IN PAPERBACKS, LOOK FOR THE

In every corner of the world, on every subject under the sun, Penguin represents quality and variety—the very best in publishing today.

For complete information about books available from Penguin—including Pelicans, Puffins, Peregrines, and Penguin Classics—and how to order them, write to us at the appropriate address below. Please note that for copyright reasons the selection of books varies from country to country.

In the United Kingdom: For a complete list of books available from Penguin in the U.K., please write to *Dept E.P., Penguin Books Ltd, Harmondsworth, Middlesex, UB7 0DA.*

In the United States: For a complete list of books available from Penguin in the U.S., please write to *Consumer Sales, Penguin USA, P.O. Box 999— Dept. 17109, Bergenfield, New Jersey 07621-0120.* VISA and MasterCard holders call 1-800-253-6476 to order all Penguin titles.

In Canada: For a complete list of books available from Penguin in Canada, please write to *Penguin Books Canada Ltd, 10 Alcorn Avenue, Suite 300, Toronto, Ontario, Canada M4V 3B2.*

In Australia: For a complete list of books available from Penguin in Australia, please write to the *Marketing Department, Penguin Books Ltd, P.O. Box 257, Ringwood, Victoria 3134.*

In New Zealand: For a complete list of books available from Penguin in New Zealand, please write to the *Marketing Department, Penguin Books (NZ) Ltd, Private Bag, Takapuna, Auckland 9.*

In India: For a complete list of books available from Penguin, please write to *Penguin Overseas Ltd, 706 Eros Apartments, 56 Nehru Place, New Delhi, 110019.*

In Holland: For a complete list of books available from Penguin in Holland, please write to *Penguin Books Nederland B.V., Postbus 195, NL-1380AD Weesp, Netherlands.*

In Germany: For a complete list of books available from Penguin, please write to *Penguin Books Ltd, Friedrichstrasse 10-12, D-6000 Frankfurt Main 1, Federal Republic of Germany.*

In Spain: For a complete list of books available from Penguin in Spain, please write to *Longman, Penguin España, Calle San Nicolas 15, E-28013 Madrid, Spain.*

In Japan: For a complete list of books available from Penguin in Japan, please write to *Longman Penguin Japan Co Ltd, Yamaguchi Building, 2-12-9 Kanda Jimbocho, Chiyoda-Ku, Tokyo 101, Japan.*

FOR THE BEST IN HISTORY, LOOK FOR THE

FOR THE BEST IN HISTORY, LOOK FOR THE

☐ **THE FACE OF BATTLE**
John Keegan

In this study of three battles from three different centuries, John Keegan examines war from the fronts—conveying its reality for the participants at the "point of maximum danger."

366 pages   ISBN: 0-14-004897-9

☐ **VIETNAM: A HISTORY**
Stanley Karnow

Stanley Karnow's monumental narrative—the first complete account of the Vietnam War—puts events and decisions of the day into sharp, clear focus. "This is history writing at its best."—*Chicago Sun-Times*

752 pages   ISBN: 0-14-007324-8

☐ **MIRACLE AT MIDWAY**
Gordon W. Prange
with Donald M. Goldstein and Katherine V. Dillon

The best-selling sequel to *At Dawn We Slept* recounts the battles at Midway Island—events which marked the beginning of the end of the war in the Pacific.

470 pages   ISBN: 0-14-006814-7

☐ **THE MASK OF COMMAND**
John Keegan

This provocative view of leadership examines the meaning of military heroism through four prototypes from history—Alexander the Great, Wellington, Grant, and Hitler—and proposes a fifth type of "post-heroic" leader for the nuclear age.   *368 pages   ISBN: 0-14-011406-8*

☐ **THE SECOND OLDEST PROFESSION**
Spies and Spying in the Twentieth Century
Phillip Knightley

In this fascinating history and critique of espionage, Phillip Knightley explores the actions and missions of such noted spies as Mata Hari and Kim Philby, and organizations such as the CIA and the KGB.

436 pages   ISBN: 0-14-010655-3

☐ **THE STORY OF ENGLISH**
Robert McCrum, William Cran, and Robert MacNeil

"Rarely has the English language been scanned so brightly and broadly in a single volume," writes the *San Francisco Chronicle* about this journey across time and space that explores the evolution of English from Anglo-Saxon Britain to Reagan's America.   *384 pages   ISBN: 0-14-009435-0*

FOR THE BEST IN HISTORY, LOOK FOR THE

☐ **THE WORLD SINCE 1945**
T. E. Vadney

This magnificent survey of recent global history charts all the major developments since the end of World War II, including the Cold War, Vietnam, the Middle East wars, NATO, the emergence of sovereign African states, and the Warsaw Pact.   *570 pages   ISBN: 0-14-022723-7*

☐ **THE ECONOMIC CONSEQUENCES OF THE PEACE**
John Maynard Keynes
Introduction by Robert Lekachman

First published in 1920, Keynes's brilliant book about the cost of the "Carthaginian" peace imposed on Germany after World War I stands today as one of the great economic and political works of our time.
                    336 pages   ISBN: 0-14-011380-0

☐ **A SHORT HISTORY OF AFRICA**
Sixth Edition
Roland Oliver and J. D. Fage

While the centers of European culture alternately flourished and decayed, empires in Africa rose, ruled, resisted, and succumbed. In this classic work, the authors have drawn on the whole range of literature about Africa, taking its study a step forward.   *304 pages   ISBN: 0-14-022759-8*

☐ **RUSSIA**
Broken Idols, Solemn Dreams
David K. Shipler

A national best-seller, this involving personal narrative by the former Moscow bureau chief of *The New York Times* crystallizes what is truly Russian behind the facade of stereotypes and official government rhetoric.
                    404 pages   ISBN: 0-14-007408-2

FOR THE BEST IN PAPERBACKS, LOOK FOR THE

☐ **GOD'S TROMBONES**
   Seven Negro Sermons in Verse
   James Weldon Johnson

The inspirational sermons of the old Negro preachers are set down as poetry in this classic collection, which has been frequently dramatized, recorded, and anthologized.   *56 pages*   *ISBN: 0-14-042217-X*

☐ **A PASSOVER HAGGADAH**
   Central Conference of American Rabbis
   Drawings by Leonard Baskin

"As it is said: You shall tell your child on that day. . . ." This beautifully illustrated, large-size Haggadah includes the prayers, lessons, and preparations for the Seder, the ceremonial feast of Passover.
                              124 pages   *ISBN: 0-14-004871-5*

FOR THE BEST IN PAPERBACKS, LOOK FOR THE

☐ **FAITH, SEX, MYSTERY**
A Memoir
Richard Gilman

Gilman's memoir tells of the making and unmaking of a Catholic—as a young Jewish atheist undergoes a conversion, enjoys eight years of believing, and then gradually loses faith.   *254 pages*   *ISBN: 0-14-010587-5*

☐ **THE EARLY CHURCH**
Henry Chadwick

The first volume of the *The Pelican History of the Church* follows the emergence of Christianity from the apostolic age to the foundation and explosive expansion of the Church of Rome.
                    304 pages   *ISBN: 0-14-020502-0*

☐ **WESTERN SOCIETY AND THE CHURCH IN THE MIDDLE AGES**
R. W. Southern

Volume 2 of *The Pelican History of the Church* is the story of the birth and decay of a great Western ideal—that of an ordered society, religious and secular, as an expression of a divinely ordered universe.
                    376 pages   *ISBN: 0-14-020503-9*

☐ **THE CHURCH IN AN AGE OF REVOLUTION**
1789 to the Present Day
Alec R. Vidler

The fifth volume in *The Pelican History of the Church* is a masterful assessment of a doubt-ridden and turbulent period in Christian history; it offers an incisive appraisal of the Church's endurance in the Age of Revolution.
                    302 pages   *ISBN: 0-14-020506-3*

☐ **A HISTORY OF CHRISTIAN MISSIONS**
Stephen Neill

The sixth and final volume of *The Pelican History of the Church* traces the expansion of Christianity via missionary activity, from the Crusades to Colonialism to the present day.   *528 pages*   *ISBN: 0-14-022736-9*

FOR THE BEST IN PAPERBACKS, LOOK FOR THE

Other religion books available from Penguin:

☐ **THE DEAD SEA SCROLLS IN ENGLISH**
  G. Vermes

The discovery of the Scrolls in the late 1940's was an epoch-making event for the study of Judaism and Christianity; this definitive English translation also serves as an introduction to the customs and history of the community responsible for the Scrolls.   *320 pages   ISBN: 0-14-022779-2*

☐ **THE REFORMATION**
  Owen Chadwick

Volume 3 in *The Pelican History of the Church* covers the work of 16th-Century Reformers Erasmus, Luther, Zwingli, and Calvin and discusses the special circumstances of the English Reformation as well as the Jesuits and the Counter-Reformation.   *464 pages   ISBN: 0-14-020504-7*

☐ **THE CHURCH & THE AGE OF REASON 1648-1789**
  Gerald R. Cragg

Volume 4 of *The Pelican History of the Church* charts the response of the Church to the widespread strife of mid-seventeenth century Europe; as the state began to have more of a hand in religious affairs, order, moderation, and stability became the rule.   *300 pages   ISBN: 0-14-020505-5*

☐ **THE ORTHODOX CHURCH**
  Timothy Ware

Ware, Bishop Kallistos of Diokleia, retells the 2,000-year history of the Eastern Church and explains its views on such widely ranging matters as Ecumenical Councils, Sacraments, Free Will, Purgatory, and the Papacy.
                  352 pages   ISBN: 0-14-020592-6

You can find all these books at your local bookstore, or use this handy coupon for ordering:
                  Penguin Books By Mail
                  Dept: BA Box 999
                  Bergenfield, NJ 07621-0999
Please send me the above title(s). I am enclosing _____
(please add sales tax if appropriate and $1.50 to cover postage and handling). Send check or money order—no CODs. Please allow four weeks for shipping. We cannot ship to post office boxes or addresses outside the USA. *Prices subject to change without notice.*

Ms./Mrs./Mr. _____

Address _____

City/State _____ Zip _____